D0501102

ELICITING CHILDREN'S FULL POTENTIAL

Designing & Evaluating Developmentally Based Programs for Young Children

Brooks/Cole Publishing Company
A Division of Wadsworth, Inc.

Printed in the United States of America

10 9 8 7 6 5 4 3 2 1

Library of Congress Cataloging-in-Publication Data

Feinburg, Sylvia G.
Eliciting children's full potential : designing and evaluating developmentally based programs for young children / by Sylvia G. Feinburg, Mary Mindess.
p. cm.
Includes bibliographical references and index.
ISBN 0-534-22244-7
1. Early childhood education—United States. 2. Child development—United States. I. Mindess, Mary. II. Title.
LB1139.25.F45 1994
372.21—dc20 94-461
CIP

Sponsoring Editor: *Vicki Knight*
Editorial Associate: *Lauri Banks Ataide*
Production Editor: *Nancy L. Shammas*
Manuscript Editor: *Catherine Cambron*
Permissions Editor: *Roxane Buck Ezcurra*
Interior Design: *Leesa Berman*
Cover Design: *Laurie Albrecht*
Art Coordinator: *Susan Haberkorn*
Photo Editor: *Diana Mara Henry*
Indexer: *James Minkin*
Typesetting: *Graphic World*
Printing and Binding: *Malloy Lithographing, Inc.*
Cover Graphic: *"The Battle Between the Wolves and the Poodle Dogs" by Valerie Gruber was drawn when she was not yet six years old. Collection of Sylvia Feinburg.*

Chapter Opening Photos: Chapter 1, © Michael Siluk; Chapters 2, 3, 5, 6, 7, 8, 10, and 11, © Elizabeth Crews; Chapters 4 and 9, © Jeffrey High/Image Productions.
Excerpts on pp. 271–272 from *Constructivist Early Education: Overview and Comparison with Other Programs* by R. DeVries and L. Kohlberg, 1990. Copyright © Rheta DeVries. Reprinted by permission.
Excerpt on p. 319 from C. Lewis "Cooperation and control in Japanese nursery schools." *Comparative Education Review,* February 1984, *28,* No. 1. Copyright © 1984 by Comparative and International Education Society. Reprinted by permission of the University of Chicago Press.

ELICITING CHILDREN'S FULL POTENTIAL

Designing & Evaluating Developmentally Based Programs for Young Children

Sylvia G. Feinburg
Tufts University

Mary Mindess
Lesley College

Brooks/Cole Publishing Company
Pacific Grove, California

This book is dedicated to our children, who have been and continue to be a source of inspiration about the nature of growth and development and the learning process.

David, Todd, and Doug—S.F
Karen, Tom, Tracy, and Richard—M.M.

A child is a person who is going to carry on what you have started....

He is going to sit where you are sitting, and when you are gone, attend to those things which you think are important.

You may adopt all the policies you please, but how they are carried out depends on him. He will assume control of your cities, states, and nations....

He is going to move in and take over your churches, schools, universities, and corporations....

The fate of humanity is in his hands.

Abraham Lincoln

BRIEF CONTENTS

CONTENTS

PREFACE

In this book we clarify the term "developmentally based early childhood education" and explain how high-quality programs for children from three to eight years old can be developed, nurtured, and maintained. In working with preservice and inservice teachers and administrators we have found that there is still considerable confusion over exactly what the developmental model is and is not and precisely how it is like and unlike other approaches to early education.

The book is intended for a wide range of professionals in preschools, day care centers, kindergartens, and the primary grades, including preservice and inservice teachers, curriculum specialists, early childhood and special needs coordinators, and administrators. It is appropriate for anyone who seeks a general understanding of contemporary high-quality early education programs. We have responded to the need of many public schools to incorporate an early childhood unit. We recognize the value of continuity of learning experiences for children in the 3-to-8 age range and respect individual rates of development.

Special Features

Key Characteristics

The text is organized in relation to the key characteristics of the developmental model, which are introduced in Part 1 and summarized by the forms in the "Compendium of Observational Instruments" in Part 5. In Part 1, "Seeking Quality in Early Childhood Programs," we introduce and describe the key characteristics of the model and link them to the philosophical, historical, and psychological bases of developmental education. We analyze the polarities in educational thought that have influenced the field, and contrast the histories of nursery school, day care, kindergarten, and primary grade education. In Part 2, "Challenging Children Intellectually," Part 3, "Stimulating Creative Thinking," and Part 4, "A Cognitive Approach to Social-Emotional Issues," we define the key characteristics and elaborate on them. Each part contains a theoretical overview followed by a set of observational characteristics that translate the objectives into operational terms, that is, succinct statements of the specific strategies teachers use to realize these objectives. The operational characteristics make the term "developmental education" unambiguous.

Examples

Specific classroom examples vividly illuminate the key characteristics. The classroom vignettes, representative of the full 3-to-8 age range, demonstrate the flexibility of the model. The vignettes are illustrative, not prescriptive; they are designed to stimulate the practitioner's creative involvement in the teaching process, suggesting important values and objectives that teachers can translate to fit their own needs. The developmental model by its very nature demands ingenuity and creative thinking on the part of the adult.

Although the book is not organized around traditional academic content areas, Parts 2, 3, and 4 contain rich material related to curriculum development. Examples are drawn from all areas: literacy and mathematics, the social sciences, science, physical education, and the arts. We also include the traditional content of the early years, such as spontaneous and dramatic play and the use of such expressive materials as blocks, sand, and water. We emphasize the importance of providing children with programs that are provocative and challenging, because the intellectual component of early childhood programs is so frequently misunderstood.

We highlight examples that reflect integrated and interdisciplinary curriculum that is fundamental to the developmental approach. However, not all learning takes place in this way, and there are major differences in how teachers work with children at different stages of development, depending on the nature of the task and the adult's objectives. Thus, some of the examples illustrate discrete skill practice that is not part of an integrated approach (although the teacher or the child usually finds ways to address these skills so they are meaningful and relevant). Nonetheless, because the concept of integration is a key aspect of developmental education, it is a theme that pervades this text. We show the integration of concepts and skills and of various domains of learning, and also how the principles of integration influence human interactions. The examples highlight some fundamental values related to integration such as the critical importance of cultural diversity and the inclusion of children with a wide range of special needs in the regular classroom.

In Chapter 10, "The Observational Process in the Developmental Classroom," and Chapter 11, "A Compendium of Observational Instruments," we stress the critical importance of classroom observation as a means of strengthening our understanding of the teaching and learning process. We emphasize learning by observing one's own and one's peers' classrooms and by engaging in reflective practice. We also explain methods of gathering data and how to develop objective observing and recording skills.

Forms

The classroom observation and evaluation forms in Part 5 summarize our approach to the developmental model, succinctly denoting the key characteristics of high quality programs that adhere to the "constructivist" or "cognitive-developmental" model. The forms are the basis for an ongoing process of evaluation, ensuring that a given program is, in fact, consistent with the tenets of developmentally based education. A method for evaluation is necessary for quality control and to prevent the model from becoming vague, all-inclusive, and open to varying interpretations. The observation and evaluation process serves two central objectives: (1) clarifying the complexities of the model, and (2) providing a brief, efficient method for examining the degree to which certain characteristics are realized within a given program.

The evaluation forms can be used in a variety of ways by individuals at many different professional levels. They are a teaching tool, focusing attention on a cluster of characteristics and thus deepening the observer's understanding of certain teaching behaviors. They are also an instrument for evaluation and assessment, helping to determine the degree to which certain developmental principles are actually realized. Self-evaluation and program evaluation are more scientific when the criteria are readily identifiable and specific. For example, two teachers may maintain that they value and promote creativity in their classrooms, although their methods differ significantly. The classroom observation forms enable one to examine directly the degree to which key creative characteristics are being addressed. Assessment and evaluation are tools for sharpening awareness and understanding, not the basis for narrow judgment. The purpose of the evaluation process is to help practitioners set goals for themselves as they refine their understanding of developmental education, engage in continuous re-evaluation of their programs, and identify areas that require attention. The forms can be used as a mechanism for reflective practice, helping teachers become more introspective about their own teaching and the challenge of teaching in general.

Two of the forms in Chapter 11 are designed for evaluating a classroom in terms of the major characteristics that are fundamental to the developmental model. Form A-1, "Characteristics of a Developmentally Based Early Childhood Program," is comprehensive, and Form A-2, "Characteristics of a Developmentally Based Early Childhood Program," is abbreviated. They are of particular benefit in clarifying the strengths and weaknesses of a given program and establishing a focus for implementing change. When small groups of people engage in this process together the ensuing discussion of the teaching dynamic will be rich and provocative.

The other four observation forms reflect specific topics that closely correspond to material in respective chapters of the text. These are: Form B, "Critical Qualities of the Teacher," Form C, "Curriculum in the Dynamic Classroom," Form D, "Stimulating Creative Thinking," and Form E, " Social-Emotional Issues." We advise reading the corresponding chapter and then using the relevant form while observing a classroom. The forms let the reader view teaching as a continuum from the traditional to the developmental approach.

From the developmental perspective, education is a process in which children are actively involved in successively more complex learning situations in a context where there is respect for their changing capabilities. The learning process is viewed as dynamic, not static. If teachers are to challenge children and provide an environment that engages them intellectually, socially, and emotionally, they too must be challenged in comparable ways. When teachers are in the process of growing and developing themselves, they are in the best position to provide powerful leadership within the classroom. It is our hope that Eliciting Children's Full Potential will both deepen understanding of the nature of developmental education and stimulate the important process of growth and change in teachers, engendering an infectious spirit that will be transmitted to children.

Acknowledgments

A number of people helped in the creation of this book and we are indebted to all of them. We thank the many teachers who opened their classrooms to us and were willing to share the situations we included as examples. We also thank the many college and university students and colleagues who stimulated our thinking through their sensitive documentation and analyses of classroom life. In addition, we acknowledge the children who demonstrated love and affection toward each other, argued about sharing, wrote stories, drew and painted pictures, built with blocks, and otherwise provided the necessary drama and action that are central to meaningful learning experiences. Without all these contributions our efforts would have been greatly compromised.

In particular, we acknowledge David Alexander, Betty Allen, Linda Beardsley, Chery-Render Brown, Holly Carroll, Virginia Chalmers, Margaret Consalvi, Janice Danielson, Andrea Doane, Valerie Gruber, Ruth Japinga, Rebecca Keenan, Felicia Lee, Judy Lazarus, Charna Levine, Jennifer McGuinn, Alyssa McCabe, Danielle Mindess, Katie Mindess, Jayanthi Mistry, Jennifer Morrison, Florence Bailey Poor, Marion Reynolds, Lynn Rosen Schade, Michael Sexton, Janet Stork, Sharie Verruso, David Waldstein, Nikki Waldstein, Enid Wetzner, Deborah Zalkind, and Janet Zeller.

We are also grateful to the following reviewers: Hugh Fox; Marcia Jorgenson, University of Northern Colorado; Judy McKee, Eastern Michigan University; Sandy Miller, Ohio Department of Education; Linda Ruhman, San Antonio College; and Carol Seefeldt, University of Maryland

Special thanks to the directors and staff of the Eliot-Pearson Children's School of Tufts University and the Tufts Educational Day Care Center. These two sites were of major importance to our efforts. We also appreciate the Lesley College librarians and the staff and students associated with the Lesley College Expanded New England Kindergarten Conference for research and manuscript assistance.

Finally, this undertaking could not have been completed without the care of key people on the Brooks/Cole editorial staff, particularly our editors, Vicki Knight and Nancy Shammas.

Sylvia G. Feinburg
Mary Mindess

ELICITING CHILDREN'S FULL POTENTIAL

Designing & Evaluating Developmentally Based Programs for Young Children

PART 1

SEEKING QUALITY IN EARLY CHILDHOOD PROGRAMS

High-quality early childhood programs are based on understanding the relationship between child development and educational practice and providing a continuum of developmentally based learning experiences for children from preschool through grade three.

Early childhood education has come into its own. At no time in history has there been such respect for this field nor such wide support for the concept of high-quality early educational experiences for young children. The past three decades have had a profound impact on how we view and understand the importance of learning in the early years. This increased understanding is reflected in the views of parents, educators, and political leaders and is influencing a redefinition of the field itself.

For many years the term **early childhood education** was used primarily to refer to educational programs for preschool- and kindergarten-aged children. It was considered an introductory set of experiences that prepared the child for eventual entry into formal schooling, which began at the first-grade level. The term **preschool** itself suggests that schooling for three- and four-year-olds was viewed not as "real" school but rather as preparatory; in fact, many people considered it an optional experience, rather than an imperative one for all children.

Although the kindergarten experience (for five-year-olds, or the year before first grade) has been common for well over fifty years, it, too, was traditionally seen as optional. Not until the 1960s did kindergarten become mandatory in most of the United States, with public school systems required to provide kindergarten programs (Hymes, 1991; Osborn, 1991; Williams & Fromberg, 1992).

Traditionally, preschool and kindergarten experiences remained separated from the grades in both form and content, and the gulf between the two worlds was well recognized. Preschool and kindergarten have been seen as focusing primarily on social and emotional issues, with heavy emphasis on play and what were once called "readiness" experiences; and the grades have been seen as the place where real learning takes place and basic skills are mastered. Although situations differ from one location to another, for the most part a clear distinction has been drawn between the worlds of preschool and kindergarten and between kindergarten and the elementary grades.

In recent years, however, the meaning of the term *early childhood education* has changed. It has been expanded to include all educational experiences for children from birth to eight years of age (or through grade three), and the distinction between preschool and kindergarten experiences on the one hand, and the early elementary grades on the other, is eroding. Great efforts are being made to provide continuity throughout this entire age span and to eliminate the sharp separation that has prevailed historically (Webster, 1984; Bredekamp, 1987; NASBE, 1988; Hymes, 1991; Bredekamp & Rosegrant, 1992; Kostelnik, Soderman, & Whiren, 1993).

This text focuses on the age span from three to eight years. The authors acknowledge the critical importance of the infant and toddler period, but coverage of that area is beyond the scope of this book. The attempt to provide continuity of learning experiences in programs serving children three to eight years old reflects the view that the developmental processes that take place during this age span have more in common with one another than once was believed to be the case, and that drawing a sharp distinction between the preschool/kindergarten period and the grades is inappropriate in view of what is currently understood about cognitive growth and development. Associated with this change in thinking is the concept of **developmental education**—an approach based on the idea that classroom activities should be driven by what is known about child development.

This apparently simple concept is more complex than it appears. For example, one commonly reiterated principle of development is that children differ in their rate of growth. In the physical domain, this principle is easy to observe and document. Teachers and parents readily observe this principle in action and willingly accept it as fact. More difficult, however, is transferring this principle to concepts of cognitive growth. Cognitive growth, unlike physical growth, reveals itself in ways that are somewhat more difficult to ascertain; the observer must have a more in-depth understanding of developmental theory in order to see this growth clearly. Between the ages of three and eight years, children's way of thinking undergoes many changes. However, like the rate of physical growth, the rate of cognitive growth differs from one child to another. Failure to understand this principle often results in provision of educational experiences that hinder rather than aid development.

Rate of development is one important factor to consider in planning educational experiences for young children. Many other factors must be considered as well—some related to the child's unique qualities and others related to the child's family and culture. The extensive body of information we have about how children grow and develop makes it imperative that educators view early childhood education as a continuum and establish learning environments responsive to the individual and group needs of the children with whom they work. Developmental education offers this perspective. It includes a wide range of child-centered programs, emphasizing play, concrete learning, children's active participation, and experiences related to children's interests. The curriculum is matched to each child's level of understanding.

The goal of this text is to make explicit the concept of developmental education—in particular, the **cognitive developmental** model, a specific approach to developmental education. This model emphasizes the processes of cognitive growth, as articulated by Piaget, Vygotsky, and other cognitive psychologists, as well as the work carried out by Freud, Erikson, and others in the area of **psychodynamic theory.** An additional objective of the text is to provide guidelines for making the concept operational within the classroom.

Chapter 1 identifies the cognitive-developmental model's key characteristics and explains the model's theoretical basis. The chapter also discusses the appropriateness of the model for today's children. In short, the goals of Chapter 1 are to identify key characteristics of the cognitive-developmental model; provide classroom examples of the model in operation; describe some common misperceptions about the model; and put forth a rationale about the appropriateness of the model.

Many aspects of developmental education are not new. They are rooted in a long history of philosophical ideas, societal changes, and educational practice. Understanding the cognitive-developmental model's theoretical and historical roots is essential to implementing the model. Thus, Chapter 2 links the key characteristics of the developmental model with child development theory; traces aspects of the history of early childhood education that have influenced the model's development; identifies factors associated with the current movement toward providing a learning continuum from prekindergarten through grade three; and describes some identifiable early childhood models. Together, these two chapters set the stage for the implementation discussions that follow. They also provide the basis for the chapters on observation and evaluation that conclude the text.

The process of planning, implementing, and evaluating developmentally based programs for young children is a circular one; it depends on fully understanding the model. The reader will have frequent occasion to refer back to this first section of the text.

CHAPTER

1 DEVELOPMENTAL EDUCATION DEFINED

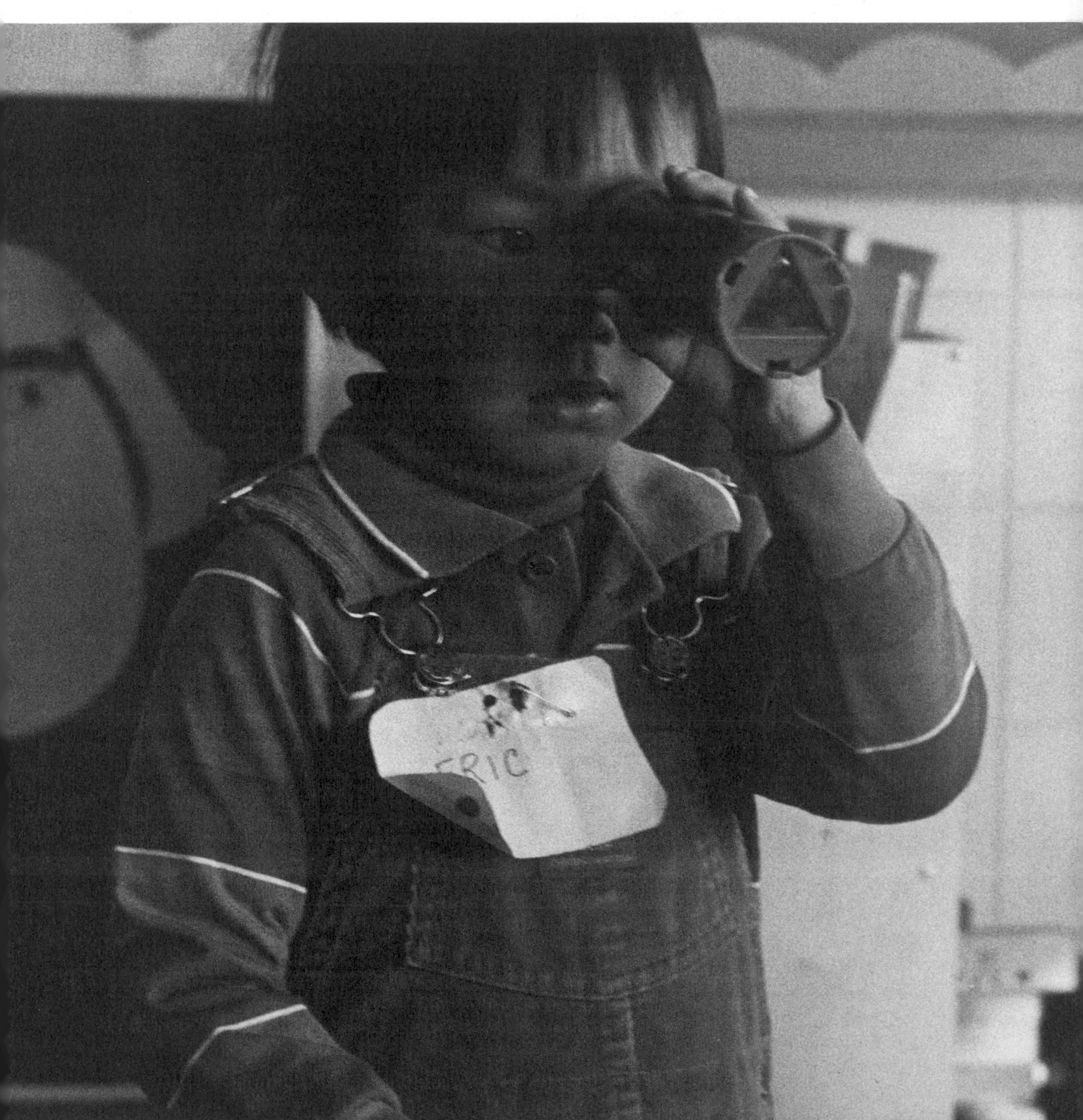

- *The Key Characteristics of the Developmental Model*
- *The Key Characteristics Described*
- *Classroom Manifestations*
- *Developmental Education: Some Common Misperceptions*
- *The Importance of the Model for Today's Children*
- *Summary*

This chapter identifies the **key characteristics** of developmentally based programs for young children and explains why each characteristic is critical to the model. It describes classroom manifestations of the characteristics in operation and discusses some common misperceptions about the model. In addition, the chapter gives a rationale for the appropriateness of the model for today's children. This discussion provides the foundation for Chapter 2, which traces the historical roots of these ideas and links the characteristics of the developmental model with its basis in psychological, sociological, anthropological, and linguistic theory, thus clarifying the relationship between theory and practice.

Many sources have identified characteristics of developmental education (Bredekamp, 1987; NAEYC, 1991; Connecticut State Department of Education, 1988). Although definitions of these characteristics differ in wording and sometimes in primary focus, they reflect general agreement on the model's basic tenets. The reason for this agreement is that developmental programs by their very nature rely on a specific body of knowledge about how children grow and develop, derived from research in the fields of psychology and child development.

Even when developmental education's characteristics are stated explicitly, often the links between them and the developmental principles on which they are based are not clearly set forth, and justification for the characteristics is overlooked or taken for granted. People tend to pay lip service to the characteristics without fully understanding their real meaning, the rationale behind them, or for that matter the way they are expressed in the classroom. Sometimes educators use these characteristics as slogans, catch phrases, or educational jargon without fully understanding their implications and connection to developmental theory. As a result, these people have difficulty implementing developmentally based programs or explaining these programs to parents and other educators. Linking psychological information which frames the planning, implementation, and evaluation of developmentally based programs with classroom practice is of critical importance. A first step in this process is to clearly articulate the model's key characteristics.

The Key Characteristics of the Developmental Model

No brief set of characteristics set forth to guide teachers can embrace everything that must be considered in handling the complexities of a classroom, and any set of guiding principles is vulnerable to important omissions. The set of characteristics described here is not exhaustive, but rather represents a distillation of the central components of a developmental program as shaped by contemporary developmental theories of child psychology. The characteristics are expressed so as to facilitate the reader's understanding of both values and actions. In some cases, a set of beliefs and attitudes is outlined; in others, procedures and specific ways for teachers to act and behave are addressed. Subsequent chapters detail how these characteristics are operationalized.

The key characteristics of a developmental program are as follows:

1. The physical environment is designed to optimize concrete learning and to enable children to explore a wide variety of objects and materials.
2. Children have the opportunity to work alone, with one or two other

children, in small groups, and in large group situations. Children have some options in choosing learning experiences.

3. The teacher observes, records, and assesses child and group progress and bases instruction on this information. Children's special talents, as well as areas of difficulty, are addressed.
4. The teacher is vibrant intellectually. He or she understands the importance of motivational strategies in stimulating children's intellectual and expressive activity and is alert to the teacher's role in shaping children's activity. The notion of **cognitive conflict** is respected. Hence, the adult shares information, raises questions, and provokes experimentation in a wide variety of ways.
5. The academic areas of literacy and mathematics are crucial aspects of the curriculum, but they are taught in an interdisciplinary manner that makes them relevant to the child and builds respect for their importance.
6. Creativity is valued highly; hence, every effort is made to capitalize on children's imaginative, expressive thinking and productivity.
7. Social and emotional issues are viewed as an important part of intellectual development and are integrated into both classroom management and the curriculum.
8. Since young children are egocentric emotionally and intellectually, subject matter that is of personal interest to them is important in designing learning experiences. Consideration is given to family, cultural, and community concerns.

As you can see, the characteristics are organized to address intellectual, creative, and social-emotional development. Each of these areas is discussed explicitly in subsequent sections of the book. Although the areas are identified independently of one another, it is important to recognize that they are vitally interrelated. Cognition, or intellectual development, cannot be divorced from creative and social-emotional development. Cognition—the process of thought—governs the child's behavior in the creative as well as the interpersonal and emotional areas. Although development in the physical-motor domain is of great importance, we have not identified it as a separate characteristic. Instead, principles and activities related to physical-motor growth are incorporated into the other key areas. The rationale for this organizational structure is that well-planned physical-motor activities also contribute to growth in the cognitive, creative, and social-emotional realms.

The Key Characteristics Described

The characteristics identified as key to the developmental model also define **constructivism,** a particular approach to developmental education. Constructivism describes a way of learning in which the child actively engages with the environment and builds his or her own knowledge and understanding. Thus, constructivism accentuates the processes of cognitive or intellectual growth. This text uses the term *constructivism* as a synonym for *cognitive-developmental* philosophy. Constructivism recognizes the vital role of teachers' interactions with children, as well as the setup of the physical environment. The nature of cognitive-developmental philosophy will be apparent in the following elaboration of the characteristics of the developmental model.

The Physical Environment

Nature has programmed the human organism to use the senses to acquire understanding of the physical and social world. Young children, in particular, use all their senses to gain firsthand knowledge about their environment. They pick up and examine things in their environment in a curious and intense manner, using their senses of smell, taste, hearing, sight, and touch. Children shove objects under or behind other objects and then go searching for them; they push and poke and throw, not because they are being unruly or obstreperous, but because that is their way of finding out about the nature of things and coming to understand their environment.

Certainly we know that children learn in a wide variety of ways: through imitation, listening, and watching TV, to name a few. All these modes of learning are useful, and all are a part of the developmental classroom. The dominant mode of learning in the developmental classroom, however, is through manipulation and exploration of available materials. Hence, this characteristic implies that developmentally based classrooms for young children are full of firsthand materials that children can use and investigate—materials for writing and drawing, classifying and measuring, constructing and experimenting, and studying in great detail.

As children progress through the early childhood years, the need for direct sensory experiences and concrete learning diminishes, for a number of reasons. First of all, as the child builds a repertoire of knowledge about how particular materials and objects respond, and as information is accumulated about the nature of the physical world, the child has less need to examine things directly, having learned what to expect. In addition, the capacity to function symbolically is increasing, and the child is less dependent on using objects as a means of understanding concepts. Abstract thought is developing. This shift in thinking is one reason that classes for five- and six-year-olds look different from classes for three- and four-year-olds. It is easy to be deceived, however, by the apparent verbal maturity of five- to eight-year-olds and to be lulled into thinking that children of this age can learn effectively predominantly by listening and reading. That older children can sit still longer and rely a bit less on their senses as a way of learning does not mean that they do not need the opportunity to use concrete materials and to be actively engaged in learning. Although reliance on the senses diminishes with experience and maturity, human beings never lose their need and tendency to explore firsthand, in a direct and concrete manner, new ideas with which they have had limited experience. *Thus, the first key characteristic of the cognitive-developmental model: the physical environment is designed to optimize concrete learning and to enable children to explore a wide variety of objects and materials.*

Grouping Patterns

If the goal is to have children exploring and manipulating materials in increasingly complex ways, and we know that young children within a group are at varying levels of development, then it follows that grouping patterns should be variable. Sometimes children should be working in the group as a whole; at other times, it is more appropriate for them to work in small groups, with one or two other children, or alone. Obviously, the nature of the particular experience influences the grouping pattern.

In many kinds of situations, children learn best in a total group—for example, singing, storytelling, recounting a shared field trip, sharing a class visitor, or discussing class norms. In these types of activities, a group identity and an esprit de corps are evolving, which are valuable in children's development. The Japanese recognize this value and begin each day with a fixed ritual in which all the schoolchildren participate (Hendry, 1986). In Great Britain, many schools, including those that value children's choosing of activities, usually begin the school day with an assembly, an experience that the whole school shares. Many early childhood teachers follow a similar routine. They plan times, usually near the beginning of the day and at the end of the day, to plan or review what has gone on in the classroom. Sometimes, the discussion focuses on tasks in which the children are engaged; at other times, the conversation centers on how the children are interacting with one another and caring for the classroom environment. The review often pulls together children's cognitive activities, the physical and motoric challenges they have encountered, and the specific social skills on which they are working. The feeling of belonging and the sharing of norms that comes from this experience usually can be achieved only in a total group setting.

Total group experiences are also appropriate when the nature of the activity is such that the enthusiasm of the entire group contributes to the impact of the experience. In one class the teacher introduced a construction lesson involving a marble-rolling apparatus. The materials were so stimulating, and interest was so high, that in place of her usual method of having different small group activities take place simultaneously, the teacher had everyone create a marble-rolling apparatus. The collective situation intensified children's interest and awareness of potential strategies for creation.

In the developmental classroom, much of children's learning takes place as children work in small groups, with a partner or alone. This flexible grouping encourages children's active involvement in learning. They do not need to wait until other children respond; they can discover their own questions and search for solutions. The teacher who offers guidance and instruction individually or to small groups of children can tailor the example and the rate of presentation so that it is responsive to the needs of particular children.

The grouping pattern itself is not fixed, and group composition varies with the activity. This variation enables the program to respond to differences in children's level of cognitive and social-emotional functioning. In any classroom, a range of capacities, temperaments, and learning styles can be found. Given this range of difference, children should not be expected—nor are they able—to move through the curriculum in the same way and at the same rate. To be respectful of the range of capacities in a particular classroom, one needs to find ways to make the curriculum responsive to children's needs. Flexible grouping is one way to achieve this end.

In the developmental classroom, flexible grouping avoids the establishment of fixed grouping patterns that may create the feeling that one group's skills are more

While several of the children in this class are working alone—at a table or on the floor with unit blocks—others are engaged with a partner or with a small group of peers. All are taking responsibility for their own learning, leaving the teacher free to work with individuals or small groups. © Elizabeth Crews/The Image Works

advanced or more valued than another's. Instead, groups are established as the need arises. The members of the group are identified so that they can help one another, build on one another's strengths, and provide opportunities for one another to grow.

Deciding who will play and work together in a developmental classroom depends on a variety of factors: the nature of the task, its complexity, the kinds of material involved, the skills required, the teacher's assessment of the needs of particular children, and children's own preferences. Small groups often provide the setting through which children become engaged in projects or learn and practice specific skills. In a classroom of three- and four-year-olds, children often choose those with whom they want to work in the block corner or in the dramatic play area. Sometimes the teacher will make a suggestion: for example, "I think Lynishia would be really interested in the zoo you have been working on in the block area. She's been to a zoo and has a lot of information about the kinds of cages that the different animals live in." In a first-grade class, children may group themselves in a particular learning center, or the teacher may specify those who will be working together. Children can be, and are expected to be, resources for one another.

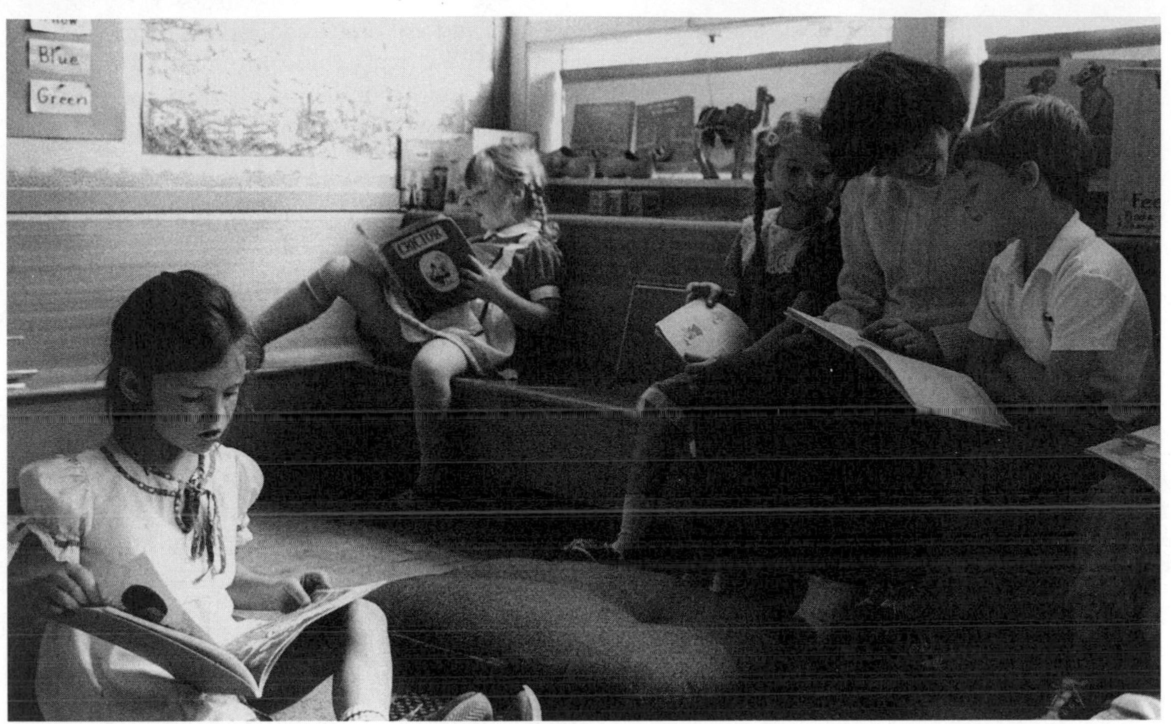

Individual conferences between teacher and child are an important part of the writing/reading process. They stimulate the child's thinking and provide an opportunity for teachers to gain an understanding and an awareness of a child's progress that is not readily accessible when teaching groups. © Elizabeth Crews

In classes for five- to eight-year-olds, the teacher may have individual conferences with children—for example, about the writing that they are doing in their journals. To teach a particular skill that can best be learned in a small group setting, the teacher may call to a designated area children who are ready to learn the skill. To take advantage of children's learning from one another, the teacher may decide that children should work in pairs—for example, in paired reading activities. Simultaneously some children may be working alone, others with a partner, and others with an adult (teacher or aide). Grouping in the developmental classroom depends on the activity, the children, and the goals to be achieved. *Thus, the second of the key characteristics: children have the opportunity to work alone, with one or two other children, in small groups, and in large groups. Children have some options in choosing learning experiences.*

Observing, Recording, and Assessing Progress

If instruction is to be individualized and at the same time take place in a group setting, the teacher needs to observe the children carefully and systematically. Developmental classrooms recognize that children differ in their rate of learning, temperament, learning style, interests, and cultural background. Some children have identified talents or special needs. These qualities are important aspects of the child. The teacher finds out about each child's unique qualities through careful observation and systematic recordkeeping. The information that is gathered becomes a key component in program planning.

This focus on the needs of the individual and on how the individual functions in a group is characteristic of the developmental model. This basic orientation differs from the approach frequently employed in traditional classrooms, where it is assumed that all children are or should be at the same level of development and that the curriculum materials should interest and challenge all of them. Usually in these programs, teachers attempt to fit children to the prescribed curriculum rather than fitting the curriculum to the child. Of course, in traditional classrooms, some attempts are made to individualize learning experiences—usually, by grouping some children in a more advanced group, some in an average group, and some in a slow group. But the focus remains on the curriculum and on how the individual is able to fit into it. In the developmental classroom, the focus is on the child and what needs to happen in the school environment to facilitate the child's learning.

A teacher who understands the learner's interests, learning style, temperament, and other emotional factors is in a better position to fit the materials to the child. Taking this approach doesn't mean, nor is it intended to imply, tutorial or one-to-one teaching. Rather, it reflects an orientation that begins with the child. This orientation may be reflected in the subtle ways the teacher responds to the child—ways that indicate respect for the child's temperament or build on the interests the child displays. The child-centered approach may be reflected in grouping practices that vary with the task and with the children involved. This orientation certainly is present in the feedback the teacher provides.

Recordkeeping is a key component of this characteristic. The framework for the recordkeeping is often based on naturalistic or **authentic assessment** procedures. In other words, children are observed as they function in their regular settings, rather than in traditional testing-type situations designed to assess the presence or absence of certain abilities. The recordkeeping component is built on the notion that the child is constantly changing, growing, and learning. Recordkeeping is a documentation of the process rather than a finite measure of the child's accomplishments or lack of accomplishment at a certain point in time. When keeping records in an authentic assessment approach, the initial focus is on what the child can do and how the child can be helped to progress. This focus contrasts with that of the common testing model, in which particular skills and information are identified and a test is designed to measure which of these skills the child does not possess (commonly referred to as a deficit approach). The developmental educator does not ignore areas in which a particular child may be having difficulty; however, the approach to the difficulty is not one of remediation, but rather a positive look at what the child can do on his or her own and what the child can be helped to do as a next step.

The authentic assessment process also documents children's special talents. Usually, teachers rely on samples of the child's work, anecdotes about the child's interactions, checklists indicating skills the child possesses, the child's self-evaluation and reflective comments, and parental observations about the child's progress. All these provide valuable information about each child, which is of critical importance in constructing the curriculum.

In schools where the developmental philosophy pervades all the grades and where authentic assessment is the mode, questions about age of school entry, retention, and promotion become relatively unimportant. These schools encourage apprenticeship learning and take into account developmental principles of how children grow and learn. Such schools allow for differences in rate of learning and in learning style, and carefully monitor and plan for each child's progress. *Thus, the third characteristic: the teacher observes, records, and assesses individual and group progress and bases instruction on this information. Children's special talents, as well as areas of difficulty, are addressed.*

Intellectual Vibrancy of the Teacher

The development of children's thinking skills is closely linked to the intellectual vibrancy of the teacher. What does it mean to be intellectually vibrant? It means many things. Most obviously, it involves the teacher's own breadth and depth of interests. In early childhood programs, subject matter areas are quite varied. No one person can be equally knowledgeable in all these areas. However, the teacher with a passion for studying history, or classical music, or any other subject can whet young children's appetites for learning and help them to gain the satisfaction of a sustained interest in a topic.

Intellectually vibrant teachers are those who, in addition to their own interests, have a passion for studying children. These teachers understand developmental stages and are able to translate this understanding into action. They view individuality as a stimulating aspect of teaching. They know what three-year-olds are like and how they differ from children who are six. These teachers can take almost any topic and fashion it in a way that makes sense to the children with whom they are working. Such teachers perceive the clues provided in children's behavior as guidelines for their own professional practice.

Intellectually vibrant teachers are knowledgeable about what is going on in the field of early childhood education. Their minds are open to current research and new approaches. They have the confidence to evaluate this information and to consider its implications for their own teaching practices. They demonstrate their skills as constructivist teachers by adopting, modifying, or rejecting ideas that they have carefully considered and thoughtfully analyzed.

Intellectually vibrant teachers are able to motivate and inspire learners. Their methods of delivery make content meaningful. They know what is important to children and why. They have a sense of how inquiry drives intelligence. They know how to engage children in inquiry and how to set up situations that provoke cognitive conflict. They are able to help children make links between what they already know and new information. To do this effectively takes enormous skill, energy, and drive; it is a competence that must be continually exercised and developed.

Intellectually vibrant teachers are dynamic. They find connections and reorganize material so that it makes sense to children. They take advantage of the moment when an interest is sparked or a breakthrough is occurring. They provide germane background information. Their vocalizations are not routinized or stereotypic. They are not mechanistic in the workbook sense; nor do they rely on the past for all they need to use in the present. In short, intellectually vibrant teachers are "orchestrators of learning." They are empowered to respond to the current call for increased student achievement and to meet the educational needs of an increasingly diverse population of students. They are empowered to construct their own responses, ones that reflect their "understanding of children and subject matter goals and how to relate one to the other in the context of their own classrooms" (Black & Ammon, 1992). *Thus, the fourth characteristic: the intellectually vibrant teacher understands the importance of motivational strategies in stimulating children's intellectual and expressive activity and is alert to the teacher's role in shaping children's activity. The notion of cognitive conflict (Kohlberg & Mayer, 1972) is respected. Hence, the adult shares information, raises questions, and provokes experimentation in a wide variety of ways.*

The Approach to Academics

Let's assume that a parent is trying to decide to which school he should send his child. He visits a first-grade classroom in one school and sees the children playing with concrete materials. Some are seated at tables; others are working on the floor. Some are working alone and are very quiet; others are working in groups and are continually talking. This, the teacher tells the parent, is the developmental approach.

Then the parent visits another school. In the classroom, children are in their seats working busily on a math worksheet that requires them to practice addition. The parent is familiar with this approach; it is what he experienced when he went to school. In addition to this sense of familiarity, the approach seems to be more responsive to the recent criticisms of education. Are not math scores (according to the media) lower than ever? Aren't workbooks more rigorous than playing with math manipulatives? Do children need this more rigorous program? Something makes him think twice, and he goes back to ask some questions about the first classroom. Do children really learn math by playing around with all these materials, or is this approach simply designed to make school more enjoyable? Is the developmental approach contributing to declining scores, or can the model provide a way for children to reach greater levels of proficiency in the basic skills?

Very often those who do not understand developmental education or the value of constructivism in programs for young children interpret children's being engaged with materials in the classroom as evidence of minimum regard for the importance of language development and the acquisition of literacy, mathematical, and scientific skills. This interpretation is one of the common misconceptions about developmental programs.

In fact, acquiring skills in language, mathematics, science, and social studies is critical in developmental programs. These areas receive attention in programs for three-year-olds as well as in programs for children of eight. Teachers are aware of the developmental progression through which children acquire the skills of writing, reading, mathematics, science, and social studies. Teachers also appreciate children's natural desire to attain these skills and the importance of the teacher's role in nurturing, supporting, and stimulating this desire.

The ways literacy and mathematics are incorporated into the developmental program are often very different from what many people associate with "real" learning. Since developmental education is based on constructivism, the ways developmentally based programs encourage skill development are frequently different from those used in traditional classrooms. In the developmental classroom, the child and the child's activity, rather than a prescribed curriculum, are the focus of attention. Children are encouraged to construct their own knowledge. Learning is viewed in a holistic sense: knowledge, attitudes, and feelings are equally important. The basic premise is that if children are to be successful in the areas of reading, writing, and mathematics, they need to participate in the process of learning and to perceive themselves as competent writers, readers, and mathematical and scientific thinkers.

Educators in developmental programs recognize that when children are expected to engage in activities that are beyond their comprehension or ability, they often experience frustration and develop lifelong attitudes that stand in the way of learning. Developmental educators seek to avoid these frustrating experiences for children, as well as to avoid having children engage in activities that are not sufficiently challenging to them. At one time most educators thought that avoiding frustration for some children meant that the teacher, the parents, and the child had to sit back and wait for the child to mature. When children were not challenged in programs, the traditional idea was to encourage the child to adapt, rather than to modify the curriculum.

Neither of these attitudes has a place in developmental education. Instead, the teacher in the developmental classroom constantly observes children, looking for ways to engage them in activities in which they can experience success and appropriate challenge. As a result, children in the developmental classroom may be doing different things at different times. They may be working alone, or with other children; using paper and pencils, or manipulative materials; engaged in convergent tasks with right and wrong answers, or in more open-ended tasks in which it is more difficult to document efforts and progress. Whatever the method, whatever the activity, in the developmental classroom the goal is to have children gain increased enthusiasm, interest, and skill in the areas of reading, writing, mathematics, science, and social studies.

Interdisciplinary teaching that integrates the various subject areas is often criticized for using an unstructured approach to teaching literacy and mathematical skills. Often people interpret play experiences as lacking in structure or direction. In fact, the opposite may be true. Play provides an opportunity for children to express their ideas and construct their own meanings for related concepts. When developmental teachers incorporate play time or time for free exploration into their programs, they do so with clear goals in mind. The specific objectives may be different for different children, and the way children use time is often unlike the way they do in traditional classrooms, but the ultimate aim—that the child acquire proficiency in the skill areas as well as attitudes and dispositions that will lead to enthusiasm and love of learning—is the same for all.

The developmental teacher has a range of strategies to use for instructional purposes. These may include worksheets, usually ones designed to provoke thinking as well as drill and practice; group instruction on a particular skill; and opportunities for children to express themselves and make discoveries on their own. These activities may take the form of exploratory play. (Play also can be useful to adults; adults who have the freedom to play with objects or ideas are often the most skilled and the most productive.) The activities in the developmental program always are reaffirming to children as they gain proficiency in the basic skill areas. Whole language, process writing, mathematics programs such as Math Their Way, Box-It and Bag-It Mathematics, activity-based science, and social studies activities—these approaches are well suited to meeting this goal. Developmental teachers use these and many other approaches as ways of helping each individual child increase proficiency in basic skills.

The skills themselves are often taught in an interdisciplinary way; in other words, the subjects in the curriculum are integrated. In some programs this method is referred to as theme teaching or unit planning. This approach is similar to the **project method** advocated by Kilpatrick (1918) and described in 1932 in the *Curriculum Records of the Children's School,* published by the staff of the National College of Education (Osborn, 1991). Katz and Chard (1989) use the term **project approach** to describe the integrated approach to teaching and learning, in which children actively participate in planning, implementing, and evaluating their experiences. The aim of this approach, according to Katz and Chard, is "to cultivate the life of the young child's mind . . . [including] not only knowledge and skills, but also emotional, moral and aesthetic sensibilities" (p. 3).

In interdisciplinary teaching, many subject areas are included as children explore a particular topic in some degree of depth. This integration does not minimize the child's need to master discrete skills and acquire specific information in each of the subject areas. On the contrary, a basic premise of the developmental model is the idea that through the program children acquire increasing degrees of skill in the areas of writing, reading, and mathematics. Children also learn factual material in literature, science, social studies, and the arts. The aim is to make learning meaningful and to build respect for the importance of skills. For example, children engaged in making pancakes as part of a study of foods make a trip to the store to purchase the supplies for the pancake breakfast, talk about where the food comes from, read the recipe, measure the ingredients, and set the table. The way the teacher structures this experience provides opportunities for counting, adding, patterning, and exploring one-to-one correspondence and other mathematical relationships. The children observe, in the manner of the scientist, the changes that occur when the batter is heated. They put together their own recipe book and design the book in their own unique way. This experience incorporates social studies, science, writing, reading, drawing, and perhaps communicating feelings and ideas the children have about the recipes they have shared.

Learning that is presented in an interdisciplinary way tends to have more meaning for children. The children come to appreciate the use of skills and find ways to practice these skills. Also, interdisciplinary teaching fosters concept development. It helps children establish links between various pieces of information they are assimilating and helps them to categorize information in ways that make for easier retrieval. In this respect, interdisciplinary teaching is consistent with both a Piagetian framework and an information processing approach to cognitive development.

Why, one might ask, does this characteristic specifically mention literacy and mathematics and omit reference to other aspects of the curriculum? The reason is that literacy and mathematics are often considered areas that are neglected developmental programs. As can be seen from the example just given of makin, pancakes, integration includes all the subject areas: science, social studies, the arts, and physical education or movement. (Changes during the cooking process make excellent stimulation for creative movement experiences.) Learning in the areas of literacy and mathematics, as well as in all other areas of the curriculum, is strengthened through the relevant, hands-on experiences supported by the interdisciplinary approach.

Focus on an interdisciplinary approach does not mean that the skill areas are never addressed separately. Rather, interdisciplinary teaching calls attention to the fact that in the past, teaching these disciplines has been looked at narrowly as a pure transmission of skills. Children acquired these skills not in a way that made conceptual sense, but more through memorization, drill, and practice. Today we take a much broader view of how children learn to write, read, and engage in mathematical activities. Developing competency in skill areas is important, but learning involves much more than that. Skills do not exist in isolation. Children who fail to become writers and readers do so not because they lack skills, but because they lack the perception of themselves as writers and readers. Through an interdisciplinary approach, children come to view books as important sources of information and pleasure, cherish stories in books as they cherish the stories they themselves create, and develop a burning desire to read. The varied experiences they have with literature broaden their horizons and augment their ability to express themselves through language.

Mathematics, too, consists of more than just skills (cf. National Council of Teachers of Mathematics Standards, 1991). When children engage in interdisciplinary experiences, they come to see the relevance and importance of math. Of course, drill is still important, and workbooks have their place, but these are part of a much larger whole. What is most important is the attitude about skills that is generated through the program. *Thus, the fifth characteristic of the developmental model: the academic areas of literacy and mathematics are crucial aspects of the curriculum, but they are taught in an interdisciplinary manner that makes them relevant to the child and builds respect for their importance.*

Valuing Creativity

Creativity is a part of cognition. It involves reorganizing, reinventing, and transforming. Creativity cannot be dissociated from knowing; it is an approach to knowledge, a way of thinking. Jerome Kagan (1967), in the introduction to the book *Creativity and Learning,* clearly delineates the connection between creativity and thinking:

> Too many of our schools behave as if they believed that the task of education was to teach pieces of correct information and to eliminate mistaken ideas. . . . We give too little concern to a second goal: that of convincing the child that he can produce possible solution hypotheses, even though each might contain a little error. We do not devote enough energy to teaching the child that he can think. It is certainly easier to teach facts than to train thinking. (p. x)

Often, when people talk about creativity, they associate it with the arts. Working in any art form does require synthesis, reorganization, reinvention, and transformation. Creativity does not have to do solely with the arts, however. Creativity is a way of strengthening cognition, and thus it applies to all areas of the curriculum. To think creatively, one needs to own the material, to know the information and grasp the key ideas. Creativity, a process of reorganizing or transforming ideas, requires factual information or specific knowledge that can be transformed; it is a part of all areas of human endeavor.

Creativity has two dimensions: expressivity, which has to do with affective states and involves feelings and the processing of emotional concerns; and creative productivity, which has to do with the reorganization of ideas. Both these dimensions are related to social-emotional and cognitive growth. Both expressivity and creative productivity are essential in the development of cognition and social-emotional understanding.

Encouraging productivity involves having high expectations about the level at which children will achieve. Every piece of work should not be equally valued, or children's creativity will be stifled. It is important to help children to move forward in their understanding and their ability to express what they know. The teacher needs to expect and challenge children to take the next step rather than simply regurgitating what they have learned. Creativity, no matter what the domain—literature, art, music, mathematics, science, or social studies—is not developed when teachers adopt a hands-off policy. In storytelling, for example, as in all other areas, there is a progression based on a body of knowledge that the teacher has to help children to access. As children access this knowledge, they are expected to show progression in their creative products.

Creativity is an essential aspect of developmental programs. Developmental programs start with the notion of the self and encourage the individual to construct meaning. Creativity by its very nature is a constructivist process. What the child already knows or brings to the program is important. Through a process of construction, children continually reorganize knowledge to make it their own, take in new knowledge, and then repeat the cycle. Reorganization demands creativity. The kinds of activities teachers make available to children determine whether innate creativity will be nurtured or thwarted. How the teacher presents skill and other lessons is of key importance in nurturing creativity.

People often think you have to ignore or throw away creativity in order to teach skills. This idea needs to be challenged. Children do not need to do convergent thinking (for example, to color in all the cats, or to write the word *cats* ten times) in order to master fine motor skills or the correct way to spell. Teachers can design play activities and creative worksheets that encourage divergent thinking and at the same time achieve the program's goals. Word recognition exercises and practice with mathematical computations can be presented in a way that is not narrowly constricted. For example, children can construct dictionaries or pictionaries designed to help visitors from another country become acclimated to the classroom or to help children recognize words in languages other than their own. This activity could be adapted to fit any theme on which the children are focusing. Children who are studying their neighborhood can graph their findings about the types of houses or trees there. Based on the graphs, the children could construct word problems that require computation (Kaplan, 1980). In the developmental program, the aim is to have creative thought as an aspect of cognition pervade all aspects of the curriculum. *Thus, the sixth characteristic: creativity is valued highly; hence, every effort is made to capitalize on children's imaginative, expressive thinking and productivity.*

Social-Emotional Issues in Curriculum and Classroom Management

In developmental programs, social-emotional issues are also linked to cognition. Children construct their understanding of themselves—their feelings, emotions, interpersonal relationships, and self-esteem—using processes much the same as those they use to acquire concepts about hibernation, for example, or one-to-one correspondence, or the structure of a story. Children start with what they know; they take in new information (in a process of **assimilation**), relate it to what they know, and deepen their understanding (in a process of **accommodation**). Then they seek new experiences, and the cycle starts again. The environment or the teacher provokes cognitive conflict and the state of **disequilibrium** that conflict causes. Individuals seek resolution of the conflict and the state of **homeostasis (equilibrium)** that resolution brings. Thus, through engagement in cognitive conflict, the individual continues to grow.

Earlier, educators believed that social-emotional development took place in one way, and cognitive or intellectual growth in another. Although early childhood educators believed in paying attention to "the whole child," this concept meant that what happened in one area of a child's development affected all other areas; so that if a child had difficulty getting along with his peers or experienced emotional turmoil at home, one could expect his or her progress in school subjects to be affected. Educators' efforts to help children deal with social-emotional issues often were predicated on psychoanalytic or behavioral psychology. In the psychoanalytic view, children were encouraged to express feelings, and teachers and others in the helping professions used such concepts as sublimation, displacement, and the operation of defense mechanisms in attempting to understand those feelings. The behaviorist view, which was based on the stimulus-response phenomenon, prompted teachers to use reward and punishment to help children gain control over their social-emotional behavior. Some teachers, particularly those working with the Distar program, also used the behaviorist approach in teaching subject matter (Engelmann & Bruner, 1969).

With the advent of cognitive psychology, stimulated by the work of Piaget, educators began to consider ways to develop programs focusing on or incorporating children's thinking abilities. They became aware of how children's thinking differed from adults' and how thinking manifested itself in social relationships as well as in the acquisition of academic knowledge. This cognitive approach to social-emotional development is particularly well suited to a rapidly changing society. In the past, parents and teachers were able to provide children with clear guidelines about how to behave. Currently, technological and scientific advances, as well as sociological changes, that are occurring at an almost explosive rate make it critical for children to learn how to formulate their own behavioral guidelines to cope with both positive and negative aspects of change. Of particular concern are the increase of violence and drug abuse in our society and the AIDS epidemic, which make it essential for children to learn how to make decisions about their own behavior and identify ways to cope with personal and interpersonal challenges. Understanding behavior and identifying alternative ways of coping with social-emotional issues involves creative ingenuity and is integral to the concept of constructivism.

Of critical importance is helping children understand themselves and others and become competent in their abilities to negotiate interpersonal relationships. The developmental program's approach to dealing with feelings and interpersonal relationships is a cognitive one. The aim is increased understanding as well as acquisition of social skills. Children come to recognize that they have alternatives in the area of social-emotional behavior and that they have some basis for deciding which skills to use under which circumstances. Children become autonomous in the area of social-emotional development in the same way they become autonomous in intellectual pursuits. Moreover, social-emotional topics are integrated into all curriculum areas—in the areas of literacy through writing, reading, discussing; in science through questioning, investigating, and hypothesizing; in mathematics through graphing, interviewing, and recording; in social studies through categorizing, relating, and exploring; and in the arts through all forms of expressive activity.

In the developmental model, classroom management also becomes a cognitive process in which children are fully engaged. The teacher sets the expectations and the classroom parameters. He or she involves children in discussing the rationale for these expectations. Whenever appropriate, children are engaged in formulating the rules for the classroom and in evaluating how effectively group members are adhering to the rules. The teacher, always listening and respecting children's ideas, discusses with children how they should behave toward one another. In classrooms where behavioral issues are considered from a cognitive perspective, discipline in the negative sense is hardly an issue. Rather, the emphasis is on helping children take responsibility for their own actions and for interactions within the group. In such classrooms, children take on attitudes of self-discipline and learn skills for managing their own behavior. The teacher and the children together work at building a community in which all are respected and all are engaged in productive learning activities. *Thus, the seventh characteristic: social-emotional issues are viewed as an important part of intellectual development and are integrated into both classroom management and the curriculum.*

The Importance of Family, Cultural, and Community Concerns

Children are engaged by subject matter when it is relevant to them and is directly related to their lives. The reason is that young children are egocentric. Developmentally, young children are able to see things primarily from only their own perspective. They are most interested in things that are a part of their daily lives or closely related to their own experiences. They want to find out about the bus that they ride in to come to school, the house they watch being built, and the animals they have as pets. They also become very engaged when the discussion centers on their own emotional experiences—times they were afraid, felt especially loved, or were angry. Children also try to make sense of their world by developing their own classification systems: Who's my friend and who's not? Whose skin color is like mine and whose is not? Who is stronger than I am and who is less strong? These are compelling topics for children. They bring their own experiences to these explorations and thus have a base on which to build new learning.

Although a group of children, by virtue of their age and developmental level, may have many experiences in common, there are many other experiences that become key factors in personalizing the curriculum due to diversity in classrooms. An example is diversity in family structures. Some children live with fathers and mothers; others with grandparents, aunts, and uncles. Some children have two mothers; others have two fathers; some live in single-parent homes; and some spend time with two sets of parents and four sets of grandparents. Some family members spend a great deal of time together; and others have very little time. In some families, children have siblings who require special care; in others, children have close-knit ties with aging grandparents. Children learn most efficiently in situations where the uniqueness of their family lifestyle is acknowledged and appreciated.

Children's cultural backgrounds also represent an important area of diversity with implications for program planning. In addition to outward manifestations of culture—such as food, eating patterns, holiday celebrations, and customs—there are many less recognized but equally important dimensions. Cultures differ in their perception of relationships with authorities and in their expectations for how children react to and approach adults. Cultures differ in language and linguistic style, in body language, in patterns of telling stories, in ways of handling conflict, in attitudes toward cooperation and competition, and in many other values. Some cultures value assertiveness in children; others encourage children to be more reticent in group situations. Some value early independence; for others, encouraging interdependence is more important. How these differences are approached affects children's self-esteem and ability to learn.

Children need to have their own cultures recognized and valued before or while they are learning about other cultures. Educators who value cultural diversity need to be certain to incorporate this value into school programs so that it is central to children's concerns in their own lives—their fears, their avenues for obtaining security, their eating habits, and their other family customs. Children cannot understand other people's lives until they understand their own. Similarly, in classrooms that lack family and cultural diversity, ways need to be found to help children recognize and appreciate the human differences they will come in contact with throughout their lives. *Thus, the eighth characteristic: since young children are egocentric emotionally and intellectually, subject matter that is of personal interest to them is important in designing learning experiences. Consideration is given to family, cultural, and community concerns.*

Classroom Manifestations

One of the first steps in implementing developmentally appropriate programs is to identify the key characteristics as they appear in classrooms. The task is not only to identify what is developmentally appropriate but also to state a rationale for this judgment. The key characteristics provide the basis for making informed judgments.

Consider the following example, which illustrates children's use of concrete materials, flexible grouping patterns, creativity, and interaction with an intellectually vibrant teacher. In a first-grade classroom, two times a week the children have a time they call "math buckets." Each child chooses the bucket of materials that she or he wants to work with for the period. No more than four children can work with the same materials. Look in on the class, and you see four children in one corner of the room working with large rods. They are trying to see how high they can make a construction supported on four sides. The process is one of trial and error. The teacher spends some time with this group and asks: "Do you think you can make it higher? How can you find out?"

Two other children have chosen to work with **geoboards,** another sort of manipulative math material. The children are seated at the same table, but each is engrossed in his or her own work. The teacher visits individually with each child at the table. The teacher moves; the children continue to be engrossed in their activity. Unobtrusively the teacher sits down at the child's level, observes what the child is trying to do, and enters the dialogue. "I see you're making squares. How many squares could you make that would fit inside of that one big one?"

The teacher stays long enough to be sure that the child has the idea, even though this means that he will have spent time interacting with only six of the twenty children. Through his interactions, the teacher helps these children to identify and become engaged in some powerful cognitive conflicts. The other children also are engaged in mathematical thinking as they work with mosaic tiles, plastic animals, **unifix cubes,** and other math manipulatives—materials that lend themselves to patterning, measuring, and estimating. These children are identifying appropriate challenges on their own.

In the same classroom, once a week, math experiences are structured in a cooperative learning format. "Cooperative learning is a teaching strategy involving children's participation in small group learning activities that promote positive interaction" (Lyman & Foyle, n.d.). The cooperative learning approach has been particularly effective in helping children think about their behavior in groups. It has also proved effective as a way to respond to the learning styles of some children whose cultures emphasize group rather than individual activity and achievement. For children who have a more competitive orientation, cooperative learning provides the affective and cognitive benefits that come from participating in a group.

For one cooperative learning activity, the teacher organizes the children into groups of four. Their task is to create, record, solve, and check mathematical problems. Each member of the group has a particular role. One child, using the manipulatives provided, creates the problem. A second child records the problem on a sheet of paper. The third child solves the problem, using the manipulatives, and records the answer on the paper. The fourth child is the checker; using the manipulatives, this child is responsible for verifying the answer. In an example of their creativity, the children construct a diversity of mathematical problems. Also interesting is the way the teacher helps the children process their interactions and their contributions to the group effort. Cooperative learning involves a cognitive approach to social-emotional interactions and is thus compatible with the developmental model.

The next example, a project carried out in a school in **Reggio Emilia**, Italy, illustrates the relationship between creativity and cognition. Some of the work children did in connection with this project was part of a multimedia art exhibit titled *The Hundred Languages of Children* that toured the United States. Viewers

of the exhibit often spoke of their disbelief that preschool children were capa
of such high-quality work. However, as viewers pondered the amount of artwor
that was related to a single topic, it became apparent that the capabilities the children revealed were related to the depth with which they had explored the topic. They used all their senses to become fully immersed in an experience. The many approaches to a particular topic indicated the extended period of time children devoted to their investigations. In these investigations the children integrated many different subjects: art, science, and social studies.

The project was titled "The City and the Rain." The exhibit itself and the viewer's guide (Forman, 1989) indicated the depth of the study. The children studied the wet reflections on stone pavements. They watched the pigeons seek shelter under the eaves of a building. They traveled to the city with their cameras and tape recorders to see the city in the rain. They measured the rainfall and captured the sounds of rain as it fell on different surfaces. They studied buildings to see how architects prepared for rain. The children made connections, relating rainfall to water supply. They studied pictures of clouds and postulated theories about the source of rain. They expressed these theories through art; each piece of art was a study in itself.

What was the role of the teacher under whose guidance this work took place? Lilian Katz described the role of teachers in the Reggio Emilia school very succinctly:

> Teachers take an active role in encouraging and helping children explore the possibilities of a wide variety of materials and media. But most important, teachers do not underestimate children's capacities for sustained effort in achieving understanding of what they are exploring; nor do they underestimate children's abilities to capture and depict these understandings through a variety of art forms. (Katz, 1990, p. 11)

The children's artwork makes it clear that art and understanding are closely linked. Those who explain the Reggio Emilia philosophy stress this link.

> In the Reggio program, art is not viewed as a separate part of the curriculum but as inseparable from the whole cognitive-symbolic expression of the developing child. Teachers consider the learning process to involve both creative exploration and problem-solving. They value the children's activities and constructions, be they expressed through words, songs, dance, drawings, dramatics, block constructions, weaving, shadow-plays, or face-making before the mirror. Teachers ensure that these activities are rarely done in a casual, unguided way. Rather, though they respect the children's spontaneity and follow their lead, they see themselves as actively cooperating in the creative process. They create favorable or stimulating situations to provoke the children. They extend children's experiences by offering questions, materials, and related experiences. (Gandini & Edwards, 1988, p. 15)

The Reggio Emilia preschools have been recognized for their encouragement of an effective collaboration among parents, teachers, and children and for making clear programmatic connections between creativity and cognition. Rebecca New (1990, 5) described the philosophy on which this collaboration is based. As she pointed out, "Because teachers and parents consider isolation from one another a hindrance to professional and child development, they have designed formal and informal strategies to establish a rich community of exchange." The strategies include keeping children, as toddlers and preschoolers, with the same group for three years, and as older preschoolers, moving them to another group they stay in for the next three years. Thus, children, teachers, and families come to know one another well. Each child has an album to which both teachers and families contribute. Families accompany children, teachers, and other members of the school staff on field trips, and parents, people in the community, and teachers serve together on decision-making boards. In this way the Reggio Emilia schools take steps to implement another characteristic of developmental programs: namely, the development of a curriculum that reflects the families and the cultures of the children in the program.

Constructivism as a philosophy for teachers and children provides the framework for the developmental model. It is evidenced in developmental programs through opportunities provided for children to

- engage in concrete learning and active exploration
- have some opportunity to exercise choice about what learning experiences they will become involved in and with whom they will work
- play and work in classroom groupings that are flexible and offer chances for children to work alone, in small groups, or in total class settings
- be supported by teacher observation and assessment
- benefit from interactions with an intellectually vibrant teacher
- engage in interdisciplinary experiences
- have their creativity nurtured
- use their developing intellects to understand feelings and social relationships
- engage in activities that are interesting, relevant, and connected to their experiences in their family, neighborhood, and cultural group

One important step in delineating the developmental model's components is to address directly some common misperceptions about the model.

Developmental Education: Some Common Misperceptions

As we, the authors, work with preservice and inservice teachers, evaluate early childhood programs, and speak with parents and the larger community, we have encountered considerable confusion about exactly what developmental practice involves. Misperceptions abound. The developmental model is often thought to entail permissiveness, free choice, and random play. Many people have superficial familiarity with some qualities and practices commonly associated with the model—for example, they think that developmental education is less formal than traditional education, that children have more freedom to move about and make choices, and that play is important. The media often portray developmental education by describing aspects of the model in ways that are emotionally charged and stereotypic, focusing on the child's freedom, teacher permissiveness, and excessive emphasis on random play. As a result of the popularization of the tern *developmentally appropriate education* without comprehensive clarification of exactly what is involved in this exciting and important educational movement, confusion has been created, leaving the model vulnerable to misinterpretation. Unfortunately, many people do not realize how complex and multifaceted the model really is, and how much structure, teacher control, and content is actually in operation. A proliferation of misperceptions about developmental education persist and need to be addressed, including the following:

1. The teacher in a developmental program does not teach or has an easy job.
2. Developmental programs are not academic enough.
3. Developmental programs are not suited for all children.
4. Developmental programs are not sufficiently structured.
5. Developmental programs never employ what are considered to be nondevelopmental techniques.

The misperceptions are rampant and have been identified by many people. Kostelnik (1992) refers to them as myths, and Bredekamp and Rosegrant (1992) as misunderstandings. Writers, including the present authors, use their own wording and incorporate slightly different ideas; the concepts identified, however, are similar. It is imperative that educators give careful consideration to the misperceptions lest they continue to obstruct efforts to construct an effective developmental model.

Misperception One: Teachers in developmental programs have an easy job and do not really teach Many people have the misperception that teaching in developmental classes is easy. To them, to see children working independently or with peers, doing research, recording observations, or reading to one another means that the teacher is not doing his or her job. Many people think of teaching as telling—with the teacher presenting information to a group of children or the children sitting quietly in their seats engaged in teacher-directed tasks. If one thinks this way, it is difficult to imagine how the developmental classroom—a setting where children are engaged in a variety of projects, many of them self-initiated, and are encouraged to express their own ideas; where children confer with one another, and the teacher is the quiet one, observing and recording children's behaviors and accomplishments—could in fact be a highly productive environment.

Certainly, in some classrooms that purport to be developmental, teachers have abdicated authority, structure is nonexistent, and no productive learning is taking place. This same situation could also be found in classrooms committed to any particular philosophy. Teaching in a developmental classroom actually requires tremendous preparation when the children are not present in the room. Teachers need to respond to the children's interests, identify resources, and plan activities through which children can acquire "skills, attitudes and dispositions" (Katz & Chard, 1989) appropriate at each child's individual level of development. Furthermore, observing and reflecting—critical components of the model—are very difficult to do when only one teacher is in the classroom. Norms need to be established for how children can obtain help while the teacher is occupied and how they can work independently as the situation requires. A classroom that looks easy to manage gives this impression only when the teacher is very well organized, the environment is sufficiently stimulating to engage children's interest, and the teacher has successfully built and continues to nurture a caring classroom community.

Misperception Two: Good developmental programs do not focus on academics In good developmental programs, teachers do not abdicate their authority to children and dismiss the importance of mastering skills and acquiring knowledge; quite the contrary. Good developmental programs contain clear and unambivalent expectations for achievement and productivity, stressing learning to read and write and mastery of basic skills, and also emphasizing building children's self-control and autonomy in order to make them independent and motivated learners. The ways these objectives are achieved, however, are qualitatively different from traditional programs, and it is imperative that these differences are understood. Otherwise, creative energy that should be spent on developing quality programs, improving programs already in existence, and evaluating programs' effectiveness for the children they serve can be dissipated in futile arguments about educational practices that have been mislabeled, or that are not properly understood. The developmental teacher needs to be proactive in explaining the educational goals of the program to administrators and parents.

Misperception Three: Developmental education is not suited for all children This misperception became popular in the 1960s, when the federal government encouraged the development of a variety of different early childhood models. The proponents of the **direct teaching model** argued that children from "disadvantaged" backgrounds required a fast-paced, clearly organized curriculum in order to "catch up" with their "nondisadvantaged" peers (Bereiter & Engelmann, 1966).

Let's talk about "catching up." This notion is based on a deficit view of education. Educational programs that begin by finding out what children are unable to do feed into the development of negative self-concepts. Furthermore, children's development does not take place at an even pace. Once children gain control of their own learning, they go through spurts as they master skills involved in reading, writing, and arithmetic.

The belief that socioeconomically poorer environments are necessarily disadvantaged environments is a stereotype that is frequently fallacious. Although many children living in poverty are considered at risk for failure in school, not all such children are in this category, and many children at risk for school failure come from middle- and upper-class homes. Very often, socioeconomic status is linked with cultural stereotypes (Dimidjian, 1989) and is more acutely misinterpreted. If a teacher believes that a parent with a particular background is unable to provide the support necessary for children to succeed in school, the parent and the child will respond to this expectation, and the misperception will become a reality. Present understanding of cultural differences suggests a need to appreciate diversity and build on this diversity to provide enriched programs for children (Ramsey, 1987; Derman-Sparks & the A.B.C. Task Force, 1989). The developmental model is built on this principle. The model is flexible and responsive; at its core is the notion of empowering the learner, a process that begins with and builds on the strengths that children and families bring to school.

In the field of special education, some proponents of a direct teaching model have tended, often unknowingly, to contribute to misperceptions about the developmental model. These people argue that young children with special needs require specific skill training, which is most effectively delivered directly and often in isolation from other aspects of the curriculum. However, children with special needs are children first (Wolery, Strain, & Bailey, 1992). The special skills training they require often can and should be provided in integrated, developmentally appropriate programs. All children benefit when children with special needs are included in regular education programs.

Misperception Four: Developmental programs do not provide sufficient structure Associated with the misperception that developmental education is not appropriate for all children is the question of how structured developmental programs are. Many factors—including home background, temperament, and the child's ability to function in a group situation—influence the degree of structure with which a child feels most comfortable in school. One misperception about developmentally appropriate programs is that they are too loosely structured, particularly for children whose home life does not provide sufficient structure and also for those whose out-of-school hours are spent in an overly rigid environment. These children find it difficult or uncomfortable to function in what is perceived as the loosely structured developmental classroom environment. In point of fact, developmental classrooms have a great deal of structure, but the elements of structure are not always visible to the casual observer. There is structure, for example, in the schedule, in the organization of materials, and in what is and is not acceptable behavior. The degree of structure in a developmental classroom is flexible and is determined by the teacher as he or she works with a particular group of children. In its optimum form, developmental education can be sufficiently adaptable to provide high-quality learning experiences for all children, including those who are economically or educationally at risk. Since developmental education by definition addresses the learner's needs, it is well equipped to provide an optimal learning situation for children with a wide range of needs.

Misperception Five: Developmental programs never employ what are considered nondevelopmental techniques Developmental education is not an all-or-nothing phenomenon. In many high-quality developmental programs, teachers use strategies that when considered in isolation seem more compatible with direct teaching than with developmental education. The fact is that developmental education is inadequate when it is so narrowly construed that it rules out use of certain teaching strategies that may be necessary for some children under some circumstances. For example, although the model may include broad objectives for such qualities as self-determination and initiative, at certain times and for certain individuals the teacher may use more traditionally structured methods for helping children move toward these objectives.

Consider the practice of time out, in which a disruptive child is removed from the classroom activity for a brief period of time. This behavioristic technique, which might be considered incompatible with a developmental program, may be used as a temporary strategy for helping children gain control. The developmental teacher would ultimately want to move that child toward a more self-determining posture, but would recognize that the child is presently unprepared for this responsibility. The principles of the developmental model are both specific and broad; they are elastic enough, flexible enough, and broad enough to accommodate a wide range of learners and cultural styles. What may seem inconsistent is not always inconsistent when the ultimate aim is to achieve the common goal of empowering each child to reach his or her full potential.

This same perspective holds true in academics. Memorization is often not thought to be consistent with a problem-solving, constructivist approach. In some areas, however, memorization is useful. Children enjoy memorizing poetry and number facts that they already understand. Mnemonic devices for spelling can also be helpful. Some children benefit from a drill-and-practice approach, or from being taught a particular skill in an isolated rather than an integrated way. Here again, the developmental model allows teachers to make the judgment about specific strategies to use with particular children. What is critical in the developmental model is that teachers understand and can justify the use of a particular approach in light of the ultimate goals. This understanding is based on careful observation, a great deal of reflection, and whenever possible, discussion with colleagues.

Once these misperceptions are clarified, educators, parents, and community leaders will be in a better position to consider why the developmental model is so critical in early childhood education and why it is worth the effort to support and nurture its continual development.

The Importance of the Model for Today's Children

Teaching young children today presents a significant challenge—a much greater one than in earlier years when classrooms were less diverse, societal change was slower, and children had greater stability in their lives and fewer unmet needs. Children today are living in stressful times. The sources of stress are economic, interpersonal, sociological, and geographic. In the economic sphere, because of advertising and other means of almost instantaneous worldwide communication, people are aware of and seeking more and more material advantages. Financial policies are making credit relatively easy to obtain. At the same time that material wants are increasing, significant changes are taking place in the economic structure of society. The U.S. economy, for example, is becoming less industrialized and more service-oriented. At a time when two family wage-earners have become more important, fewer and fewer jobs are available. Changes in society—the macro environment in which children are living—affect children and their families at the interpersonal as well as the economic level.

Changes in family living patterns are bringing about increased stress in interpersonal relationships. Many children are living with divorced parents; some have multiple parents as a result of remarriage of one or both parents; others are living with gay parents, stepparents, grandparents, or other relatives. No longer are children coming to school with a relatively consistent set of values and experiences.

At one time, people lived in extended family situations. Parents of young children had the support of grandparents, aunts, and cousins. Today, with geographic mobility, the nuclear family and the one-parent family are much more common. Often couples move great distances from their families of origin in order to obtain desired jobs. When these couples break up—and statistics show that 50 percent of U.S. marriages end in divorce (Bumpass, 1990) and that almost 25 percent of U.S. children live in a single-parent household (U.S. Bureau of the Census, 1990)—the lack of extended family support becomes an increasingly significant factor in the functioning of the family unit. Sometimes friends take the place of family in lending support, but not always.

Sociologically, changes are occurring very rapidly—changes in sex-role definitions, changes in values and moral attitudes, changes in work-related opportunities and in time available for leisure activities. Rapid change, while often desirable in some ways, tends to result in the breaking down of values, contributing to some disintegration of society. Disintegration usually occurs at times of great societal shifts: for example, change from an agrarian to an industrialized society, or our current movement from an industrialized to a service-oriented, information processing society. This disintegration and the process of rebuilding are not in and of themselves undesirable. In fact, in many ways they are responsible for societal advances. Nonetheless, the disruptions do affect young children, and these effects are magnified today because change is occurring so rapidly. Values seem to be shifting continuously. What is right in one situation is totally wrong in another. Stability in values and interpersonal relationships, which is thought to have a particular benefit in psychosocial development, is for many children nonexistent. Drug addiction is more prevalent, and children who were born addicted to drugs are in school today. These societal changes and their accompanying problems affect children at all socioeconomic levels: wealthy, poor, and in the middle. Teachers today are working with children and families who are facing a great deal of stress, less stability, and many diverse needs.

Complicating the situation is the violence that children today are witnessing more than they ever have in the past: shootings, stabbings, rioting in the streets, and violence within families. This is true for children who live in wealthy suburbs as well as for those growing up in the inner city. Many children are witnessing repeated violence firsthand, and almost all children experience its effects vicariously on a daily basis as they watch television or glance at the daily newspaper. Violence in society is so widespread today that psychologists fear that children as well as adults are becoming habituated to it. "Man's inhumanity to man" is considered a part of life. Child abuse of an emotional, physical, and sexual nature is on the rise. In earlier times it was possible to protect children from turmoil, violence, and the negative aspects of society. Now children, wherever they grow up, are exposed in some way to a full range of human behaviors. Helping children make sense of their world, cope with its problems, and become productive members of society represents a real challenge for teachers.

In the developmental classroom, a teacher cannot look at a group of children as a single entity and design a program that will be relevant, meaningful, and appropriate for every child. Differences among children may be cultural, linguistic, sociological, and sexual. In this pluralistic society, teachers need to consider the individual children in a class before planning an experience as basic as celebrating Mother's Day, Columbus Day, or Thanksgiving.

For example, an Asian mother whose children were attending school in the United States recounted how offended she felt by an assignment her third-grader brought home from school. As a part of the Mother's Day curriculum, the children had been reading *Sarah Plain and Tall* by Patricia MacLachlan (1985). In the story, a widowed father advertises for a new mother for the children. As one of the activities related to the reading, the children were asked to speculate about the qualities of an ideal mother and to compose an original advertisement for this mother. Then they were to ask their mothers to write a response to the advertisement.

For the mother who had grown up in China, that a teacher could give such an assignment was shocking. In Chinese culture people have great respect for mothers. It is very offensive to talk about someone else's mother, and nobody ever talks about a mother's characteristics unless she is not living. Furthermore, the assignment brought forth for this bicultural mother many negative feelings. Having lived in China, she had witnessed and been affected by the traditional Chinese practice of a man's taking many wives as concubines. At first, this mother refused to do her part of the assignment and suggested that her son explain the reason to his teacher. When she recognized how difficult this would be for the child, she decided to comply. She wrote out two or three lines in an apparently bland but, in reality, agitated response to the child, so that the teacher would not continue to hound him for the incompleted assignment.

She then made an appointment to talk with the teacher. She explained to the teacher her feelings about the assignment. She acknowledged that for a traditional Chinese person, thinking of a situation such as the teacher created might not be as difficult as it was for her. For traditional Chinese, concubinage was a fact of life, and therefore discussions suggesting it might not be as painful. Also, for someone who had not been exposed to the traditional Chinese culture, feelings may not be so intense; but for this mother, as an individual who had been transplanted from one culture to another, the assignment stirred up too many unpleasant, almost unbearable feelings. The parent asked the teacher in the future to be more sensitive to these feelings and possibly give a different assignment to children who because of difference in cultures would find a particular assignment offensive. The teacher's response was that she couldn't possibly give a different assignment just because a child's family had a different cultural background: "You're in America now and you need to expect these things to happen." This response aggravated the parent's feelings, and she left with a negative sense of what it meant to go to school in the United States.

In another situation, a teacher who had been accustomed to celebrating Thanksgiving as a coming together of Native Americans and Pilgrims found himself almost in the midst of a riot on the day of the school play. The family with Native American roots and those who supported their point of view became very angry at the biased way the teacher had presented the Thanksgiving story. The fact that the teacher was totally unaware of the stereotypes he was conveying made the situation all the more volatile.

These clashing of values occur in schools over and over again. They should not be ignored or swept under the table; rather they should be viewed as opportunities for growth and change. As attitudes are discussed more openly, in some situations certain practices will change; in other situations the attitudes surrounding the practices will change. As a result, schools will be better positioned to prepare children for life in a culturally diverse world, which will be enriched by an appreciation of differences.

Of course, problems related to the complexities of cultural differences are not simple ones, with simple solutions. On the contrary, they are very complex. The developmental model is not a panacea, but it is an approach that addresses the complex issues arising in schools today. It offers clear parameters and within these parameters a great deal of flexibility. It is designed to empower teachers, children, and parents so that they can all be active agents in addressing specific problems as they arise. It focuses on the development of creativity and problem solving, essential skills in times of change and uncertainty, and it values diversity and the notion that society can be enriched by its diversity and by the varying contributions of all its members.

As schools struggle to be inclusionary, they also are becoming more complicated. It is difficult for teachers to know what the central values are and at the same time to be flexible and accepting. On the one hand, it is important to communicate values that are universal across cultural groups—the values of empowering children, working hard, respecting differences, being responsible for oneself as well as the group, making one's own decisions, and being productive. On the other hand, it is important to take into account differences in values that exist among cultural groups, among people with varying sexual orientations, and among people with varying skills, abilities, and limitations.

The developmental model in its best form is the optimal model for helping children deal with the wide range of issues prevalent in society. The model—with its emphasis on problem solving, adjusting to the needs of the children and the situation, and continuous modification—is of critical value in programs for today's children. We do not know what will be asked of children twenty years from now. What we do know is that within their lifetimes, children can expect many changes—in occupation, leisure pursuits, and lifestyles (Naisbitt, 1982). Life was once more predictable, and flexibility and responsiveness in educational programs were not as critical then as they are today. Current knowledge about child development and how it is affected by environmental factors suggests that the developmental approach in educational programs for young children has enormous potential for addressing the complex challenges of educating young children in today's society.

Summary

In this chapter, we have set the stage for the quest for high-quality early childhood programs. We have defined what is meant by early childhood education and established the need for viewing the early childhood years as a unit so that children and families can have continuity in their educational experiences throughout this period. We have also defined the term *developmental education,* attempted to clarify some misperceptions about it, and established a rationale for the applicability of this model to all children living in today's complex world.

CHAPTER 2

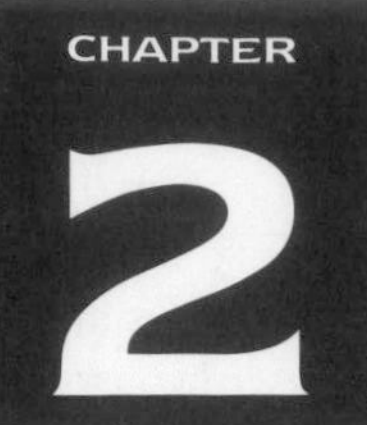

THEORETICAL AND HISTORICAL CONNECTIONS

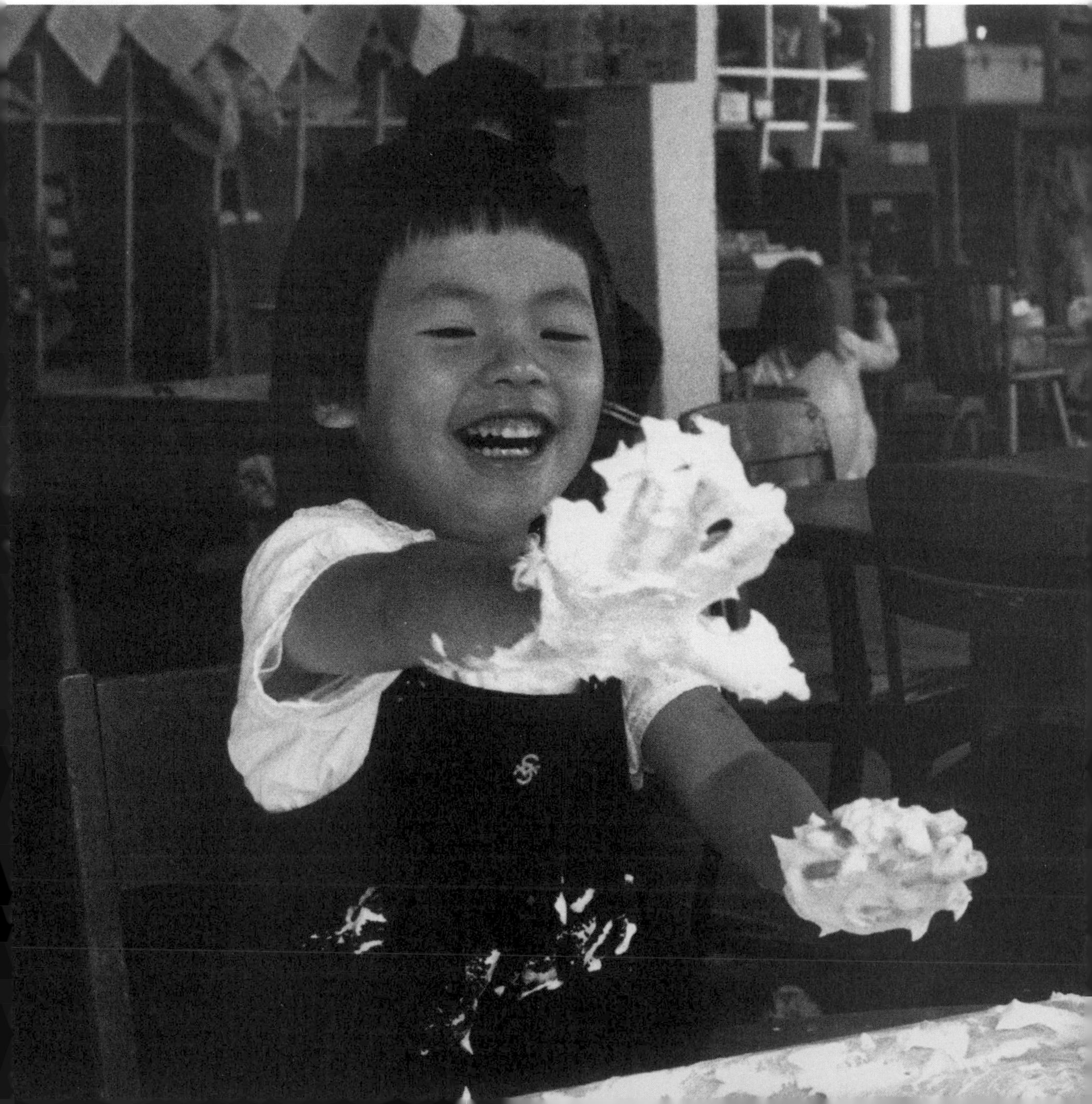

- *Influences from Developmental Psychology*
- *Historical Roots of Developmental Education*
- *Some Identifiable Developmental Models*
- *Summary*

This chapter links the key characteristics of developmentally based programs to the theory and the history on which they are based. Emphasized are the origins of the child-centered curriculum and the movement toward curriculum continuity in prekindergarten through grade three programs. Also contrasted are some identifiable developmental models. These themes combine to provide a sense of the excitement and challenge that currently exists in the field of early childhood education.

The previous chapter presented an expanded definition of the cognitive-developmental model based on the eight key characteristics that illuminate its implementation. A few examples were provided to illustrate how these characteristics manifest themselves in the classroom. Also discussed were some common misperceptions about the model and how these misperceptions tend to obstruct optimum implementation.

Another factor that often stands in the way of thoughtful implementation of the cognitive-developmental model is the tendency to separate knowledge in the fields of developmental psychology and child development from the realm of educational practice. Often people are able to state the explicit characteristics of the developmental model. However, the link between these characteristics and the developmental principles on which they are based is not clearly understood, and justifications for the characteristics are overlooked or taken for granted. People tend to pay lip service to the characteristics without fully understanding their real meaning, the rationale behind them, or for that matter how they are expressed in the classroom. Sometimes educators tend to use these characteristics as slogans, catch phrases, or educational jargon without fully understanding their implications and connection to developmental theory. As a result, these educators have difficulty implementing developmentally based programs or explaining them to parents and other educators. To avoid this pitfall, the psychological information that frames the planning, implementation, and evaluation of developmentally based programs must be linked with classroom practice.

The study of child development tells us much about the nature of the child, how growth and thought take place, and the complexities of individual development as it occurs within the context of general development. What child development theory does not tell us, however, is how those ideas and principles are manifested in child rearing and education. That separate, but crucial, topic is the subject of this chapter.

Some aspects of developmental theory speak clearly about the implications for practice, whereas others are more elusive, contain greater ambiguity, and are more susceptible to bias. Nonetheless, much in developmental theory speaks loudly and clearly about how the parent and teacher should proceed. It is to this body of knowledge that we turn our attention. This chapter links the key characteristics of the model with the major influences that provide its theoretical, historical, and philosophical foundation. The aim is to provide deeper understanding of the integration of theory and practice, leading toward the development of a framework for implementing and evaluating the model.

Influences from Developmental Psychology

The study of child development is a vast and complex area, representing a wide range of beliefs and theories. Although developmental early childhood education is eclectic in nature and draws upon a number of perspectives, its dominant thrust is derived from two major areas: psychodynamic theory, including the work of Freud and Erikson; and cognitive-developmental theory, as set forth by Piaget, Werner, Vygotsky, Kohlberg, and other developmentalists. Developmental theory has enabled us to see isolated patterns of behavior as part of a larger whole, providing an invaluable logic and coherence to information and thinking about development. For example, although sensitive observers of children have long been able to recognize that young children were predisposed to move, play, and touch things—in other words, to learn by concrete means—developmental theory enables us to see that inclination more comprehensively, as part of a particular stage of development, along with a host of other characteristics. Understanding stage theory helps us to understand why certain behaviors take place; it moves us beyond simply making factual observations.

Thomas (1992) attempted to clarify the distinction between a theory and a cluster of facts about how children behave as follows:

> I define theory as an explanation of how the facts fit together. More precisely, I intend the process of theorizing about child development to mean the act of proposing (1) which facts are most important for understanding children and (2) what sorts of relationships amongst the facts are most significant for producing this understanding. Theory is what makes sense out of facts. Theory gives facts their meaning. Without theory, facts remain a clutter of disorganized specks on the canvas, unconnected spots that form no picture of how and why children grow as they do. (p. 4)

Play is a critically important part of children's development. In psychodynamic theory, play serves as an avenue for expressing feelings, a way of working out emotional conflicts (Isaacs, 1933/1992) and gaining control over real or imagined fears (Erikson, 1963; Singer & Singer, 1992; Williams & Fromberg, 1992). In cognitive-developmental theory, play assumes a critical role at each stage of development. It is related to constructivism, which describes development as a process of creating understanding and envisions a clear role for play. Both Piaget (McKee, 1986; Piaget, 1962) and Vygotsky (Thomas, 1992) have recognized its importance. Play is a vital aspect of each stage of cognitive development. In sensorimotor play, children engage in repetitive actions. Later, in the preoperational stage, children develop a capacity for symbolic or pretend play, and then for dramatic and sociodramatic play, in which they reenact situations. These reenactments help children better comprehend various aspects of the interpersonal relationships they observe or in which they are involved. Through play children come to understand rules (an ability most closely associated with the concrete operational stage) and grow in their skill in negotiating a rule structure (Piaget 1962; Kamii & DeVries, 1980). Many authors have described the relationship between theoretical discussions about the value of play and practical aspects of developing a curriculum that relies heavily on play opportunities for children (Dimidjian, 1992; Wasserman, 1990; Monighan-Nourot, Scales, Van Hoorn, & Almy, 1987). The cognitive-developmental model depends on teachers' understanding play, identifying frameworks for observing children at play, and using this information in curriculum planning. The next section describes specific theoretical frameworks that aid in observing and understanding behavior.

Major Theoretical Influences

Two major theories have profoundly impacted developmental education: **cognitive-developmental theory,** as espoused by Piaget, Vygotsky, and other cognitive psychologists; and **psychosocial theory,** as described by Erikson. These theories are vast in scope. Identified here are a few of the theories' essential components, which illuminate the key characteristics of the developmental model.

Piagetian Theory and the Cognitive-Developmental Movement

The dominant figure in shaping the theoretical underpinnings of developmental education was Jean Piaget, a Swiss psychologist. Piaget provided us with a complex theoretical framework for understanding the nature of children's thinking from a developmental perspective. Although during recent years, Piaget's work has been challenged and debated boldly, his contribution remains an important and highly influential force and continues to guide our thinking.

Jean Piaget (1896–1980) was a **genetic epistemologist**: in other words, he was concerned about children's thinking and the way in which they construct knowledge and understanding. His interest was not in the field of education, although his theories have had a profound impact on educational practice, particularly as they have been used in defining and articulating the concept of constructivism (by, for example, DeVries & Kohlberg, 1990; Kamii, 1982; Elkind, 1967).

Piaget's work clearly supports the key characteristic concerning the observation and recording of children's behavior, particularly behavior related to how children think. Piaget closely observed children—primarily his own three children—from infancy onward, documenting their behavior in elaborate detail across a number of domains of functioning, including language; memory; understanding of space, time, and number; working with rules; and learning right from wrong (Singer & Revenson, 1978). He also interviewed children extensively, using what he called the **clinical interview,** a research method that involves asking open-ended questions in a controlled situation, to document how children responded to a series of specific experimental tasks. Piaget was particularly interested in children's errors, since he believed that they provide important information about children's thought. In this area, too, the developmental model is indebted to Piaget. Observing children's errors often provides the teacher with important information. From the data gained from his study of children, Piaget constructed a stage theory that attempts to explain the child's progression in cognition as it unfolds during development.

Jean Piaget (1896–1980) The Bettmann Archive

A premise of stage theory is that the nature of children's thinking changes as they grow and interact with the environment: at different stages of development, children process information and solve problems differently. Prior to Piaget's work, educators tended to view the child as intellectually an empty vessel, with knowledge something that was deposited into the child. Piaget's stages helped us to recognize that the same knowledge is addressed by a child at one stage of development in a way different from the way a child at another stage would handle it; it is the interaction between the child's organizational abilities and the new information that is of key importance. Piaget stressed the importance of the child's constructing knowledge, meaning that new experiences and information must be processed and reorganized in relationship to existing structures of understanding. Hence, Piaget saw the child as actively involved in learning, not simply a passive recipient of what others deliver. This aspect of his work forms the basis for the key characteristic of the developmental model that concerns the *physical environment,* providing a clear rationale for making available to children concrete, hands-on learning materials and ample opportunity to explore these materials.

To illustrate that children construct their own knowledge, Piaget described in his book *The Child's Conception of the World* (1960) his son's explanation of the origins of a large body of water. This anecdote can be particularly useful to educators who are trying to explain the concept of constructivism to parents and the community. Most people who interact with children will be able to recount a similar experience.

As a prelude to the story, Piaget speaks of the importance of children's acting upon new knowledge and learnings, emphasizing that the new learnings must be incorporated into existing understandings.

> When [Piaget] and his son were out walking, they noticed a large body of water. "How did that water get there?" the son asked. The father explained: "Years ago in the ice age there was a large glacier. As the earth became warmer, the glacier moved down and melted in this spot." "No," said the son, "that's not what happened. There was a great big giant who had a large bucket of water. He spilled the water right here." Despite the father's words the child persisted in his own interpretation of the natural phenomenon. The next day when the two were out walking, the child asked the father the same question; he received the same answer and persisted in sharing his own story about the giant. (p. 326)

Piaget's theory provides the basis for constructivism, a movement within developmental education that remains closely linked to his theoretical contribution. Although all programs that purport to be developmental draw generally from Piagetian theory, the constructivists are more closely attached to the theory, designing curriculum and approaches to instruction that are more specifically derivative (Forman & Kuschner, 1983; DeVries & Kohlberg, 1990; Kamii & DeVries, 1980; Forman & Hill, 1980). According to constructivist theory, each individual builds his or her own concepts through a process inherent in human development. All individuals are born with the capacity for organizing their experiences. This organization is an ongoing process through which new information is taken in (assimilated) and present mental structures change (accommodate) to take account of the new information. Thus, cognitive growth is a process of continual reorganization; the individual takes in new information and makes it fit with what is already known.

The message here for the developmental educator is that teachers need to have faith in a child's ability to construct knowledge. This faith pervades the characteristic related to grouping practices. It justifies the practice of having children work alone or in groups and take responsibility for their own learning. It diminishes the need for total group instruction in which the teacher imparts information and children follow directions.

Piaget differentiated between **arbitrary social learning,** learning **physical knowledge,** and learning **logico-mathematical knowledge.** Arbitrary social learning includes learning names of objects, customs, skills, and other information that can be learned through association or by rote. It also consists of information that can be easily transferred from one individual to another: for example, that January 1 is the first day of the year, or that it is important to say "thank you" when someone gives you something. Arbitrary social learning is very different from constructivism, which Piaget describes as operating when children learn about rules, make decisions about moral behavior, and are involved in more complex transformations of knowledge. Physical knowledge includes information about the physical world: for instance, that a wheel rolls, a magnet attracts metal objects, or some objects sink in water while others float. Logico-mathematical knowledge involves understanding relationships: for example, how to classify, compare, recognize one-to-one correspondence, and understand rules. According to Piaget, neither physical knowledge nor logico-mathematical knowledge can be taught by others. The individual needs to construct his or her own understanding through an ongoing process of activity that makes possible personal transformation of knowledge (Peterson & Felton-Collins, 1986).

Piaget identified four stages of cognitive development: (1) the **sensorimotor stage**; (2) the **preoperational stage**; (3) the **concrete operational stage**; and (4) the **formal operational stage.** Each of these stages is based on a particular kind of thinking. Of particular interest to educators who work with children aged three to eight are the preoperational and concrete operational stages. These two stages are defined in relation to each other by the presence or absence of certain abilities. In the preoperational stage, a child is unable to keep two ideas in mind at a time. Moreover, thinking at the preoperational stage is **perception-bound.** In other words, the child focuses on the most salient aspects of a given situation—such as what can be seen, heard, or felt at the moment—and is unable to focus on more than one attribute at a given time. In the visual realm, this is termed "before-the-eye reality" meaning that the child attends to those elements that seem most obvious. As the child matures, his or her quality of thinking changes. The child acquires the ability to conserve—to keep two ideas in mind at the same time—and is no longer perception-bound in his or her thinking. At this stage the child is described as a concrete operational thinker. Concrete operational thinking is less egocentric than preoperational thought and involves a greater capacity to consider multiple aspects of a situation simultaneously. The child is increasingly able to **decenter,** that is, to become less bound to his or her own point of view, known as **egocentricity,** and gain in the capacity to consider other people's perspectives.

Although these two stages are identified as separate entities, in reality there is constant moving between them when the child is in transition from one cognitive orientation to another. Piaget refers to this as "intuitive thinking." For example, a child who is dominantly in the preoperational stage may, when attempting to solve a particular problem, show evidence of more advanced thought characteristic of the concrete operational stage. The process of decentering is long and arduous; intuitive thinking is a valuable mechanism by which the child makes the transition from one stage to another.

Understanding the child's thinking is important for the teacher who is attempting to match curriculum to the child's developmental level. Piaget's theory provides guides for assessing the child's level of development. For example, a teacher who is aware of a preoperational thinker's limitations can modify the presentation of material so that children's perceptions are paramount and children are not asked to consider too many variables at the same time. This understanding of development will aid the teacher in making sense of the inaccuracies and inconsistencies in children's thinking.

When a child is clearly at the preoperational stage or clearly at the concrete operational stage, making observations about development and planning experiences are relatively simple processes. However, frequently children are neither clearly preoperational nor clearly concrete operational. The child may be in what Piaget calls the **intuitive stage,** the period of time between the preoperational stage and the concrete operational stage when children show some evidence of concrete operational thinking, but not on all occasions nor with all types of tasks. The important point is that children progress from one stage of cognitive thinking to the next at varying rates. This progress occurs with maturation and with the child's experience in operating on—or in other words manipulating—concrete objects and materials in the environment. As the child grows, the quality of thinking changes. The child becomes concrete operational and gains increasing skill in being able to decenter from experiences and take into account more than one factor at a time. Thus, the child is able to avoid distracting thoughts and focus more consistently.

Table 2.1 provides an overview of Piagetian stages. The age identification for each of the stages is approximate. Since children differ in rate of growth, the age at which they achieve a particular level of thinking varies.

Criticisms of Piaget

Many criticisms of Piagetian theory have been advanced. One argument focuses on evidence that concrete operational thinking is not an all-or-nothing quality. Children may be perception-bound in one situation and not in another. They may be capable of conserving at one time and not at another. The critics of Piagetian theory argue that children's cognitive abilities seem to grow gradually rather than by stages. Berk (1991) explained the criticisms of Piaget's notion of cognitive stages as follows:

> If [stages] exist, children must display new competencies that they did not have before. . . . [However,] most cognitive changes proceed slowly and gradually; very few abilities are absent during one period and then suddenly present at another. . . . [Rather,] within each of Piaget's stages, children appear to be constantly modifying structures and acquiring new skills. (pp. 243–244)

TABLE 2.1

An Overview of Piagetian Stages of Cognitive Development

Stage	Approximate Age	Principal Characteristics
sensorimotor	birth to 2 years	object permanence means-end relationships
preoperational	2 to 7 or 8 years	perception-bound thinking inability to keep two ideas in mind at the same time
concrete operational	7 to 11 years	ability to conserve—that is, keep two ideas in mind at the same time reversibility—the understanding "that any change of position, shape, order, etc., can be reversed"
formal operational	12 and up	abstract thinking propositional thinking

SOURCE: Based on information from Peterson and Felton-Collins (1986).

Even though conclusive information about the validity of Piaget's stage theory is not currently available, the orientation and structure Piaget's theory provides can be of great help to teachers as they observe behavior.

Application of Piagetian Theory to Classroom Practice

Consider the following incident, observed in a kindergarten classroom. The teacher asked the children to think of words that rhymed with *fan*. The children identified several words: *can, man, Dan, Nan, ban*. At this point one child blurted out, "I have a Band-Aid on my knee. I fell down and . . . " The teacher tried to get the child's attention back to the task of rhyming words; however, the child, hearing the word *ban,* had associated it with *Band-Aid* and was unable to focus both on his Band-Aid experience and the need to continue the rhyming pattern. If this child revealed the same type of thinking in a variety of situations, one could postulate that the child is not yet a concrete operational thinker (that is, he is not yet able to keep two ideas in mind at the same time, but is instead perception-bound) and thus may have difficulty in tasks requiring phonetic analysis. **Phonetic analysis** involves focusing on the visual appearance of the letter and the sound that the letter represents.

The following is another example of how Piagetian principles manifest themselves in the classroom. Narison (age five and a half), a kindergartner, and Taylor (age eight), his third-grade buddy, were playing a Milton-Bradley game called Guess Who. In this game there are three duplicate sets of 24 character cards. Each of two players has a rack with a set of the individual characters cards arranged randomly. At the start of the game each player draws a character card from the third set of cards. The object of the game is to be the first to identify the character card the opponent drew from the third set. This is done by asking a series of yes/no questions through which characters on the player's rack can be eliminated or turned face down. Narison had drawn a girl character. When Taylor asks, "Is your character a boy?" the answer is no so she turns down the nineteen boy cards on her rack, leaving only five cards to eliminate. On Narison's turn, he asks the same question: "Is your character a boy?" Since Taylor's character is a boy, she answers "Yes." Narison is puzzled by the fact that he, through the same question, gets to turn down only five cards, while Taylor could turn down nineteen cards. Narison notices that there are more pictures of boys than girls. He recognizes that the object of the game is to be left with one card standing, the card that matches the opponent's. His facial expressions and tone of voice reflect real puzzlement that his question did not lead to turning down the greatest number of cards. This puzzlement is an example of cognitive conflict.

Trying to explain this situation to Narison is useless. Narison has identified a thinking problem for himself. He looks for every possible opportunity to play the game over and over again so that he can figure out this problem. Watch him play, listen to his questions, observe the way in which he hesitatingly eliminates the characters, and you will get a sense of the intellectual challenge he is experiencing.

As a third example, consider the following incident, which involves Chekeska, a four-year-old interacting with her teacher. Chekeska is working on a puzzle. She usually is skilled at putting puzzles together. This time she has chosen a puzzle with twenty pieces. She has tried repeatedly to match up shapes, but these efforts have not led to the completion of the puzzle. The teacher notices that Chekeska is having difficulty. She sits down beside her and tries to offer helpful clues: "Look at the picture on the cover of the box. See the blue sky and the green grass. The puppy is golden brown. See if you can put all the blue pieces for the sky together." Chekeska does this without too much difficulty. Then the teacher says, "Can you find the piece of the sky that goes right here in the corner?" On the first three tries, Chekeska is unable to identify the corner sky piece. She overturns the puzzle board, brushes all the pieces to the floor, and declares, "I don't want to do this anymore." Then she runs to the sandbox and starts to disrupt the play of the children who have been engaged in setting up a bakery shop. What is the teacher's response to this behavior? What factors does the teacher need to consider before deciding how to react? How does the teacher's reaction affect Chekeska's development?

The sensitive, astute teacher is aware that a child's behavior may be viewed through many lenses. Using an understanding of development to inform educational practice, the teacher in the example just given considers what she knows about Chekeska as an individual: her genetic makeup as evidenced through her temperament, her willingness to take risks, her rate of development, her previous experiences, the sociocultural context in which she is growing up, the kinds of experiences she is having in school and outside of school, and the factors operating in the present situation. In this particular situation, the teacher purposely selects the cognitive lens as a way of making sense out of Chekeska's behavior, recognizing that under different circumstances Chekeska's reaction may be different or a different lens may be more appropriate.

Using the Piagetian stages as a guide through which to view this behavior, the teacher hypothesizes that perhaps the cognitive challenge was too great for Chekeska, and cognitive frustration contributed to her behavior. In this case the teacher might review the cognitive challenge she presented to Chekeska. The teacher then would recognize that she asked the child to shift focus and consider two or more dimensions of the puzzle picture (the shape, the color, and the contextual meaning) at the same time. This task seemed to be beyond Chekeska's cognitive capacity. The cognitive frustration she experienced caused her to react in anger and frustration. Looking through the cognitive lens, the teacher would recall that children aged four to seven are often in transition between a preoperational mode of thinking and a concrete operational mode. This in-between stage, which Piaget labeled the intuitive stage, is characterized by inconsistency in the child's ability to perceive two dimensions of a situation at the same time. Should the teacher help Chekeska avoid puzzles of this complexity until she shows signs of being more ready for them? In some cases that interpretation would be appropriate, but the analysis does not stop there. With some guidance and under different circumstances, Chekeska may be able to complete a puzzle of comparable complexity. Of key importance is that the adult understand the potential cognitive source of the child's behavior and not interpret it as simplistically negative.

Although the cognitive stages of development do not provide us with definitive answers, one thing is certain: Piaget helped clarify our vision, providing us with an important lens through which we can observe and study behavior. This lens, like any other lens we may choose to use to study behavior, does not provide unambiguous information. However, it certainly constitutes a useful tool.

The Contrast Between Piagetian and Vygotskian Perspectives

Vygotsky (1896–1934), a Russian psychologist who during his short lifespan was a contemporary of Piaget's, shared Piaget's ideas on stage theory (although he defined stages differently) and on the importance of activity in learning. Vygotsky, however, expanded on Piaget's stress of the use of concrete materials as a dominant means of concept formation. In addition to the importance of concrete materials, Vygotsky emphasized the critical importance of social interactions in shaping cognitive development. The social interactions (or the **dialectic,** as Vygotsky calls the discussions between the learner and an adult or a more knowledgable peer) provide a way for learning to take place. Vygotsky (1978) coined the term **zone of proximal development,** which, in the context of instruction, he defined as

> the difference between the actual development level as determined by independent problem solving and the level of potential development as determined through problem solving under adult guidance or in collaboration with more capable peers. (p. 86)

In the case of Chekeska, the child who was working with the puzzle, the teacher, possibly on another occasion, might try to enter a dialogue with the child and engage in the puzzle completion task with her. In this way the adult could provide the script, or the verbal representation of the activity, which the child could then follow.

Piaget and Vygotsky also viewed the role of social interaction in cognition differently. Piaget emphasized the importance of peer interactions when children are at the same, or close to the same, cognitive level, emphasizing the importance of stage compatibility. For Vygotsky the interpersonal process occurs first.

An interpersonal process is transformed into an intrapersonal one. Every function in the child's cultural development appears twice: first, on the social level, and later, on the individual level; first between people *(interpsychological),* and then inside the child *(intrapsychological).* This applies equally to voluntary attention, to logical memory, and to the formation of concepts. All the higher functions originate as actual relations between human individuals. (Vygotsky, 1978, p. 57)

Thus, a basic difference between Piaget and Vygotsky is that Piaget saw thinking as emanating from within the individual and then being used in relationship to others, whereas Vygotsky, who espoused a **sociocultural theory** of development, saw thought as originating in interpersonal relations and then moving inward for greater understanding.

Piaget and Vygotsky also viewed the role of language in cognition from differing perspectives. Piaget saw **inner speech** as egocentric, immature, and disappearing as the child matured. Vygotsky viewed inner speech as a way of directing one's own thinking, an ability that becomes more refined with maturity. Vygotsky emphasized the critical importance of language in concept formation. For Piaget, actually manipulating the object was of greater value than having words to describe the activity.

Thus, the Vygotskian perspective provides a broader cognitive lens through which teachers can observe evidences of children's thought processes. It expands the notion of cognitive conflict to cover not only the child's interactions with materials and personal struggles to make meaning, but also interpersonal factors, such as discussions between the child and a more knowledgeable individual. Language plays an important role in this expanded view of cognition. Language facilitates the adult and child's engaging in joint problem solving, with the adults supporting and challenging the child. The adult provides a **scaffolding** for the development of abilities, by breaking particular tasks into small discrete subsets and, as the learner becomes more skilled, gradually transferring responsibility for the task to the learner (Rogoff, 1990).

Links Between Vygotskian Ideas and Developmental Education

These Vygotskian ideas are most closely related to the key characteristic of the developmental model that emphasizes the teacher's *intellectual vibrancy.* To engage the child effectively in the dialectic, the teacher needs to identify the key concepts central to an educational task and to be skilled in asking questions.

Vygotsky's work also highlighted the need for teachers to be aware of and take into account *children's cultural background*—another of the key characteristics of the developmental model. For Vygotsky, culture played an important role in cognition. He believed that it is impossible to separate culture from cognition, since the former provides the context within which interactions take place. Hence, Vygotsky's is a sociocultural or sociohistoric theory. This orientation is gaining increased recognition and appreciation today because of its implications for education in a multicultural society.

Some of Vygotsky's ideas, particularly the notions of the dialectic and the zone of proximal development, are a part of the theory underlying the **Reading Recovery** program developed by Marie Clay. The Reading Recovery program is designed to help children avoid failure in literacy learning. Children in the program who at the end of the kindergarten year, or at the beginning of the first grade, appear to be at risk for failure in the area of literacy learning can be helped when the teacher is trained to be a keen observer and to identify the child's zone of proximal development. The role of the Reading Recovery teacher is to engage the child in tasks that the child can accomplish alone and then to provide materials and dialogue within the child's zone of proximal development as a way of helping the child to progress in the development of literacy skills (Clay, 1991). The same principle has important implications for all aspects of curriculum planning.

New Directions in Cognitive Psychology

Other cognitive psychologists—Allan Collins, John Seely Brown, and Susan E. Newman (1989)—are building on Vygotskian ideas. They emphasize two ideas that help to make the link between children's natural capacity to learn and the role of education in the learning process: namely, **situated learning** and **apprenticeship.** Situated learning is learning that occurs in a meaningful, authentic context—for example, learning about writing in order to serve a specific purpose, like preparing a memo, writing a letter, or assisting in producing the school newspaper. Situated learning provides motivation as well as opportunity to practice skills and gain knowledge. Note that situated learning substantiates a key characteristic of the developmental model: namely, an *integrated approach* to academics.

Apprenticeship is working alongside someone who already possesses the knowledge and skills the learner needs to acquire. Allan Collins, John Seely Brown, Susan E. Newman (1989), and other cognitive and developmental scientists and educators have been working on pulling together the findings of cognitive psychology and defining its implications for education. In their view, apprenticeships in schools represent one scientifically based way to restructure schools. Barbara Rogoff is also contributing to this effort. In her book *Apprenticeship in Thinking*, she considered

> children as apprentices in thinking, active in their efforts to learn from observing and participating with peers and more skilled members of their society, developing skills to handle culturally defined problems with available tools, and building from these givens to construct new solutions within the context of sociocultural activity. (Rogoff, 1990, p. 7)

The notion of the *cognitive apprenticeship* provides support for the flexible grouping characteristic of the developmental model. Children differ in the skills they possess, and they certainly can learn from one another. Farnham-Diggory (1990) described what schools based on the cognitive-developmental model should be like: "Schooling is reconceptualized as a cognitive apprenticeship, a place where people go to develop skills in learning to learn, problem solving, and the creative application of ideas" (p. 56).

One curriculum approach that embodies the ideas of situated learning and cognitive apprenticeships is **process writing.** In process writing, emphasis is on conveying ideas first and then revising and editing several drafts of a written piece. Learning to express ideas precedes learning detailed strategies about how to write.

Children write about topics they know and care about, and they have the opportunity to observe teachers and other peers as writers. Children also have the benefit of conference time with adults and peers who can help them think more deeply about the ideas they are sharing.

A second example of this kind of curriculum approach is **whole language,** in which children gain literacy skills through active engagement in authentic literacy situations. Children learn through naturalistic processes rather than direct instruction (Weaver, 1990). Included among the conditions of learning in the whole language classroom are "demonstration of how texts are constructed and used and the engagement of learners in these demonstrations." Teachers and children examining texts together is a beautiful example of how affect and skills are transmitted to children.

Another condition for learning described in cognitive-developmental theory is called **approximation.** In an environment that encourages approximation as a step toward mastery, children are rewarded for their efforts to match a model, rather than being corrected for the ways their approximation fails to come up to the standard of the ultimately desired behavior. Thus, children feel free to make mistakes and eventually to learn from these mistakes as their efforts come closer and closer to the desired model. "Proponents of whole language believe that keeping children from making the mistakes that occur in approximations is a sure way to make them insecure and inhibit their development" (Crispen, n.d.). In whole language classrooms, there is a continuous interaction between reading and writing. Weaver (1990) described several naturalistic studies that demonstrated the potency of whole language learning in children's development as readers and writers. These studies also illustrated the power of learning in authentic situations as well as in an interdisciplinary setting. The teaching practices that support whole language learning are consistent with the findings of cognitive psychologists and are clearly related to the developmental model.

Information Processing Approach

A challenge to cognitive stage theory is the work being carried out in the area of information processing. Information processing theorists see children's performance as context-specific and view cognitive growth as a continuous process rather than occurring in discrete stages. As Berk points out, however, "the existence of cognitive stages is still an unsettled issue" (Berk, 1991, p. 244). It behooves the intellectually vibrant teacher to keep abreast of the findings of the information processing theorists. These theorists are paying particular attention to how children take in information, process it, store it in long- or short-term memory, and retrieve it for use at appropriate times—an approach stimulated in part by computer technology. Information processing theory emphasizes encouraging children to think about *how* they learn as well as what they learn and to focus on metacognitive strategies. The approach is thus clearly related to aspects of cognitive conflict and how *social-emotional issues* are incorporated into the curriculum. Researchers are currently exploring how information processing approaches may apply to children's learning to read, to think mathematically, and to solve problems. It is important for the cognitive-developmental teacher to be aware of this and other directions in the field of developmental psychology, so that findings consistent with the developmental model can be incorporated into it, and inconsistent ones can be thoughtfully avoided.

One tendency of the information processing approach is to atomize learning. If under some circumstances this approach appears beneficial to children's progress, the developmental educator should be able to assess its effectiveness and continue to move toward a meaningful, integrated approach. As developmental programs continue to evolve, the intellectually vibrant teacher will keep abreast of new developments and use new findings to better understand how children develop.

Eriksonian Theory: The Psychodynamic Influences

Up to this point we have discussed the work of cognitive psychologists, with particular emphasis on the work of Piaget and Vygotsky. Let us turn now to psychodynamic influences on the developmental education model. Erik Erikson (1902–), a major psychodynamic theorist, has provided us with a dynamic model for examining the psychosocial stages of development as people move from infancy through old age. Highly influenced by Freud, Erikson set about the task of plotting the major challenges that the individual confronts in moving through the life cycle. Each stage presents the individual with a social or emotional challenge; accompanying this challenge is the threat of a liability if the stage is not mastered effectively. The notion of a contest between resolution and lack of resolution is central to the Eriksonian perspective. The stages are not hierarchical—that is, the resolution of one is not dependent upon full realization of preceding stages—but they are progressive and developmental in nature.

Erikson's stages are also closely related to physical changes that are taking place as the individual grows and develops, and are consistent with Freudian psychosexual stages (the oral, anal, oedipal, latency, and genital stages). These physical changes are of major significance in the manifestations of a particular stage of development.

Most educators are familiar with Erikson's theory of "eight stages of man" (1963); however, educators frequently have not thought through the theory's implications for working with children. In addition to providing a lens through which behavior may be viewed, Erikson's psychosocial stages, combined with the work of the cognitive psychologists, provide a useful framework for structuring the social-emotional component of curriculum and classroom management—one of the key characteristics of the developmental model. When teachers recognize the psychosocial conflicts in which children are immersed at a particular stage of their development, teachers are in a better position to structure experiences that will help children understand the conflicts they are experiencing and work toward a more positive resolution of these conflicts. Erikson's stages may be summarized as follows.

In infancy, the stage of conflict centers on **trust versus mistrust.** Throughout the first eighteen months of life, infants are constantly struggling to determine whether or not they can trust the environment to be responsive to their needs—for food, human contact, and stimulation. Infants who emerge from this stage with a feeling that the environment is dependable and responsive, and that they can influence the environment to fulfill their needs, will develop a sense of trust as a

Erik Erikson (1902–   ) Jon Erikson

firm foundation on which to base their struggles to resolve subsequent developmental conflicts. Erikson does not suggest that if the positive resolution of a given stage does not take place at the critical time, it is impossible to achieve a future resolution. Rather, certain developmental periods are more optimum, or facilitative, of effective mastery of a given dynamic.

Toddlers, from eighteen months to about two and a half years, are working through the conflict of **autonomy versus shame and doubt.** It is no accident that the most common word in the vocabulary of the two-year-old is *no*. Through using this powerful word, children express their autonomy, or their power to be self-directed. Adults who understand children of this age help them find ways to both express their autonomy and at the same time provide the sense of security that children derive from knowing that adults have set clear parameters for behavior. This stage, characterized by what Erikson calls "holding on and letting go," is intimately connected to the period of toilet training. In both bodily and behavioral functions, the child is engaged in this dynamic contest.

The conflict that looms the largest for preschool children, ages three to five, is a conflict between initiative and guilt. In the **initiative versus guilt** stage, children develop their psychosocial sense of self by intrusively acting on their environment. Their emerging language abilities enable them to create imaginary situations and to engage in play through which they can express ideas and emotions. This is a heightened period for fantasy and imagination—for bold experimentation and exploration. Thus, often a child will have an imaginary playmate whose creation is uniquely the child's and whose presence the child literally forces on others (Fraiberg, 1959). Particularly interesting is how the child uses the imaginary playmate to solve problems of a psychosocial nature: "I did not spill the juice. Petey [the imaginary friend who is very real to the child] did it." The imaginary playmate indicates the child's ability to think in ways different from those of the adult.

The imaginary playmate is only one example of how children, using their own ideas and objects in the environment, find ways to deal with problems they are encountering. In effect, children through fantasy play can become their own mental health advocates. They can create situations like those they are concerned about and develop their own strategies for resolving or dealing with these concerns. They create these situations in many ways: sometimes through symbolic play, other times through exploration of art materials, blocks, or use of their bodies in creative movement activities. In this stage, children are propelled by a sense of initiative, and process is of the utmost importance. If children are not provided with a time to use this initiative in ways that are empowering and bring them positive feedback, they will come to doubt and feel guilty about having their own ideas and will lack a sense of purpose in their interactions with the world.

For teachers of young children, this stage has deep implications. Preschool, kindergarten, and day care classrooms that provide rich stimulation and materials, as well as options for children to choose activities that involve play and creative activity, are providing a forum for children's full exploitation of the stage of initiative. Constricting environments—where narrow conformity and particular, correct ways of drawing and working are expected—are counterproductive to this developmental agenda.

As they grow older and become involved in what Erikson calls the **industry versus inferiority** stage, ages six to ten, children struggle to master the fundamentals of technology and the tools through which they can acquire and demonstrate competence in areas important in their particular culture. Teachers working with children of this age become keenly aware of how important it is for them to master skills. No longer are children content with bold, undifferentiated exploration; they are looking for products and are not satisfied only with process, as they may have been at a younger age. The struggle is no longer an individual one. It now becomes a matter of evaluating oneself in relation to others, one's peers, and engaging in the contest between feelings of industry and inferiority. In discussing industry versus inferiority, Erikson (1963) focuses on the notion of competence, which he defines as "fitness or ability to transact with the environment in such a way as to maintain self, flourish and grow." Developing competence involves activity, manipulation, and exploration, and the mastery of basic skills. The areas considered important for the development of competence in one society may not be valued in another. In the industrialized United States, learning to read and write are important. In other cultures in which it is necessary to hunt for one's own food, for example, hunting skills are more valued. Whatever the culture, productive activity is key to resolution of the industry versus inferiority conflict.

Erikson's stages provide an important tool for helping teachers understand what to expect of children's behavior and learning at different stages of development. For example, a teacher who is aware of a four-year-old's need to be assertive in his or her play will not overreact when small incidents of aggression occur. Instead, the teacher will examine behavior with deference to the child's developmental agenda and provide guidance with an understanding of what motivates particular actions. Teachers working with children in the stage of industry can provide constructive support by helping children in their quest to achieve and master skills and will recognize why sometimes children reveal what seems like excessive frustration, insecurity, and competitive behavior. Programs that support children's sense of trust and encourage the expression of autonomy, initiative, and industry are consistent with the developmental model.

Although Erikson's stages continue throughout the entire life cycle, we are addressing only those stages most closely associated with children aged three to eight. The reader is encouraged to examine the remaining stages in the accompanying chart and to read more extensively for a full appreciation of the complexity and continuity of the various stages. It is important to recognize that, according to Erikson, one does not progress through these stages and leave each one behind. On the contrary, the stages identify the principal focus of developmental issues at a particular time. Under some circumstances, individuals do regress and deal with earlier issues. Moreover, how one works through the issues of a particular stage influences development at subsequent stages, as well as one's lifelong stance toward certain issues. Age ranges for these stages are not fixed and universal; they are presented as general guidelines.

As teachers observe children's behavior, Erikson's theory can be particularly helpful. It can provide some insight in helping teachers differentiate between children who are struggling with initiative versus guilt as opposed to those whose main concern is with industry versus inferiority. Interpreting children's behavior is not easy, particularly in cultures that are product-oriented and value achievement. For example, when children are in the stage of initiative versus guilt, the meaning

TABLE 2.2

Erikson's Psychosocial Stages of Development

Stage	Major Conflict	Mode of Learning	Outcome	Approximate Age
1	trust vs. mistrust	incorporative mode	hope	0 to 18 months
2	autonomy vs. doubt or shame	retentive mode	self-will	1 to 3 years
3	initiative vs. guilt	intrusive mode	purpose	3 to 5 years
4	industry vs. inferiority	industrious mode	competence	6 to 11 years
5	identity vs. role confusion	exploration mode	fidelity	12 to 18 years
6	intimacy vs. isolation	love	commitment	18 to 35 years
7	generativity vs. stagnation	care	sharing	40 to 60 years
8	ego integrity vs. despair	wisdom	support of cultural institutions	60 and up

SOURCE: Based on Erik Erikson's eight stages of man, in *Childhood and Society* (1963).

of their play is not always discernible to an adult. Nonetheless, the play is serving an important purpose in development. To try to redirect this play and connect it more to industry when the child has not reached that stage can result in increased conflict within the child and may impede the child's creative development. Similarly, some children who chronologically may appear ready for the stage of industry may still need time to work through conflicts related to an earlier stage of development.

Another important dimension of early childhood programming on which Erikson's psychosocial theory can shed some light is the use of competition. Teachers who understand development will avoid setting up competitive situations with three- to five-year-old children. Children of this age often have cognitive difficulty processing instructions like "Let's see who can be the first to finish putting away the materials." It is not uncommon to see some children continue to pursue their own ideas despite this prompt from the teacher. The response they receive often contributes to their lowered self-image. For this reason teachers of children in the three- to five-year-old range often use techniques that stimulate imagination as a way of directing behavior.

The question of using competition with children six to ten years of age is also a complex one. If children are about equally matched in their skill level, they may enjoy competition without undue implications for the industry versus inferiority conflict. However, even with children at this stage, resourceful teachers can find ways to stimulate industry and competence that build confidence and self-esteem.

Erikson's stages of development provide support for the child's need to exert autonomy and make choices, to take initiative, and to move on to achieve industriousness and competence. These needs are well addressed by the developmental model.

Individual Differences

Stage theory is most helpful in plotting the progression through which most children move; stages provide the practitioner with a baseline for making general judgments about how most children think and behave. However, general stage theory must also be viewed in relationship to what we know and understand about individuals' similarities and dissimilarities. Developmentally based programs are committed to the notion of each child's uniqueness in terms of interests, intelligence, temperament, special needs, language, and prior experiences including those often associated with socioeconomic status.

Respect for the concept of individual differences is revealed in Gardner's (1983) notion of multiple intelligences. With his book *Frames of Mind,* Gardner has broadened our view of intelligence by identifying seven different kinds of intelligence: linguistic, musical, logico-mathematical, spatial, bodily-kinesthetic, intrapersonal, and interpersonal. Gardner maintains that the traditional view of intelligence is too narrow, since it focuses primarily on linguistic and logico-mathematical competences and fails to acknowledge the wide range of other kinds of intellectual power that exist. Gardner's objective has been to expand our understanding about the complexities of intelligence and to encourage us to look more broadly and specifically at the various ways individuals can reveal their cognitive capabilities.

In one undertaking, Project Spectrum, based on the work of Howard Gardner and David Feldman (Gardner, 1983), an assessment system was developed for identifying young children's intellectual proclivities. In addition to demonstrating respect for these different intelligences and for the way one area of intelligence operates in concert with another, the people involved in Project Spectrum investigated how teachers' sensitivity to children's intellectual proclivities can have a positive impact on children's behavior and learning (Krechevsky, 1991). In a first-grade classroom where Project Spectrum materials were being field-tested, one of the authors observed a child who was having great difficulty with reading, writing, and behavioral control reveal totally different behavior when the tools made available and the learning tasks demanded were related to what Gardner calls bodily-kinesthetic and spatial intelligence. According to Krechevsky, the director of Project Spectrum, "The general Spectrum approach can be used on many levels: as assessment, as curriculum, or as a powerful philosophical framework through which to view children and their particular sets of strengths and working styles" (1991, p. 138). The tasks that are a part of the Spectrum approach are based on real-life activities. For these reasons the approach is well suited to developmental classrooms.

Another example of how psychologists have taken into account the concept of individual differences is the important work carried out in the area of temperament by Thomas and Chess (1977). **Temperament** is defined as the individual's "characteristic style of emotional responding" (Berk, 1991). Temperament refers "to the *how* of behavior. It differs from ability, which is concerned with the *what* and *how well* of behaving, and from motivation, which accounts for the *why* a person does what he is doing. Temperament, by contrast, concerns the *way* in which an individual behaves" (Thomas & Chess, 1977, p. 9). Thomas and Chess have identified clusters of characteristics grouped into "three temperamental constellations" (p. 22). These are summarized below:

Easy—has a positive approach; is easily adaptable; is generally in a positive mood; maintains regular schedules for sleeping and eating; accepts rules easily.
Difficult—has irregular eating and sleeping patterns; usually has a negative response to new experiences; has difficulty adapting to new situations; reflects intense and often negative moods; reacts strongly, often with a tantrum, when frustrated.
Slow-To-Warm-Up—is slow to adapt; reacts mildly either on the positive or negative side; over time gradually shows "positive interest and involvement." (p. 23)

Other researchers (Buss & Plomin, 1975) have suggested somewhat different categories:

Emotionality—the intensity of reaction
Activity level—total energy output
Sociability—desire to be with others
Impulsivity—tendency to respond quickly. (pp. 7–8)

Studies conducted by Stephen Suomi with uptight monkeys and by Jerome Kagan with extremely shy children "support the belief that shyness is a part of a person's basic temperament" (Santrock & Yussen, 1992, p. 99). Temperament is believed to be an inborn characteristic. Although amenable to some degree of modification based on the individual's experiences, a child's temperament is believed to remain somewhat consistent throughout life. However, experiences do influence an individual's ability to accept, adapt, and maximize aspects of temperament. When there is a **"goodness-of-fit"** (Thomas & Chess, 1977; Chess & Thomas, 1984) between the child's temperament and the parenting or teaching style to which the child is exposed, optimal development results. When there is conflict between the temperament and the environment, development often takes the form of maladaptive functioning. Maladaptive functioning is most likely to occur in North American society when children with difficult temperaments receive punitive, intrusive, and inconsistent reactions from parents or teachers, or when slow-to-warm-up children take longer to become engaged than is allowed.

One temperament is not better than another. Each has its positive and negative side. Of critical importance is the goodness-of-fit between the child's temperament and the environment. A child with a slow-to-warm-up temperament may fare very well in circumstances in which caution is important, but less well in situations in which a high degree of sociability is valued. A child with an easy temperament perhaps has a better chance of faring well in most environments. Nonetheless, such a child's parents or teachers may possibly respond more favorably to children who are less predictable and more of a challenge.

Teachers have found the study of temperament and the compatibility of temperament between adult and child to be provocative. The concept of

Each child brings to the classroom his or her own basic temperament and way of interacting. © Elizabeth Crews temperament is particularly useful when discussing interaction patterns between an adult (a parent or a teacher) and a child with special needs, especially in cases in which the child's temperament makes it difficult for the adult to manage the child's behavior. Adults who engage in discussions about temperament as a way of helping children understand and manage their own behavior also find these discussions useful.

It is interesting to consider temperament in the light of cross-cultural research. "Chinese and Japanese babies are calmer, more easily soothed when upset, and better at self-quieting than Caucasian infants" (Berk, 1991; see also Caudill & Frost, 1975, Freedman & Freedman, 1969). The researchers point out that child-rearing patterns support this behavior, thus indicating the relationship between heredity and environment. Moreover, what is considered to be difficult in one culture may not be considered difficult in another. "Difficult children from working class Puerto Rican families are not more likely to be maladjusted, presumably because they are exposed to more accepting child-rearing attitudes and practices" (Berk, 1991, p. 411, citing Gannon & Korn, 1983).

One aspect of temperament is the individual's cognitive style. Impulsivity and reflectivity are aspects of cognitive style that clearly influence how a child reacts in a learning situation. The impulsive child blurts out answers and interjects comments before a reflective child has even begun to process the information. Cognitive style as manifested in individuals should be viewed as lying on a continuum. Some individuals are highly impulsive, others are highly reflective, and others are somewhere in between. Some teachers tend to value impulsivity; others, reflectivity. How a child fares in a group depends, to some degree, on how the teacher and the other children respond to the child. One basis for their response is the reflectivity or impulsivity of the parties involved.

Temperament, like stages of development, provides a lens through which teachers can view children's behavior. As teachers' understanding of temperament increases, they can consider and respond to this aspect of diversity among individuals. Responding to individual differences is a key component of the developmental model. In addition, information about temperament is clearly related to and has important implications for several of the developmental model's key characteristics: the need for thoughtful observation, the importance of social-emotional issues in the curriculum and in classroom management, and the emphasis on family and community.

Children with Special Needs: An Inclusionary Model

Research has demonstrated the benefits of educating children with special needs in classrooms together with typical children. These benefits include fostering social interaction and friendship among children, providing role models for behavior and approach to school-related activities, enhancing self-concept, and encouraging appreciation of the wide range of human diversity (Walter & Vincent, 1982). The publication *Hand in Hand* (Massachusetts Department of Education, 1991b) describes the benefits of an **inclusionary philosophy** as follows:

> The fundamental principle [in an inclusionary philosophy is the acceptance of the idea] that every person is a composite of both strengths and weaknesses. [As children come to appreciate] the existence of *both* within themselves,

> children with and without special needs may develop a realistic self-concept as well as the ability to focus on *capabilities* rather than disabilities. (p. 12)

Determining which children with special needs can benefit from and contribute to an inclusionary classroom is a judgment teachers, special educators, and parents need to make collaboratively; they then need to work toward curriculum planning that maximizes opportunities for all children in the class.

Many of the strategies that cognitive-developmental teachers employ work equally well for children of all ability levels, including those with special needs. In some cases, however, modifications are necessary. Frequently, modifications enhance learning opportunities not only for the child with identified special needs but for other children in the class as well. In an article in *Young Children,* several educators report on how they used guided dramatization to foster social development in children with disabilities (Brown, Althouse, & Anfin, 1993). The authors detail a multistep process through which they engaged the children, provided modeling opportunities, used photographs to encourage reflection, and stimulated repetition of parts of the story during free play time. This example showed that detailing the steps in the planning process makes a difference in how children become engaged in the activity. By following new developments pertaining to inclusionary classrooms and constructing their own modifications, teachers increase the repertoire of strategies they can use to benefit all children. Another useful suggestion made in the Massachusetts Department of Education publication (1991b) relates to the importance of encouraging reciprocal social interactions while ensuring that one-way tutor relationships do not develop.

These suggestions are linked to the developmental program's key characteristic of having an *integrated* and *interdisciplinary* curriculum. They also are based on appreciating the importance of *observation*, as well as on open discussion, addressed by the program's characteristic of incorporating *social-emotional issues* in the classroom.

Sociocultural Factors

In addition to the topic of individual differences, which permeates all aspects of developmental theory, a large body of research relates more directly to the individual's development within a social context. Reviewed here is research on second language learning, cross-cultural research, and studies that highlight socioeconomic issues.

Second Language Learning

For many children in schools today, English is a second language. Considerable effort has been spent researching how children acquire a second language, the role education can play in this process, and the influence of individual and societal factors (Krashen, 1987; McLaughlin, 1984, 1985). Currently this area of developmental psychology is receiving considerable attention. Reviewed in this section are selected aspects of this research that relate to the key characteristics of the developmental model.

The way children acquire language is, by its very nature, compatible with the developmental orientation, since language acquisition requires active organization and reorganization of information. Chomsky postulated that a **language acquisition device (LAD)** in human beings enables them to master language. The LAD is a part of the human brain that makes possible and directs language learning. Bruner added to this concept the need for a **language acquisition support system (LASS),** which provides the social scaffolding necessary to support language learning (Santrock & Yussen, 1992). These same systems operate as children acquire first and second languages (Krashen, 1987).

In his summary of current second language acquisition theory, Krashen identifies important hypotheses that explain this process. The first is that there is a distinction between acquisition and learning. Acquisition is a "subconscious process," the result of informal or natural learning. Acquisition is akin to constructivism. In contrast, learning, in this context, refers to "knowing the [grammar or] the rules, being aware of them, and being able to talk about them" (Krashen, 1987). Krashen maintains that children acquire rather than learn both first and second languages. He calls this the **acquisition-learning hypothesis.**

Krashen also makes the case for the **natural order hypothesis**—namely, that second language acquisition follows the same pattern or natural order as first language acquisition. For teachers working with young children, this hypothesis means that they can expect a period of time when children will take in language but be unable to use it as a mode of expression (the silent period), and that children will make errors that tend to disappear as they acquire greater competency. For example, early in the process of developing language, children overregularize rules for forming plurals; thus, they say "foots" instead of "feet" or "mouses" instead of "mice." Children also form their own past tense of irregular verbs, saying "goed" instead of "went" and "breaked" instead of "broke." These patterns continue "for many months and sometimes years until the child has managed the difficult task of sorting out the exceptions from the regular instances" (Berk, 1991). Making these types of errors are part of the natural order of language acquisition and occur in learning both first and second languages.

In explaining second language acquisition, Krashen also describes the **input hypothesis.** He emphasizes the need for comprehensible input and points out how this input resembles "caretaker speech," a form of speech adults use with children to help them understand meaning. Caretaker speech is not a deliberate attempt to teach language; rather, it represents an intuitive modification of adult speech so that the child comes to understand language. One characteristic of caretaker speech is that usually it is talk about the " 'here and now,' about what the child can perceive, what is in the immediate environment" (Krashen, 1987, p. 23).

The input hypothesis describes how an individual moves from one level of competence to the next in the acquisition of language. This movement depends on the learner's ability to gain meaning from interactions. In language learning, individuals go for meaning first and then acquire structure. It is not necessary or desirable to deliberately teach the structure of language. What is important is to provide as much comprehensible input as possible. Production ability emerges when the learner is ready. It occurs at different times for different people. It is not taught directly (Krashen, 1987).

Referring to the work of Dulay and Burt (1977), Krashen (1987) also described the **affective filter hypothesis,** which emphasizes the role played in second language acquisition by affective variables including motivation, self-confidence, and anxiety. The publication *Young Lives: Many Languages, Many Cultures* (Massachusetts Department of Education, 1992) contains an anecdotal description of the experiences of two cousins as they first entered school in the United States. Each was assigned to a different classroom. In one classroom, the teacher was friendly and comforting. She helped the child feel secure and competent as she recognized the child's accomplishments in learning English and in teaching classmates words and songs in Spanish. In the other classroom, the teacher's reaction to the child and to the child's speech made him feel angry and ashamed. When he refused to speak, he was punished. For him, the school year was very unsuccessful.

Many studies have been done that reflect the influence of teacher-child interactions on the affective filter. Jackson and Costa (1974) contrasted teacher interaction with Mexican American (also referred to as Chicano) and white (Anglo) pupils in public schools in five southwestern states. They found that "teachers praised and encouraged Anglo students 35 percent more often than Chicanos, and directed 21 percent more questions to Anglos than to Chicanos" (p. 227). McLaughlin (1985) cited a study by Arias and Gray (1977) that "found that student teachers rated those third-grade Mexican American children who had good voice quality (defined by pronunciation, speed, intonation, etc.) more favorably than those children who had poor voice quality" (p. 190–191). According to McLaughlin, this study "suggests . . . that the way a child talks may influence a teacher's judgment as to how good a student the child is" (p. 191).

The affective filter is also influenced by the child's attitude toward learning the second language, as well as by the teacher-child pattern of interaction. As Krashen (1987) points out: "Those whose attitudes are not optimal for second language acquisition will not only tend to seek less input, but . . . even if they understand the message, the input will not reach that part of the brain responsible for language acquisition, or the language acquisition device" (p. 31). McLaughlin (1985), in his analysis of the social factors that influence the affective filter, describes as an important consideration the attitude of the child and the child's family toward the target language group. Children with an integrative orientation—who want to be like the target group—have a stronger motivation to learn the language (Wong, 1976). Another factor influencing the affective filter is the compatibility between modes of interaction in the classroom and those customary in the child's culture. Some cultures emphasize peer-to-peer interaction as a mode of learning; others rely more heavily on an adult-child pattern. The teacher's sensitivity to behavior patterns and appreciation of the cultural diversity represented in the classroom are significant factors in influencing the affective filter and consequently the process by which a child acquires a second language.

The hypotheses Krashen describes as a basis for studying second language acquisition support the developmental model's appropriateness to meet the needs of children learning a second language in school. The flexibility of *grouping patterns* in the model permits maximum comprehensible input. The affective filter hypothesis is supported by considering *social-emotional factors* in classroom management and curriculum. The acquisition hypothesis may be clearly linked to the setup of the *physical environment* to allow for hands-on manipulation of concrete materials.

The link between these widely accepted hypotheses about how children acquire second language competency and the key characteristics of the cognitive-developmental model is clearly articulated in the Massachusetts State Department of Education publication *Young Lives: Many Languages, Many Cultures* (1992). This publication includes a description of a developmentally appropriate curriculum design that would be responsive to the needs of children learning English as a second language. Concerning grouping patterns, the publication stated: "The program should include individual, small group and large group activities, self-directed activities, and cooperative activities" (p. 22). Regarding creativity, the publication recommended: "Open-ended activities that can have multiple outcomes, rather than a single or preset outcome, can help children experience success and foster creativity. . . . Children need opportunities . . . to develop creativity through art, music, movement, and imagination" (p. 22). In support of the characteristics related to the *physical environment* and the need to incorporate *social-emotional issues* into the curriculum, the publication stated:

> Learning for young children should be active and engaging. Children need opportunities to master physical and cognitive tasks. . . . Young children learn about the world through interacting with people and the physical environment, through direct experience of working and changing real objects, by manipulating symbols, using language and by "trying on" a variety of roles. (p. 22)

Cross-Cultural Studies

Closely related to the discussion of children who are learning English as a second language—in fact, often part of the same discussion—are cultural differences that affect both language development and success in school. Children's culture, as well as their personalities, influence the kinds of linguistic interaction patterns with which they are most comfortable. In some cultures children receive verbal instructions from a very early age. In less technologically advanced societies, instructions may instead be provided through nonverbal means. In such cultures, children learn through observation and participation rather than through questioning designed to assess specific knowledge (McLaughlin, 1985). Some cultures emphasize the expressive and aesthetic use of language rather than its problem-solving uses.

Cultures differ not only in language, but also in both material and nonmaterial ways. In *Breaking the Ice: A Guide to Understanding People from Other Cultures,* Kabagarama (1993) explained, "culture has two major components: the material which refers to artifacts and other tangible objects including such items as cars, books, television sets, houses, clothes, and wedding rings; and the nonmaterial including values, norms, beliefs, emotions, attitudes, aspirations, laws, and symbols" (p. 15). As an example of cultural values that may be in conflict, consider that the core U.S. values of individualism, competition, and winning may be of little importance to or conflict with the values of other cultural groups. Cultural differences may also manifest themselves in the way time is viewed. In the United States there is a tendency to value promptness, whereas some individuals in other cultural groups may find this emphasis on time to be insulting. Many aspects of behavior are regulated by culture, such as when and how people show emotion, and their attitude toward the future (Kabagarama, 1993). Schools in some cultures emphasize verbal performance, whereas in other cultures children are expected to observe carefully before they perform.

The child development literature, particularly work prompted by increased appreciation of Vygotskian concepts, incorporates many studies that demonstrate the *impact* of culture. Cultures differ in how thinking is organized, the emphasis placed on different types of intelligence, the context in which children learn mathematical skills, the role of peers in development, and the patterns of interaction that influence achievement orientation. (Hetherington & Parke, 1993). Teachers who place a high value on cultural diversity must recognize that observing carefully and learning about each child's family and culture is essential.

Socioeconomic Issues

The following two areas of research provide justification for the cognitive-developmental model's appropriateness for children of all socioeconomic classes. It is important to recognize that not all children at a particular socioeconomic level manifest the same qualities. Researchers acknowledge this fact. However, they feel they have enough information about the effects of poverty on school success that this information needs to be shared and steps taken to alter the situation.

The first area addresses differences in sociodramatic play among children with lower socioeconomic status and those from higher socioeconomic status groups. This research is cited here because it provides support for the key characteristic of the developmental model related to the physical setup of the classroom. Sara Smilansky, a leader in the study of the sociodramatic play of young children, conducted several studies in which she refined an assessment instrument for measuring the richness of sociodramatic play. She used this instrument in Israel to compare the play of children from different socioeconomic levels. She found that lower socioeconomic status (SES) children preferred toys that were exact replicas of the original object, in contrast to upper SES children who showed a greater degree of symbolization and were content to use a variety of objects as representative of real things. Lower SES children were interested in the toys as ends in themselves, whereas higher SES children used toys as symbols to execute a set of ideas. In addition, Smilansky found differences in language use and ability to resolve conflict. She pointed out that language use, rich sociodramatic play, and success in school were all part of the same process. A good cognitive-developmental classroom, through the setup of the physical environment and the interactions it encourages among children and teacher, can provide for the needs of children from all socioeconomic levels (Smilansky & Shefatya, 1990).

Jeannie Oakes (1990) and others who have been concerned with equality of educational opportunity for children of all races and all social classes focused their study on the association between minority status, socioeconomic level, and tracking. Although the researchers recognize that minority status and low socioeconomic status are not always linked, they refer to statistics indicating that more minority students are represented in the low socioeconomic groups. In "ability-grouped classes at racially mixed elementary schools . . . white classes were found to be about equally likely to be identified as low- or high-ability, [whereas] disproportionately minority classes were *seven times more likely to be identified as low-ability than as high-ability*" (Oakes, 1990, p. 23).

Oakes identified differences in teachers' emphasis of various objectives with classes of different ability levels. In low-ability classes, teachers set sights lower and did not emphasize problem-solving and inquiry skills or science concepts. Adults engaged in more discussion with higher-ability classes. With lower-ability levels, teachers relied more on tests and quizzes. In science at predominantly minority schools, teachers spent twice as much time on tests and half as much time on hands-on and laboratory work.

Oakes concluded that "if schools hope to make science and mathematics accessible to diverse groups, they will need to redesign both curriculum and instruction" (Oakes, 1990, p. xiii). Schools need to eliminate tracking and ability grouping (Bredderman, 1983)—practices that begin in some schools as early as kindergarten. Oakes pointed out that

> Knowledge gained from research in education, cultural anthropology, and sociolinguistics can support new approaches that may be especially appropriate for low-income and minority students. Non-traditional instruction can be more effective than conventional techniques for minority children. African-American and Hispanic children tend to succeed better in classrooms featuring cooperative small learning groups (Au and Jordan, 1981; Cohen and DeAvila, 1983; Slavin and Oickle, 1981; Slavin, 1987) and experienced based instruction (Cohen and DeAvila, 1983). Recent analyses of the effectiveness of activity-based science curriculum, e.g. the Elementary Science Study, Science—A Process Approach, and The Science Curriculum Improvement Study, have concluded that while all students profit from such curricula, ('so-called') disadvantaged students make exceptional gains. (1990, p. 111)

The Kamehameha Early Education Program (KEEP) in Hawaii exemplifies the changes Oakes and others identified as necessary. The program was "specifically designed to be compatible with the cultural background of the children which it served" (Bukatko & Daehler, 1992, p. 675). Classrooms were organized into small groups of four to five children in order to foster collaboration and cooperation, traits highly valued in the Hawaiian culture. The program also capitalized on the Hawaiian children's tendency to engage in rich dialogue with peers. Recognizing this point, teachers were "less disturbed by children's interruptions and rapidly paced speech" (p. 675). With these modifications of "classroom practices to incorporate cultural patterns of language, communication, and social organization" (p. 675), the children's school performance improved.

The findings of sociocultural research support the *key characteristics* of the cognitive-developmental model. The model depends on an intellectually vibrant teacher who tries to find out as much as possible about the cultural backgrounds of the children in the class—by reading, talking with members of the particular group, and listening carefully to parents. The model also relies heavily on observation, recording, and assessment—of particular importance to teachers working with children from diverse cultural backgrounds who place a value on responding to family, cultural, and community concerns.

Historical Roots of Developmental Education

When an idea becomes popular, there is a tendency to think that it originated in the present. In fact, this is rarely the case. Most ideas are rooted in history. Tracing these roots is usually helpful in refining and implementing the "new" idea. This is certainly true of some pervasive historical issues embedded in the developmental model, such as the importance of the child-centered curriculum and the value of continuity in the early childhood curriculum. The following discussion highlights some aspects of the history of early childhood education that support the child-centered philosophy.

The Origins of the Child-Centered Curriculum

Although developmental education may seem a contemporary phenomenon, many notions associated with it have roots in education's history. Educational ideas characteristic of the model can be traced as far back as the writings of the Greek philosophers Plato and Aristotle. For example, in the *Republic,* Plato (428–348 B.C.) noted that "knowledge which is obtained under compulsion obtains no hold on the mind" (Braun & Edwards, 1972, p. 15), and Aristotle in the *Politics* noted that children "should nevertheless be allowed enough movement to avoid bodily inactivity; and this exercise should be obtained by means of various pursuits, particularly play" (Braun & Edwards, 1972, p. 19). In these ideas of Plato and Aristotle on education, one may recognize the notions of the importance of play and activity as a way of learning, as well as the value of providing options for children. One sees the beginnings of support for the physical setup of the environment, a key characteristic of the developmental model.

Comenius (1592–1670), a Polish bishop, in his *Great Didactic* expressed educational ideas that foreshadowed later work by Pestalozzi, Froebel, Montessori, and Dewey (Williams & Fromberg, 1992). His educational plan was activity-oriented and employed the use of actual objects whenever possible (Webster, 1984). He advocated educational activities matched to children's developmental level, and he set forth as basic principles that everything must be related through sense impression, if possible (Braun & Edwards, 1972), and that education should proceed from the "known to the unknown" (Webster, 1984).

Much later in history, Rousseau (1712–1778), a philosopher whose ideas influenced all aspects of society—politics, art, literature, and most profoundly education—emphasized the need to "teach the child what is of use to the child" (Farnham-Diggory, 1990). "In any study whatsoever, the symbols are of no value without the idea of the things symbolized" (Rousseau, 1911/1762, p. 11). Rousseau was a leader in recognizing that children's development should influence the type of education they receive. He was a strong proponent of children's *learning through active exploration*, a forerunner of integrated learning, one of the key characteristics of the developmental model.

Pestalozzi (1746–1827), a disciple of Rousseau's, expressed appreciation of the child's need for self-discovery: "Before the child learns, he must experience something for himself and gain his own impressions" (Osborn, 1991, quoting Pestalozzi, 1951, p. 40). In the early 1800s, Pestalozzi established a school that embodied many of Rousseau's ideas. In his book *How Gertrude Teaches Her Children,* Pestalozzi (as quoted in Braun & Edwards, 1972) described how children learned mathematics:

> The instruction she gave them in the rudiments of arithmetic was intimately connected with the realities of life. She taught them to count the number of steps from one end of the room to the other. . . . She also made them count their threads while spinning, and the number of turns on the reel, when they wound the skeins. (p. 59)

In the Pestalozzi schools, children engaged in the tasks of daily family living and through these activities learned to read and write. In addition, Pestalozzi emphasized the goal of "awaken[ing] a feeling of brotherhood amongst the children, and mak[ing] them affectionate, just, and considerate" (Braun & Edwards, 1972, p. 52)—a precursor to the *social-emotional* characteristic (although no evidence indicates that Pestalozzi took a cognitive approach to these issues).

In more modern times, John Dewey in his philosophy of education emphasized the interdisciplinary nature of the curriculum and the notion that curriculum must be relevant to children's lives. In his *Pedagogic Creed* (1897), he emphasized the need for children to act on their environment in order to develop reasoning powers and powers of judgment (Braun & Edwards, 1972). He and other proponents of progressive education emphasized the need for integrated, project-oriented education rather than a focus on specific subjects as a way of developing the student's mind. Mayhew and Edwards (1936) describe how children in the Dewey school built their own playhouse in the classroom.

> The older children measured and cut all the paper for the walls. The little children tacked down the matting on the floors, made a table for the dining room by fastening legs on a block. For chairs, they nailed a back to a cube and tacked on a leather seat. The older children made tables and chairs from uncut wood which they measured and sawed by themselves. . . . Some of the children painted the outside of the house so that its walls should "be protected from the weather." Inside it was papered "for ornament." (pp. 68–69)

Through this project children gained in their ability to carry out their own ideas and also experienced a sense of accomplishment. In her analysis of the Dewey School, Sylvia Farnham-Diggory (1990) emphasized how in this approach children engaged in the "scientific activities of observing, analyzing, investigating, quantifying, and making predictions; social cooperation; and exchange of ideas" (p. 17). She also described how dictating reports of their activities and making up stories about people who lived in the house provided the children with written records that some of the children could begin to read.

The progressive movement in education, an outgrowth of Dewey's theories, is often thought of as having similarities with the developmental approach. For this reason it is particularly interesting to consider some reasons that progressive education eventually became less popular. For one thing, progressive education was not buttressed by a strong theoretical rationale in psychology that supported its basic tenets. In addition, the progressive movement did not retain a firm hold on education for young children because of difficulties in teacher training. Many educators sensed the value of the child-centered approach that was the embodiment of the progressive movement; but though they bought into the approach, they often lacked the skills and depth of understanding required to carry it out. Thus, the learning climate in many classrooms labeled progressive began to degenerate.

Another important factor that contributed to the demise of progressive education was the changing social climate of the early 1900s. Factories were becoming more efficient in their procedures and the prevailing attitude was that this efficiency could be translated into school management. Emphasis was on designing school organizational patterns, exploring new recordkeeping procedures, and preparing curriculum manuals (Farnham-Diggory, 1990). In psychology, Thorndike and other behaviorists emphasized the measurement of attitudes, abilities, skills, and knowledge in theories consistent with the factory model for thinking about human development that prevailed at the time. Curriculum manuals focused on behavioral objectives with clearly measurable outcomes. This change in emphasis in society and in psychology was not consistent with child-centered education and served to weaken its impact.

The mid-1900s brought a change from a factory management orientation to a more technological focus. The United States and the former U.S.S.R. became engaged in a scientific race to see which country would be first to put a man on the moon. This period, often referred to as the Sputnik era, created an interest in how schools could better prepare young people both academically and creatively to compete with the Russian ability to launch Sputnik. People became very interested in Piagetian ideas and in cognitive psychology as a mechanism for achieving this goal. Activity-oriented, project-centered, meaningful learning experiences received renewed support from the Piagetian orientation.

Movement Toward a Prekindergarten Through Grade Three Continuum

This emphasis on constructivism, together with the Piagetian descriptions of cognitive stages, also is contributing to the establishment of a prekindergarten–grade three continuum. Supporting this movement is the convincing body of research indicating the benefit to society of providing educational experiences for three- and four-year-old children (Schweinhart & Weikart, 1993), as well as efforts at the national and state levels to support children's transitions from one level to another (National Head Start, 1987), collaboration between programs providing services to young children (the Massachusetts Department of Education & Massachusetts Department of Public Health, 1991a), and new directions in curriculum development and assessment at the primary grade level. The National Council of Teachers of Mathematics (1991) standards and the work being done in the area of authentic assessment (Bredekamp & Rosegrant, 1992; Meisels, 1992; Engel, 1991; Grace & Shores, 1991) are two examples of the movement toward a prekindergarten–grade three continuum. The developmental model is committed to the notion of curriculum continuity. In the history of early childhood education, many leaders in the field—including Maria Montessori, Patty Smith Hill, and those active in the British infant school movement—have attempted to address this issue.

Traditionally the early childhood period, ages three to eight, has been divided into three separate entities for purposes of education:

1. Preschool, for three- and four-year olds, including nursery school—usually a half-day program—or day care or child care programs—a full day program. **Head Start** programs were established by the federal government as a part of the War on Poverty and have been in existence since 1965.
2. Kindergarten, for five- and six-year olds.
3. The primary grades, for six- to eight-year olds.

Among these programs have been clear-cut differences in terms of philosophy, curriculum, teacher training, and method of financial support. That these differences exist is not surprising when one considers the different historical roots of the preschool, kindergarten, and primary grade movements.

Differing Historic Roots

The preschool had its origins in the child study movement of the early 1900s, with the work of people like G. Stanley Hall, the founder of the movement in the United States; Lawrence K. Frank, who was deeply committed to children's emotional growth; and others heavily influenced by the work of Freud and Erikson in the psychosocial domain. Preschools traditionally stressed the social and emotional needs of the child: the needs to express feelings, to be creative with materials that are largely unstructured, and to learn to get along with others. The cognitive aspects of development were not considered as important.

In the 1960s and 1970s, a burgeoning body of theory and research concerning children's intellectual development dramatically altered the way the early years were viewed (e.g., Piaget, 1960; Wann, Dorn, & Liddle, 1962; Bloom, 1963; Lavatelli, 1973). Developmental psychologists began attending to the role of early experience as a powerful force in intellectual development. Nonetheless, the public—and many educators—continued to value preschools primarily for their contributions to children's emotional and social development

Usually parents paid tuition for their child to attend nursery school and selected the school with which they felt most comfortable. Some nursery schools were affiliated with colleges and universities, serving as laboratory schools for college students studying psychology and child development. Some were parent cooperative nursery schools, involving a great deal of parental involvement. Some schools were run by churches or social agencies, and many were privately run programs. In 1933, during the Depression, the U.S. government through the Works Projects Administration (WPA) supported nursery schools to provide work for unemployed teachers and "to combat physical and mental handicaps being imposed on young children by conditions incident to current economic and social difficulties" (Braun & Edwards, 1972). During World War II, some companies, including the Kaiser shipbuilding company, set up day care programs to provide for the children of women who were needed in the wartime workforce, marking the beginning of employer-sponsored child care programs.

The kindergarten movement began in the 1860s, about 50 years earlier than the preschool movement. It was strongly influenced by the work of Pestalozzi and

Froebel. Froebel, considered the founder of the kindergarten movement, developed a system of education that "respected [both] the individuality of each child and an organized articulated curriculum designed to ensure the step by step progress of that child through the subjects necessary for his education" (Braun & Edwards, 1972, p. 69). In this curriculum, Froebel emphasized the value of play and its importance in encouraging "self-active determination." He also included materials called "Froebelian gifts," which were "used to teach the child the nature of form, number, and measurement" (Braun & Edwards, 1972, p. 69) and "occupations" including weaving, sewing, and paper tearing. The first kindergartens, established from 1850 to 1860, were based on a strict interpretation of Froebelian philosophy.

Early kindergartens were established mainly as philanthropic efforts. In the 1870s, when kindergartens were incorporated into public schools, other educators often did not regard them highly. Teachers in primary schools viewed their responsibility as helping children to acquire academic skills and necessary subject matter information. The kindergarten teachers, with their philanthropic orientation, were interested in children's health and family conditions. Many viewed kindergarten as a year of socializing to the world of the public school, but kindergarten was not seen as critical to intellectual development.

In 1990, Osborn reported, 94 percent of all five-year-olds in the United States were attending kindergarten, and most states were requiring that school systems make kindergarten experiences available (1991). The benefits of a developmentally appropriate kindergarten experience are becoming more widely recognized. Nonetheless, in times of fiscal constraint kindergarten is still one of the first places school systems cut back services.

The primary grades have traditionally been a part of the elementary school, and their history predates both the kindergarten and the preschool movements. Most frequently, primary grade programs emphasize the formal aspects of schooling, with traditional didactic approaches to teaching and learning. Preschools and kindergartens have usually been more informal, process-oriented, and child-centered in nature; elementary schools have tended to be skill- or subject-oriented.

These different historical roots have resulted in entirely different orientations, readily recognized by the population at large. Even young children are sensitive to the dramatic distinctions between preschool, kindergarten, and the first grade.

The following incident represents one example of how firmly entrenched are the stereotypes of a typical kindergarten and first grade. One kindergarten teacher, who was particularly effective in working with young children, in June decided to introduce the notion of first grade to her class. Her aim was to relieve anxiety and clarify any misconceptions the children might have. She planned several experiences around the theme of what it would be like in first grade. She began this theme study by asking the children how they thought first grade differed from kindergarten. (These children were in a private school, associated with a nursery school, in a physical plant far removed from the public school they would attend.) She had them talk about and play first grade.

In the mode of a teacher who understands young children and how they learn, she encouraged the children to express their ideas concretely, allowing them to rearrange the kindergarten classroom. They did this with great conviction. They arranged the tables so that they were no longer in a circle or in clusters, but rather in rows that simulated a first-grade classroom. They got caught up in a pencil-and-paper environment for a whole week. For many children this experience was a real turn-on. For others it was very scary.

The teacher was fascinated not only with the children's description of first grade, but also with how quickly they set about requesting lined paper for writing and expressing a desire to learn how to read. They arranged the tables in rows, and in their play they emphasized following directions, doing what the teacher said, and working very hard at learning to read and write. The experiences they depicted in their play of first grade were qualitatively different from those they had experienced in kindergarten.

In a discussion of the experience, the teacher asked children, "What do you do in first grade?" The responses included the following:

- "You get yelled at."
- "You have to sit at desks in your own chair, and not talk to other kids."
- "You learn to read like big people read."
- "You can't do what you want anymore."
- "You get to use paper with lines . . . and make your letters straight."
- "You gotta do gym with a big gym teacher."

The children's responses reflected common stereotypes of first grade as contrasted with the kindergarten experience. In these stereotypes, kindergarten is free of intellectual challenge and academic expectations. One has many more choices in kindergarten and play is valued, whereas first grade is a place where skills and seriousness of purpose prevail. In short, many think that in kindergarten there is no rigor, and in first grade there is no joy.

Consider instead the value of a continuous orientation that doesn't divide the child artificially. We know that development is a continuous, evolving process, not a series of discrete, separate stages. In schools where curriculum reflects this knowledge, prekindergarten, kindergarten, and primary grade teachers attend in-service workshops together. They learn about the use of portfolios in the classroom (Grace & Shores, 1991; Meisels, 1992) and how to implement whole language with children at various developmental levels. When people visit classrooms at any of the early childhood levels, children are engaged in whole language experiences, in process writing, and in hands-on explorations of mathematical and scientific material. Obviously children differ in what they can do at the various levels, but the teachers view growth as a continuous process. At each level they are able to adapt experiences to meet the individual child's needs. In these settings the program is responsive to the needs of all children: the gifted, the child with special interests, and the child with special needs. The power of providing for continuity of learning experiences is obvious.

Current Trends Influencing the Prekindergarten Through Grade Three Continuum

The beginning of this section indicated that several factors were influencing the movement toward the prekindergarten–grade three (or preK–3) continuum. Described here are two particularly important factors. The first is the trend toward increased emphasis on the value of preschool programs. The High/Scope Foundation carried out research, which has since been highly popularized, indicating that

> high-quality preschool programs [have been] found to improve adult status. . . . Adults born in poverty who attended a high-quality, active learning preschool program at ages 3 and 4 have fewer criminal arrests, higher earnings and property wealth and greater commitment to marriage. . . . Over the participants' lifetimes, the public is receiving an estimated $7.16 for every dollar invested [in preschool education]. (Schweinhart, Barnes, & Weikert, 1993, p. 1)

The preliminary findings of this longitudinal research study (Berrueta-Clement et al., 1984) as well as other sociological factors, have stimulated efforts to provide a preschool experience for all children. This trend is reflected in the first of the national education goals set forth by President Bush in 1992, referred to as "Readiness 2000": "By the year 2000 all children in America will start school ready to learn." The executive summary of the National Task Force on School Readiness begins with an identification of the challenges posed by this goal: Readiness 2000

> is a bold challenge to our personal values, our public policy, and our professional practice. We are challenged to believe that every child can be successful. We are challenged to support the preparation of every child for school. And we are challenged to bolster schools to accommodate success for every young child. . . .
>
> The school readiness goal reflects our increased awareness of the importance of early childhood experiences on eventual school performance—and our increased concern about the equity and quality of our present efforts to support young children and families. (NASBE, 1991, p. 6)

A national task force has been established to identify ways to define the Readiness 2000 goal's specific objectives and ways to measure attainment of these objectives. The research going on in this area will have significant impact on early childhood programs.

Presently, support is growing for universal preschool education (Massachusetts Early Childhood Advisory Council, 1992; Marx & Seligson, 1988). In many instances, programs for three- and four-year-olds are being linked to the public schools and supported by public funds. Agencies outside the public schools continue to provide much-needed early childhood services, and attempts are being made to strengthen collaboration between these groups and public schools. Particularly emphasized are efforts to support transitions from preschool to kindergarten. The goal is to implement useful policies that will enable children and families to make smooth adjustments as they move from one educational setting to another (National Head Start–Public School Transition Demonstration Project, 1991; Love & Logue, 1992). Although the transition programs themselves do not emphasize continuity between programs, they do encourage communication and the sharing of in-service training opportunities. Curriculum continuity is frequently a by-product of these efforts.

Accompanying these efforts, however, are feelings of anxiety and some degree of controversy. Since many schools do not embrace the developmental model, early childhood educators feel threatened by the idea of joining prekindergarten with the primary grades. They fear that the traditional values of the primary school will dominate and impose themselves on young children in inappropriate ways. The primary grade teachers also worry that their programs will become watered down and more like kindergarten programs. This feeling is particularly strong as the media bombards the public with questions: Are children learning what they need to learn in school? Are they mastering basic skills? Are their education programs making them aware of important historical as well as current information? Are children acquiring attitudes of caring and concern for the environment and for other people? With these questions on primary grade teachers' minds, it is difficult for them to build relationships with preschool teachers. In many communities, however, both groups are recognizing their common goals and are focusing on the best way to achieve them collaboratively.

Many important efforts are directed at supporting this collaboration. For example, the National Association of State Boards of Education assembled a task force to study this issue. The task force conducted public hearings at various sites throughout the country and made two major recommendations: "We recommend that early childhood units be established in elementary schools, to provide a new pedagogy for working with children ages 4–8 and a focal point for enhanced services to preschool children and their parents" (NASBE, 1988, p. vii). The aim of the fusion between preschool and primary education is to extract the best from both realms and combine them to arrive at an optimal synthesis. Preschool, kindergarten, and primary grades should all provide intellectually challenging programs. They should combine this intellectual component with the learning of academic skills, subject area content, and social-emotional strategies that empower children to take charge of their own lives and become contributing members of their society.

For the many preschool programs sponsored by groups outside of public schools, the task force also recommended "that public schools develop partnerships with other early childhood programs and community agencies to build and improve services for young children and their parents" (NASBE, 1988, p. viii).

Another trend supporting the movement toward the prekindergarten–grade three continuum is occurring in the area of teacher certification. The current direction in many states—including Alabama, Arizona, Arkansas, Illinois, Massachusetts, New York, Vermont, and Washington (McMahon, Egbert, & McCarthy, 1991)—is toward early childhood teacher certification, encompassing nursery school through grade three, or a prekindergarten endorsement to a primary certificate. This new trend encourages preschool, kindergarten, and primary grade educators to share a developmentally based philosophy. It also encourages preschool and primary grade educators to influence one another so that each child throughout the early childhood years benefits from challenging educational experiences.

Certifying teachers to work with young children with special needs introduced another element to the certification process. For many years, there was a separate certificate for teachers of young children, aged three to eight, with special needs. Currently, however, in many states the standards for this certificate are embedded in the new certification requirements, making it essential that all teachers of young children be able to provide education for children with special needs within the regular classroom. This change in certification reflects the restructuring of programs serving young children with special needs. Formerly many programs provided educational experiences for young children with special needs in substantially separate classrooms. The current trend in preschool through grade three is to provide education for children with a wide range of abilities and special needs in the regular classroom, a concept formerly referred to as mainstreaming and now, in a redefined form, as inclusion. The inclusionary classroom is consistent with the developmental model.

The addition of the nursery (N) level in the early childhood certificate, and the emphasis on teachers developing skills and attitudes for working with all children, represent a significant step forward in teacher certification. For pragmatic reasons, an overlap still exists between the N–3 and the 1–6 certificate. However, the new directions in teacher certification are being reflected concurrently in hiring practices. Many administrators and school committees are recognizing the benefits of hiring teachers who have had the specific N–3 background to fill positions in the early grades and of hiring those with the 1–6 certificate to work with older children.

Another trend in teacher certification is to require all teachers to have a liberal arts major in their undergraduate program. This trend emphasizes the importance of teachers' developing a significant interdisciplinary knowledge base and strengthening their intellectual powers. This requirement, which pervades programs for preschool teachers as well as those teaching in the primary grades, represents a shift in thinking that brings the programs closer together. The requirement also prepares *intellectually vibrant* teachers, a critical part of high-quality developmentally based early childhood programs.

Some Identifiable Developmental Models

The impetus for the development and refinement of clearly definable developmental models came in the 1960s when the U.S. government launched its War on Poverty. As part of this effort the government funded many Head Start and Follow-Through grants, which were intended to identify the most effective way to help "disadvantaged" children become more successful in school. Head Start programs served preschool children. The Follow-Through programs were usually linked to particular Head Start models and represented an effort to carry the specific philosophical orientation into the primary grades. The grant requirements included strong community and parental components as well as a clear statement of goals, procedures, and methods of evaluation.

Studying these distinctive program models is valuable. It enriches one's understanding of similarities and potential differences among models within the developmental framework. The most notable identifiable models are the Montessori method, the Bank Street model, and the cognitive-developmental model. The overview of these models presented here is too brief to convey fully their richness and the scope of the impact each has had on the field, but it will give readers a sense of the range of programs. Each of the developmental models adheres in varying degrees to the tenets of developmental education:

1. Growth proceeds in hierarchical stages.
2. Education is interactionist in nature.

3. Problem solving and creative thinking apply to social as well as physical and logical situations—hence the term **social cognition.**
4. Individual differences, both personal and cultural, are respected and nurtured.
5. The model, due to its dynamic nature, requires continuous evaluation and ongoing modification.

Since the developmental model is responsive to the learner, to development, to the teacher and to society, it can be neither static nor prescriptive. The model itself is always in a state of flux, and it cannot be disseminated easily in a prescribed way. Although there are universal concepts in the developmental model, effective implementation of the key characteristics rests in the hands of the individual teacher and the total school community. The model allows for individual interpretations and stylistic differences. Analysis and reflection, and avoiding a search for simple solutions, are key aspects of the developmental approach.

The models we are going to discuss identify themselves with a particular label and retain distinctive features. Those studying developmental education will find it useful to compare the developmental orientation with other perspectives. One example of a nondevelopmental model is the Distar program, which will also be described in this section.

The Montessori Method

Let's consider, first, the Montessori method (1964). Many interesting debates center around whether or not the Montessori method is developmental. These debates are worthy of consideration because they heighten awareness of what is and what is not developmental education. Although numerous aspects of the traditional Montessori method are clearly not considered developmental (for example, the absence of free play, specificity in the way children are permitted to use materials, and reliance on a carefully prescribed curriculum), many of the principles Montessori espoused share much in common with developmental models. Montessori emphasized the value of a **prepared environment,** in which the teacher—or in Montessori's terms, the directress—makes available materials appropriate for children at various developmental stages. The variability is particularly wide in Montessori classrooms, because the method is based on interage grouping, with three- to six-year-olds in one class and six- to nine-year-olds in another. Montessori recognized that children learn differently from adults and need to manipulate concrete materials in order to learn. She developed a program in which every facet of learning was based on the use of manipulative materials. For the most part, the materials are autotelic—that is, they are designed to be self-correcting. Her notion that children pass through sensitive periods, times when they are most receptive to certain types of learning, may be viewed as a forerunner to Piaget's hierarchical stages in cognitive development. Montessori emphasized the importance of the teacher or directress observing children to determine their individual levels of development and then individualizing the curriculum.

Montessori attempted to individualize the curriculum by developing carefully sequenced materials and methods for their use. The math materials in particular—

The Montessori method emphasizes independent learning through use of concrete materials. The method also defines individual workspace by using trays, placemats, and pieces of carpet. © Elizabeth Crews

which include beads, number rods, and other manipulatives—are worthy of mention. Specifically designed beads are grouped in units: ones, tens, hundreds, thousands. These materials are stored and used in very systematic ways—for matching, counting, substituting, and, later, depicting solutions to problems. The beads lend themselves to manipulation and to clear visualization of mathematical concepts. Many of the subsequently devised materials found in developmental programs today (for example, manipulative math materials such as **Cuisenaire rods** and **unifix cubes**) bear similarities to Montessori materials, especially number rods and beads.

Montessori developed materials in three categories: didactic, sensorial, and practical life. The materials designed for teaching mathematics are one example of the didactic materials, which include those designed to teach academic skills and specific subject matter (reading, writing, geography, and science). The sensorial materials nurture the development of acuity in each of the five sensory areas. Many of the sensorial materials require children to use their senses of seeing, hearing, touching, smelling, and tasting to make gross and fine discriminations. For example, there are color tablets that children arrange according to very fine color gradations; tonal bells for auditory matching; **baric tablets** of the same size that children distinguish by their varying weights; and various fabric pieces all the same size that children, blindfolded, attempt to match. For increasing discriminatory acuity in the sense of smell, Montessori provided tubes containing various scents that children also try to match. The practical life materials include practice boards for tying, zipping, and buttoning, and materials children use to care for the environment—for example, to clean tables and wash mirrors.

All these materials encourage children's active involvement and to some degree their sense of autonomy. Thus, the Montessori method may be considered developmental. If one delves deeper into the method, however, one discovers that Montessori materials are based on the belief that children have an innate capacity to learn—a capacity Montessori called "the absorbent mind." As DeVries and Kohlberg (1990) pointed out, though, "there is a difference between absorption and intellectual construction." Absorption means soaking up or taking in what already exists; intellectual construction involves each child's unique building process. The end result of the building process depends on the individual builder's experiences. The Montessori method, in which children are expected to take in information and end with the same result, stands in contrast to the intellectual construction model.

Moreover, the Montessori Teacher's Manual prescribes in detail how these activities are to be carried out. This aspect of the Montessori Method is not considered developmental because it does not allow teachers or children the opportunity to infuse the curriculum with their own ideas, interests, and approaches. Nonetheless, it is interesting to note Maria Montessori's rationale for this approach. She believed that children need a sense of order before they can be creative. This sense of order, although restricted to certain types of activities, is apparent in many highly effective developmental programs.

As an example, consider the procedures used when children move chairs to and from a group circle. In some programs that call themselves developmental, methods of chair-carrying may be left to children's whims: some pushing the chairs along the floor, others carrying the chairs on their heads, and some using the chairs to push other children out of their way. This approach usually results in bedlam, which is not characteristic of a developmental classroom. More appropriately the developmental teacher would work with children to help them identify and articulate the problem and agree on a safe way to carry chairs. Not every activity in a developmental program, however, needs to be seen as an opportunity for problem solving. In some cases the developmental educator establishes the procedures and, in a manner very similar to the Montessori method, demonstrates and models these procedures for children to emulate. As Montessori predicted, this ordered approach helps children feel safe, in control, and free to engage in other productive tasks.

The Montessori materials themselves have proved cross-culturally appropriate. Maria Montessori was a medical doctor concerned about environmental influences on the lives of poor children, many of whom appeared retarded. She developed her materials in Italy to substantiate her theory that the problems these children faced were educational rather than medical. In 1907, under the aegis of the city of

Rome, Montessori established day nurseries for children living in housing developments. She called these nurseries *casa's dei bambini* (children's houses) and in this environment demonstrated the effectiveness of her method with normal children (Essa, 1992). When unable to gain the extended support she was seeking in Italy, Montessori took her ideas to India. There they took root, flourished, and were transported throughout the world. Some American Montessori schools retained the developmentally appropriate aspects of the Montessori method, modified other aspects of Maria Montessori's original ideas, and are operating today, usually with teachers who have received special Montessori training provided by the American Montessori Society. In some traditional Montessori schools, teachers often have been trained in programs linked to the International Montessori society, with its seat of training in Perugia, Italy. Whether or not a specific Montessori program is developmental, the method itself has had a profound influence on developmental education.

The Bank Street Model

Another identifiable developmental model is the Bank Street model. This model has evolved over a long period of time. It was affected by the child study movement that began in the early 1900s, with roots first in Freudian and later in Eriksonian theory. People like G. Stanley Hall, Lawrence Frank, and Abigail Eliot—and at Bank Street more specifically, faculty members Barbara Biber and Edna Shapiro—influenced the model. The Bank Street model is often called developmental-interactionist. This label represents the Bank Street theoreticians' attempt to articulate clearly the developmental perspective. Framing it as a model would allow it to be easily contrasted with the direct teaching approach of programs like Distar, based on the work of Bereiter and Engelmann (1966), which commanded considerable attention as one of the defined models of the Head Start Variation Studies.

Prior to this period of time many developmentally oriented models were eclectic in nature, and it was difficult to assign a label to them. Educators in these eclectic programs usually understood developmental education, but they had considerable difficulty explaining their goals and objectives to the general public. In the field of early childhood education was a clear dichotomy between those who believed in developmental education and those who did not. The latter usually were in the direct teaching camp. In the 1960s, with the War on Poverty and support available for the development and refinement of various models, proponents of the direct teaching model came out with clear statements of goals, procedures, and methods of evaluation—statements that were easily comprehended by the general public. After all, what was school for if not to learn to read, write, and do arithmetic? Reading, language, and arithmetic were the three basic components of the direct teaching model.

Although the direct teaching approach was in clear opposition to the developmental model, it did have a positive effect in the field of early childhood education. It encouraged developmental educators to articulate more clearly the goals and methodology they were using. Prior to this clear articulation of the model, developmental educators expended a great deal of effort criticizing programs that were not developmental and that relied predominantly on total group instruction and paper-and-pencil tasks, instead of explicitly describing the specific characteristics of the developmental model.

Developmental educators argued that young children are not ready for learning primarily in the symbolic mode; they need concrete experiences on which to base their learning. Developmentalists also believed that the direct teaching of skills to young children before they are able to attach meaning to the skills or perceive their usefulness resulted in the establishment of attitudes and dispositions that impeded learning later. Furthermore, developmental educators argued that many children in direct teaching programs are not ready to learn the skills when they are presented to them and thus experience failure in school-related tasks before they have had an opportunity to succeed. Most important, however, developmental educators perceived the direct teaching approach as obstructing children's developing sense of autonomy, a characteristic they considered essential if children are to assume responsibility for their own learning and behavior.

One direct teaching program that received considerable attention was the Distar program, based on the work of Bereiter and Engelmann (1966). When this model was first articulated, it caused a great furor in the early childhood education community. The program was designed to help "disadvantaged" children catch up with their "nondisadvantaged" counterparts in as short a time as possible. The Distar program was presented by specially trained teachers to small groups of children. These teachers were trained to be enthusiastic and to use positive reinforcement and group response techniques to help children feel successful. Teachers were trained to use a behavioristic approach, with its emphasis on stimulus-response learning. Observers who visited these programs were often encouraged to come during direct teaching periods rather than during free play times, "when nothing of interest was happening"—in direct contrast to the role of play in the developmental models.

Developmental educators invested a great deal of effort in describing the direct teaching programs, emphasizing the inappropriateness of the direct teaching practices and the absence of such practices in developmental programs. The tendency was not to describe developmental programs themselves in positive terms, but rather in terms of all the negative features of the direct teaching model that do not exist in developmental programs.

Because Distar programs received widespread, positive media coverage that communicated ideas about the program in ways that parents and community people could easily understand, and because Distar was portrayed as making it possible for four- and five-year-old children from "disadvantaged" environments to do multiplication and division as well as some simple forms of algebra, many people sat up and took notice. This widespread coverage, together with federal government requirements that funded programs clearly articulate their goals and expected outcomes, provided a challenge and an opportunity for developmental educators.

Shapiro and Biber at Bank Street College in New York were among the first developmental educators to pick up the challenge and clearly articulate the developmental approach. They described the Bank Street model as developmental-interactionist, explaining the term as follows:

> Developmental refers to the emphasis on identifiable patterns of growth and modes of perceiving and responding which are characterized by increasing differentiation and progressive integration as a function of chronological age. Interaction refers, first, to the emphasis on the child's interaction with the environment—adults, other children, and the material world—and second, to the interaction between cognitive and affective spheres of development. The developmental interaction formulation stresses the nature of the environment as much as it does the patterns of the responding child. (Shapiro & Biber, 1972, pp. 59–60)

The Bank Street model emphasized the importance of linking school experiences with children's real-life situations. Bank Street materials were developed specifically for urban children from low economic backgrounds. Many of the stories and large picture cards depicted scenes familiar to the children and thus particularly well suited to stimulating language development and rich dramatic play. Many of those who have adopted the Bank Street model have identified materials for the population of children the particular program serves—whether these children come from low, middle, or high economic backgrounds. Those who adhere to the Bank Street model and consider themselves developmental-interactionist tend to be primarily concerned with children's social-emotional development and with setting up an environment that fosters this development. They are concerned with cognitive development, but not independent of affective development.

Those who refer to their programs as cognitively oriented or constructivist in orientation differ from the developmental-interactionists in one important regard—namely, the emphasis each places on cognition. In constructivist programs, all aspects of growth are viewed through the cognitive lens, and emphasis is on the development of thinking processes (classifying, seriating, experimenting, and recording in areas of physical, social, and emotional, as well as intellectual, growth). (The difference between the traditional child-centered models and the cognitively oriented or constructivist models was explained earlier in this chapter.) The cognitively oriented models rely heavily on the work of Piaget and his notion of hierarchical stages in cognitive development.

As an example of the difference between the developmental-interactionist and the constructivist programs, consider the programs' different goal orientation in movement activities, an aspect of physical education. Both the developmental-interactionist models and the cognitive models often include physical development in their goal statements. Movement activities in both types of programs involve problem solving and creative thinking, and are often linked with other aspects of the program. However, the specific objectives ascribed to physical activities tend to vary with the program orientation. In the developmental-interactionist models, the focus frequently is on physical activity as a way of releasing energy, building healthy bodies, and developing feelings of competence. The developmental-interactionists tend to emphasize the affective, physical-motor, or whole child aspects of the experiences. In the cognitive models, the focus in the area of physical activity, as well as in all other areas of the curriculum, tends to be on thinking, risk taking, and decision making. Sometimes these orientations are reflected in program practices, and sometimes they are apparent only in the goal statements of the particular program.

The Cognitively Oriented Curriculum

One example of a cognitive model that has had widespread impact is the High/Scope model, commonly referred to as the cognitively oriented curriculum and developed in Ypsilanti, Michigan, by David Weikart and his colleagues. This model is described in the publication *Young Children in Action* (Hohmann, Banet, & Weikart, 1979) and in various films produced by the High/Scope Foundation. The model incorporates a "plan, do, review" format, which encourages children to think about what they are going to do, do it, and then evaluate their efforts. The High/Scope curriculum includes key experiences in seven areas: active learning, language, representation, classification, seriation, temporal relations, and spatial relations (Hohmann, Banet, & Weikart, 1979). Ongoing staff training and parental involvement are critical components of the program. The model shows a clear appreciation of the skill required to engage children in cognitive activity.

The Relative Effectiveness of the Models

Many attempts have been made to evaluate the relative effectiveness of these various models (Shipman, 1973; Lazar, Hubbell, Rosche, & Royce, 1977). One interesting study, carried out by Miller and Dyer at the University of Kentucky, was titled *Four Preschool Programs: Their Dimensions and Effects* (1975). It was part of a group of longitudinal studies that became known as the sleeper effect studies. These studies have had an important impact on the formulation and refinement of developmental programs. The study focused on the school performance of children who had attended four different programs: (1) the Distar program, based on the work of Bereiter and Engelmann; (2) DARCEE, a George Peabody College program that focused on academics and preparation for school; (3) a Montessori program; and (4) a traditional child development program that emphasized children's selection of materials and active engagement in the use of the materials (a program similar to the Bank Street model). The study used as controls children who had no preschool experience. Children's progress in academic areas was evaluated at the end of preschool, the end of kindergarten, in the sixth grade, and when children were in high school.

The Miller and Dyer study attempted to answer the question whether preschool intervention programs have significant long-term impact. As one might expect, the direct teaching model had the greatest impact in the short term; but in the long term the developmental programs had a more significant "sleeper" effect. Long-term research of this type is subject to many criticisms, because it is very difficult to isolate the variables that impact development over a long time span. Nonetheless, the sleeper effect studies served a valuable purpose. They emphasized the distinction between learning skills and acquiring critical attitudes and dispositions toward learning. The studies helped people appreciate that early skill learning is often achieved at the expense of certain attitudes critical for lifelong learning. This idea has become a basic tenet of developmental education. It has manifested itself in a practical, observable form in the authentic assessment movement, and it is inherent in the whole language philosophy.

Another study that contrasted three "theoretically distinct approaches to preschool programs" was carried out by Schweinhart, Weikart, and Larner (1986). This study, like Miller and Dyer's, was an attempt to define quality in early childhood programs. Essentially the study "randomly assigned 68 impoverished children in Ypsilanti, Michigan, . . . to three different programs: the High/Scope cognitive model, the Distar model, and a model in the nursery school tradition" (p. 15). The study found that school-related results were the same in all three programs; thus, the type of curriculum did not seem to be a factor in later school success. Preschool curriculum choices had important social consequences, however. Thus, the study tentatively concluded that "a high quality preschool curriculum is based on child-initiated learning activities" (Schweinhart et al., 1986).

Although many earlier efforts have been made to provide quality early childhood experiences for young children, at no other time in history has there been such a widespread, organized attempt to bring together in a coherent way what is known and understood about child development and educational practice. Ideas from psychology, classroom practice, and curriculum development are presently being systematically fused. The National Association for the Education of Young Children has exerted considerable leadership in formulating and disseminating guidelines for programs and establishing accrediting procedures. The National Education Association, the Association for Supervision and Curriculum Development, the National Association of State Boards of Education, the Association for Childhood Education International, and the National Elementary Principals Association are among the many groups contributing to this effort. These are exciting and challenging times as educators work with other professionals—psychologists, sociologists, anthropologists—to define and describe a comprehensive approach to early childhood education.

Summary

In this chapter we discussed aspects of developmental theory that provide the basis for the cognitive model. We also identified in the history of early childhood education some major themes that have influenced this model. Described more fully was the concept identified in the introduction to this section: namely, that high-quality early childhood programs depend on providing a continuum of learning experiences from prekindergarten through grade three. As a way of highlighting the need for clarity of definition, we also described some of the clearly identifiable models. We now turn to a consideration of the developmental perspective in relation to other educational orientations, in order to deepen our theoretical understanding.

Part One: Questions for Discussion

1. Select two of the eight key characteristics of the developmental model. Describe a classroom vignette that illustrates each of these characteristics in operation.
2. Select an additional characteristic. Identify factors in theory and history that support it.
3. Explain why the developmental model is appropriate for children of all races, abilities, and socioeconomic levels.
4. Describe why early childhood movements in the past have failed. What are the implications for ensuring the success of the cognitive-developmental model?

PART 2 CHALLENGING CHILDREN INTELLECTUALLY

In developmental programs, the teacher understands the importance of motivational strategies in stimulating children's intellectual and expressive curiosity and is alert to his or her role in helping to shape the nature of children's investigations. The notions of cognitive conflict and the dialectic are respected. Hence, the adult shares information, raises questions, and provokes experimentation in a wide variety of ways.

Some classrooms that teachers have labeled developmental are not inspiring. In observing activities in these classrooms, we feel a sense of the mundane, of randomness and repetition. Children do not seem to be involved in productive ways, and we may question whether enough real learning is taking place. Sometimes this feeling comes when we observe classrooms where children seem to be responding routinely to tasks that they have already mastered or that are not really relevant to their lives. Other times this same feeling occurs when we observe classrooms where children seem to be just playing, as opposed to being truly engaged. We may feel that there is a lack of challenge and productivity in the environment and sense apathy and indifference on the part of the children. Often we see this lack of meaningful involvement reflected in negative behavior, with a high level of aggression or misbehavior among the children. In such situations we may question whether children can learn anything meaningful in an environment that offers either so much structure or so much freedom and that seems to lack teacher direction. We may, in fact, come to question the basic concept of child-centered classrooms and grow to doubt that they can provide young children with the skills and concepts we know they must master.

Yet in other classrooms that are also referred to as developmental, we are genuinely moved and stimulated and can see without question that something meaningful and powerful is occurring. We feel a sense of excitement and power in these classrooms, and they stir within us respect and commitment for the developmentally based model. We see children working with dedication, exploring materials and mastering skills, establishing objectives for themselves. They are genuinely excited about the potential in the environment; they are engaged and productive, and there is a sense of harmony and involvement that is inspiring. In both kinds of classrooms the same basic materials and equipment may be present—social studies materials, blocks, manipulatives, a reading center, science and art material—yet the difference between these situations is patently clear.

The distinction between the dynamic classroom—an environment that engages, stimulates, and challenges—and its mundane counterpart, where there is a sense of boredom and stagnation, or even of chaos and confusion, deserves our careful consideration. Critics of child-centered educational models are often right in maintaining that children in some classrooms are not being genuinely challenged and that classroom activities look superficial and seem to lack a clear focus and sense of purpose. The difference between the dynamic classroom and one that falls short of our expectations does not rest narrowly on the physical organization, or the presence or absence of particular materials, important as these factors may be. The difference between these two kinds of settings is the teacher and his or her role in leading and channeling the potential in the environment. This role cannot be underestimated. The teacher is the most critical factor, the essential variable; and in the final analysis, it is the teacher's power and competence that determine the quality of the educational experience. Concerning the teacher's critical importance, John Fischer wrote:

> Rapport is the cutting edge of the whole business. It is like a great machine tool. You have a tremendous structure providing the position, providing the power. But it ultimately comes down to an infinitesimally thin edge of metal that cuts into another piece of metal. If that contact isn't right, you may just as well forget the machinery. (Fischer, 1967, p. 33)

When we are stirred by a particular classroom and feel conviction about what transpires within it, it is because the adult is a skillful diagnostician and clinician as well as teacher and is unambivalent about his or her role as the significant adult with responsibility for everything that takes place in the classroom. The teacher feels secure in the position of a leader, exercising authority in a wide assortment of ways. The teacher is not only the orchestrator who sets up and organizes the environment initially; he or she also has a pivotal role throughout the learning process. Although not exercising authority in the traditional way—characterized by excessive reliance on large group lecturing and the use of didactic methods—teachers in dynamic classrooms recognize that what they say and do, the questions they ask, and the materials they present are all part of the instructional process. In particular, such teachers recognize their centrality in designing situations that stimulate, inspire, and challenge children's thinking, and are able to design learning encounters that are relevant and intellectually engaging.

This ability to challenge children intellectually is the critical ingredient that differentiates the ordinary classroom from the distinguished one. It demands our full attention. The adult must be engaged intellectually on his or her own level and be able to promote the process of inquiry and exploration. Without these abilities on the part of the teacher, the learning situation is seriously compromised.

This section is dedicated to clarifying the teacher's role in stimulating children's intellectual activity in the developmentally based classroom. The **cultural transmission classroom,** which is didactic and not child-centered, and the **romantic classroom,** which is laissez-faire in its approach, are both distinguished from the **cognitive developmental** classroom, where the teacher provides clear and unambiguous intellectual leadership (Kohlberg & Mayer, 1972; DeVries & Kohlberg, 1990). In particular, this section addresses ways that the classroom can be made dynamic, as opposed to static and unchallenging. The purpose of this part of the text is to assist the teacher in recognizing the range of ways the adult can create what Kohlberg and Mayer called cognitive conflict, thereby provoking substantive thinking, exploration, and learning on the part of each child.

CHAPTER 3

RATIONALE FOR THE COGNITIVE APPROACH

- *Kohlberg and Mayer's Three Streams of Educational Thought*
- *The Cultural Transmission Classroom*
- *The Romantic Classroom*
- *The Cognitive-Developmental or Dynamic Classroom*
- *The Cognitive-Developmental Model Analyzed*
- *Summary*

Kohlberg and Mayer's Three Streams of Educational Thought

This chapter extends the discussion of early childhood models by considering the cognitive-developmental perspective in relation to other major educational orientations, specifically those identified by Kohlberg and Mayer (1972) as three streams of educational thought: the romantic, cultural transmission, and cognitive-developmental. Early childhood classroom manifestations of each of the three streams are described in terms of physical environment and the nature of the learning process, behavior management, lesson planning and curriculum, and assessment. The chapter highlights the key components of the cognitive-developmental model: the teacher's role, the organization of classroom groups, and the incorporation of the Vygotskian concept of the zone of proximal development. The chapter concludes by revisiting the points of contrast between the two orientations that are most often confused—romantic and cognitive-developmental—and emphasizes cognitive conflict and the dialectic as key points of difference.

In 1972 Kohlberg and Mayer wrote a seminal article about education that has had profound implications for the way we think about providing children with intellectually stimulating experiences. The article, entitled "Development as the Aim of Education," maintained that all educational practice can basically be classified into one of three streams of educational ideology and that each of these streams is associated with a corresponding theoretical framework within the field of psychology. As we have seen, the three streams are the romantic, cultural transmission, and cognitive-developmental.

Kohlberg and Mayer's article is theoretical in nature. It does not translate theory into practice. Nor does it describe theory as it pertains specifically to early childhood classrooms. However, it does provide a framework for understanding the wide range of approaches to teaching children and helps us to recognize their underlying values. In this chapter, we discuss the theoretical framework Kohlberg and Mayer describe and then explain how this framework is manifested in early childhood classrooms.

Although the idea of classifying the wide range of existing educational practices into three basic streams may seem like an oversimplification, this organizational system is most useful. It clarifies and sharpens our understanding of common classroom practices and their inherent philosophical biases. Studying the streams gives one a rich understanding of the means and ends of particular classroom practices. The role of the teacher, the nature of the curriculum, and the way discipline and control are exercised, for example, all become strikingly clear as a set of overt or covert biases when viewed through the lens of each of these three perspectives. A brief overview of the three streams and their accompanying psychological biases is presented here. The reader is encouraged to review the original material for a fuller understanding of this rich source of information.

In reviewing the three streams of educational thought, keep in mind that it is somewhat artificial to separate them from one another in an absolute way. We are making this distinction in order to highlight the differences, and we recognize that no single mode will be totally divorced from the others. At particular times in any classroom, characteristics of more than one stream of thought apply. The question is which stream is dominant in a particular classroom. Recognizing the dichotomies and identifying the dominant orientation is useful because this process helps to clarify the significant differences among the streams and makes the teacher more thoughtful about his or her own classroom practices.

The Romantic Stream

Romantics feel that the adult's main responsibility in a classroom is to provide children with a warm and nurturing environment that is sufficiently stimulating to enable them to pursue those activities and ideas that seem important and relevant to each individual child. Although romantic teachers may provide some basic structure to a given activity and to the program at large, they are reluctant to influence the child's thinking too much, fearing that they will impose and not be respectful of the child's agenda or developmental capacities. They value what comes from the child to such an extent that they are reluctant to interfere, often withholding questions, information, and suggestions that will shape the direction of a given experience. Romantic teachers fear getting in the way of the child's internal motivation and curtailing investigation by being too heavy-handed or didactic. Kohlberg and Mayer see romantics as overly preoccupied with a narrow concept of creativity and self-expression, so concerned about stifling creativity that they are not willing to provide the necessary stimulus for its full realization. In essence, Kohlberg and Mayer view the romantics as too passive in the learning situation, giving the child so much responsibility for shaping learning activities that they abdicate their responsibility as teachers and run the risk of creating an intellectual vacuum.

Kohlberg and Mayer associate this group with figures such as Arnold Gesell, Sigmund Freud, and G. Stanley Hall in psychology, and with A. S. Neill and John Holt in the field of education. The free school movement that took place during the 1960s and 1970s in the United States represents the far left of the romantic movement. Nondirective, highly permissive preschools and kindergartens, where child-initiated play completely dominates the day, constitute another example of this laissez-faire approach. The open classroom movement that gained impetus during the 1960s and 1970s, in part inspired by informal education in England, was sometimes romantic in nature, although its original advocates never intended it to be.

Romanticism is driven by the maturationist orientation in psychology. Stages of development are perceived as unfolding in an organic, natural manner. The metaphor that Kohlberg and Mayer provide for understanding this stream is that of *the plant.* Children are viewed as needing to be cared for and provided with the basic needs that will enable them to grow and flourish, but the adult must exercise a light hand in the process, allowing nature to take its inevitable course. This view posits that barring traumatic events, and given a supportive and stimulating environment, growth and learning will occur as part of a predictable program of development.

The Cultural Transmission Stream

Cultural transmission is the model most immediately identified with traditional education and the one that the largest number of people have experienced in their own educational backgrounds. The transmission of information and societal rules are considered of key importance, and the teacher is responsible for imparting the culture's values and accumulated knowledge. Information is given to the child as content that must be learned and mastered. The child has little influence on the learning situation and is expected to subordinate his or her own interests and objectives in order to acquire the knowledge the adult world deems important. Feelings are of minimal concern; experiences that can be measured and evaluated are of key importance. This model is culture-driven and readies the child to be a contributing member of society; little attention is given to individual differences. The model is characterized by a predictable, established curriculum, which is systematically taught to the child. In large public school programs, this body of knowledge is often presented systemwide, with little variation from one school or teacher to another. Some of the cultural transmission proponents argue that statewide or countrywide curriculum should be transmitted to children in classrooms.

Kohlberg and Mayer's metaphor for cultural transmission is *the machine.* Input—the skills and knowledge the culture views as crucial—is provided; the product is the output, the child's capacity to deliver clear evidence that he or she has mastered the information. Testing is used to determine whether or not expectations have been met and mastery has occurred.

In psychology, cultural transmission is associated with a stimulus-response orientation and is exemplified by such figures as Locke, Thorndike, and Skinner. In early childhood education, the Bereiter-Engelmann model, introduced to poor, "disadvantaged" children in the 1960s, serves as a strong example (Bereiter & Engelmann, 1966). Traditional public school education—with its heavy emphasis on such techniques as rote teaching, didactic worksheets, consistent large group instruction, authoritarian discipline and lack of individualization—is another example. Kohlberg and Mayer criticize cultural transmission as value-relative. Reflecting the biases of a given culture, cultural transmission does not strike at the heart of what Kohlberg and Mayer see as the central objective of education: influencing the nature of the thinking process in its own right. They view cultural transmission as too narrow, focusing on the acquisition of skills and information while ignoring the critical issue of how children think and function developmentally.

The Cognitive-Developmental Stream

Kohlberg and Mayer present a persuasive argument on behalf of the cognitive-developmental orientation, which they see as the only ethically and morally appropriate stance for educators to embrace. This orientation is Piagetian in nature, resting on the notion of hierarchical stages and the dynamic interaction between organism and environment. The central role of education is to foster the process by which children engage in rational thought and to assist them in the crucial task of increasing their capacities to function cognitively. The educator's responsibility is to provide learning situations that challenge children's analytical and problem-solving abilities, and to propel them toward higher-level thinking. The notion of how children construct knowledge—namely, constructivism—is fundamental to the cognitive-developmental orientation. Skills and information are certainly important, and the teacher is responsible for seeing that children master them, but the way knowledge is taught should be challenging intellectually and require children to integrate new learning into what is already known and understood. It is not enough for children to simply master the information the teacher provides; they must act upon it, wrestle with it, and make sense of it in relationship to their own capacities to think critically. Unlike the proponents of cultural transmission, the cognitive-developmentally oriented teacher is concerned not only with the acquisition of knowledge, but also with how children use this knowledge and integrate it into their basic cognitive functioning. For integration to take place, according to the cognitive-developmentalist, knowledge must also have relevance and meaning.

Kohlberg and Mayer see the cognitive-developmental model as morally and ethically superior because it is dedicated to freeing the child from a narrow imitation of what adults tell them to be good and right. When adults strengthen children's abilities to reason and engage in debate, for example, they help children make judgments based on logic, rather than on blind obedience. Hence, when an adult engages a group of children in discussing why it is important to have certain rules in the classroom, and allows the class to engage in establishing and justifying these rules, the learning that takes place goes far beyond knowing what one can and cannot do in a particular situation. The children are learning about solving an issue intellectually—an experience that can be generalized to other events. Of central importance is the inseparability of emotional and cognitive elements. Children's social and emotional behavior is inextricably bound together. Conflicts and fights between children are an opportunity to teach simple concepts about human behavior. Children learn about the impact their own behavior has on others and what they can do to affect constructively other people's ways of behaving toward them.

Although the process of teaching children to think critically is a long and complex undertaking, influenced by maturation as well as teaching, the strategies central to its realization are important ones to introduce early in the educational process. Kohlberg and Mayer adopted the metaphor of *the poet* or *the philosopher* to conceptualize the cognitive-developmental model. The metaphor means that ideas must be played with—continuously reorganized and sharpened—and that a contest among competing points of view is crucial. Hence, Kohlberg and Mayer speak of the importance of cognitive conflict and the dialectic—with the educator's role being to present children with challenges that are appropriately confounding, and to provide them with the opportunity to wrestle with these challenges in active, meaningful ways.

The cognitive-developmental model is clearly derived from the work of Piaget, and its educational roots are in the work of Dewey. Its philosophical bias is interactionist—committed to the notion that organism and environment function dynamically. In sum, Kohlberg and Mayer argue that the child's cognitive development is the basic objective of the educational process and that all skills and specific information taught to children, although important in their own right, are subordinate to the larger task of helping children over time to become more logical, rational thinkers.

The following is a summary of some characteristics of each of the three streams, as manifested in early childhood classrooms. Keep in mind the idea expressed earlier in this chapter that the characteristics described here vary widely in how they are represented in actual classrooms—which individually may clearly illustrate one stream or another, or may have characteristics of a combination of streams.

The Cultural Transmission Classroom

Some characteristics of a classroom organized on the typical cultural transmission model are set out in this section.

Physical Environment and the Learning Process

Tables and chairs, or desks, dominate the cultural transmission classroom. Few objects, toys, manipulatives are readily accessible. Those that are available are stored most of the time and used only when the teacher presents them in conjunction with a specific lesson or during free play. Worksheets, workbooks, programmed readers, and structured paper-and-pencil tasks are the central materials for instruction.

Free play with blocks, puzzles, art materials may be allowed for brief periods during the daily program, but these periods are independent from instruction. Free play is viewed as something children need to do, but not as a significant part of the teaching process. In some classrooms, free play is used as a reward for finishing one's work or for behaving appropriately.

Outside of free play times, the teacher decides what children do and how long they spend on a given task. Children have few opportunities to exercise their own judgment about what is meaningful activity, and they have few choices.

Children are primarily organized in large groups, with everyone undertaking the same task at the same time. Activities are planned for the whole class with little regard for differences in developmental capabilities, although there may be some ability grouping for reading and math activities. Children have few opportunities to work in small groups and to have individual attention from the teacher.

Behavior and Management

Teachers view themselves as the exclusive decision maker about behavior in the cultural transmission classroom. They expect children to follow their expectations for behavior. Hence, they state rules, moralize, and demand obedience. The reasons behind expectations for behavior are not always established, and children have little opportunity to participate in discussions about conflict or appropriate individual and group behavior. Teachers are not

Stereotyped patterns of Lincoln's and Washington's profiles dominate the windows of this school, suggesting that cultural transmission prevails in the classroom. Sylvia G. Feinburg

particularly concerned about whether children understand the reasons behind what is expected of them.

Cultural issues center primarily on white middle-class values and traditional family life; little attention is given to the wide range of values, cultures, and lifestyles that reflect contemporary society. Teachers avoid dealing with, or dismiss, patterns of behavior that are not conventional.

Lesson Plans and Curriculum

In the cultural transmission classroom, basic skills are emphasized and taught in didactic, mechanistic ways. Subject matter and areas of study are predominantly determined by curriculum guides and conventional worksheets. Stereotyped ideas from commercial sources are presented—fall leaves, spring flowers, farm animals, city workers—with little opportunity for relating the ideas to children's interests or lives. Publishers control a substantial part of the curriculum. Interdisciplinary teaching is not emphasized.

Emphasis is on tasks with predetermined outcomes, such as completing commercial worksheets, filling in mimeographed forms with pictures created by adults, and following directions to arrive at identical products. Individual creativity is not emphasized, and children's unique expressive products are not displayed or are given minimal attention. The product represents the imposition of adult values with no opportunity for the child to function creatively.

Teachers do not plan lessons and activities that focus attention on social and emotional issues in decisive ways. Children's spontaneous expressions about what they love, hate, fear, or wish for are not built on, encouraged, or addressed in the curriculum. When teachers do deal with such concepts as being kind, caring about others, being angry, and so on, they do so moralistically—making a point of conveying expectations about how one ought to behave, rather than increasing understanding about human beings and how they function.

The concept of the dialectic, of debate and inquiry, is not a central value. Children have little opportunity to engage in controversial discussions, whether they focus on academic or personal and social issues.

Assessment

Standardized achievement tests and paper-and-pencil tasks are the primary means of evaluation. Systematic observation and recording of children's behavior and performance in a naturalistic manner does not occur. Teachers use assessment only to measure a child's capability to accomplish group tasks, as contrasted with identifying individual strengths and weaknesses across a broad range of capabilities.

The Romantic Classroom

Some characteristics of a typical romantic early childhood classroom are set out in this section.

Physical Environment and the Learning Process

Many open-ended materials are provided for children to explore, and play is valued highly. Conventional early childhood equipment like blocks, manipulatives, and books are available, as are dramatic play and science area activity centers, but the teacher does not attempt to influence the exploration in any significant way. She is tentative about making suggestions, raising questions, or stimulating thinking in specific ways. Children's discovering for themselves is of key importance. Learning centers and activity areas are options for children to select.

The classroom does not change significantly throughout the year. Basic equipment and activity areas remain relatively constant. Few changes are evident. For example, the same books remain; painting always takes place in the same location and in much the same way; water table equipment does not represent differing degrees of complexity and challenge.

Emphasis is placed on children's expressivity, and materials are provided for children to use freely. The teacher is reluctant to make suggestions and offer possibilities for fear of limiting the child's thinking. Exploration and discovery are valued as they evolve with minimal intervention by the adult. The term *creativity* is used to cover everything children produce, without differentiating products that represent true ingenuity on the part of the child.

Children determine what activities or tasks they will participate in. The teacher rarely redirects or influences the child's decision about what activity to engage in and for how long. Hence, a child may be permitted to remain at a given activity repeatedly and avoid dealing with certain areas of the curriculum. Self-direction is honored without always considering the complex reasons that a child may select or reject a particular pursuit.

There are minimal expectations for children to focus attention, listen to others who are speaking, and achieve their best. The label "not ready developmentally" may be applied inappropriately, and concern for the child's individual level of development may be confused with having few expectations for children to realize their maximum capabilities to concentrate or to pursue a set of ideas. Children are not always challenged to deliver their best.

Teachers are often remiss in terms of the physical organization of materials and the classroom in general. Teachers may not have high expectations for children to care for materials and deal with them respectfully. Children neglect returning things to their proper places and do not take responsibility for cleaning up after themselves and others.

Behavior and Management

Teachers may be sensitive to children's emotional and social development, but may focus on these areas excessively without paying equal attention to intellectual and academic concerns. Teachers are predisposed toward psychodynamic interpretations and do not always recognize the critical interplay between productive work and behavior. How children are feeling is viewed in isolation, making it difficult for competence to be influential in building self-esteem. Teachers often verbalize explanations for children's behavior instead of helping children understand that they can take responsibility for how they act.

Teachers value understanding how people feel about a given situation and encourage children to share their point of view with others. However, teachers are less likely to structure particular learning situations around key behavioral issues.

Teachers accept a wide range of children's behavior and do not always set limits that make the classroom safe and secure for all children. Strategies such as time out and simple reinforcement techniques that may be helpful for children who have problems with self-control are not considered viable alternatives to discussion. Talking and discussion are the exclusive strategies used to manage behavior.

Lesson Plans and Curriculum

Although activity centers and daily projects are available, the main way children are encouraged to become involved is through presentation of materials. The adult is reluctant to motivate the lesson or provide a set of concepts or skills for children to address.

The teacher provides materials somewhat randomly, without thinking about sequence and progression in its use. Thus, children may be given mathematics, painting, collage, and journal-writing activities on a repeated basis to use informally, but the presentation is not altered so as to challenge the child's thinking in successively demanding ways.

Challenging children to struggle with a difficult concept is avoided. Children are allowed to find their own level of participation all the time, sometimes resulting in boredom and repetitive, hackneyed work.

Skills are taught only haphazardly or not at all. Creativity and mastery of skills are not distinguished as separate functions. Teachers are so respectful of the child's own product in art, writing, and other expressive activities that they do not recognize the importance of helping children to master skills. Hence, teachers may be reluctant to help children learn such things as how to paste effectively, how to apply paint using particular techniques, and how to form letters more precisely.

Assessment

Teachers indiscriminately praise or applaud work without providing information about why the product or activity is praiseworthy. Teachers may be inclined toward vague reinforcement, such as "I like that" or "Isn't that terrific?" They may see process as so important that they always ignore the significance of the product, even in situations where addressing the product seems especially warranted. All the child's efforts are responded to comparably.

Careful records are not kept to document the child's capabilities in a given area of performance. Children, and in particular their behavior, are observed casually, but systematic documentation of intellectual progress and skill acquisition is neglected. The adult may be unaware of the child's capabilities across a broad spectrum of performance.

The Cognitive-Developmental or Dynamic Classroom

Some characteristics of a typical cognitive-developmental classroom are set out in this section.

Physical Environment and the Learning Process

In addition to basic equipment and media generally associated with an early childhood program (blocks, puzzles, books, math and other manipulatives, and art materials), the cognitive-developmental classroom reveals a wide variety of materials for children to observe, touch, and manipulate. These materials invite investigation and imaginative use. The unique and imaginative (for example, a broken telephone, a meat grinder, menus from a local restaurant) are included, and the materials change throughout the year.

The classroom is well organized physically, with sufficient order and clarity to communicate a sense of harmony and security. Children can easily determine where things are and how to clean up, and they are expected to participate actively in maintaining the environment.

The classroom is aesthetically pleasing. To engage interest and stimulate thinking, both children's and adults' work (including high-quality adult work as well as reproductions of works by famous artists) are displayed.

Teachers are knowledgeable about child development and how cognition affects intellectual and social-emotional behavior. They view development comprehensively, considering its implications for a given age range as well as for the individual child. Knowledge about development is central to the design of learning experiences.

Teachers work in a range of ways with children, individually and in both small and large groups. Children are organized in relation to individual interests and developmental capabilities. Since the importance of concrete activity is respected, many concepts are taught in small groups, allowing children the opportunity to directly manipulate materials. Literacy and mathematics activities are sometimes addressed in large groups, sometimes in small groups, and sometimes individually.

Teachers appreciate of the complexity of human performance. They recognize that children may function quite differently in different areas of the curriculum. Teachers are aware of and responsive to, not only children's special difficulties in learning, but also children's unique talents and interests.

Teachers understand the impact of lifestyle and culture on children's learning styles and ability to feel comfortable in the classroom. Teachers create a sense of community at the same time as they are acutely aware of individual differences.

Behavior and Management

Teachers use management and behavioral issues, as well as the curriculum in general, as opportunities for children to reason, solve problems, and analyze events. Critical thinking and social cognition are clear objectives. Teachers model negotiation strategies by focusing on alternative points of view.

Teachers strive to help children gain autonomy and a sense of personal power while strengthening their understanding of group dynamics. Teachers are not reluctant to assert their authority when a situation requires, but they do so in a way that strengthens children's self-esteem and lessens vulnerability. Teachers rely on a range of strategies to maintain order and control and apply them with sensitivity to individual needs.

Lesson Plans and Curriculum

Although teachers respect the spontaneous and what comes from the child, they see it as their responsibility to stimulate children's thinking in direct ways and to move children beyond what they are able to uncover on their own. Hence, teachers present lessons with clear objectives that challenge thinking. Using cognitive conflict and the dialectic are valued teaching strategies.

Children with exceptional capabilities or areas of concern have activities planned specifically with them in mind. Teachers extend their own knowledge base on behalf of gifted children and are able to challenge them in progressively more complex ways.

The teacher capitalizes on children's interests so that such themes as dinosaurs and fantasy figures, birthday parties, sibling relationships, and family and neighborhood events are strategically integrated into key activities, including language arts and mathematics. Interdisciplinary units are designed around areas compelling to many children.

Creativity is valued highly; every attempt is made to capitalize on children's imaginative, expressive thinking. Many opportunities are provided for children to invent and create across media. The distinction is made between teaching skills and encouraging creative thinking. The teacher is deliberate in intervening to promote both skill mastery and creativity.

The curriculum routinely includes activities that encourage children's expression of social-emotional issues, and the teacher actively builds understanding about human behavior in planning activities. Subject matter includes children's fears, anger, aspirations, and friendships. Social cognition—knowledge about social behavior—is an integral part of curriculum development.

Assessment

The teacher uses observation and recording to document children's strengths and weaknesses. Children's work is reviewed comprehensively to determine their level of performance across domains of learning. Competence is not evaluated narrowly; for example, numerous drawings of a person are analyzed, rather than a single one, in order to evaluate concept formation.

The Cognitive-Developmental Model Analyzed

This book emphasizes the cognitive-developmental model as offering the greatest opportunity to challenge children intellectually. The next section analyzes in depth the key components of this model: the teacher's role, the organization of classroom groups, and the presentation of learning experiences. Some contrasts with the other models of early childhood education are pointed out in order to highlight the rationale for implementing the cognitive-developmental model.

The Teacher's Role

In the traditional classroom (which follows the cultural transmission model) the teacher is often guilty of assuming too much importance in the learning experience, lecturing and delivering information in didactic ways. In addition, children may not have enough opportunity to use concrete materials and be involved in direct exploration; they have little opportunity for self-initiated activity. Conversely, in the permissive, overly child-centered classroom (the romantic model), teachers value the child's play and discovery almost to a fault, seeing their role as one of setting the stage, providing appropriate materials, and then standing back and leaving the rest to the child.

In the dynamic classroom (the cognitive-developmental model) the teacher views these two processes—setting up and presenting materials, and guiding activity and imparting information—as complementary. The teacher intervenes in a wide variety of ways: to help the child to focus, to raise challenging issues that incite critical thinking, and to deliver information directly in order to extend the child's frame of reference. The teacher strikes a balance between, on the one hand, standing back and allowing the child to lead the way, and, on the other hand, moving forward and providing the stimulation and direction that will guide

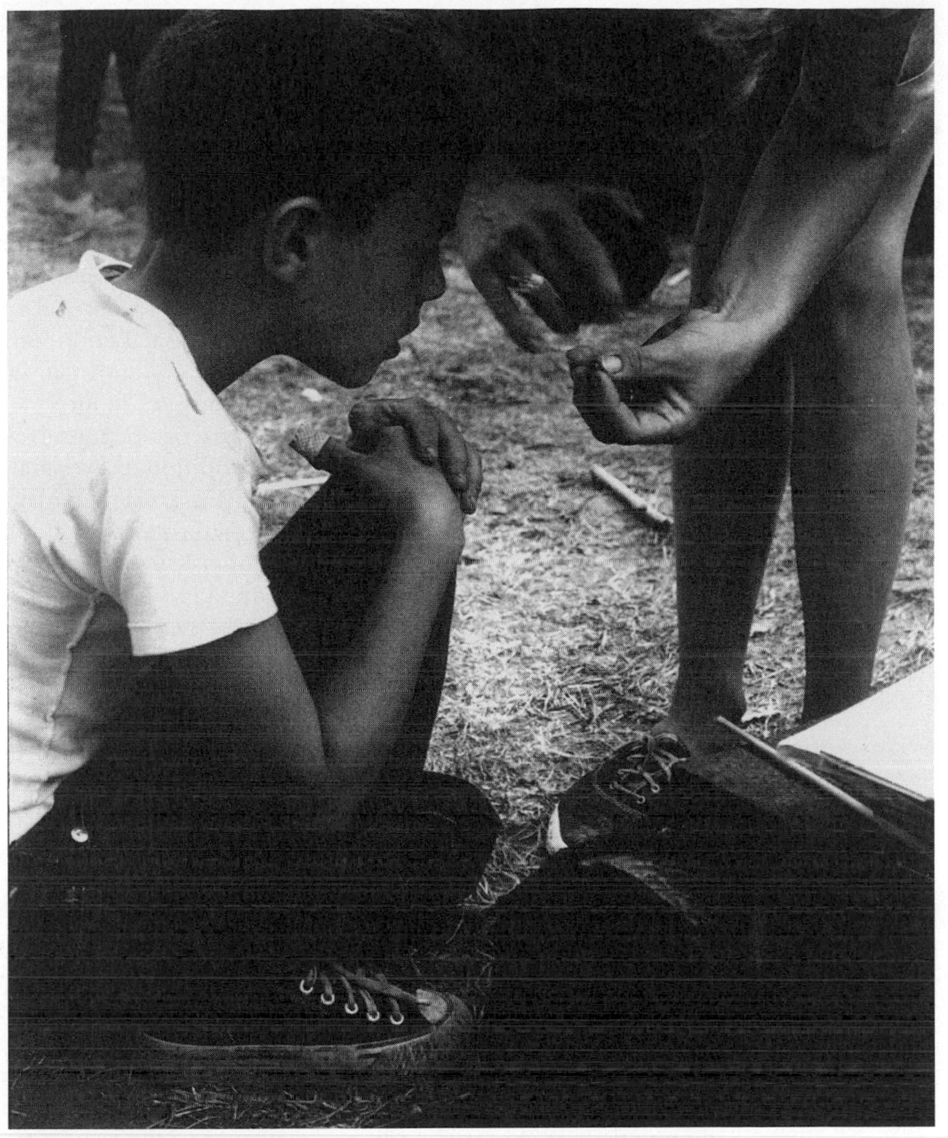

The cognitive-developmental teacher is not reluctant to share information in a direct manner. This teacher is identifying and labeling critical features of the insect. Sylvia G. Feinburg

subsequent learning. In the dynamic classroom the notion of interaction is central, not just the interaction of child with materials, but also the interaction of child with child. The child's independent discovery is valued, but it is not seen as contradictory to appropriate adult guidance.

In the dynamic or cognitive-developmental classroom, the teacher has no ambivalence about sharing information and shaping the child's thinking. The teacher recognizes that his or her role in stimulating interest and concept formation is critical.

Organization of Classroom Groups

In the cultural transmission classroom, it is customary to treat the members of a class as a single homogeneous group, dealing with everyone as if all the children were developmentally ready for identical experiences across most curriculum areas. Sometimes separations are made for key academic areas, like math and reading, and children are placed in ability groups that remain relatively constant. This approach ignores the complexity of developmental and motivational factors and creates rigid and artificial distinctions among children that can have deleterious effects, resulting in grade retention and a sense of failure.

Conversely, romantic teachers may ignore distinctions in ability levels entirely, treating every child as though he or she will flower eventually if surrounded by ample stimulation and support. The romantic teacher may ignore differences among children in the same way traditional teachers do, but for a different set of reasons. The romantic—dedicated to minimizing competition and differences in children's intellectual abilities, and committed to helping children to be independent and self-sufficient—may provide a rich environment and options for children. The romantic teacher, however, allows children to be completely self-determining about what they will work at and for how long, neglecting the wide number of variables that influence interest, motivation, and performance.

Certainly children are different in their academic abilities, but these differences do not fit into neat compartments. Differences are influenced by such factors as special needs and learning problems, critical social-emotional factors (self-concept, self-discipline, shyness), experience in a particular domain of learning, comfort and familiarity with media and with certain approaches to working, family and cultural influences, and interest levels. For example, a child who is shy or fearful of the boisterousness in the block corner may nevertheless want to be an active participant, but may avoid becoming one for fear of rejection in the entry process. Or a child who is apprehensive about his capacity to do well in reading or math may avoid the activity, given the choice, even when the child is secretly hungry to become involved. Or, again, a child may want to become involved in a cooking project, but she may reject this involvement because in her culture, food is prepared differently, and she feels insecure about eating what will be made. Motivation and performance in a given learning situation can vary substantially, depending on the specific circumstances involved and whether they are enabling or inhibiting for the individual. Furthermore, shifts in development are always occurring, sometimes subtly and sometimes rather dramatically. The cognitive-developmental teacher understands that he or she can elicit the most from students using a multifaceted approach, and organizes learning experiences in a range of ways.

The dynamic teacher works individually, with small groups of children, and with large groups throughout the day, depending on the nature of the activity, its specific objectives, and what is in the best interests of individual children. Sometimes children are able to select what they will do and how they will go about it on their own. On other occasions the teacher actively determines what the children will do and what the context will be. Hence, during some periods of the day, children will choose to draw or to write alone, without teacher intervention; at other times, there will be teacher-initiated small group activities, which children may choose or reject; on other occasions, children will be assigned to a given activity without choice. Some large group experiences will be required for everyone; but occasionally, exceptions will be made for one or two children for whom the expectation seems inappropriate. A myriad of situations will occur, some representing choice and independence for the child, some reflecting firm teacher expectations and leadership, and some representing collaboration between teacher and children.

The Importance of Aides and Assistants

Under the best of circumstances, more than one adult will be in the classroom, making it possible for a variety of learning situations to occur simultaneously. An assistant teacher or part-time aide must be made aware of program objectives and the curriculum. Assistants in the classroom can be of enormous benefit and should not be viewed as just another pair of hands. Many untrained people can make a significant contribution to a classroom if the head teacher assumes a leadership role and provides clear information about her objectives and expectations for participation.

Many teachers who do not have the advantage of an assistant or student teacher are able to identify parents, elderly people, or others in the community interested in donating their time to the classroom. For example, in one community parents and other adults are invited to the classroom for the first half-hour of the day to read with individual children. It is important and exciting for the children each to have the complete attention of an adult with whom to read and interact over a book.

Whether or not an assistant is available, the learning environment must be organized so that certain activities can function relatively independently, allowing the teacher to determine which situations require his or her sustained presence at a particular period of time. Boxed projects, purposeful worksheets, games, and other independent or collaborative tasks are all important ways to allow individuals or small groups of children to work constructively without an adult present.

Presentation of Learning Experiences

In the dynamic classroom, concrete activity is emphasized, and modes of presentation are flexible, varying with the situation.

The Importance of Concrete Activity

Materials play a central role in teaching young children, since nature has programmed them to learn most effectively through direct, concrete experiences involving multiple senses. One could argue that learning this way is a powerful approach all through life, since it is clear that such experiences enhance adult learning as well. For adults, however, words and abstract symbols are viable learning options, and adults are able to gather knowledge and develop concepts without necessarily being engaged in concrete ways. Children, though, form concepts through direct observation and through the actions they perform—touching, manipulating, taking things apart and putting them back together again, creating and destroying. Words are not totally useless for the child as a means of learning, but they are limited, and they must rest on concrete experience to become significant. Words increase in meaning as they are joined with live, dynamic experiences; play and materials are the mechanisms through which knowledge is constructed. Consequently, in planning learning experiences for young children, the teacher will want to provide many first-hand opportunities for children to use various media, equipment, and tools. Naturally, the teacher will also use words and language as teaching strategies, but will reinforce them with as many concrete activity-based experiences as possible.

Developmentally based classrooms are designed to provide a rich physical environment that offers children the opportunity to explore according to their individual interests. The following activity materials and areas are considered basic: blocks, mathematics, science, water and sand, reading and writing, art, dramatic play, puzzles and manipulatives, and music (McKee, 1986). Time periods are provided sometime during the day, usually during free play and planned activity time, when children are free to select some of these areas for spontaneous investigation. The idea of having activity areas available for children to use on their own terms is extremely important and should not be underestimated.

There will also be times throughout the day, however, when the teacher will plan specific learning experiences with identifiable objectives—lessons and activities introduced independently of the times children are involved in spontaneous activity. These lessons may be focused directly on a given area of the curriculum—reading, writing, mathematics, art, science—or they may be interdisciplinary, involving a range of subject areas. Some lessons will be narrowly focused on skills; others will be more comprehensive and thematic in nature. The developmental teacher does not see a contradiction between teaching skills and providing more integrated experientially based activities. Both kinds of experiences are crucial for children to acquire. Sometimes skills will be strengthened as a part of informal play and activity, and sometimes addressed directly, for their own sake.

Three Forms of Presentation in the Dynamic Classroom

Activities and lessons may take one of the following three forms. Teachers select the instructional option that facilitates their specific objectives in a given situation.

In the first presentation option, children are free to select spontaneously from basic materials and activities within the environment. In these circumstances the materials are familiar to the child, or what to do with them is readily apparent. The materials are part of the basic organization of the room, or if they are novel, they are within a context that makes their use understandable. Although there may be continuity from a previous experience, spontaneity and the child's self-determination are important. The teacher may intervene strategically or remain removed from the situation. The teacher makes certain that subtle and strategic shifts in the environment take place as the year progresses. For example, children may go to the reading area and look at books; get art materials from shelves and use them at a nearby table; go to the block area and bring salvage scraps to help make a rocket launching pad; or go to the water table and play with the funnels

This three-year-old is observing carefully to see the impact of having placed two blocks on a wooden gear apparatus. For young children, the opportunity to act on materials and observe the results is crucial for intellectual development. Sylvia G. Feinburg and cups that are usually there. Children in one classroom we observed spontaneously traced puzzle shapes and called the shapes new countries; the teacher helped them name the countries and record their ideas.

In the second presentation option, materials are set up in a particular location or context (arranged or combined in a different way) to stimulate learning experiences. Materials are the dominant thrust of the activity. Teachers prearrange the physical environment so as to provoke a particular kind of investigation that would likely not take place without their intervention. This preparation may take place within the basic learning areas (the blocks, art, water, or science area, for example), or it may be set up on tables or in another specified area so that it is identifiable as an activity. Teachers are critically aware of why the materials are being presented and what learnings they think the materials will engender. Teachers are purposeful in their presentation. They may say nothing or make only a few introductory comments; the power of the motivation is less with the teacher and more with the dynamic way the materials have been arranged and presented. Essentially, teachers transfer their intellectual authority to the materials, allowing them to stimulate the activity (as Montessori attempted to do with her didactic materials, although the Montessori materials are presented in a more systematic, programmed way than is typical of a more eclectic classroom). The teacher employs some of the following strategies to achieve her objectives:

- novel juxtapositions—combining materials that are not usually together or eliminating an expected tool or material
- novel environmental elements—placing materials in a new area of the room
- presenting materials in ways that command attention and inspire

Examples include the following:

- The teacher arranges hunks of styrofoam; strips of thin, brightly colored electrician's wire; and cellophane drinking straws on the table. Three- and four-year-olds quickly see the potential in the situation and begin to make sculptural forms of all different shapes. When she visits the table periodically, the teacher asks probing questions like "How did you get that straw to stay on your construction?" or "Would those beads over there help you with what you're doing?"
- The teacher assembles a number of pop-up books on the table, along with materials that will enable first and second graders to make their own (heavy paper, cardboard strips, scissors, accordion-folded paper strips). She arranges strips of cardboard to suggest accordion and slotting techniques. Children see the potential immediately and become involved in making picture books with parts that move and pop up. At group time children share the concepts they have uncovered.
- The teacher places dollhouse furniture and small table-sized blocks next to the area usually reserved for large blocks. Kindergartners immediately create apartment houses and other constructions, and discussion emerges about living upstairs or downstairs from another family.
- A large windowsill, usually reserved for plants, is set up for measuring the lengths of things brought in from outside. Pieces of bark, tree branches, rocks, bricks, and so on are assembled, along with measuring tapes and yardsticks. A chart has been made in advance for first graders to enter measurements for the various

objects. The teacher drops by periodically to guide the activity; she is flexible in her expectations of their recording abilities.

- First graders make collages of tree forms by tearing large sheets of paper; no scissors are allowed.

In the third presentation option, the teacher stimulates or motivates the situation directly and is actively involved in teaching the lesson. In these situations the teacher's presence, at least initially, is crucial to the unfolding of the lesson. Teachers bring the children together, in either a small group or a large group, and make certain to have children's attention before beginning. Teachers may use a wide variety of motivational strategies to focus attention and engage interest. Since they have specific objectives in mind in terms of learning outcomes, teachers stimulate the activity in a purposeful way. They do not rely on hackneyed phrases such as "We're going to do something special today"; rather, they command children's interest through the vitality and incisiveness of their presentation (for example, "When you look out the window, how can you tell whether or not it is windy outside? Look carefully and see if you can find any evidence or clues"). Children are clearly expected to attend to the task, but teachers strive to make it worthy of their attention. They may leave the activity once it has been initiated and come back periodically to steer its direction when the initial energy begins to dissipate.

The Zone of Proximal Development

Vygotsky cautioned us not to think about developmental stages too narrowly. In terms of learning he believed that we must consider two developmental levels that apply to children. The first is what he labeled the "actual developmental level": the level of functioning established by evaluating the child's capabilities within a given area of functioning—in other words, the completed developmental capacity. With testing, for example, we can determine the specific level at which a child is able to function in a given area, and we can make some developmental judgments based on this mastery. The second level Vygotsky called the "zone of proximal development": capabilities of the child that are in transition, in the process of becoming. When children are working at a difficult problem with adult assistance and guidance, they can often move beyond their actual developmental level and perform at a more advanced stage. Vygotsky (1978) wrote:

> The zone of proximal development defines those functions that have not yet matured but are in the process of maturation, functions that will mature tomorrow but are currently in an embryonic state. These functions could be termed the "buds" or "flowers" of development rather than the "fruits" of development. The actual developmental level characterizes mental development retrospectively, while the zone of proximal development characterizes mental development prospectively. (pp. 86–87)

Vygotsky argued that "developmental processes do not coincide with learning processes." Instead, development lags behind learning, so that educational practice must reach beyond the established developmental stage and assist the child in moving to the next stage. Pedagogical practices that challenge children to reach beyond their current stage of mastery are thus of key importance. In optimal learning situations, stimulation is aimed slightly beyond the reach of the learner—not at the existing level of functioning, and certainly not well beneath it.

Cognitive Conflict and the Dialectic

The cultural transmission model is clearly at variance with the values central to a developmentally based classroom. The cultural transmission model, as it is most commonly practiced and frequently used at the primary grade levels, relies heavily on such procedures as teaching skills in isolation, having the entire class work on the same activity the majority of the time, using pencil-and-paper tasks and repetitive worksheets extensively, and providing limited opportunities for play and for using manipulatives and other concrete materials. Cultural transmission is information-oriented, not child-oriented; hence, it has little in common with developmentally based practices.

The romantic and cognitive-developmental streams are both child-centered and respectful of developmental factors. Distinguishing them, however, is of central importance to the developmental educator, because the distinction between the two orientations strikes at the heart of what distinguishes the dynamic from the static classroom, the stimulating environment from the mundane one. Both streams are committed to encouraging children's activity—open-ended investigation, play, creativity, and self-expression—and to considering children's individual needs and interests. Where the two orientations part company is over how active the teacher should be in influencing learning situations, as well as how she should set about her work.

Romantic teachers (whether they so call themselves or not) are often ambivalent about how much direction and stimulation they should provide. They may be very successful in setting up a child-centered physical environment, but their profound respect for the child's own motivation and initiative or their lack of understanding about how to motivate children often prevents them from intervening when that intervention could be pivotal. These teachers may be predisposed to withhold certain information and instruction or may avoid raising focused questions for fear of imposing themselves on the child and thwarting discovery.

In the cognitive-developmental stream, Kohlberg and Mayer argue for purposeful and relevant adult intervention, which goes beyond simply providing a child-centered environment and basic materials, and then stepping back and leaving subsequent responsibility with the child. Kohlberg and Mayer feel that the adult must be provocative and influential in a wide assortment of ways and appeal to the child's innate desire to attain a higher level of mastery and understanding of a given set of ideas. The argument is not for aggressive and controlling teacher influence of an inappropriate nature—quite the contrary. It suggests, instead, careful observation of progress on behalf of both the individual and the group, followed by purposeful interventions by the adult. For example, during a first-grade writing time when a child has written the statement, "I went to a haunted house," the cognitive-developmental teacher, intending to provoke thought, might say, "What does it mean when a house is haunted?"—whereas the romantic teacher might say, "That's a wonderful start!"

A teacher in a cognitive-developmental classroom will not, of course, interfere continuously in children's activity and is not unaware of how important it is to respect children's needs to be left alone under certain circumstances. But neither is the teacher reluctant to seize opportunities for teaching and extending a child's cursory investigation. A distinction should be made between allowing children to follow their own objectives to their logical conclusion, and withholding assistance and stimulation that can be crucial to the child's ultimate objectives. Romantic teachers are often guilty of not providing the necessary materials or verbal input that enable and free the child to examine new possibilities. Romantic teachers may also be satisfied with work habits and products that are shoddy and do not reflect children's full potential. It is critical that the teacher establish standards and expectations for performance, although these expectations should be based on an understanding of individual children's needs and capabilities.

Kohlberg and Mayer's emphasis on such notions as cognitive conflict and the dialectic reflects their sense of how important it is to challenge children in deliberate ways, instead of leaving the quality of the learning encounter to chance as a romantic teacher might. Using cognitive conflict to teach children means providing children with sufficient stimulation and provocation so that they feel an intellectual challenge and excitement about the ideas at hand. Kohlberg and Mayer take issue with classrooms so benign in this regard that they do not do all they can to provoke the child's thinking. An example of a situation that relies on cognitive conflict to teach kindergartners is the following: Kindergartners are studying birds and their nesting habits. The teacher has helped them construct the knowledge that when building nests, birds seek relatively strong materials that can be shaped easily and joined readily with other materials, and that provide warmth and ventilation. During activity time, a wide assortment of materials is set out, such as nails, fabric scraps, grasses, string, acorns, aluminum foil, and styrofoam. Children are asked to build nests on their own and to decide which of the available materials the bird would select or reject.

To Kohlberg and Mayer, using the dialectic means encouraging children to debate and discourse about ideas, and in the process to raise questions and examine possible answers. The dialectic is based on the concept of confronting contradictions and weighing alternative hypotheses—in short, of wrestling with ideas and examining them analytically. In the example of the kindergartners' learning about birds, the teacher uses the dialectic in teaching by asking, "How do you think a mother bird decides where she is going to build her nest?" The children provide many different ideas. The teacher records them and stimulates discussion. The children are encouraged to discuss the relative value of the various suggestions. They consider what additional information they should have in order to answer the question and where they can find this information. The teacher follows up on their recommendations and plans future discussions.

In the cognitive-developmental model, the teacher is central to this process of inquiry and investigation. Although at times the teacher is a passive observer (particularly when materials are new or children are able to establish goals and objectives for themselves), at other times the teacher structures the learning situation so as to focus the child's attention on a given set of ideas. Furthermore, the teacher does not feel reticent about raising questions, sharing information, and providing additional materials to lead a child's thinking in a particular direction.

The teacher recognizes that providing meaningful content is a central responsibility. In short, the cognitive-developmental teacher is willing to be what DeVries and Kohlberg called "a guide, companion, and stimulator." The romantic teacher, conversely, is all too often only a companion (DeVries & Kohlberg, 1990).

Summary

Juxtaposing the cognitive-developmental model with the romantic and cultural transmission models clarifies the key qualities of all three perspectives. The distinguishing feature of the cultural transmission model is its focus on conveying information. In contrast, the cognitive-developmental model emphasizes an orientation that encourages the child to construct meaning. The romantic model shares the child-centered view of the cognitive-developmental model, but it does not articulate as clearly the role of purposeful adult interventions. The cognitive-developmental model emphasizes these interventions as a way for teachers to create cognitive conflict and encourage discussion as an important component of learning.

Classrooms dominated by these philosophical perspectives look very different from one another in terms of the physical setup, the way classroom management is viewed, and the approach to lesson planning and assessment. The cognitive-developmental model is a dynamic model: interactions between teacher and child, child and child, and child and materials form the basis for discovery learning. The teacher in the dynamic classroom uses a variety of approaches in presenting lessons, including encouraging children's free selection of materials, arranging materials so as to stimulate thinking, and teaching directly in a way that provokes children to search for information. Both through modeling and stimulating children to go beyond the level at which they are functioning comfortably, the cognitive-developmental teacher incorporates the Vygotskian perspective of development.

This chapter compared the distinguishing classroom characteristics of the models, enabling the reader to comprehend more fully how philosophical orientation manifests itself in classroom practice. The next two chapters focus on the cognitive-developmental model and how it is implemented. These chapters are structured around basic **operational characteristics** that educators can use to translate key aspects of the model into action.

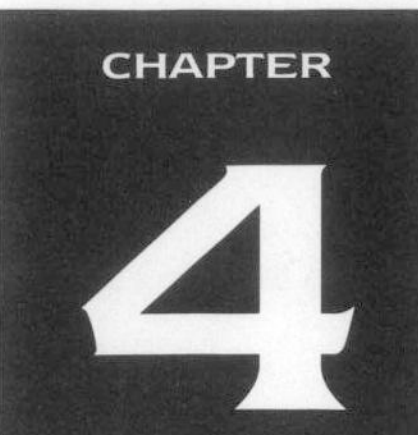

CHAPTER

4 CRITICAL QUALITIES OF THE TEACHER: OPERATIONAL CHARACTERISTICS

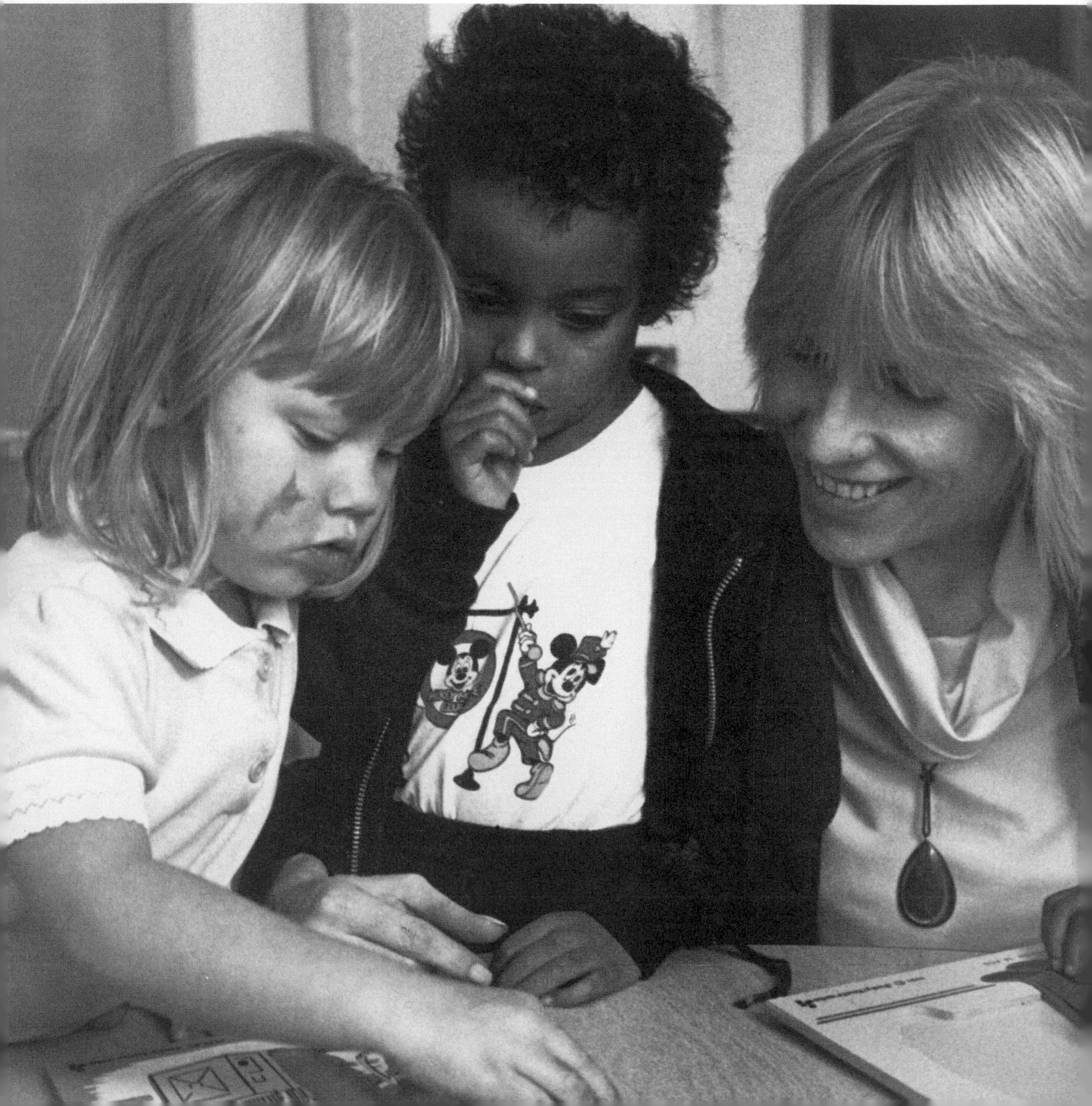

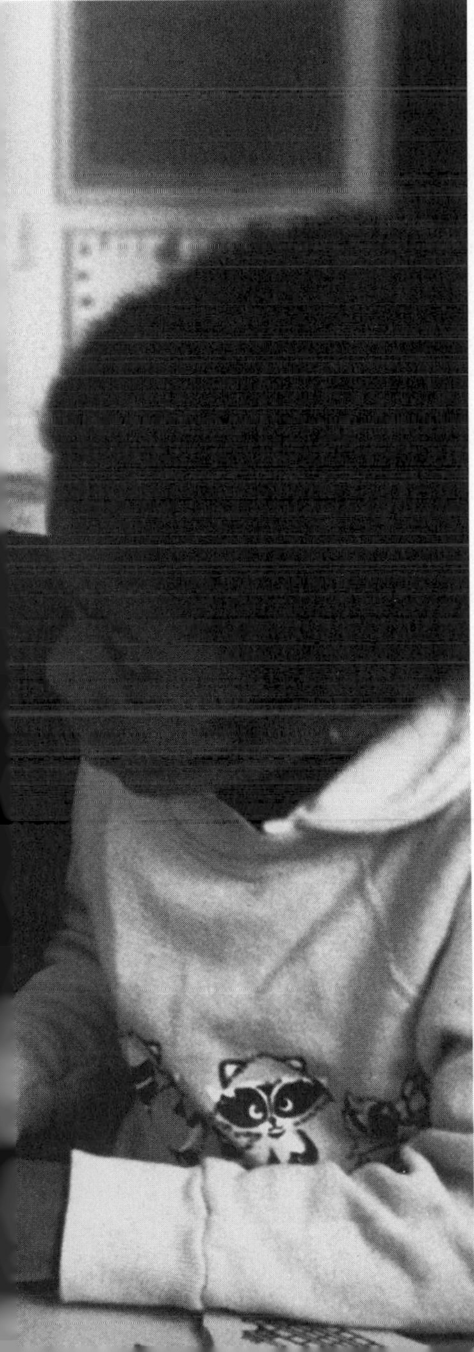

As we learned in Chapter 3, the cognitive-developmental model is distinguished from other educational orientations primarily in the emphasis it places on cognitive conflict and on purposeful and relevant adult interventions. This chapter identifies four critical teaching qualities that support these interventions and enable teachers to provide children with an appropriate degree of cognitive challenge.* Cognitive-developmental teachers must develop and nurture the four qualities to be effective in carrying out the model's goals.

These teaching qualities are described as **operational characteristics**—that is, specific clusters of teaching behaviors critical to the model's implementation. Each behavior is accompanied by anecdotes that focus on particular aspects of the model in action. The operational characteristics in this chapter also provide a reference for those interested in refining specific aspects of their teaching, particularly their intellectual vibrancy; ability to translate into practice knowledge about development, learning, and teaching strategies; use of questions and other verbal interaction skills; and empowerment of children to take responsibility for their own learning.

Teachers are the most important force in creating a learning environment that stimulates and challenges children. Their intellectual vitality and the way they deal with ideas, communicate, and influence others are of major importance. Guiding all their actions is their understanding of child development, the developmental model, and its effective implementation. This chapter addresses the qualities essential to the teacher's being a significant force in the learning process:

1. The teacher is alert intellectually.
2. The teacher assumes a leadership role in shaping thinking.
3. The teacher recognizes the power of speech for challenging children intellectually.
4. The teacher empowers children to be in charge of their own learning.

The Teacher Is Alert Intellectually

The first of the four operational characteristics critical to a successful developmental program focuses on the teacher's intellectual vibrancy. The teacher is alert and responsive to issues and ideas and models these qualities.

Current Events

The successful developmental teacher is aware of current events and identifies issues appropriate for children to address. The teacher uses his or her knowledge of child development, as well as individual and group needs, in identifying relevant areas for consideration and designs the curriculum accordingly. The following examples are illustrative.

◗ A fall hurricane has created considerable damage in the area, and newspaper and television news reports have been full of information about it. Since the children in a third-grade class are intensely interested, the teacher introduces a unit on storms. The children learn about different kinds of storms and how they are

*The classroom evaluation guide, Form B, in Chapter 11 relates to this chapter.

defined (thunderstorms, hurricanes, tornadoes), as well as some basic concepts about the impact of storms on a community (home destruction, insurance, the declaration of a national disaster area). The teacher recognizes that the storm is important to consider not only because it is a major event in the children's lives, but because these third graders are developmentally ready to study a specific storm in relationship to a larger category of storms. The subject matter is an opportunity for them to learn to classify, to identify similarities and differences in weather patterns, and to learn important safety information.

◗ A fight between two baseball players has dominated the news over the weekend. Television and newspapers have given the event a lot of attention. The teacher brings newspaper articles and pictures about the situation into her first-grade classroom and engages children in discussing the incident, which involved a rookie player. The teacher encourages an exchange about why people fight; inappropriate fighting, particularly during a game; and appropriate behavior when people are frustrated and angry. The concept of fair play emerges and is examined in depth. This subject has special significance for this group of children because a good deal of antagonism has been arising among certain classroom members, sometimes erupting into fights.

◗ The local newspaper reported that a much-loved school bus driver has HIV, the virus that causes AIDS. This topic is the subject of many conversations. One child announces: "My father says that I'm not riding on that bus." The teacher has a responsibility to help children recognize that it is all right to discuss a threatening and emotionally laden subject in school. The teacher needs to determine what is appropriate for children at this age to understand and to clarify children's misconceptions. What is HIV? Is it like the measles or a cold? Do children catch it? Can you catch it if you sit next to somebody who has it? The teacher needs to be informed about the subject, to share this information with parents and children at appropriate times, and to help children develop a positive attitude about their own responsibility for healthy living habits.

Cultural Diversity

A good developmental teacher is informed about cultural diversity and pays particular attention to learning about the cultures of children in his or her classroom. A teacher who takes the time to become familiar with the cultures of the children in the classroom increases the likelihood that individual children and their families will feel comfortable in the new surroundings. Such a teacher also enriches the curriculum for all children.

◗ A new child in a kindergarten classroom is from India. The teacher seeks information about celebrations, customs, language, and values, and shares this information in appropriate contexts. At lunchtime, for example, she arranges a menu that includes chapati (a kind of Indian bread), some vegetables, and some yogurt. She asks the new child to show how his family sometimes takes a little piece of the chapati and uses it to scoop up and roll the food before they eat it. When they eat this way, they do not use knives and forks (Knowlton and Wright, 1988).

◗ For children from kindergarten to grade two interested in setting up a store, the teacher provides a variety of pictures and books showing marketplaces in other countries. She helps the children discover from books and from talking to people that in India the marketplace is set up so that the stands selling a particular item are located on the same street. On one street, fruit is sold; on another, candy; and on still another street, fabric. (This activity also provides an excellent opportunity to help children integrate their play experiences with classification, an important mathematical concept.)

Enrichment from Parents and Other Adults

The developmental teacher identifies parents and other key adults as sources for classroom enrichment. The following examples illustrate.

◗ The school building is near a pizza shop whose owner is warmly disposed toward schoolchildren. The second-grade teacher plans a visit to the shop, where the owner teaches children about what is involved in the pizza business. The owner provides exciting information, demonstrating how pizzas are made, how he uses the large ovens, how he keeps the pizzas warm, and how he figures his profits.

◗ A parent is knowledgeable about Japanese paper folding and is invited to give the first-grade class a lesson with origami paper. He introduces the concepts of symmetry and mathematical equivalents and the skill of scoring and folding paper precisely. The teacher continues the project after the parent leaves.

◗ A group of senior citizens have oil painting lessons in the school building every Friday morning. The teacher takes her class of first graders to watch the adults painting. The children are encouraged to pay close attention to the work being produced and to ask the painters questions. Later, when the children are back in their classroom painting, the teacher asks them to include something in their work that they learned from watching the adults. The children share their products with the senior citizens.

Children's Areas of Interest

The developmental teacher gathers information about an area in which children and their families have shown an interest. The teacher selectively builds this information into the program and provides additional stimulation.

◗ Four- and five-year-olds indicate an interest in ants. The teacher gets books and pictures and borrows an ant farm. At group discussion time, the teacher helps children recall their interest in the ants. She describes ants as very hard workers that scurry about trying to find food to bring back to their homes. "Isn't it amazing," she says, "how ants can carry things that are bigger than they are? Next time you see an ant colony, look closely and see if you can tell how the ants manage to do this." During a subsequent discussion, the teacher shows the children the first page from *The Icky Bug Alphabet Book,* by Jerry Pallotta (1986). The children study the pictures and identify the ant's six legs, the three parts of its body, the antennae, and the feelers. They observe in one picture how the ants carry a large green leaf. When something is too big for an ant to carry alone, the ant finds other ants and asks them to help. "Can ants talk? How can they ask for help?" The teacher continues to gather more information about ants and shares it with the children.

◗ A parent (Dr. Alyssa McCabe) shared this account of her son Nicky's positive experience in a kindergarten classroom in a letter to the author in 1990:

> Nicky for his fourth birthday received some polished rocks and was so struck by them that he put them into a stuffed bear and took them to school. This first time his teachers let him show the rocks to the class during group meeting. His peers and teachers were very enthusiastic, and so Nicky began taking the rocks to school every day to show everyone. His teachers, in fact, would recognize new potential audiences for whom Nicky could display his rock collection, and point this information out to Nicky. In the process of sharing Nicky used and learned the names for many rocks: amethyst, garnet, polished and unpolished rose quartz, snowflake obsidian, pyrite (the real name of "fool's gold"), adventurine, stilbite. One of his teachers brought in her rock book and gave it to him to help with the identification process. After this teacher left the school to give birth to her daughter, she returned to give Nicky her favorite rock for him to identify (pyrite with bornite). Another teacher in a different classroom told Nicky about a specimen he had. When Nicky reminded him to do so, that teacher brought in a specimen of pyrite in slate along with a sledgehammer and broke up the large specimen in front of all the children in school. He gave Nicky a small piece to put in his bear. Several teachers wore jewelry made of polished rocks and asked Nicky to identify the piece (for example, Nicky aptly identified a necklace as either jade or adventurine). But not only did these teachers build on and extend Nicky's interest in a variety of ways, they correctly recognized the important social function it had. Nicky had been a rather shy child for about a year and a half. But through his rocks, he "discovered a bridge to other children that he used with great success thereafter," to quote one of his teachers.

◗ Katja, a four-year-old, shows tremendous interest in a mushroom after having found one in the schoolyard. She asks many questions and continues to examine the mushroom after the children have come back into the classroom. The teacher builds on this cursory investigation by bringing in a number of picture books about mushrooms and collecting a number of interesting ones from the market. The teacher provides a magnifying glass so that Katja can examine the mushrooms closely. Katja begins to learn the names of various kinds of mushrooms, how to identify the mushroom's parts (caps, gills, spores), and how to classify different mushroom shapes (umbrellas and parasols, sponges, turkey tails, shelves, and so on). The teacher also introduces the process of spore printing (printing the various patterns with paint). Other children are involved in Katja's "independent study"; she shares what she learns about mushrooms with them and they with her. Once an area of interest has been identified, it is amazing how many people have relevant information to share.

The Teacher Is a Leader in Shaping Thinking

The second operational characteristic of the developmental teacher is assumption of a leadership role in shaping children's thinking. The teacher recognizes that the

The teacher provides four-year-old Katya with materials and information that enable her to learn about mushrooms. Sylvia G. Feinburg

dynamic interaction between adult and child is central to the learning process and is not reluctant to take a leadership role.

Such teachers realize that the specific way they present materials, plan learning experiences, and interact with children is of major importance in stimulating intellectual activity. Although appreciating the importance of children's exploring and discovering on their own, these teachers engage in direct instruction as well.

Knowledge of Child Development and Learning

Teachers' understanding of development and how children learn is translated into classroom practice.

Developmental Stages

The developmental teacher applies his or her understanding of developmental stages of cognition. The teacher is aware of the qualitatively different ways that children function intellectually during one period of development as contrasted with another (for example, the preoperational stage as contrasted with the intuitive or concrete operational stage). Furthermore, the teacher recognizes that children may perform at different levels in one domain of activity as contrasted with another (horizontal décalage). The teacher is thus able to accommodate children's different levels of understanding across a range of activities.

◗ During bookmaking time, some children are drawing pictures in the books they have constructed, using only a few letters. Other children are writing and illustrating simple stories, and others are writing and illustrating complex ones. Every ability level is accepted and recognized as reflecting a particular child's current cognitive capacity.

◗ Hans has extraordinary musical ability and is able to translate spontaneous singing into written notes. In other areas of the curriculum his giftedness is not apparent, and he has some fine motor problems that make it difficult for him to write easily. The teacher provides opportunities for Hans to use his musical competence. The other first graders invent songs and create words for them. Hans records the notes on a staff, crudely; another child with strong fine motor skills copies the notes over so that they are more legible. All the children play the music on an electronic instrument.

Concrete Learning

Since concrete learning is an important way for young children to learn, the teacher provides many opportunities for specific skills and concepts to be reinforced through direct contact with materials. The teacher is purposeful in the way he or she designs these experiences.

◗ Shallow trays of sand are available for four-year-olds to draw and create numbers and letters. Plastic forms to help the children be accurate are nearby for reference.

◗ Five- and six-year-olds are setting two large tables for a Thanksgiving meal. To determine how many plates they will need, the teacher has the children each get a plate and put it in front of them while sitting in a circle at group time. The children are counted; the plates are counted. Then the plates are collected for setting. One-to-one correspondence mathematically is demonstrated vividly.

Using Children's Errors

The teacher recognizes that children's errors reveal important data about how they think and may be used constructively to propel learning forward. The teacher does not perceive errors negatively and helps children feel the same way. Piaget spoke of constructive errors—errors that help children master information and skills.

◗ One third grader announces at group time that the reason old photographs are in black and white is that years ago, there was no color in the world. She explains, "It's only since they invented color television that everything in the world got to be different colors; everything used to be just black and white." Some children laugh and ridicule her contribution. The teacher validates the girl's having shared her point of view and, instead of telling her that she is mistaken, uses the incident as an opportunity for the children to problem-solve about whether or not the information is valid. A rich discussion follows, and eventually the issue is clarified. The teacher thanks the girl for having introduced "such an important idea to talk about."

Identifying Children's Interests

The teacher identifies children's interests and uses them in designing lessons. Some of children's interests are predictable, since many children share them. Some are strongly associated with gender: for example, for boys, monsters and dinosaurs, superheroes, and sports; and for girls, rainbows, hearts and princesses, and horses. Other interests may be related to what is going on at home, in a given neighborhood or culture, or nationally. Interests may be identified by listening to children's conversations, identifying what they draw and write about, and observing recess and dramatic play.

◗ In group time one of the children mentions that her grandmother is getting very old. The teacher asks, "What does it mean to be old?" The four- and five-year-olds attempt to define the concept of old age. Children respond with statements such as these: "When you're old, you live alone"; "Being old means living in an apartment"; "Old means you can't have a baby anymore." Interest is strong and is transferred to dramatic play and informal conversation. The teacher decides to build a unit on the subject. She identifies key concepts, such as that all living things are young, then mature, then grow old; that even nonliving things grow old; that some things show their age, and others don't; and that time is involved in things' growing old. One planned activity involves setting up a display of potatoes in a sunny spot and watching them grow progressively older from day to day. Children become involved in the physical transformation and begin to make potato people, using the withered potatoes for heads, steel wool for hair, and collage materials for clothes. Stories and dramatic play emerge.

◗ First graders are deeply involved in jump rope chants and take pleasure in jumping and rhyming. The teacher builds activity around many jump rope chants, including those from other cultures. The teacher records the chants on large pieces of paper on an easel, and the children sing and read them together at group time. Rhyming and clapping are coordinated.

◗ A child in a group of second graders has a rich fantasy life and tells outlandish stories. Some children call him a liar. The group becomes involved in defining a lie. The teacher distinguishes lying from storytelling in a variety of ways and attempts to clarify the distinction. The teacher plays a game with one group of children: when they are called on they must tell either a "story" or a "lie." Other children try to guess which one it is, and why. (Lying is a common behavior at this age, making this particular intervention by the teacher especially important.)

Physical Knowledge

The teacher recognizes that physical knowledge—understanding about the nature of materials and how they respond under specific circumstances—is a crucial part of the curriculum. The teacher seizes opportunities to extend children's understanding of physical knowledge through the materials he or she provides, the kinds of comments he or she makes, and the lessons he or she plans. The teacher takes advantage of spontaneous situations to further physical knowledge and also designs specific activities with that objective.

DeVries and Kohlberg (1990) offered four criteria for good physical knowledge activities:

(1) The child must be able to produce the phenomenon by his own action;
(2) The child must be able to vary his action;
(3) The reaction of the object must be observable;
(4) The reaction of the object must be immediate.

They also identified nonverbal methods the teacher can use to intervene, including these:

(1) Helping the child with practical problems to facilitate experimentation and observation;
(2) Offering materials to facilitate comparisons;
(3) Modeling new possibilities.

The criteria that make physical knowledge activities appealing to children, and nonverbal methods of teacher intervention, both merit thoughtful attention.

◗ A four-year-old is engaged in trying to attach two empty orange juice containers together with a wire. She is attempting to punch holes in the bottom of the cans with a pencil in order to string them together. The teacher observes the process and sometimes holds the cans firmly to facilitate the punching process. When the child is unsuccessful, the teacher brings the child to the tool area and asks, "Which of these tools do you think would be the most helpful? Why?"

◗ Five-year-olds have been pressing fall leaves and bits of crayon between two pieces of waxed paper. When they are finished and the iron has fused the crayon scraps and leaves into new configurations, the teacher takes time to discuss the children's creations: "Which part of the leaf made this section?" "Can you tell what color that section over there was before we ironed it?" "How did the heat change this part?" "I wonder if it matters how long the iron stays on the paper, what do you think?"

◗ Three- and four-year-olds are playing with "ooblick" (a cornstarch, water, and food coloring mixture) at the water table. The substance is colloidal in nature, and it shifts back and forth from liquid to solid. After much time for play and experimentation, the teacher wanders over and asks casually, "I notice that sometimes it's watery and sometimes it isn't. I wonder if anything you do makes it change?"

◗ A kindergartner is using wire cutters with wire and collage materials. The teacher observes briefly and then says, "You figured out a way to make the cellophane stay on the wire. Have you ever used this tool before? It's called a wire cutter. Would it be interesting to see whether or not it cuts cellophane, too?"

◗ A small group of children is making collages out of "scrounged" materials. The teacher says to one boy, "You found a clever way to connect those rings with a long wire."

Although the kinds of verbal interventions identified here are important and central to the child's comprehensive investigation, the teacher must be judicious in deciding when to use words to extend a child's thinking, and when to remain silent

A three-year-old, stimulated to experiment with finding the best way to get tape off the tape holder, has made many attempts and is now gaining control over the process. Gaining competence with tools and an understanding of physical knowledge are of crucial importance for young children. Sylvia G. Feinburg

or simply provide additional materials. Too much verbalization on the teacher's part can be distracting and controlling. Sensitive observation of the situation is critical.

Dynamic Qualities

The teacher identifies critical dynamic qualities that engage children emotionally and intellectually, and addresses these in designing learning activities. The teacher understands that the desire to explore and pursue things is closely related to the presence or absence of these dynamic qualities.

Dynamic qualities are certain aspects of the child's actions and ways of playing that have readily identifiable physical characteristics. These characteristics may be apparent in the child's casual play with objects; in his or her drawing, painting, or work with clay; or in the activities the child selects to investigate.

These qualities are sometimes important to an individual child but more often are important to many children during a particular stage of development. These qualities are frequently gender-related, as well: some are more compelling to one sex than to the other, although not exclusively. Obviously, all children can benefit from activities with a range of dynamic qualities, but the teacher's awareness of the powerful role they may be playing for certain children is important in curriculum planning.

For example, sometimes parents and teachers try to extinguish children's desire to throw, propel, and make things move, instead of finding constructive ways for these preferred ways of playing to be expressed positively. The sensitive teacher can use dynamic qualities as a way of involving children constructively and enhancing the learning process. Some examples of dynamic qualities are the following.

- the quality of *containing*—putting things in and taking things out, enclosing, filling, and dumping—which is common among two- and three-year-olds
- the quality of *elaborating and repeating*—repetition and sequencing, building patterns and repetitive forms—which is especially common among five- and six-year-old girls
- the quality of *projection*—shooting, throwing, making things move rapidly through space—common among boys
- the quality of *motion*—rolling, spinning, moving things rapidly from place to place—common among boys
- the quality of *penetrating*—tearing, slicing, punching holes in things—common among boys
- the quality of *layering*—piling things on top of one another—common among girls
- the quality of *classifying*—grouping and sorting things by arbitrary categories, seriating, sequencing
- the quality of *transforming*—changing something from one state to another, such as liquid to solid, three- to two-dimensional, an object to another object

The observant teacher will identify many other dynamic qualities important to children in his or her classroom. Some ways to address these qualities in planning classroom activities are illustrated in the following examples.

- Three-year-olds are fascinated by putting things, particularly small objects, inside other things. The teacher allows the children to explore the notion of containing by designing a range of activities, including an art lesson with gummed stickers and paper reinforcers that can be pasted inside large cardboard circular forms, and a floating activity at the water table involving floating forms filled with variously colored plastic discs. These activities engage the dynamic quality of classifying as well as containing.
- Many third graders are interested in toy fantasy figures with interchangeable parts that allow them to be transformed into new creatures. The teacher captures this interest in a writing lesson. Children are expected to create a new figure out of the various plastic parts available, to give their character a three-syllable name, and to create a relevant story. Children are expected to develop a simple plot that involves two identities. Children are encouraged to work collaboratively as well.
- A first grade math lesson is designed to reinforce the notion of creating patterns mathematically using paper punches and long strips of black construction

FIGURE 4-1

This drawing by Douglas (3.2 years old) illustrates the young child's preoccupation with making small circular forms and containing them within a large shape.

paper. A series of exercises are involved (counting by twos and fours; creating sequences of odd numbers; creating a beautifully visual pattern on one piece of paper and giving it to a friend to copy). Many children find the lesson exciting because they enjoy the dynamic quality of penetration when using the paper punches.

Motivational Strategies and Lesson Planning

Other operational characteristics relate to teaching strategies and curriculum planning skills.

Presenting New Material

The teacher understands that when a material is new to children, it is not usually necessary to provide extensive additional stimulation. Thus, children are allowed to use a material in an open-ended way when it is new to them. When they are well aware of its potential, however, and productivity has waned, the teacher provides challenges that encourage exploration in more meaningful ways.

▶ When Cuisenaire rods are presented to kindergartners the first few times, they are allowed to use them in any way they choose, making trains and other imaginative constructions. Eventually, the teacher introduces controlled lessons—

for example, asking them to recreate a given configuration numerically using different colored units.

◗ Five- and six-year-olds have been printing with paint, sponges, and potato scraps for a few weeks, inventing shapes and forms. Interest has waned, and the children's work does not reflect genuine involvement any longer. The teacher introduces the notion of making complex units out of many small pieces and then repeating them to make designs. She relates this notion to creating fabric and wallpaper patterns. In future lessons she introduces the concept of symmetry using these same materials.

Cognitive Conflict

In both spontaneous and planned situations the teacher stretches children's thinking to provide cognitive conflict. Ambiguity and problem solving are valued as teaching strategies. The teacher presents situations that challenge the child cognitively, within reasonable limits. The teacher is not fearful of providing stimulation that stretches children's thinking and requires them to struggle intellectually.

◗ Among kindergartners and first graders, block play has become repetitive and uninspired. The children are creating the same forms over and over again. The teacher places a book that reveals some simple architectural principles in the block area, and many of the children are stimulated by the principles. Eventually a few children identify the concept of the cantilever, and the teacher demonstrates how one block can be extended to hang over another, if it is sufficiently weighted on one end. Children begin, with great enthusiasm, to create structures that include the cantilever and to use the word in sharing their work with others. The teacher provides other books on architectural techniques to engage further interest; a unit emerges.

◗ During group time when discussion comes up about the concepts of yesterday, today, and tomorrow, the teacher asks, "If today is Thursday, what was the day before yesterday?" She lets the kindergartners and first graders know that this is not an easy question and that she does not expect that everyone will know how to answer it. Much animated discussion takes place among the children. A few children can solve the problem; others are completely baffled and focus on the issues of yesterday and the days of the week. The teacher is accepting all attempts to deal with the question.

Progression in Creative Areas

The teacher recognizes that progression in learning applies to expressive, creative areas, not just those traditionally associated with academic skill development, such as math and reading. Hence, the teacher considers increasing levels of complexity in designing learning objectives in such areas as writing stories, painting, collage making, and dramatics.

◗ During journal writing time, second graders are given the opportunity to write about whatever they like in their personal notebooks. The teacher reads and responds to these. The teacher periodically challenges the children to improve the quality of their writing. On one occasion, the teacher discusses using descriptive language to let the reader know the quality of something—what it was really like. The teacher provides concrete examples that make comparisons. One child changed her journal entry from "an old dog came out of the alley" to "an old, ragged dog who looked moth-eaten came out of the alley."

◗ Second and third graders are involved in creative dramatics. When they are first assigned a particular role to play, the teacher is accepting of their interpretation of the person or creature. As time goes by, however, the teacher provides clear information about how to strengthen the fantasy images that the children are projecting. Discussing the role of an angry witch, for example, the teacher heightens children's awareness of how to make one's body reflect anger. The teacher helps them understand that when the child playing the witch bends her body and fingers in an angular manner, the child assumes a menacing posture (Heathcote, 1972).

Modeling

The teacher is not reluctant to model procedures and skills when it is apparent that children will benefit from such input. The teacher recognizes the distinction between making things for children to copy and imitate in mechanical ways, and stimulating them to see the potential in a given media. George Forman (1990) spoke to this issue in writing of the educational program for young children in Reggio Emilia, Italy. In "Lessons from Reggio Emilia," he wrote:

> They (the teachers) seem to have mastered the balance between direct instruction and self-regulated learning. They are not afraid to give the child direct tutelage on an expressive technique, such as painting or sculpting. But tutelage is used in a manner, that I do not often see in the United States, as a cognitive tool for reflective thinking about the physical and social world. The self regulation comes in the children's use of that technique. Children may be taught how to use the brush or the sculptor's knife, but they then invent in their own renderings. For example, children discuss how the eyes sometimes look sleepy, angry, even cautious. Then it remains to the child to invent some metaphorical rendering in clay of "an angry eye" or "the eye watching television and is bored." These renderings are always made public, discussed by others, and even improved through several children working together. This communication context of art is a mainstay of their social constructivism. The objective is not to learn how to make good art, but to use art as a medium for discussion about some concept, such as boredom, caution, or anger. (Forman, 1990, p. 2)

Other examples of teachers using modeling to stimulate children include the following.

◗ First graders are using watercolors in a way that does not exploit their potential, drawing lines using the brush like a pencil. The teacher demonstrates how one can brush water onto a piece of paper freely, dropping paint on the surface and allowing the colors to bleed. The teacher continues this demonstration, helping the children recognize that experimenting—with pigment, water, and variations of wet and dry—is central to the painting process. The teacher does not create a particular image for them to replicate.

◗ Three-year-olds are trying to wash a tabletop with water and soapsuds, and are using a sponge without squeezing out the excess water. The teacher demonstrates how to use a sponge effectively and how to minimize dripping.

◗ First graders are involved in paper folding in conjunction with a math lesson. Accuracy is important. The teacher asks each child to watch carefully while she demonstrates how to fold the paper accurately. Emphasis is placed on lining up edges, pressing the paper to achieve a fold, and opening the form carefully.

Teaching skills versus providing models It is sometimes difficult for teachers to feel comfortable about teaching skills directly, for fear that they will be thwarting children's creativity and independent thinking. Controlling children's thinking by imposing forms for them to copy and imitate is not the same as helping them to understand techniques and procedures that facilitate the expression of an idea. Children need help in understanding such things as how to control a paintbrush, how to cut efficiently, how to glue with care and dexterity, and even how to manage a sponge during a cleanup task. Teachers need to introduce and help children master these skills and techniques, since they are central to expressing ideas with satisfaction. This issue is of particular importance as children grow older. A three-year-old may be satisfied with a crude product; but as children grow older, their capacity to evaluate and set standards develops, and skill mastery becomes central to achieving satisfaction. Under some circumstances the child may develop skills on his or her own, without too much help from the adult. Often, however, simple demonstrations or discussions can provide the child with much-needed assistance to move forward. Teachers who, ignoring the child's need to gain mastery, withhold instruction may be considered romantic in orientation.

Themes for Teaching Skills and Concepts

Themes are an important part of designing interdisciplinary curriculum (Katz & Chard, 1989). In presenting themes, the successful developmental teacher is aware of the opportunity for teaching both skills and concepts. Skills are defined as discrete tasks, such as counting, memorizing multiplication tables, learning to hold a pen, aligning blocks precisely, and repeating back a pattern of words. Concepts are defined as ideas that represent the organization of thought, or "an idea generalized from particular instances" (Webster, 1984).

◗ The teacher invites a football player to come to class a number of times to share information with a kindergarten class about the game of football. This activity allows a number of important skills and concepts to be addressed. Similar lessons are created throughout the year in other areas of study by inviting others to class (for example, a male dancer, a female bus driver, and a reporter). The following concepts are addressed: (1) Football players are members of an organized group called a team. (2) Players wear similar uniforms to identify their team. Uniforms are also worn to protect them from injury. (3) Players have numbers on their shirts so that they may be identified by it. (4) Football is played on a vast field with yard lines. Downs and counting are involved in moving across the field. (5) Players use a number of signals to communicate to one another about their strategies for moving the ball and winning points. In the following activities, skills are addressed: (1) Mathematical skills are practiced by counting yard lines and downs, identifying numbers on shirts, counting the number of men on a team, watching the clock and learning about the minute hand. (2) Children make football shirts out of old sheeting, with skills involved including measuring, cutting, and sewing. (3) Children learn specific signals to communicate intended moves with the ball, learning the skills it takes to listen to a pattern, memorize it, and repeat it back. (4) Children learn skills for handling the ball—positioning it for a kick, throwing it, making a quick pass.

BOX 4-1

Development of a Theme: An Example

In the following extract from an informal, course paper on the observation of a kindergarten unit on the theme of trees (written by teacher Jennifer McGuinn, 1990) it is apparent that many skills are being addressed, but they are embedded in meaningful activity. Note the skills of observing, sorting, classifying, creating surveys, counting, writing, and inventing simple stories.

> The theme of trees was foremost in the curriculum for two weeks prior to my visit. The room was full of activities building on this theme. I believe the teacher chose this theme because it contained activities which are interesting and compelling to children. The room has a long window on either side of it looking out onto many trees which were changing into beautiful colors. The children were surrounded by these magnificent trees and the theme served to highlight and celebrate them.
>
> Within the theme there were plenty of high interest activities, such as observations of weevils [grublike creatures] which came out of the acorns the children had collected. They made leaf creatures by pressing the leaves onto paper and drawing legs, arms, and fur.
>
> A huge bucket with many different kinds of pressed leaves was placed in the middle of the table surrounded by trays on which to put the sorted leaves. There were leaves on laminated cards labeled with words like, big, small, prickly, sharp, round, and pointed, so that the children could sort the leaves according to the categories the teacher invented . . . or their own. For instance, while I was there I noticed a child sorting by color . . . brown, gold, green, or red.
>
> There was also a survey that the children were conducting to determine all the things in the room which were made out of wood. They usually went in pairs and counted the number of objects made out of wood, using whatever strategy they came up with. Some children used invented spelling to write down the things that were wood. Other children copied the names of objects that were already labeled, as many of the things in the classroom were, for instance, small blocks. This turned into a counting activity as well as a language experience. It was surprising to me that many children didn't really know what was wood and what wasn't.
>
> Another activity allowed the children to create stories about trees. The teacher made books in the shape of trees which interested the children very much. They made stories out of pictures, used invented spelling, and I observed the teacher taking down dictation from some children.

Kindergarten children painting on snow are initially involved in spontaneous designing and painting around frozen footprints. The children paint around one another's shadows at different times of the day. They attempt to measure the various lengths with a yardstick; the teacher helps them record their findings and devise some simple hypotheses about what is happening and why. Sylvia G. Feinburg

Kindergarten children are given the opportunity to paint on snow for several days. Initially they work freely and spontaneously, delighting in creating vivid designs on the broad expanse of white. The vastness of the painting surface is tremendously exciting. They become deeply involved in the painting process and explore various qualities of paint and snow. Eventually they discover the excitement of seeing one another's shadows. The children become captivated by the way their shadows change in size and shape because of their own body movements as well as the sun's moving across the sky throughout the day.

The teacher builds on this discussion, and the theme of shadows emerges as an important focus. The teacher builds a series of interdisciplinary experiences that are studied for a number of weeks. Science, art, and mathematics are all integrated into meaningful activity. The following concepts emerge: (1) Paint goes on snow differently, depending on how hard or soft it is. (2) When snow melts, the paint forms change in shape and color intensity. (3) The temperature outside affects the way the paint and snow respond. (4) Shadows change in size and shape when you move; they're different when you crouch down, for example. (5) Shadows change in length depending on where the sun is in the sky.

The Scientific Method

The developmental teacher encourages use of the scientific method. Strategies based on the scientific method are promoted in the following examples.

The teacher helps children distinguish guessing (forming a judgment without knowledge), estimating (forming a judgment with some knowledge), and predicting (anticipating what will occur or has occurred).

◗ A wagonload of pine cones collected by kindergartners and first graders is on top of the sand table. The teacher asks the children to visit the spot sometime during activity time and estimate how many pine cones are there. Small groups of children estimate the number. Later on at group time, the children's different answers are presented and contrasted with the number actually present. Answers range from 29 to 600 to "a real, real lot." The teacher encourages children to share the strategies they used to arrive at their decisions. Special reinforcement is given to children who worked cooperatively.

The teacher encourages children to compile information in systematic ways, such as classifying, counting, poll-taking and voting, and weighing and measuring.

◗ A chance to hold an earthworm is offered in the science corner. The kindergartners vote on whether or not they like to hold worms. Poll-taking procedures are introduced, and votes are counted. It becomes clear that not everyone feels comfortable about holding earthworms!

◗ Kindergartners make simple graphs to plot the months of class members' birthdays.

◗ The teacher provides a graph for first graders to record their eye color, their hair color, how many of their teeth are missing, and so on.

The teacher also encourages children to raise and test hypotheses.

◗ A small group of kindergarten children is trying to figure out how to distinguish north, south, east, and west without a compass. Many answers are given about shadows, light and dark, and where the sun rises and sets. One child contributes: "My cat follows the sun as it moves around the house all day. So I can always tell the east from the west."

◗ First grade children are involved in a unit on temperature, and discussion emerges about how long various frozen things take to defrost when left at room temperature. Children are discussing how long it will take for a pint of ice cream and a quart of ice cream to melt. Will it take the same length of time? Individual children raise hypotheses about which one will take longer and why.

The teacher encourages children to observe, analyze, and record.

◗ To a small group of kindergartners at a table loaded with plastic lids and containers of various sizes and shapes, the teacher says, "I'd like you to look at these closely. What observations can you make about them?" The children respond in a variety of ways, identifying things that are the same and different. The children notice that some things are larger than others and that some can be inserted in others. One child exclaims,"If I had a stick for a propeller, I could make these things here into an airplane." He is encouraged to do so.

◗ Four-year-olds are involved in a project with stones, which are going to be used to make mathematics games like "Kalah." The children are washing, painting, and shellacking the stones. The teacher asks the children to focus on the size, shape, and weight of the various stones. The teacher asks, "What do you notice about the stones?" Children's responses include the following: "That one's shaped like a triangle." "Mine is like an egg." "That one is small and flat." "Hers is big and rough." "Yours has a bump."

The teacher helps children learn to form conclusions.

◗ Kindergartners have been involved in weighing on a scale various objects and materials in the room (a ball of twine, a stapler, a piece of paper, and a

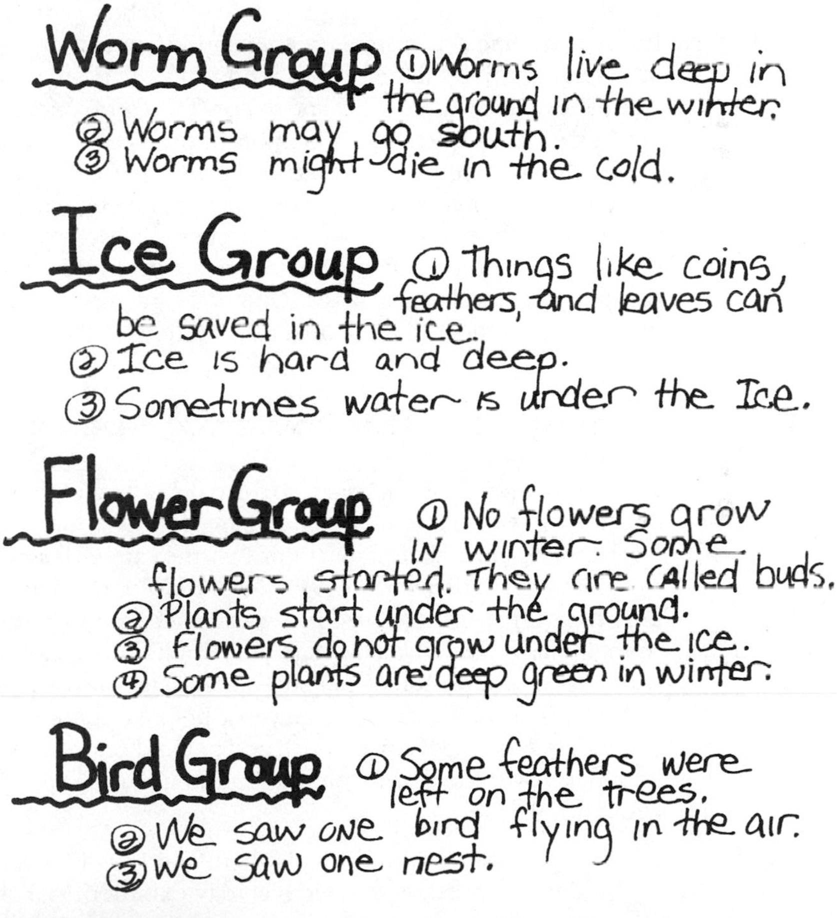

Worm Group ① Worms live deep in the ground in the winter.
② Worms may go south.
③ Worms might die in the cold.

Ice Group ① Things like coins, feathers, and leaves can be saved in the ice.
② Ice is hard and deep.
③ Sometimes water is under the Ice.

Flower Group ① No flowers grow in winter. Some flowers started. They are called buds.
② Plants start under the ground.
③ Flowers do not grow under the ice.
④ Some plants are deep green in winter.

Bird Group ① Some feathers were left on the trees.
② We saw one bird flying in the air.
③ We saw one nest.

FIGURE 4-2

Kindergarten children were placed in four groups to go on an outdoor discovery walk and observe worms, ice, flowers, and birds in winter. The teacher made this chart to share some of their findings.
Tufts Educational Day Care Center

styrofoam bat) to determine whether large things weigh more than small things. The teacher says to the group, "We need to find some conclusions to our problem about whether or not big things weigh more than small things. Let's look at our evidence—the number that tells how much each of the things weighed—and then look at how large each one is."

Children's Reactions

When teacher-planned activities are met with passivity or resistance, the adult analyzes the reasons for these reactions and adjusts expectations accordingly. The teacher does not persist with an agenda once it becomes clear that it is failing, but reorganizes priorities instead.

◗ The teacher is trying to involve second graders in making a supermarket for a unit on shopping. She brings in lots of kitchen salvage (such as empty cereal boxes, cylindrical containers with rotating covers, and plastic containers). She attempts to guide the discussion to the way various products are organized by categories at the supermarket and to how things are priced, but interest is not great. One girl picks up a rectangular box and announces, "I could make a great computer out of that box, and I could use the round plastic thing on top for making the printer." Other children are very responsive and begin to build on her idea, sharing information about computers. The teacher abandons the supermarket project for the time being and encourages the children to use the salvage materials to make computers and other machines. One child invents a game-making machine that generates a number of mathematical problems.

The Teacher Recognizes the Power of Speech

Good developmental teachers recognize the power of their own speech and verbal interactions with children in encouraging children's intellectual development. Such teachers maximize their impact through the range of strategies they employ.

Heath and Mangiola (1991), in *Children of Promise: Literate Activity in Linguistically and Culturally Diverse Classrooms,* made a strong case for strengthening children's language while being respectful and appreciative of the wide range of communication styles that may coexist in a given classroom. The authors emphasized the importance of helping children develop language skills beyond their own personal, social, and cultural orientation and to "see themselves as experts over their own communication abilities" (p. 47). Heath and Mangiola wrote:

> We argue here that the what, when, and how of schooling should enable all students to break with their everyday experiences. Schooling should provide such a range of ways of seeing, knowing, thinking, and being that it will be equally challenging to all students and teachers to imagine other possibilities, take risks with learning, and transcend the boundaries of immediacy of personal experience. Let us then not think of students of diverse backgrounds as bringing "differences" to school, but instead as offering classrooms "expansions" of background knowledge and ways of using language. (1991, p. 17)

The teacher's stance toward language is thus a major factor in shaping children's attitudes about its importance and in helping them want to achieve in this crucial area. The teacher must accept and validate the linguistic capacities children bring to school at the same time as he or she extends their capabilities in this fundamental area of learning. The teacher's role is an active one, and a number of important behaviors must be considered.

Listening and Modeling Respect

The developmental teacher uses strategies that help children feel valued and encourage them to engage in discourse with one another. The teacher intervenes in ways that stimulate thinking.

Attentive Listening

The teacher listens to children attentively to communicate to them the importance of what they have to share. The teacher makes it patently clear that what children have to say is important at the same time that he or she helps them to monitor and express themselves in appropriate ways.

◗ A first-grade teacher says, "I'm sorry, Sophie, I can't come with you right now; I'm listening to Jennie tell me about how she solved the balance problem with the bridge, and it's really interesting. I'll have time for you later."

◗ "I'm so glad you took the time to share that with me, Ahmed; it helped me to understand why you were in such a hurry," the teacher responds after a child clarifies a misunderstanding.

◗ When a first grader with a speech problem evokes laughter from a few of the other children because he cannot express his idea clearly, the teacher terminates the teasing and helps the boy to share his idea once again, speaking more slowly. She expects the other children to give him their full attention and makes it clear that all members of the classroom will listen to one another respectfully.

Dialogue and Discourse

The teacher creates organized ways for children to engage in dialogue and discourse with the teacher and with one another. The teacher guides these interactions strategically, communicating respect for the process of discussion. The teacher realizes that a lack of responsiveness from children is often caused by developmental immaturity, lack of self-confidence, and cultural differences. The teacher is thus able to wait and does not pressure children inappropriately.

◗ The teacher focuses on each kindergartner as he or she speaks at circle time, demonstrating through eye contact and general concentration that each contribution is important. When the teacher must terminate a child's speech, she does so with sensitivity: "I know you have a lot more to say about your new kitten, Rebecca, and I do want to know about it all. We don't have time to discuss it right now, but I'm sure that there will be time later; maybe you could make a picture of the kitten during activity time."

◗ Kindergartners and first graders share news with one another during group time. They are encouraged to give their full concentration to the child who is speaking and to think about the ideas being presented. When each child has finished, children are encouraged to make comments on their peers' contributions. When a boy tells about being afraid to cross a main street in the center of town, one child says, "I don't blame you for being scared; I am always scared when I cross big streets like that." Children learn how to focus on what is being said and to feel a sense of responsibility about providing others with feedback.

◗ A game that involves cumulative recall ("My grandmother went to Europe and in her suitcase she took . . . ") is being played. Children are expected to repeat the phrase, recite all the objects the other children have listed, and then add a new one. When the turn comes around to Gracia, a child who is new to the group, she is silent and gazes vaguely around the room. The teacher recognizes that Gracia is feeling stressed and leads her in becoming involved in the task. Gracia joins tentatively, but participates. The teacher realizes that it is not lack of interest that makes Gracia hesitant.

Supporting and Extending Ideas

Developmental teachers provide information, extend ideas, and serve as language models.

Opportunities for Extension

The teacher recognizes opportunities in the child's spontaneous activity for extension and builds upon these by asking pertinent questions, providing information, and establishing links between this event and prior ones. The teacher watches carefully to make certain that his or her interventions are meaningful to the child. The teacher recognizes that interventions must be appropriately timed. For instance, intervention is not helpful when children have just initiated an activity or seem to have a different objective from the teacher's.

◗ A five-year-old accidentally creates a syphon while engaged in water play. The teacher shares the child's enthusiasm and asks simple, basic questions that encourage the child to consider how it was accomplished, such as "Was the end of the hose above or below the pail of water?" The teacher encourages replication and sharing with others.

◗ A four-year-old who is building with blocks is attempting to create a complex building, which ends up falling down. The teacher assists the child and engages other children in figuring out how to avoid another such collapse. The teacher says: "It looks pretty steady over on this side; but I'm not sure that it's steady here. What do you think?" "Remember this same thing happened last week to Lesley; let's get her help."

◗ First graders have been showing great interest in spiders and have been drawing them with markers on scrap paper. The products are crude and not very elaborated. The teacher provides magnifying glasses and calligraphy pens and asks them to look carefully at the spider's body and legs before they draw. She helps them to see how various parts of the insect can be drawn by holding the pen at different angles.

◗ The teacher shares with a large group: "I want to show you all something that some kids taught me this summer. They showed me how to make a book. I asked them, 'How do I know what's the front of the book?' Do you people know the difference between the front of a staple and the back of a staple?" The children describe the flat, long side of the staple as opposed to its bumpy, short side. A child says, "Or you could draw a picture on the front!" The teacher responds, "That is another strategy, isn't it? This is why we wanted to solve the dilemma—deciding where to start can be a problem. But in the English language we read from left to right, so we need to try to make sure that our books open the right way." Jeremy adds, "Hebrew books open from left to right."

◗ A bilingual child who is in her first week of school is deeply involved in playing with small blocks at a table. She looks to the teacher with pride and points silently to her simple block construction. They make eye contact and the teacher says with enthusiasm and clarity, " 'I'm making something wonderful with the small blocks!' I'll bet that's what you're thinking!"

Guidance at Critical Times

The teacher guides children verbally at critical times when intervention can be central to their continued thought and involvement.

◗ When a second-grade boy asks the teacher how to spell *start,* the teacher replies, "Do you remember how you spelled *start* yesterday?" Inspired to think for himself, the boy begins, renewed.

◗ A first grader is standing listlessly, watching other children at the writing table. The teacher says, "Are you planning to illustrate the part of your story about the dragon fly and the baby? If you are, I have some small feathers that might be helpful."

◗ A kindergartner is insecure during journal writing time and usually produces terse stories and drawings. On one occasion he makes a small, minimal drawing of a person on the center of the page and says, "That's me uptown." The teacher responds, "I wonder who you were with that day and what you were both wearing." The boy resumes the task with real enthusiasm, adding another person and elaborating the clothing on each one.

Sharing Appropriate Information

Although the teacher recognizes the dangers of excessive lecturing and explaining to young children, the teacher is not reluctant to share appropriate information when the situation warrants. Informing, elaborating, and explaining in ways that are vibrant and relevant, the teacher provides children with new knowledge that increases interest and challenges further thought. The teacher avoids being redundant or explaining things children already understand.

◗ Second graders are engaged in dialogue about whether or not the Loch Ness monster really exists. They share all kinds of disparate information—some of it accurate and some not. The teacher talks briefly but comprehensively about the history and ambiguity of beliefs surrounding this phenomenon—not closing the issue, but providing important information to anchor the discussion. The teacher explains that *loch* means lake and that Loch Ness is the name of a large lake in the northern part of Scotland. The children refer to a map and relate the geographic information to their own experiences. The teacher helps to frame the discussion. She writes the following on a chart:

> WHAT WE KNOW ABOUT THE LOCH NESS
> It is a very deep lake (500–734 feet deep).
> The water in it never freezes completely because it is so deep.
> The water is murky. If you put your hand in the water, it is almost impossible to see your fingers.
> At the bottom of the lake there is no oxygen.

The sheet is taped to the bulletin board and the children continue to bring in information about the lake. "The water is anaerobic," Mario quotes his father, who has done some research on the subject. This term means that no living things, as we know them, can live in the lake. It also means that "when an object falls to the bottom—including people who have drowned—it never returns to the surface" (Aylesworth, 1982).

The children share the story of Saint Columba, the missionary who frightened off the "very odd-looking beastie" that looked something like a huge frog, only it was not a frog. Saint Columba frightened the monster away from a man who was trying to bring back a boat that was on the lake. Saint Columba shouted: 'Go thou no further nor touch the man. Go back at once!' On hearing this word . . . the monster was terrified and fled away again more quickly than if it had been dragged on by ropes" (Aylesworth, 1982). With this background, the discussion about whether the Loch Ness monster is real takes on a different flavor.

◗ A teacher tells a group of four-year-olds that when he was a small boy growing up in Georgia, because he was African American he had to sit at the back of the bus and was called nasty names. The teacher goes on to explain that some of the laws (serious rules) were very unfair then. One child, Nicky, is very impressed with the information and tells his parents about it in great detail.

Use of Language

Good developmental teachers model rich and vibrant language. Teachers encourage an interest in words and their meanings—in vocabulary building. They speak clearly and articulate well. They use a vocabulary that stretches children's capacities to understand. For example: "That's a good strategy, Ben." "Yes, that number is divisible by four." "What a complicated block structure you people made!"

Teachers describe things using words that are descriptive and compelling. For example: "That's absolutely exquisite; the lavender and blue remind me of grapes." "She's jumping up and down like a jack-in-the-box; how funny!" They reinforce understanding of new words and ideas by stating them in a variety of ways. For instance: "What I meant by strategy, Ben, was a plan—a system for getting something done." "Let's just ignore what he's doing; we'll just not pay any attention at all."

Teachers avoid slovenly, hackneyed language: "What'cha think of that, huh?" "Ya better cut that out." "Quit it, cut it out, quit it right now!" They strive to eliminate verbal tics, like "you know," "right?" "okay?" and "you guys." They speak neither too fast nor too slowly. They avoid "talking at" children—shifting into a manner of speaking that dominates and curtails their verbal interaction with the teacher.

◗ A four-year-old asks the teacher what *several* means. The teacher explains that it means "a few of something—just a little bit." The child considers this explanation, becomes confused, and seeks a definitive answer, since the ambiguity is difficult. "How many exactly?" he persists. "It's more than two, but not a large amount," she explains. "Is it three," he inquires, "or four?" The conversation continues, and the teacher realizes that the child has difficulty dealing with the word's ambiguity.

◗ Kindergartners are discussing an insect "limping home" after jumping in a pot of glue. One child offers ideas about how fractures are different from breaks. The teacher says: "Let's talk about the word *limp;* what does it mean when you limp?"

◗ Two five-year-old girls are enthusiastic about their cardboard structures and say, "Look, ours are pretty much just the same!" The teacher responds, "Yes, the way you placed them together makes them look *identical*."

◗ The teacher plays rhyming word games while waiting for straggling four-year-olds to join the group. One child presents the word *bird*. Children call out all the words they can think of that rhyme with it—*heard, turd, word, absurd,* and so on. They clap for every new word that is identified.

◗ A child is making a drawing on thin paper and decides that she can draw the front of a person on one side and the back on the other. She is pleased and shows the drawing to the teacher, who responds: "Drawing the back of the person on the back of the paper was quite *ingenious!*"

◗ Two girls are discussing a boy who says that he has two mothers. Another child overhears and insists that this is impossible. The girls explain to him, "You have to understand—they're girl gays!" The teacher overhears and explains, "David's two mothers are *lesbians* who live together. They are two women who love each other, just as a man and woman might love one another."

◗ A teacher makes up compelling stories of his own and shares them with four-year-olds on a daily basis. He emphasizes interesting words and compelling plots. Children are encouraged to make up stories to share with the group as well. Each day another child is the storyteller and sits in a special place; children in the group give the storyteller their full attention. Sometimes the storyteller uses props.

◗ A group of kindergartners are engaged in discussing how they should design plasticene dinosaurs that they are making for a three-dimensional display. The conversation becomes tedious and unfocused. The teacher says with vitality, "In order to *expedite* this procedure, this is what I propose . . . "

Questioning Effectively

Developmental teachers use effective questioning techniques.

The Power of Questioning Skills

The teacher is particularly respectful of the power of questioning skills in the learning experience and uses these skills with care and consideration. The teacher asks questions in ways that maximize children's thinking processes and interest. The teacher asks probing questions that engage children.

Developmental teachers avoid random use of rhetorical questions like "Wasn't it fun? What'd ya think?" or "Is everybody listening? I'm waiting. Is everybody listening?" Teachers recognize that these questions can lead to boredom and disinterest. Teachers avoid repetitive questions as well as those that lack substance and challenge. They avoid asking questions when it is obvious that everyone knows the answer. They avoid asking questions when children clearly do not have the appropriate answer—questions like "Guess who's coming to our class next week?" or "Who knows what we're going to do this afternoon?" They select questions that do not necessarily have a single correct answer, encouraging children to think independently—for example, "So what might Andrew have done to find his way back to the hotel when he lost his way?"

◗ A teacher asks first graders to analyze information: "In what ways are birds and kites the same? In what ways are they different?" The children have many responses and eventually agree that birds are alive and kites are not.

◗ First graders are having difficulty deciding how to price the lemonade they are planning to sell. The teacher asks them to synthesize information by saying, "Let's consider who the customers are going to be—children and teachers in this school. What is reasonable for this group of people to pay? Could they pay 50¢ easily? Could they pay $2.50?"

◗ While playing a Halloween word search game, the teacher asks, "What is a body that has only bones?" A five-year-old child responds enthusiastically: "A skeleton!" Guiding the children to evaluate their responses, the teacher adds, "Check and see if it says that. Yes, it does. You did it!"

◗ A group discussion among four-year-olds is centered on dogs and cats. One boy contributes, "Dogs eat cats and chase them." The teacher asks, "What can cats do about this problem? What can they do to keep the dogs from getting them?"—probing questions that engage the child in using analysis to solve problems. The child responds, "They can run up trees."

◗ Kindergartners are building mouse traps. Corey is trying to poke airholes in a shoe box. He is holding small but dull scissors, while a teacher is holding larger, sharper scissors. The teacher asks, "Which scissors have the smaller point and would be easier for poking holes, Corey?" He looks at them both and automatically says the smaller one. Engaging him in comparing and analyzing aspects of size, the teacher says, "Corey, look carefully. Which has the smaller point?" He studies both pairs and finally realizes that the larger pair has the smaller point.

Bloom's taxonomy One way to look at questioning strategies is to use Bloom's taxonomy (Krathwohl, Bloom, & Masia, 1967). The taxonomy identifies six levels of questioning: knowledge, comprehension, application, analysis, synthesis, and evaluation. Questions that provoke thinking require knowledge and understanding of the material. In addition, such questions require analysis (looking at the various parts of a piece of information), synthesis (putting together information from a variety of sources), or evaluation (making a judgment about information's usefulness or accuracy).

The teacher needs to be skillful in assessing children's level of understanding of a topic and their ability to engage in the higher levels of thinking (analysis, synthesis, and evaluation). Generally, the greater children's understanding of information about a topic, the more they will be stimulated by higher-order questions. All children need some experience with thinking at all levels. However, children who are academically gifted or talented need to become more engaged in tasks that require higher-order thinking.

To use a discussion about the Loch Ness monster as an example, the teacher might ask the following questions:

- *Knowledge:* "Where is Loch Ness?"
- *Comprehension:* "How did the Loch Ness monster get its name?"
- *Application:* "How can you use the information from the sightings of the monster to draw a picture of what the monster looks like?"
- *Analysis:* "Compare Loch Ness with Lake Sebago. How are they alike? How are they different?"
- *Synthesis:* "What information do we have about the monster that would make us believe that it is real?"
- *Evaluation:* "What information could you use about the monster to convince scientists that it really exists?"

The Torrance creative thinking model Another framework for looking at questioning skills is provided by the Torrance creative thinking model (Torrance, 1966). In this model, the teacher uses questions to promote fluency (the ability to generate many ideas), flexibility (the ability to generate ideas in a variety of different categories), and elaboration (the ability to provide additional details).

- The teacher and a first grader, Paran, are sitting together discussing the book she has made. The book has a picture of a person saying "Hi" and another of a person saying "Bye." The product is terse. To encourage *elaboration,* the teacher and student have the following exchange.

Teacher: I see that there are two characters in your story. Who are they?
Paran: I don't know.
Teacher: Are they people you know?
Paran: No.
Teacher: Are they in your imagination? (Paran does not respond.)
Teacher: What are their names? Paran shrugs her shoulders. The teacher continues: "Everyone in the world has a name. You have a name. What's *her* name? (pointing to the picture).

Paran: Jennifer.

Teacher: Okay—how old is she? Is she seven?

Paran: Yes.

Teacher: Or is she older than seven or younger than seven?

Paran: She's eighteen and she's going to the park.

Teacher: Who does she say 'Hi' to?

Paran: Me—I am her friend.

Teacher: Is she a pretend friend that no one else knows?

Paran: No; my mom knows her also.

Teacher: Who is she saying 'Bye' to?

Paran: (with enthusiasm) Me—it's a faraway park and that's her horse.

Teacher: Paran, there are so many things you know about you and about the world. You need to share them in your work. You turn your books in without doing your very best. You need to work harder. I am going to work with you now and help you do your very best. (They go to a table; the teacher writes down questions, and Paran writes down answers to elaborate her story.)

◗ In an activity involving paper, the teacher uses questions to stimulate *fluency,* such as the following: "How many different ways can you find to attach these pieces of paper together?" The teacher also uses questions to provoke *flexibility*—for example, "You have thought of three ways that you can get them to stick together. Can you think of a way that you can get one piece to fit into the other?"

Convergent and divergent questioning A third framework for looking at questions is to consider whether they are convergent (requiring only one correct answer) or divergent (allowing for many different responses). For example, contrast the question "What do firefighters wear?" (a convergent or closed question) with "How do firefighters protect themselves?" (a divergent or open-ended question). Both types of questions are useful. (Guilford, 1967).

Wasserman's framework Wasserman suggested a different framework for helping teachers ask stimulating questions. In her model, teachers structure experiences to provide children with opportunities for firsthand observation. After children have had a firsthand experience with materials—for example, in the science center with a variety of seeds and tools for examining them (flower, fruit, and vegetable seeds, seeds from trees, an assortment of fresh flowers, photographs of flowers, plants and trees budding and in full bloom, magnifying lenses, scissors, measuring tools, and knives)—the teacher asks the children to record their observations: "What observations did you make about how plants grow?" "What observations did you make about how plants change?"

Later, in what Wasserman called a debriefing, the teacher asks one or two questions that challenge children to go beyond their observations: "What are some differences among flower, fruit, and vegetable seeds? What are some similarities?"

"What makes seeds grow? What hypothesis can you suggest to explain this?" These questions challenge children to reflect on their experiences and to generate new ideas (Wasserman, 1990).

Waiting for Answers

The developmental teacher realizes that in group situations it is important to wait at least ten seconds after asking a question, since the ability to conceptualize a response takes longer for one child than another. The teacher does not always call on the first person to raise a hand. The teacher avoids competition by helping children recognize and respect individual differences.

- During group times when a question is asked, four-year-olds are expected to wait ten seconds until everyone has had a chance to do their thinking. The teacher and children often count silently together on their fingers.
- Children who are consistently quicker than others in arriving at a response to a question are encouraged to think of hints that will help others decide on an answer. For example, the teacher points to the letter *b* in the word *bear* on a chart of the lyrics to the song "The Bear Went Over the Mountain" (after the song has been shared in its entirety for pleasure many times and children are familiar with the text). The teacher says, "Tell me something you know about this letter" (an open question), rather than "What letter is this?" (a closed question). After wait time, some children may guide others by saying, "That's the first letter in the word *bear*," or "That's a letter in Roberto's name."

When to Ask, When to Tell

The developmental teacher uses questioning as a means of helping children uncover information for themselves. On the other hand, the teacher is not hesitant to deliver information directly when it seems appropriate to do so.

- Children are involved in a styrofoam printing project—making designs and carving their names into the styrofoam for printing. The teacher asks, "Did you have any problems?" "The print came out backwards!" answers the child. "How did you solve that?" the teacher challenges the child. "I wrote my name backwards," the child responds victoriously. Another problem involved getting enough ink on the plate. The teacher again asks how the children handled the obstacle. "I couldn't solve it," one child answers. "But you got a lot of ink in other places," the teacher persists. "The problem is that before you printed, the ink dried up in certain spots. Does anyone have any solutions?" One boy offers, "Bang real hard." "That's one way," replies the teacher, "but also it's okay to use a little more ink and to work quickly"—and the teacher holds up an example of a child's product where the printing worked effectively.

Using Analogies and Metaphors Strategically

Teachers of young children have many opportunities to engage children in metaphoric thinking. The use of analogies and metaphors is an effective tool to help children understand a concept. They provide a vehicle to relate what the child is trying to understand to something that the child already knows. Analogies often add a sense of playfulness and challenge, particularly with young children. They deepen understanding and contribute to involvement in learning. To generate analogies, teachers of young children must have a wide range of knowledge from which they can draw to create comparisons and stimulate vivid imagery.

- In creative movement children are asked if they can move the way a sponge would move if it was being twisted, squeezed, or dumped in a bucket of water. They respond by gleefully imitating these motions.
- While watching leaves fall from the trees on an autumn day, a three-year-old child announces, "Those are kite leaves!" The teacher reinforces this verbal imagery and asks children what else the leaves remind them of. They add such thoughts as "spinning tops" and "hand leaves."
- During a physical education activity, kindergartners and first graders are asked to "jump like a frog; prance like a colt; slither like a large snake." Later, children invent their own analogies for other children to execute.
- A teacher of three-year-olds turns a name-calling session into a round of metaphor. When a little boy calls her an idiot, she says playfully, "Oh, there are better names than that one that can hurt my feelings. How about if I called you an apple? You know why I might do that?" He got the joke—he was wearing a bright red sweatshirt.
- A kindergarten teacher asks children why they think the birds kept in a cage in the classroom are called zebra finches. The children eventually realize that the birds' black and white striped feathers are similar to the markings of a zebra. The teacher supplies photographs of zebras and allows the children to make a visual comparison.
- A blind kindergartner is asked to imitate the sounds of birds in the classroom. She chirps with discrimination, revealing a good deal of understanding of the patterns and intonations involved.

Praising, Reinforcing, and Correcting

Developmental teachers use praise selectively. Praise and reinforcement are delivered in substantive, not superficial, ways. The teacher avoids hollow praise that does not extend thinking, as well as didactic corrections of a negative nature. Examples of substantive praise include the following:

- "That painting has many more shapes in it than the ones you usually do. Also, I notice how many different *sized* shapes are there."
- "What's interesting to me about the way you solved that math problem is that you tried three or four different strategies for laying out the cubes before you found this one. That was important planning."
- "You and Brian have been working well together. I overheard you telling him that you needed his assistance in getting the totem pole finished; that was really helpful."

These kinds of comments are minimized:

- "I just love your painting."
- "That's a wonderful story that you wrote; it's really nice."
- "How terrific!"

Didactic corrections are avoided. Critical comments are minimized in order to encourage communication and participation. Too much correction can inhibit exchange even if it speeds up the exchange of information.

- When a three-year-old mispronounces *three* as *free,* the teacher does not say, "No, that's a number *three,* not *free.*" Instead, the teacher says, "Yes, you're right, that is a number three."
- A child is unusually concerned about spelling correctly when the teacher is encouraging the group to generate ideas for a play that the children are writing. The child thrusts her rough draft in front of the teacher and asks, "Did I spell the word *dragon* right? Is it right? I want to know if it's right!!" (The child spelled it *draygun.*) The teacher responds, "You're absolutely right. The spelling is wrong, and we can change it, if you'd like. It's *dragon* not *draygun*. But having a dragon be frightened by a small chipmunk is a wonderful idea, Valerie. I'm so pleased that you came up with it!"

The Teacher Empowers Children to Take Charge of Their Learning

The developmental teacher reinforces the importance of work and productivity in a variety of ways. The teacher empowers children to expect the best from themselves and to be in charge of their own growth and learning.

Control over Learning

The developmental teacher creates situations that help children understand how people learn. The teacher makes it clear that children have control over their own learning.

- First graders are expected to write daily in their journals about any subject they choose. The teacher initiates a discussion about where ideas come from, pointing out to the group that ideas are connected to things that people have been hearing or thinking about. The teacher asks children to share their thoughts about where they get their ideas. The teacher points out the importance of being interested in things.
- At the end of group time, before children select what activity they will go to, the teacher says, "When you make a decision about where you're going to work during activity time, think about what you haven't done lately. Think about what you need to learn more about. Sometimes you just want to go where your friends

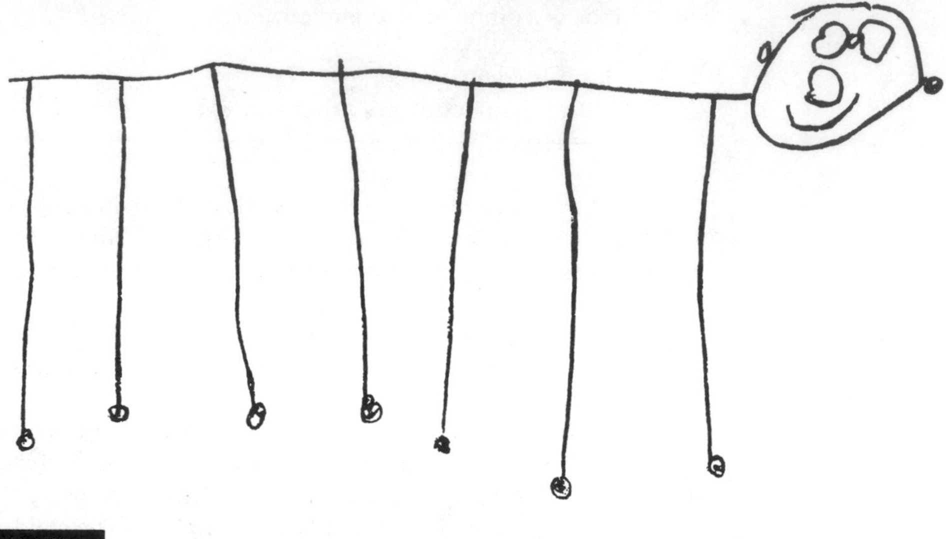

FIGURE 4-3

Heidi's horse—drawn when Heidi was four years, three months old.
From *Heidi's Horse* by Sylvia Fein, Exelrod Press. Reprinted with permission.

go, but it's important to think about what you want to learn, as well as thinking about your friends, even though they're very important."

◗ The teacher provides a sharing time for second graders to talk about how things are going with their work. The children are encouraged to discuss what is particularly difficult for them to learn right now, how their writing and bookmaking are progressing, what is giving them pleasure, and what is giving them trouble. Children are encouraged to provide their classmates with possible solutions to their concerns.

◗ At the beginning of the school year, children respond to the teacher's question "What do you want to learn this year in kindergarten?" The responses are written in large letters on a chart so that parents and others who are sometimes in the classroom (such as specialists and student teachers) can learn what individual children said. Some answers include the following. Alexander: "I want to learn about creative movement and how to feed the fish." Colleen: "I want to learn how to climb a tree. I want to learn how to plant flowers." David: "I want to learn about big blocks and small blocks." Duncan: "I want to learn how to be Batman when I grow up and to climb a building but not to fight crime. I want to learn all about bugs and where cliffs are." Joey: "I want to learn how fish swim and how the turtle swims and how they build this classroom." Lily: "I want to learn about dogs and cats, trucks and cars, about how to draw a horse. I want to learn how to stilt." Luci: "I want to learn about patterns, about reading, about trees. I want to learn how to climb trees." Natasha: "I want to learn how to add. I want to learn how to spell. I want to learn how to subtract numbers. I want to learn how to fly." Nicholas: "I want to learn how to play sports. I want to learn about boats and ships." Sara: "I want to learn about unifix cubes." Zachary: "I want to learn how to spell. I want to learn the kids' names. I want to learn about how to be a spy. I want to learn how to

FIGURE 4.4

Heidi's horse—drawn when Heidi was five years, one month old. From *Heidi's Horse* by Sylvia Fein, Exelrod Press. Reprinted with permission.

break the Empire State building." Ruby: "I want to learn about sewing and reading and writing." The children also discuss which of the things mentioned could be learned in the kindergarten class and which could not. The idea that kindergartners can make important decisions about what they want to learn more about is emphasized.

◗ *Heidi's Horse,* a book by Sylvia Fein (1984), is particularly useful in helping children understand how ability levels change—partly because people grow older, but also as a result of practice and work at improving one's skills. The book is a longitudinal presentation of one child's drawing of a horse. It allows the reader to see Heidi's development in art in pictorial form and to review the myriad representational problems she addressed as she struggled to become competent at drawing her beloved horses. Children are fascinated by her progress and like to discuss how the drawings changed over a ten-year period of time. (See Figures 4-3 to 4-6.)

Individual Differences

The teacher builds understanding about individual growth and capabilities in working. The teacher helps children understand that people perform differently from one another and that the same person may perform differently from one activity to another. The teacher builds respect for work and achievement, as well as for differences in performance.

◗ A classroom for four-year-olds has a basket of cards reading "Please Save," for the children to use to keep ongoing projects from being abused.

◗ The teacher has worked hard to help the kindergartners learn that Lainey, a blind child, experiences some things differently from the other children. The

FIGURE 4-5

Heidi's horse—drawn when Heidi was ten years, ten months old. From *Heidi's Horse* by Sylvia Fein, Exelrod Press. Reprinted with permission.

teacher encourages Lainey to let children know about some of these differences. One morning, after having worked with attribute blocks and creating a complex organization, Lainey says to another child, "Do you want to feel my playground? It's really interesting!"

◗ A kindergartner is having difficulty tying her shoelace. The teacher directs her to ask another child; "You know, Ahmed is really an expert at shoelaces; why don't you ask him? He's particularly good at that—the way you are in handling the ant farm."

Work and Effort

The developmental teacher helps children understand that achievement and mastery are the result of work and effort, and that people can grow in their ability to perform in a given area. The teacher establishes the connections between the children's work and adult work.

◗ Throughout the instructional period the teacher continues to give encour-

FIGURE 4-6

Here we see how Heidi drew a horse's head at six different times from age four to eleven. Children are fascinated to see this visual documentation of one child's progress and are encouraged to pursue a task that matters to them. From *Heidi's Horse* by Sylvia Fein, Exelrod Press. Reprinted with permission.

agement that emphasizes the difficulty for her personally and the need to practice. For example: "It takes a while to learn. It takes lots of practice. You're right, Andrew, it is hard. I did it over and over and over this weekend until I got it."

◗ A first-grade teacher takes the entire class to a room in the school where senior citizens have a weekly oil painting course. The children are free to wander around the room and watch the people painting at easels, mixing paint. The children engage in conversation about what is involved. Afterward children view adult paintings on display and create their own work based on ideas stimulated by the adults. They share their work with the adult artists and seek feedback.

◗ The teacher invites adults in as guests to talk about their work and hobbies and how they got interested in them. One man shares his interest in bees and generates a unit for the second-grade class.

Attitudes

The developmental teacher reinforces attitudes that increase learning potential. For example, the teacher encourages children to learn that it is all right to not understand or not know an answer.

◗ A child asks, "Miss Guarante, how do you spell *know,* as in 'I know something'? Does it start with *k* or *n*?" The teacher answers, "Both are silent in some cases. So which one is it?" Another child says, "I know, I know. It's both!"

◗ "Does anyone want to learn the 'eye winker game'?" the teacher asks. As she begins her step-by-step narrated demonstration, the pattern falls apart. The teacher collapses to the table in laughter, holding her head. She begins again—another failure. "I got it wrong," she says humorously.

◗ Children are trying to do complex string games, which are illustrated in a book. When a child comes with a picture of a very advanced one and says that he'd like to try it, the teacher responds, "That one is very complicated. I tried and tried all weekend and I couldn't do it. I could not learn that one!"

◗ In one classroom, there is an "I don't know" period during group time when children share what they don't know enough about. In one kindergarten a boy introduced an "I don't know cookie" that he had made. He didn't know "how to describe its taste." Another child contributed, "I want to know more about why two-wheeler bikes keep you up without a third wheel."

The teacher also helps children understand that mistakes and errors are natural occurrences and part of the learning process.

◗ A second grader is trying to copy over a story that she had written in "invented spelling," using the correct spelling provided by the teacher for a final draft. She is working in magic marker, making her letters carefully, when she accidentally copies a word incorrectly. She becomes very upset. The teacher reassures her, "It's okay, Yomi, I know that you're disappointed, but everyone makes a mistake once in a while. Let's figure out what we can do about it."

◗ The teacher asks a child why she has copied words in her journal where stories are supposed to be written. The child explains, "I wrote them and then I forgot about them." The teacher responds, "Well, maybe you ran out of things to do, so you copied words. That's not a terrible thing to do. As a matter of fact, it was good that you decided for yourself what you wanted to accomplish."

The teacher encourages children to see that they can make independent decisions.

◗ "If you feel like it's done now, you can put it in the finished work folder, or if you want to keep going you can save it in the unfinished work folder."

◗ The teacher, Isadora, and Lauren, who is blind, are working at the writing table. The teacher is reading Lauren's story back to her to make sure the teacher has written it down properly. In the story, "Siren dies and then goes in his car and drives to the store." Isadora says, "That doesn't make sense. People can't die and then get up and just drive to the store." Lauren responds, "Siren is not a person, he's a creature." Isadora says, "Creatures can't get up either after they die." The teacher intervenes: "Isadora, it's Lauren's story and they are her creatures. If they die and come back, it's her ideas and it's okay."

The teacher helps children learn that they can correct adults or provide them with important information.

◗ At lunch one of the children saw the teacher using a knife to cut an apple. She ran over to her excitedly and told her that she should use a special apple slicer they had that divides the pieces up equally. The teacher responded joyously, "You're right, Christina, I forgot all about it!"

◗ "Jared," asks a second-grade teacher, "what was that word you used when somebody changes a story around a little bit in the middle?" The child responds, "Adaptation."

The teacher reinforces the idea that children can learn from one another and that it is all right to seek one another out for help at appropriate times.

◗ A four-year-old is struggling to tie her shoelaces. The teacher suggests, "Why don't you get Emil to help you? He's just figured out how to tie, and I bet he'd be happy to help you."

The teacher encourages children to remember that all people need feedback from one another.

◗ One kindergartner writes in his journal "lick tev." Another child corrects him casually, "TV is spelled *T-V,* but I knew what you meant."

The teacher stresses that process is important. Not all learning involves a finished product.

◗ A child is upset because, while experimenting with color mixing, she lost the beginning part of her painting. The teacher explains that she learned so much about how to get certain colors that making the first part was still very productive.

Evaluation of Work

Discussion and evaluation of children's work and the work process are an integral part of the developmental program. Specific times are allocated for reviewing what children have accomplished, as well as establishing future objectives.

◗ A small group of kindergarten children have been making paintings of "interesting shapes," a lesson motivated by one of the teachers during activity time. During large group time, when children share what they have been doing in their different small groups, the teacher calls on members of the shape-painting group

Kindergarten children discuss the shapes they've drawn. Sylvia G. Feinburg

to explain what they had been doing and to share the products. One child explains: "When you paint, you can make many different shapes—round, skinny, wiggly. That's what artists do. Artists like shapes—even if they aren't shapes of something in particular. They can be a dog or a house—or they can just be shapes. Do you understand?"

Summary

The process of challenging children intellectually depends on certain critical teacher qualities, which are influential in making the classroom a vibrant and stimulating environment. These qualities are contained within four major categories: (1) the teacher is alert intellectually; (2) the teacher serves as a leader in shaping thinking; (3) the teacher uses verbal strategies that challenge intellectual development; and (4) the teacher empowers children to be in charge of their own learning. In this chapter, each of these qualities has been operationalized so as to make explicit how they are manifested across the developmental continuum. Of central importance is that the teacher must be intellectually vibrant, informed, responsive to ideas, imaginative, generative, and stimulating. The teacher's capacity to embrace and understand differences in culture and learning, ability to model certain skills and techniques, and strength in communicating and interacting with children—describing, questioning, elaborating, using analogies, providing support and praise—are all important. In addition, the teacher must extend these values to children so that they, too, feel in charge of their own learning and acquire some of the rudimentary skills and attitudes central to becoming an alert and responsive person intellectually. The next chapter addresses how the developmental teacher furthers intellectual development by the way he or she observes, records, and assesses progress; organizes the classroom environment to maximize concrete learning; deals with academic skills; and makes curriculum decisions in the best interests of the child.

CHAPTER 5

CURRICULUM IN THE DYNAMIC CLASSROOM: OPERATIONAL CHARACTERISTICS

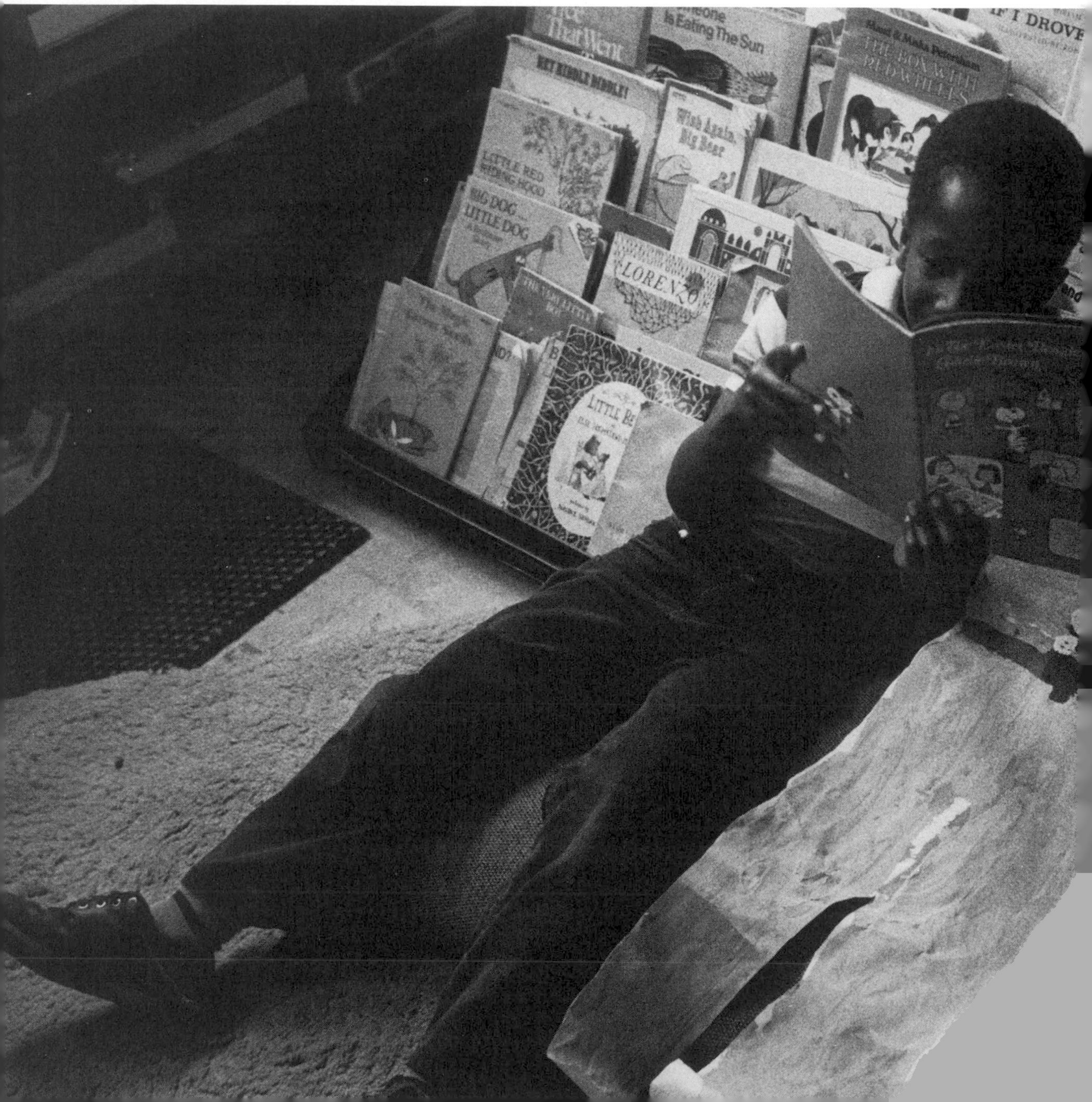

- *The Teacher Observes, Records, and Assesses Progress*
- *The Physical Environment Optimizes Concrete Learning*
- *Literacy and Mathematics Are Critical Aspects of the Curriculum*
- *The Teacher Makes Curriculum Decisions Based on the Child's Best Interests*
- *Example of an Outstanding Lesson: Marble Roller Boards*
- *Summary*

This chapter identifies ways teachers can create a classroom environment that is dynamic intellectually and challenges children's full potential.* The chapter emphasizes factors that contribute toward creating a cognitive-developmental or constructivist classroom, as opposed to a cultural transmission or romantic one. The chapter describes in detail four major categories of teaching behavior:

1. The teacher observes, records, and assesses progress.
2. The physical environment optimizes concrete learning.
3. Literacy and mathematics skills, as well as content in social studies, science, health, and the arts, are of fundamental importance in the curriculum. Both skills and concept formation are emphasized.
4. The teacher makes curriculum decisions based on the best interests of the child.

The Teacher Observes, Records, and Assesses Progress

In the cognitive-developmental classroom, teachers are critical observers of child and group progress. They use a range of strategies to collect, record, and assess children's progress, and they base instructional activities on this information. Teachers are aware of fundamental issues, such as children's strengths and weaknesses, special interests, levels of concentration, interest spans, and peer relationships. Teachers recognize that all these considerations are crucial for evaluating children's strengths and weaknesses, as well as for designing learning experiences.

Techniques for Information-Gathering and Evaluation

The teacher employs informal and formal techniques for gathering information and uses direct observation to evaluate children's individual progress. Lessons and activities reflect a range of levels of achievement.

Informal and Spontaneous Techniques

The teacher captures children's behavior and progress in a variety of ways: for example, through notes, photographs, videos, and collections of drawings and stories.

◗ A Japanese parent of a four-year-old at a child care center writes English relatively well, but is uncomfortable attempting to speak to the teacher. Teacher and parent engage in a weekly writing exchange in which they each share what is happening for the child in each environment, home and school. The parent shares sensitive material concerning cultural differences, explaining what makes the child feel comfortable and uncomfortable in school. Parent and teacher share important information about school values and differences in early education between the United States and Japan.

* The classroom evaluation guide, Form C, in Chapter 11 relates to this chapter.

The following is an excerpt from the teacher's letters to the parent:

> As for books that Kazufumi really enjoys, I will certainly pay attention to which ones interest him and let you know. Kazufumi really enjoys *Where the Wild Things Are* by Maurice Sendak. He very often asks if I will read it to him. It is certainly a favorite of many children. Kazufumi has also shown great interest in Halloween stories. I'll let you know more titles as they come up.
>
> Everything is going wonderfully at school. Kazufumi certainly has been enjoying our Halloween preparations. Trick or treating on Halloween will certainly be a delight for him. One more thing—Kazufumi had a bathroom accident and did not want to change into dry clothes. He said that his mother would get mad at him. We assured Kazufumi that everything would be okay and that he would be more comfortable in dry clothes. I hope that was okay. Let me know how you handle it at home so that if it happens again we can try to have some consistency. Thanks, and happy Halloween!*

An excerpt from one of the mother's letters follows:

> It is difficult to explain my response to Kazufumi's bathroom accident. Actually, both I and my husband blame for his frequently bathroom accident. He parted with his diapers when he was 1 year and 6 months old. Now, he is 4 year and 3 months old. He is too elder to make accident frequently. He has enough ability to prevent his accidents. You may think 1 year and 6 months old was very early compared with American children. I think this difference based on difference in culture. We Japanese usually not used paper diapers. (Recently, few women used paper diapers all day.) And we don't have all-automatic washer and dryer. So, baby's diapers asked great effort for women. We try to remove the diaper as early as we can possible. Anyway, in our country, four-year-old boy's bathroom accident should be blame. But don't worry, we never blame him severely.
>
> When he was in Japanese child care center, he would blamed from his teachers frequently. He couldn't wear his shoes himself. He sometimes took too long time for eating lunch. In Japan everyone began to eat a lunch at the same time. Before eating lunch, they said a word, "Itadakima," all together. This word means thanks for everyone who prepared meals. It is not a pray. In Japan it is regarded very bad to leave any food on his dish. If children left something, he was blamed. Children should eat everything even if it was unfavorite dishes. When he was entered child care center in America I had a culture shock about Kazufumi's meal treatment. He left some foods, and he asked me to put them in a trash!
>
> I know he feels very comfortable at the current child care center. He is blamed much less than when he was in Japan. But he must go back to Japan next summer. I'm afraid he will have a lot of trouble after he go back to Japan.†

Note how much important material the parent and teacher are able to share. They influence each other's understanding about this child's behavior and school experience.

* From correspondence of teacher Deborah Zalkind, Tufts Educational Day Care Center, 1992.

† Reprinted by permission.

◗ In a special folder for each child, a first-grade teacher records anecdotal material about individual progress in relation to the key curriculum areas (reading and writing, art, block and dramatic play, math, and science). The teacher also includes information related to social and behavioral factors that influence achievement. For example, in writing about Marguerite, a particularly reticent and shy child, the teacher writes:

> Today Marguerite initiated conversation with other children related to her writing. She asked Elan if he wanted to read her story and explained that she wrote about having gone to her grandmother's house for the weekend. She seems much more comfortable in sharing with other children spontaneously.

◗ Photographs of four-year-olds' block structures are taken periodically for the children to review. Occasionally the photographs are placed on the bulletin board near the block area to increase children's awareness of the range of ways of working that are available.

◗ Portfolios are maintained for storing kindergartners' paintings and drawings. The teacher collects any work that seems particularly important—for example, work that incorporates new approaches to using media or new subject matter, or that manifests shifts in representational ability. The work is dated.

◗ An administrator meets with a group of first-grade teachers to discuss which methods of collecting data about children and their progress are most effective. The administrator recognizes the importance of teachers identifying methods for collecting data that are meaningful for them in terms of specific objectives at a given time. For example, one teacher is presenting a major unit about different kinds of families, and cooperative learning is being emphasized. The teacher records information about which activities and skills individual children are working on, along with information about how well they are able to work together cooperatively. The teacher jots down: "Irma is very stimulated by the unit on families. She immediately understood that even in animal groupings there are roles that the various creatures play (mother, hunter, baby, siblings). She and José worked well together making a list of the activities in which each family member engages."

◗ Second graders are encouraged to bring photographs, newspaper clippings, and small artifacts into the room to share. The teacher emphasizes the importance of sharing interesting things with others and collecting ideas for writing and drawing, and provides storage space.

Formal or Systematic Techniques

◗ Time sampling is done to determine how four-year-olds use the block corner as contrasted with the dramatic play area. Every twelve minutes, the assistant teacher records what children are in which area and how they are occupied. Results are analyzed along such dimensions as gender; whether play is solitary, parallel, or cooperative; and how much conversation children engage in.

◗ A list of "emergent reader skills" is used to document the progress of children in prekindergarten through first grade. Evidence of emergent writing and reading includes scribbling, drawing, making nonphonetic letter strings, using invented and conventional spelling, mixing scribbling and drawing, creating picture stories, pointing to pictures in books, paying attention to print, running fingers along print, and elongating pointings or pointing slowly so it matches the spoken word (Sulzby, 1990).

◗ A notebook is maintained with a section for each child of a group of five- and six-year-olds. The teacher designs sheets for gathering data about particular critical areas of concern, such as initial adjustment to school, friendships, activities selected by the child, mathematics skills, and so on.

◗ Teacher's observe kindergartners and first graders on a regular basis during the course of the day. Several clipboards are strategically placed around the room. On each clipboard is a supply of white adhesive labels, on which is written the child's name, the date, and the comment. The label is later peeled off and placed in a notebook under the child's name. The material is then reviewed during team meetings. Care is taken to keep the observations objective and without interpretation. Any noteworthy behaviors are recorded: for example, academic skills mastered, new concepts, difficulties, language use, and motor skills.

◗ Kindergartners maintain journals for documenting their own progress in science, reading, writing, and art. One child records a picture of a block structure that he has created, translating a three-dimensional structure into a two-dimensional drawing. The teacher elicits discussion about the structure, bringing up such things as the kind of building it is, how the parts are related to the whole, and how long the child worked on the structure.

◗ The teacher creates two file boxes for first and second graders' writing work, with folders for each child. One box contains work in writing that is in process; the other box is for work that has been completed. The same setup is created for math work that is in process and completed. The brightly colored folders are organized so that it is easy for children to identify their folders (four greens are together, then four reds, then four yellows, and so on). Children file their own work and refer back to particular papers that have been completed.

◗ Conferences between the teacher and individual second and third graders take place periodically at predetermined times in order to discuss each child's progress. Children are asked to identify areas in which they feel confident or insecure, to share information about interests and hobbies, and to identify skills that need attention. The teacher and the child discuss how these issues can be dealt with on a daily basis. This information is jotted down (by the teacher or the child) and placed in a special folder for periodic review and analysis.

◗ The teacher tape-records second graders' oral reading and storytelling. Other children listen to the tapes; they are also used to help parents understand growth and development over time.

Documentation of Growth and Performance

The teacher documents children's growth and performance in concrete forms that may be shared with others—parents, curriculum specialists, administrators, and special needs coordinators.

◗ Portfolios of the artwork, writing, and bookmaking of children from kindergarten through third grade are maintained and reviewed with parents. The portfolios help parents to understand the child's progress as well as the teacher's objectives. Key pieces of work are photocopied. In reviewing the portfolios, teachers make comments like the following ones:

> Let's look at the relationship between Leslie's writing and drawing. There are many important parallels. Look at how the *a* form that she is practicing in handwriting appears repeatedly in this drawing where she makes curl forms on people's hair. And just as she's including more and more detail in her drawing, she's doing the same thing in her stories.
>
> Even though Eric has difficulty with fine motor skills and his work looks messy, look at the complexity of the ideas in his story and drawings.
>
> Here's a snapshot of Clara's block-building just a few months ago, and here's one of what she did just last week. Look at the difference between the two. See how, in the fall, her structures were very simple with just three or four units; now they are complex and she uses props to extend her ideas.

◗ First and second graders' stories, books, and language arts and math journals are kept in readily accessible cubicles where they may be reviewed and shared. Children are encouraged to look at others' work, as well as their own, to observe unique qualities. Other children's finished books may be checked out to take home for sharing with family.

◗ The teacher identifies the subject matter that children select when it is time to do creative writing. What a child chooses to read and write about provides important information for the teacher in planning future activities and areas for study.

◗ First graders keep notes on which activities they have been involved in during times when they are free to choose activities. Simple graphs are made for them to plot how they have spent their time. This material is integrated into their individual portfolios and discussed with the children periodically.

◗ Portfolios of kindergartners' artwork and writing are maintained and dated. Children are allowed to take home only some of the material, because the teacher wants to be able to use it in conferencing with both children and parents. Specific representative examples are chosen for conferencing with parents: for example, an illustration showing that when drawing people, a child is giving the figures greater volume, rather than creating them from one line. (See Figure 5.1.)

Recognition of Multiple Intelligences

Teachers recognize that children reveal their intellectual capabilities in a wide assortment of ways. Teachers are aware of what Howard Gardner calls "multiple intelligences." These include the following:

1. linguistic intelligence, or sensitivity to the meaning and order of words, and the varied uses of language
2. logical-mathematical intelligence, or the ability to handle long chains of reasoning and to recognize patterns and order in the world
3. spatial intelligence, or the ability to perceive the visual world accurately and to recreate, transform, or modify aspects of that world based on one's perceptions

FIGURE 5-1

Development as reflected in children's art: Sophie's two contrasting drawings at age four (left) and age five and one half (right).

4. bodily-kinesthetic intelligence, or a fine-tuned ability to use the body and to handle objects
5. interpersonal intelligence, or the ability to notice and make distinctions among others
6. intrapersonal intelligence, or access to one's own "feeling life"
7. musical intelligence, or sensitivity to pitch, melody, rhythm, and tone (Gardner, 1983)

In *The Unschooled Mind: How Children Think and How Schools Should Teach*, Gardner (1991) provides an overview of Project Spectrum, an early childhood program designed to assess children's distinctive intelligences and provide appropriate supportive curricula.

Teachers observe children carefully to determine their intellectual proclivities and plan learning experiences with respect for a range of interests and abilities. Teachers teach to children's strengths, as opposed to their weaknesses. Teachers recognize that an interdisciplinary curriculum facilitates the expression of "multiple intelligences."

◗ Dwight, a second grader, is interested in anything mechanical or technical. He has learned a good deal about batteries and lightbulbs at home, as well as from the teacher. The teacher sets up an area for children to use simple motors and make contraptions that can be illuminated. Dwight is the "expert" in charge of that activity area and helps other children to learn some of what he knows.

◗ The teacher designs an activity for kindergartners and first graders to put their names to music on the piano. Piano keys are numbered with gummed stickers. Children create a pattern with the various notes to "sing" their names. Some children are able to understand the relationship between the number of syllables and the number of notes. Musical patterns are recorded on cards so that children can play one another's names on the piano. Two children are particularly gifted at recognizing various children's names when they are played. The teacher provides opportunities for these two children to share their expertise, without pressuring other children to perform as well.

Awareness of Children's Special Knowledge

Teachers are particularly aware of areas in which children have special knowledge and competence. Teachers also identify children's interests and hobbies, and utilize this information constructively. Building the curriculum around this knowledge is important. In so doing teachers motivate children and can often engage them in learning basic skills and meeting curriculum objectives.

◗ Saul, a third grader, is extremely knowledgeable about carrier pigeons, since he helps his father work with them. When the class is doing a unit on birds, Saul is placed in charge of creating an interest center on carrier pigeons. His father helps him to set up a display center with books, related objects, and slides. Saul provides a significant amount of information and stimulation about how birds communicate, travel, and find their way home.

◗ Conti, a kindergartner, lives with his deaf grandfather and knows sign language. During circle time he often teaches words and brief sentences to the group. On Valentine's Day he teaches everyone how to sign "I love you." Many children use the signs and incorporate them into their valentines.

Awareness of Cultural Differences

Teachers are aware of how cultural differences impact children's participation in the learning process. Teachers understand that different cultures are characterized by specific interactional styles, and they take this into consideration in planning learning experiences and in assessing individual children's capabilities (Cazden, 1988).

◗ The teacher is aware that Lina, a Hawaiian second grader, is reluctant to engage in tasks all by herself. The teacher speaks to the family and learns that Lina is more comfortable when working in a small group. The teacher modifies expectations for Lina to work alone until she has had a number of positive school experiences working with her peers.

◗ During creative writing time, one first grader has difficulty when asked to write an imaginary story about an animal that has never lived—one she has invented. Clara—who is from a culture in which stories are expected to be "true to the facts" and the written word is expected to reflect the truth—is unable to participate. The teacher adjusts her expectations accordingly: "Clara, if you would feel more comfortable writing a story about an animal that is real, not imaginary, that's all right."

The Physical Environment Optimizes Concrete Learning

The physical environment is designed to optimize concrete learning and to enable children to explore a wide variety of objects and materials. The environment is viewed as a central force in stimulating intellectual activity. The teacher is vigilant in maximizing its impact.*

> Children need space in which to learn through their own actions, space in which they can move, build, sort, create, spread out, construct, experiment, pretend, work with friends, store belongings, display their works, work by themselves and in large groups. (Hohmann, Banet, & Weikart, 1979)

In the cultural transmission model, the physical environment is organized so as to reinforce the teacher's position as the dominant force in the educational program. Few objects and materials are present, and desks or tables are the essential furnishings, since words, books, reading series, mathematics workbooks, and paper-and-pencil tasks are central instructional mechanisms. In both the romantic and cognitive developmental models, however, materials and child-oriented equipment are considered of key importance, and in each setting can be found a wide assortment of materials that allow children to engage in concrete experiences.

What, then, separates the romantic classroom from the cognitive-developmental classroom—and when observing, how can one distinguish these two orientations? The cognitive-developmental model is driven by the notions of cognitive conflict and the dialectic. This orientation makes use of a physical environment that is challenging and provocative; what is taking place in such a classroom should be engaging and thought-provoking, not repetitive and superficial. All child-initiated activity is not equally valuable simply because it is concrete and involves the use of media. Educators must be concerned with the quality of involvement taking place, and whether or not it represents movement and change over time. Hence, the astute observer will look not only at the apparent meaningfulness of a child's involvement at a given moment in time but will recognize the importance of making judgments over time as well—particularly because a certain amount of repetitive behavior is an essential part of the learning process and of the process of constructing knowledge.

A few key concepts are helpful in distinguishing between romantic and cognitively oriented classrooms. First, in the cognitively oriented classroom, the range of available materials is elastic enough to enable children of the same chronological age to perform on somewhat different levels; puzzles, books, mathematical material, and games range from simple to complex. Different levels of performing within particular age groups and domains of learning are respected. The romantic classroom allows for less variability within a given age group.

* This section contains numerous suggestions from Lynn Rosen Shade, Outreach Coordinator, Eliot-Pearson Department of Child Study, Tufts University.

Second, basic areas are changed periodically in the cognitive-developmental classroom, so as to present strategic problems to children. For example, hoses, pumps, and water wheels might be placed in the water table area, thus creating the possibility that children will discover siphoning. In the romantic classroom, although what is available might be changed from time to time, these changes are for the sake of novelty rather than to provide specific cognitive challenges.

Third, the environment in the cognitive-developmental classroom is reorganized occasionally in order to focus children's attention and encourage them to explore what they have been dismissing or avoiding. For example, the block corner might be closed to encourage certain children to explore another area; reading might take place in a small tent; painting might be presented on a large flat table, instead of at an easel. In the romantic classroom, the environment often remains relatively predictable.

Fourth, the cognitive-developmental teacher recognizes the strategic role of the unique and unexpected in engaging children's interest, as well as the way critical juxtapositions of materials "speak" to the child and encourage problem solving and investigation. For example, the teacher might make big holes in large paper and place the paper on the table where children usually do spontaneous drawing—thus initiating elaborate drawings of animals that live in holes and of other things in small places. In the romantic classroom, the child is expected to make all the preliminary connections that lead to discovery. The teacher there would be less likely to place the holes in the paper; the child would be expected to generate this action.

Fifth, the cognitively oriented classroom changes in significant ways as the year unfolds. In the fall, when children are new to the environment, it may be kept relatively constant; for example, not too many materials may be available at one time, and few things may be on the walls. As time goes by, however, and children learn to negotiate the environment with ease, it becomes more complex and challenging. Perhaps more diverse salvage material is introduced for art and construction work; painting may be introduced outdoors or on the floor near the block area. In the romantic classroom, few distinctions are made from one period of time to another. Painting remains at the easels in a particular area of the room; the water table and the block area are basically unchanged.

Setting up activity areas The cognitively oriented classroom is organized into distinct activity areas with logic and clarity. Each area is defined by boundaries—dividers, such as bookcases, and more abstract implied boundaries, such as the carpet color or a change in a wall or ceiling display. The size, location, and design of each area is carefully planned to facilitate the interactions planned. Issues of overcrowding, noise level, and traffic patterns are seriously considered. Adjacent learning centers support making connections among different curriculum areas.

- An entry zone, located near the door to the classroom, is designed to help children with the transition from home (or outside) to the classroom. The zone consists of personal storage space for children's belongings, colorful bulletin boards (for displaying photographs and children's work, notices to parents, and important information about the day), a welcome mat for mud removal, a bench, a large basket labeled "things to go home," a tray for incoming homework, and a box for lost and found items.

- The block area is located next to the dramatic play corner. The end of the storage unit that serves as a boundary between the two areas is positioned two feet away from the wall, creating a very narrow and inviting passageway between the areas.
- The listening center with tapes, headphones, and storybooks consists of a low, round table (one foot from the floor) on a small carpet. The library and writing areas are directly adjacent. A record player on a nearby shelf is strategically placed at children's eye level so that children can clearly see the tip of the needle as they put it on the record.

Variety of materials The classroom contains a wide variety of material that children may observe, touch, and manipulate. These materials invite investigation and imaginative use. Some of them are available for children to use spontaneously; others are reserved for lessons the teacher prepares. The materials are challenging and exciting. They reflect Gardner's notion of "multiple intelligences," engaging different modalities of knowing and working: linguistic, logical-mathematical, visual-spatial, bodily-kinesthetic, interpersonal, intrapersonal, and musical.

Materials are provided so that children have frequent opportunities to take part in a range of activities:

- To design and create with diverse materials (both two- and three-dimensional), children use basic art materials, such as markers, scissors, tapes, paints, and colored paper, as well as household salvage from which sculpture and constructions may be made—clear plastic containers, film canisters, food trays, mat board scraps, leather and wood scraps, corks, paper towel rolls, and so on.
- To problem-solve, children work with mathematics manipulatives (Cuisenaire rods, attribute blocks), giant puzzles, and games.
- To explore, children might make use of natural materials brought in from outdoors (bark, pumpkins, reeds, rocks); old typewriters, telephones, or other mechanical objects; even a meat grinder.
- To observe, record, study, and measure, children work with live animals (fish, ant colonies, birds), plants, balance scales, and various objects to weigh and measure.
- To communicate with others through speech and print, children use writing and bookmaking materials (markers, pens, folders, printing tools), tape recorders and tapes of music and stories from different cultures, and books—including **big books** (books large enough so that a group of children can see the print), magazines, and restaurant menus.
- To imagine and make-believe, children might use medical equipment (stethoscopes, Band-Aids, old casts, plastic thermometers), cross-cultural dolls, puppets, and hats.

Strategic arrangements Compelling objects are arranged strategically on tables, shelves, and display areas to invite close observation and investigation.

Objects can be examined in detail. The unexpected and unique stimulates children's thought and involvement.

- An accumulation of broken things is placed on a large shelf in a kindergarten or first-grade classroom with a sign marked "broken" and written questions: "Can you tell why this object is broken?" "Can it be repaired or fixed?" "What do you think could be done about the problem?" "Are we able to fix it?" Included are such things as a disposal top, an old clock, a can opener, a stapler, and a plastic bowl. These questions are discussed in activity time.
- The science area has a live slug and live crayfish, which children watch and take care of. Related books are carefully displayed.
- In the small block area, several of David MacAulay's construction books are displayed on the countertop.
- A beautiful braille alphabet is displayed near the writing table, along with a wall chart that shows the letters of the alphabet in sign language.
- A large piece of contact paper is attached to the underneath surface of the art table, sticky side out (facing the floor). An assortment of collage materials (ribbons, styrofoam shapes, spangles, cut straws, and strips of paper) in a large, sectioned tray rests on the floor under the table. The teacher asks, "What do you think will happen if you make a collage upside down?" Children lie on the floor in small groups to work on the mural.
- In the nature area, a balance scale, the books *The Big Fat Worm* and *My First Nature Book,* a glass "habitat" for worms, and a scientific detailed word description of how earthworms live are all displayed together.
- A third-grade class is learning to look up words in the dictionary and record the definitions. The teacher writes new words with a marker on large pieces of cardboard and suspends them from the ceiling on string. Children are stimulated by the presence of the new words dangling just above their heads. The words include the humorous and unique (for example, *frumpy, fastidious, fantasy,* and *tumultuous*). After recording the definitions in their workbook dictionaries, the children create original sentences using three or more of the words.

Consistency and change Predictability and consistency are present in the basic organization of the environment, at the same time that there is novelty and change. Stable parts of the environment (such as the water table, the writing area, the mathematics area, the block area, and dramatic play) are altered and changed throughout the year to provoke interest and to provide intellectual stimulation. The teacher, however, avoids randomness, overstimulation, and excesses, making sure that stimulation does not appear and disappear before it can be adequately explored.

- The area under the loft is periodically changed to represent different environments, depending on children's interests and the teacher's objectives. One month the area is a puppet theater; another month it is a house, a cave, or an aquarium. Activities emerge from the different concepts. On one occasion, an office is created; kindergartners visit the school office in order to document what is needed to run one. They create in and out baskets and organize supplies; someone

A grouping of natural fall objects (pinecones, chestnuts, gourds, leaves), magnifying glasses, and a book on autumn provides stimulation for children to observe closely. Concern for an aesthetically pleasing and orderly arrangement is apparent. Sylvia G. Feinburg

brings in an old typewriter from home. The children study and discuss what an office is and what is involved in creating an efficient one. The teacher encourages the children to discuss the matter at home to gain additional ideas.

- A sign in a classroom of five and six year olds reads: "Block corner is closed today. You may want to visit the new bowling alley near the cubby area."
- The water table is filled with fresh snow. Plastic squeeze bottles of colored water are available for four-year-olds to make designs and pictures in the snow.

Logical organization The physical environment is clearly and logically organized. Boxes, bins, and cubbies are used to categorize things and make it obvious where they belong. Materials are stored in locations that facilitate management and control of the classroom.

- Paper punches, scissors, containers with pencils, and tape holders are mounted on pegboard close to the drawing and writing area. Their shapes are painted on the board and labeled. It is clear where each object belongs.
- A large number of plastic bins are on a shelf where children can easily reach them. Each one is labeled neatly and plainly, in words and pictures (for example, cardboard scraps; fabric scraps; wooden pieces; straws; plastic

This set of shelves is simply and neatly organized with pictorial and written labels to designate where things belong. The clarity makes it easy for young children to know where to find things and to participate in the cleanup process. Sylvia G. Feinburg

pieces; dowels). Children help to fill the bins to provide materials for art, science, and construction.

- A rack with tools (scissors, pliers, screwdrivers) hangs on the wall. Each tool has a specific "home," marked by a picture the same color and size as the actual object.
- Unit blocks are stored on open shelves, longest side facing out. Contact paper labels, cut precisely to match the various sizes and shapes of the blocks, are attached to the shelves. Each section is also labeled with a sign (elliptical curve, quarter circle, unit arch).

The following are avoided:

- piles of disorganized papers placed randomly around the room
- markers, pens, scissors, and other materials placed in disorder on a shelf, tops missing
- a meeting area where children gather in close proximity to messy shelves with toys that invite play and disarray during meeting time
- puzzles, games, blocks stored in large toy chests

Focusing on Aesthetics

Aesthetic and other environmental features are important in creating an inviting and facilitating total environment. Adult work of a stereotyped or commercial quality is avoided as decoration. Adult work of high quality is included, such as beautiful photographs, reproductions of drawings and paintings, and artifacts representing cultural diversity. All work, including children's work, is displayed with respect and concern for neatness and beauty. Some pictures are matted, framed, or otherwise enhanced. Labeling may be present to enhance adult and child understanding of objectives and context.

- A display of fabrics from different cultures occupies one entire wall of a second-grade classroom, from floor to ceiling. Books about pattern and design, as well as books about the various cultures represented, are nearby.
- A half-dozen frames with mats are a permanent part of a classroom. Kindergartners' art and other work is periodically placed in the frames and hung. Care is taken to display everyone's work at some point and to reinforce a range of approaches to working, such as making realistic and abstract paintings, or printing, writing, and typewriting stories.
- A rocking chair and some large colorful pillows are situated in a reading area for four-year-olds. Books are scattered on a small table as well as stored on shelves.
- Plants are placed strategically around a kindergarten classroom. A few hang from the ceiling; others are grouped in a sunny spot near the window. Birds' nests, an old beehive, potting soil, and a trowel are readily available.
- Two lamps are perched on tables, one near the library area and the other near the science area. They create a sense of warmth and coziness that attract first graders to the area and help to sustain their involvement.
- In a first-grade classroom a small piece of remnant fabric has been puffed and made into a "balloon" curtain that sits over the window behind the rocking chair where the teacher leads discussion time.

The following are avoided:

- thumbtacking children's artwork haphazardly and unevenly
- allowing work that has become tattered, torn, and faded to remain on the walls
- allowing old work that is no longer relevant to remain around the room
- leaving half-dead plants on a windowsill

Orderliness and flexibility Although the teacher maintains an orderly and aesthetically pleasing environment, he or she is flexible and recognizes that while children are involved with materials a certain amount of mess and disorder is natural. The teacher balances expectations for orderliness with an appreciation of constructive messiness and the need for temporary change.

- A science table is set up to accommodate only four children at a time. On one occasion, when third graders are scooping out the insides of pumpkins and weighing the amount of seed and pulp to determine whether the size of the pumpkin is related to the weight of the pulp, interest is unusually high, and additional children want to join in. The teacher sets up a laboratory for experimenting by placing newspapers on a nearby countertop as well as the floor, enabling the whole group to work together.
- Children are experimenting with paint and making action paintings, as the abstract expressionists did. One second grader becomes concerned when she sees another child holding up a wet painting, tipping it, and getting the paint to run and drip. "The paint will go on the floor if she keeps doing that! She should cut it out." she exclaims. "It's okay," reassures the teacher. "That happens when you're experimenting with paint. We just have to get more newspaper underneath and maybe some of that plastic sheeting. And then we can experiment all we want!"
- Three-year-olds want to move blocks from block corner into the dramatic play area in order to make an "apartment house." The teacher encourages the mood and provides an appropriate place for the construction to take place.

Using Signs as Teaching Tools

The teacher uses bulletin boards, room decorations, and display surfaces as important tools in the teaching process. Signs are strategically placed near related curriculum materials and displays of finished work. The signs ask challenging questions and offer useful and clarifying information for children, parents, and visitors.

- Simple questions are written with a Magic Marker and hung on the bulletin board at first graders' eye level: "How many legs would three dogs and two cats have?" "If there are twenty-two people in our class and three are missing, how many are here today?" (The second question is repeated each day and is familiar.) Children are encouraged to discuss the problem with one another. Answers are hidden in a spot under the clock, so that children can check their own answers.
- A sign in the science area reads: "Vote here about how you feel about earthworms. Do you like to hold them?" Kindergartners' and first graders' answers are tallied and shared.
- A sign in the art area asks kindergartners: "What colors can you make with blue and red? With blue and red and white? Paint samples of what you discover on these strips of paper."
- A sign under four paintings by a four-year-old of various line configurations is displayed in the hallway: "Riana painted all these paintings. She really likes to paint lines!" Parents and children notice and discuss them.
- Three acorns and a chestnut are taped onto a piece of cardboard and mounted on the bulletin board in a classroom of three-year-olds, with a sign reading, "Joseph found these in the woods."

Maintenance of the Physical Environment

Children are clearly expected to treat materials respectfully, as well as to return them to where they belong. A system is designed to make children accountable for and committed to cleaning up after themselves. Children are encouraged to help one another, since maintenance of the physical environment is viewed as both an individual and a group responsibility.

◗ A cleanup chart hanging in the meeting area lists ten different jobs. Two first graders are assigned to each job on a weekly basis; the child's name, written on a clothespin, is clipped to the right of the assigned task. The child flips the clothespin over to indicate that the work has been completed.

◗ The teacher makes comments such as the following: "Corey, this pen needs to have its top. We need to take care of the materials in our classroom." "I'm going to take these sharp scissors off the table because you continue not to use them correctly, even though we've talked about it many times." "Isadora, you have a job to do before you go outside." "Do we need a broom, or do you think we can pick these up with our hands?" "Corey, Isadora says she needs a dustpan. Could you go and get it? Thanks." "Great job! It makes us all feel terrific when it looks so organized and beautiful. I'm impressed!"

Adaptations for Children with Special Needs

The teacher makes adaptations in the physical environment and the instructional process for children with special needs.

◗ Diana, a child in a wheelchair with limited motor control, has difficulty reaching the vertical easel when attempting to paint. An easel is made out of heavy cardboard and mounted on a table so that her chair can glide under, enabling her to work efficiently. Other kindergartners are attracted to this novel easel and use it on occasion as well.

◗ Alexander has difficulty following the group schedule posted on the bulletin board for first graders to follow. The teacher makes him an individual one with greater clarity, places it on a clipboard, and mounts it on the bulletin board where this kind of material is kept. She spends a few moments going over it with him early in the morning.

Literacy and Mathematics Are Critical Aspects of the Curriculum

Literacy and mathematics are critical aspects of the curriculum, but they are taught in an interdisciplinary manner that makes them relevant to children and builds respect for their importance. Literacy and mathematics are being isolated and emphasized here, not in order to suggest that they are the most important aspects of the curriculum, but instead to make it clear that they are not being neglected.

Academic skills are valued highly in the developmental model; they are simply dealt with in a different way from the cultural transmission or romantic models. In the cultural transmission approach, skills tend to be taught in relative isolation, with emphasis on drill and rule systems. In contrast, the romantics provide rich experiences of a general nature, hoping that the child will absorb important material in a natural, intuitive way. The developmental model uses an eclectic approach. Basic skills are considered very important, but they are not necessarily taught in isolation, nor do they dominate the teaching agenda in a narrow and constraining manner. They are taught in context.

Interdisciplinary teaching is fundamental to a cognitive-developmental classroom. Hence, art, science, health, reading, music, and mathematics may all be taught as part of a single set of learning experience—not necessarily compartmentalized into separate, independent subject areas. As a result, an observer new to the developmental approach may not recognize how much commitment there is to teaching traditional subjects, such as reading, writing, and mathematics, and may infer that the model is not concerned with academic skills. Nothing could be further from the truth.

At times, the teacher will deal with instruction in a given skill directly, in a didactic manner; at other times, children will have opportunities to engage in activities like counting, measuring, and computing at the same time that drawing and writing are taking place. Also important is the value set forth throughout this book: namely, individualization of instruction, making it possible for children at different levels of ability to be working according to their developmental capabilities.

Factors to Consider

The following approaches are fundamental to teaching literacy and mathematics in the developmental model.

- Individual and small group activities are planned along with occasional large group situations. Obviously, some learning experiences are more effectively taught in small groups, just as others lend themselves to large group situations. In addition, the range of expected abilities that might be present in a given classroom make using small groups a more efficient teaching approach.
- Academics are not taught in relative isolation, with emphasis on trite workbooks, ditto sheets, and didactic paper-and-pencil tasks. When worksheets are used, they are interesting and engage children's attention (see Figure 5.2).
- Distinctions in ability levels are respected and minimized. The teacher makes it clear that children may perform differently in various curriculum domains, and from one period of time to another. The ability grouping that does occur is flexible and is not permanent. Every effort is made to deter children and parents from thinking that how one performs in reading or math is an index of one's total intellectual capabilities.

Approaches to Teaching Literacy

Contemporary approaches to teaching literacy are also used. For example, the classroom has a writing and drawing center where children create books and

Riddle Math

The riddle: MARIA?
What beans won't grow from seeds?

The Math:

①	5 + 2 = 7	⑥	3 + 7 = 10
②	7 + 4 = 11	⑦	3 + 8 = 11
③	4 + 5 = 6	⑧	5 + 1 = 6
④	3 + 6 = 9	⑦	7 + 5 = 12
⑤	0 + 8 = 8	⑩	2 + 3 = 5

The code:

Sum	8	4	7	3	9	15	10	2	11	12	1	5	6	20	14
letter	Y	C	J	X	L	M	B	Q	E	N	P	S	A	D	F

The answer to the riddle:

①	②	③	④	⑤		⑥	⑦	⑧	⑨	⑩
J	E	L	L	Y	■	B	E	A	N	S

FIGURE 5-2

This first grade worksheet is in the form of a riddle and requires that children first do an addition problem. Children use concrete materials to determine the answer and then use a code to translate the sums into letters. The answer to the riddle is "jelly beans."

pictures and develop an appreciation for the integration of art and writing. Children's own phonetic or "invented spelling" (Chomsky, 1971) may be used. Whole language is employed—drawing, writing, storytelling, listening, bookmaking, and reading together in small and large groups are all occurring interactively. Big books are available. Process writing—in which children revise and edit their work, gain understanding of the importance of sustained effort, and build proficiency—as well as journal writing and class "publishing" occurs. An inviting reading area is set up, with pillows or a rocking chair to encourage looking at books. Print is clearly part of the total environment—in labeling objects or displaying children's messages or alphabets. Braille and sign language posters are present. The teaching of phonics is part of the curriculum; it is used selectively to strengthen skills. Phonics is not viewed as the single most important means of instruction, but as one of many teaching options.*

- *Our First-Grade Writing Book,* containing stories created by class members, rests on a shelf beside trade books about learning to read and write.
- The teacher encourages first graders to make connections from their own language learning to the printed word. On the last page of the book *The Velveteen Rabbit,* by Margery Williams, an illustration without text appears. The teacher asks, "What do you notice about this page?" One child responds, "It's a gorgeous illustration." Another says, "There are no words on the page, only a beautiful illustration." A third says, "The bunny looks a little bit like the cow jumping over the moon from a nursery rhyme we know." The teacher responds to all the answers with support and enthusiasm, but eventually says, "There are no words on this page; just enjoy the illustration." Later in the day she hears Gregory, a child in the group, reading the story to a group of children. He says, "Boys and girls, tell me what you notice on this page." A child responds, "There are no words; just enjoy the illustration." Gregory sighs and agrees, "Yeah, just enjoy the view."
- Journal writing is an everyday part of classroom life and begins on the first day of school. The expectation that you read and write every day in school is established. Reading, writing, and playing are happening simultaneously throughout the day. Emily writes in her journal "I*FL*T*L*A*K*A*R*A*N*B*O" ("I felt like a rainbow"). During a parent conference when the teacher is explaining to the mother how Emily is learning distinctions between words, letters, and about connecting words together into sentences, Emily says enthusiastically, "I love to read and to write, and I just felt like a rainbow."
- At shared reading time, kindergartners and first graders read the book *Greedy Cat,* by Joy Cowley. In the book, Mom goes shopping, and Greedy Cat eats all the groceries. Afterward, two of the children decide to make shopping lists in the dramatic play area.
- In order to teach children how to divide words into syllables and to use pronunciation marks, the teacher stimulates third graders to invent new words that might be part of the English language. The children are very excited about the opportunity to "add to the English language." The teacher records their responses on a huge piece of paper and puts it on the bulletin board. Children try to use one another's new words during creative writing time. (See Figure 5-3.)

Approaches to Teaching Mathematics

Howard Gardner (1991), in discussing the importance of immersing children in meaningful activities and creating situations in which they are apprentices to competent adults, argues on behalf of creating a comparable approach to whole language in the field of mathematics.

*This section contains numerous suggestions from Holly J. Carroll, Literacy Center Resource Teacher, Cambridge, Massachusetts.

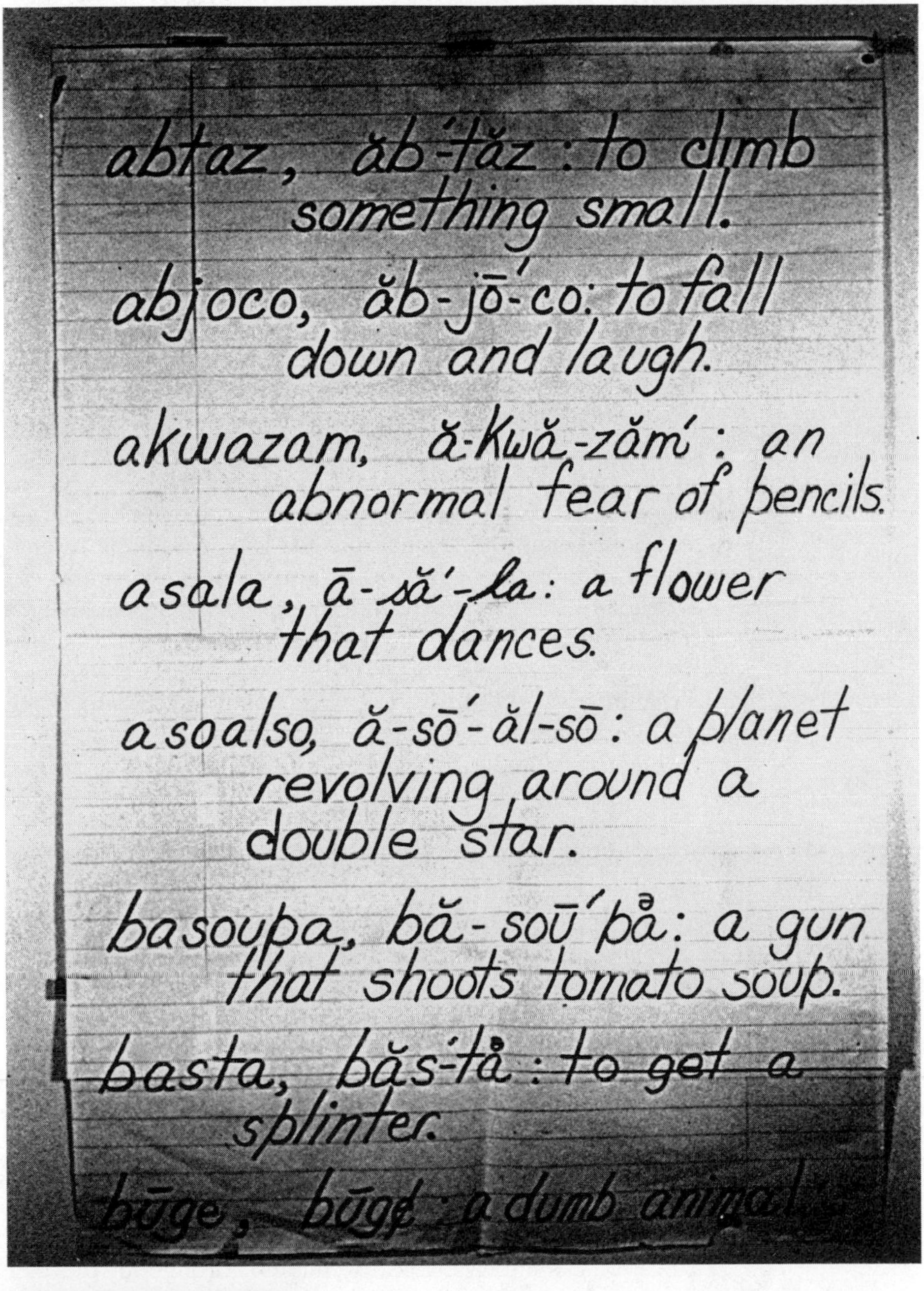

abtaz, ăb-'tăz : to climb something small.

abjoco, ăb-jō-'co: to fall down and laugh.

akwazam, ă-Kwă-zăm' : an abnormal fear of pencils.

asala, ā-să'-la: a flower that dances.

asoalso, ă-sō'-ăl-sō: a planet revolving around a double star.

basoupa, bă-soū'på: a gun that shoots tomato soup.

basta, băs-'tå : to get a splinter.

būge, būge : a dumb animal.

FIGURE 5-3

Third graders invent new words to add to the English language, while learning to divide words into syllables and use pronunciation marks. Collection of Sylvia G. Feinburg

> A fresh approach that echoes "whole language" makes mathematics part of the overall atmosphere of the primary school. Numbers and numerical operations enter the ordinary, meaningful conversation among youngsters and between youngsters and teachers. From the start, children in "whole-math" environments are encouraged to engage in games that involve measuring, counting, and comparing, not merely to rehearse number skills, but also to help out in activities that are needed and valued. Kitchen-based experiences like cooking serve as an excellent context, for arithmetical operations constitute a ready and readily understandable part of preparing and then serving a meal to a class. Telling time, going on a trip, buying food and favors for a party, and measuring clothing are but a sampling of the many other activities of consequence that call for the use of numbers. Intriguingly, once children become involved in such apparently pragmatic activities, many of them will go on to acquire—or re-acquire—a fascination with the world of numbers and numerical relationships per se." (p. 212)

A range of contemporary approaches to teaching mathematics are employed. Materials that stimulate mathematical and quantitative thinking are readily available for spontaneous and teacher-directed use, including Cuisenaire rods, Montessori mathematical equipment, and attribute blocks, as well as other tools like rulers, scales, and shoe-size measuring equipment. The commercial programs that are selected involve the use of concrete materials, such as *Math Their Way* (Baratta-Lorton, 1976), *Box It or Bag It Mathematics* (Burk, Snider, & Symonds, 1988), and *Explorations* (Addison-Wesley). Activities designed to encourage mathematical thinking are also embedded within the general curriculum, such as counting, working with one-to-one correspondence, estimating, poll taking, graphing, and comparing size relationships.

- The children keep individual math journals. Marion Reynolds, a teacher at the Eliot-Pearson Children's School, titled each child's journal in the following manner: "Things Corey Can Do as a Mathematician." Children themselves record their developing ability to count, measure, develop patterns, and demonstrate one-to-one correspondence. These abilities may be demonstrated and described through isolated activities—for example, answering the question "How many unifix cubes will it take to go all around this room?" They may also form part of an integrated experience—such as children's using string to measure a partner's height, and recording their own height in their "All About Me" booklets.
- Materials that stimulate mathematical thinking and problem solving are available to children at all times. Things like leaves, buttons, cards to be sorted, and measuring tools such as unifix cubes, tape measures, and scales are all available.
- Unit blocks are available for building and exploring mathematical concepts. These blocks are available to children throughout the early childhood years: preschool through grade 3. The teacher challenges thinking through the use of such things as activity cards that ask children to match shapes and replicate buildings. The teacher may ask the children to draw diagrams of their buildings and to recreate structures they have constructed before. The teacher encourages children to notice and record relationships among the various-sized units.
- The teacher integrates mathematics experiences in all curriculum units. The

The availability of the balance scale enables this child to create her own mathematical challenges. © Elizabeth Crews

teacher encourages children to use mathematical language in describing their projects: "This tree is about half as big as the one next to it."

◗ The teacher encourages children to estimate the amount of material they will need for a particular task and to verify their estimates and refine their judgments.

◗ The teacher increases the challenges offered to children. For example, when children record their mathematical observations in pictorial form (graphs, Venn diagrams, charts), the teacher probes in order to stimulate children to include more detail.

◗ In planning a unit, the teacher makes a web of all the mathematical possibilities within it. Consider the human body, for example: concepts include pairs, the relative sizes of various parts of the body, and comparisons. Possible activities include checking vision and heartbeat, graphing preferences for clothing and food, counting the bounces of a ball, tracing the feet of children in the room and arranging them from biggest to smallest, ordering bowls of water according to the feel of temperature and using a thermometer to verify perceptions (*Ourselves: A Unit for Teachers,* Macdonald Educational, 1973).

◗ The teacher refrains from continuously giving children direct answers to mathematical problems. Instead, the teacher provokes thinking. In one classroom, described in *I Do and I Understand* (Nuffield Mathematics Project, 1970), the children had made a block graph showing the months of their birthdays. After some discussion a clear question emerged: "Are there always more people born in April than in any other month?" To the children at first this seemed to be a closed question that could be answered either yes or no. Their subsequent investigations led them to conclude that "unless we could ask everyone in the world we couldn't find out." The children discovered that "in statistical terms the size and selection of the sample affects the validity of the conclusions." (pp. 14–15).

◗ During group time when the teacher takes attendance, the children are asked to count silently the number of people present. Afterward, they compare results, and the following conversation ensues:

Teacher: So if there are sixteen kids in our class, and one is missing, how many are there?

Child: Fifteen.

Teacher: That's a *1* and a *5,* so you put them together like this. (The teacher draws a *1* and a *5* on a piece of paper.) And how many teachers are there?

Child: Three.

Teacher: And here's a three. (The teacher draws a *3*.) So if you add fifteen and three, you have . . .

Child: Eighteen.

Teacher: That's right, we took fifteen and added three and got eighteen. Adding is a strategy that works in a sum.

◗ Lists are made of numbers that children see and use in their everyday life, such as telephone numbers, license plate numbers, bus numbers, house numbers and street addresses, and relatives' zip code numbers. Some of these lists are written on large charts and placed on the bulletin board so that they can be used by class members.

◗ The teacher is thoughtful about the props she includes in the sand and water table. She varies and extends the stimuli on a regular basis. Containers that are wide, thin, deep, shallow, round, and flat are included. The teacher also stimulates comparisons, such as the idea of "big, bigger, and biggest." The teacher encourages children to explain: "This is the biggest. It holds the most sand." Comparing and estimating how much sand various containers will hold is encouraged. The children record the answers to their experiments in pictures and words.

◗ First graders begin to count the number of pages left in their writing journals. The teacher responds enthusiastically and encourages them to record the various numbers on a large chart. Children compute the number of empty pages the greatest number of people have and write that number on the chart.

◗ During group time when the calendar is being addressed, a discussion emerges among kindergartners and first graders about "the number of days that we've come to school." This activity leads to predictions: how many more numbers are needed to get to a blue square marked on the calendar (signifying multiples of 5) and to a green circle (signifying multiples of 10)? The children learn about counting by 5s and 10s: "Does it take longer to count by 10s to 50? Why?"

- Four- and five-year-olds make a collection of tools for measuring size. Children bring in things from home to augment what they can gather from around school. Among the objects the children assemble are a shoe-size measuring tool, a yardstick, a measuring tape, and a ruler. On one occasion, the teacher plans an activity in which the children must find alternative ways to measure or estimate length without using any of these devices; rulers are also eliminated. Children use such things as their hands and feet, plastic boxes, books.
- "If your name has five letters in it, get in line. Now . . . if your name has six letters in it, get in line! You can have a friend count with you, if you like."
- The teacher poses a problem for first graders: "One Mom rides a bike; one Dad rides a bike; one eight-year old girl rides a bike; one six-year old boy rides a bike; one three year old girl rides a trike. How many wheels does the whole family need?" The children draw pictures of the family members on their bikes and then tally the answer. Pictures and computational notes are displayed together. Some children write stories about the families on their bike trips.

Other ideas include the following (some are from *Mathematics Begins,* Nuffield Mathematics Project, 1970):

- Classifying, using yarn to put objects into sets: things that float and things that don't; things that belong in the kitchen and things that belong somewhere else.
- Mathematical challenges: "What can you do with five straws?" "How many different shapes can we make from this same sized piece of paper by tearing and shaping it in different ways?"
- Weaving, which teaches children about odd versus even, alternation, and area.
- Clapping musical rhythms.
- Cooking, which involves children in measuring amounts—cups, pints, quarts; one-half, one-quarter, and three-quarters of a tablespoon; a teaspoon.

The Teacher Makes Curriculum Decisions Based on the Child's Best Interests

The teacher makes decisions about the curriculum and the teaching process based on what is in the best interests of the child. The teacher negotiates, in constructive ways, parental and institutional demands that are contrary to what is developmentally appropriate. When a school system's curriculum demands impose expectations that are not consistent with a developmental approach, the teacher integrates what he or she knows about children's capabilities in implementing these expectations. When the administration imposes inappropriate expectations, the teacher accommodates these in the best possible way and works constructively to effect change.

Communicating with Parents About the Developmental Model

The teacher communicates to parents in a wide variety of ways so that they understand the teacher's objectives and reasons for teaching developmentally. The teacher translates theoretical and pedagogical objectives into a language parents can understand.

◗ An evening slide lecture is prepared to present to parents early in the fall to inform them about the objectives of the teacher's classroom organization and program. The teacher includes critical quotes from relevant theoretical articles that can be readily understood. To help parents understand the importance of children's making choices and seeing alternatives, the teacher posts the following excerpt from a book on early childhood education on the bulletin board:

> Help Children Begin to Make Choices
>
> Help children make choices and see alternatives throughout the day, whenever the occasion arises. Making choices is basic to all planning. "What colors do you think you'll need to mix to paint your airplane, Annette?" "Since all the blocks are already being used, what else could you use to make a road for your truck? . . . What about the carpet squares or the flat styrofoam pieces?" "That was a good idea, Mark, to fly around the circle like an airplane. Who has another idea about how we could go around the circle?" (Hohmann, Banet, & Weikart, 1979)

◗ The bulletin board is covered with crude scraps of all different sizes and shapes cut by three-year-olds. A large sign is also posted, which reads, "We are learning to cut; it is difficult when you are three."

◗ While talking to a visiting parent who is concerned about academic achievement, the teacher of three- and four-year-olds says, "Play is a prelude to reading; let me show you some interesting short articles that I have over here about the relationship between the two."

◗ Worksheets of a creative nature are designed as homework for parents to do with kindergartners. The teacher helps parents learn which skills and concepts are being addressed with simple messages that clarify the objectives involved. For example, the teacher placed the class's vacation homework on a bulletin board outside the classroom for the parents and children to see. She included the following explanation so that her motives in giving the work would be understood by the community at large.

> Vacation Homework
>
> Vacation Homework can help children to remember the life of their classroom when they are at home during school vacations. It can also provide an opportunity for children to share stories, concerns and information to their families about what happens during those busy days in school. The children in the K–1 class have proudly returned their vacation homework from the February vacation. It demonstrates the careful industry with which children approach the task of being in school.

Another example of parent involvement is shown in Figure 5-4. In this worksheet, space has been left open to capture the child's own concept of a wolf

FIGURE 5-4

These two papers represent two kindergarten children's responses to vacation homework their teacher gave them to do with help from their parents. The words printed around the empty rectangle are to stimulate children's interaction with their parents over the idea. For those children able to write, the stimulus is there to encourage them to do so.* (*continued*)

* From teacher Linda Beardsley, at Eliot-Pearson Children's School.

FIGURE 5-4 (continued)

or a valentine. The parent is encouraged to read the various words around the rectangle to stimulate the child's thinking.

◗ Parents and extended family are invited to come to a first-grade class during the first thirty minutes of each day for paired reading time with their children. The teacher uses this opportunity to increase families' understanding of reading program objectives.

Communicating with Nondevelopmental Colleagues

When dealing with colleagues who are not predisposed toward a developmental approach, the developmental teacher is proactive and does not assume an adversarial position. The teacher strives to find areas of mutuality and reciprocity.

◗ A second-grade teacher attends a conference on early childhood education where she hears a lecture on the importance of skills and how they must be integrated within a developmental model. She shares the written handout with her colleagues.

◗ A curriculum specialist in reading distributes a list of vocabulary words to be mastered for all children in grade two, along with a set of narrowly didactic worksheets for accomplishing the directive. The teacher acknowledges the expectations and embeds the vocabulary words within her general curriculum, using a wide variety of ways to teach the words involved. The teacher honors the expectation in ways consistent with the developmental approach and is tactful in how she helps the specialist to understand the developmental point of view.

◗ During faculty meetings when a colleague misrepresents the developmental approach and maintains that it does not create adequate structure and expectations for achievement, the teacher does not allow the accusation to go unchallenged. The teacher is clear in articulating the importance of both these factors and engages in dialogue in a positive but firm manner.

Incorporating the Best of the Cultural Transmission Approach

The teacher joins the best of the cultural transmission approach to teaching with a developmental approach. The teacher is innovative in accommodating demands that may seem inconsistent with his or her own objectives.

◗ A kindergarten teacher designs worksheets for children's independent use that are not stereotyped or mundane. The teacher recognizes that the quality of a worksheet makes it good or bad, not the worksheet process itself.

◗ Math/block worksheets for kindergartners show various block shapes with numbers next to them (for example: "use four of this shape, two of this shape, six of this shape, and include a bridge"). Children create any structure they choose using the designated numbers of forms. They compare their solutions with other children's in order to observe the differences.

◗ A math worksheet directs children to "create an animal with two heads, six legs, and a rectangular tail made out of three one-inch sections. Color it with four different colors."

Example of an Outstanding Lesson: Marble Roller Boards

This lesson on marble rollers, for four-, five-, and six-year-olds, was presented at the Eliot-Pearson Children's School by Rebecca Keenan (her lesson plan follows). This lesson is compelling in the way it engages great numbers of children and sustains their interest for a long time. The dynamic qualities of motion and making quick transformations, along with the opportunity to use hammers and nails, make it highly appealing. The lesson challenges children to problem-solve, deal with simple physics, and create imaginative, individual structures. It also strengthens their motoric skills and understanding of physical knowledge. The lesson is one in a continuum of lessons, which move from having children make simple structures with styrofoam and Popsicle sticks to more elaborate lessons that demand greater planning, purposefulness, and mastery of materials.

Lesson Plan

General idea, including needs and goals In order to build on the experience that children had a week ago with hammers, nails, and styrofoam, we will provide an opportunity for them to build and sculpt with soft wooden bases. Children are beginning to feel a sense of mastery working with hammers, and we hope that this experience will move them further in this direction.

Creating marble rollers is also an extension of the work that children have been doing with the marble blocks at choice time. The blocks have various configurations of grooves and holes that, when combined in different ways, allow marbles to roll through them. Most of the children already have a basic schema about the ways that marbles can roll and seem to enjoy the motion and action that they can create. This activity will allow them to design their very own structures for controlling the marbles; the opportunity is there for containing, trapping, moving them through a maze, and so on (much like mini-pinball machines).

Materials Hammers; soft pine scrap boards (approximately 10 to 14 inches long); long miscellaneous nails; rubber bands; cardboard tubes of various lengths; small paper cups; marbles. Materials will be set up on tables throughout the room before the children begin. Small elements (rubber bands, nails) will be placed in plastic trays so that the table reveals clarity and order. A few additional materials (washers, discs with holes) will be added while the children are working in order to incite fresh thinking about new possibilities.

Presentation The lesson will be introduced to the entire group at the end of meeting time. Everyone will participate. The teacher will motivate the experience in front of the group at the end of meeting time. She will talk about the hard work the children have done in working with their marble blocks and elicit comments about the structures they have created in the past. She will then hold up one of the long boards with a few nails already pounded into it and ask such things as

- "How could I get this rubber band to stay on this structure?"
- "Look what happens when we do this . . . or this . . ." (demonstrate stretching the rubber band over nails to create various configurations)

- "What if I tried to roll a marble down the board while the nails and rubber bands are in place? How can I control how the marble travels?"

She will demonstrate a few of the potential combinations of nails and rubber bands. (This will be done quickly and in a suggestive way, in order to stimulate and arouse interest in experimenting, not to create a product to be replicated.) She will quickly, and coincidentally, talk about being safe with rubber bands—that it is not okay to create sling shots! She will ask more questions to get children thinking:

- "How could you use these materials to construct a marble catcher?"
- "How can you prevent the marble from rolling off of the side of the board?"
- "What else could you construct? There are so many possibilities!"

Each child will go to a wooden board set up at one of the four different tables. Two teachers will float around the room while children serve themselves from the trays of materials placed in the centers of the tables. Initially, teachers will remain relatively passive. As the lesson develops they will point out certain things that are

This marble rolling activity, using a long board, nails, rubber bands, marbles, and simple salvage materials, stimulates children who are attracted to motion and rolling forms. Stretching rubber bands over nails and creating mazes and traps for capturing the marble are key dynamic qualities of the activity. Sylvia G. Feinburg occurring and ask pivotal questions. Teachers will be careful not to dominate the activity with their conversation.

Summary

This chapter has described four major categories of teacher behavior and curriculum development, which contribute toward creating a cognitive-developmental classroom:

1. The teacher observes, records, and assesses progress. It is important that the teacher gather specific data concerning individual children's level of development, interests, and academic progress. Strategies for documenting progress include maintaining records and portfolios, sharing these with parents and other teaching personnel, and guiding children's understanding of their own needs and progress.
2. The physical environment optimizes concrete learning. Particular principles and techniques facilitate the important objective of creating a challenging and provocative environment. Especially critical qualities of the physical environment are clarity, logic, and order, in order to guide and facilitate the child's investigations. Aesthetics and visual harmony are additional key elements for the teacher to consider, since a classroom that is complex and multidimensional can become chaotic and unwieldy without such consideration.
3. Academic skills in the areas of literacy and mathematics, as well as content in social studies, science, health and the arts, are of fundamental importance in the classroom. Both skills and concept formation are important. Interdisciplinary teaching, bringing together different subject areas into a single experience, is an optimum approach. Skills can be taught in and of themselves on occasion, but should be integrated into the full spectrum of classroom life so that they are rendered significant and relevant. The distinction between skills and concepts has been introduced so that teachers will be vigilant about addressing both of them as two complementary processes. Themes are a valuable mechanism for unifying certain teaching objectives as well.
4. The teacher makes curriculum decisions based on the child's best interests. The teacher who is committed to the developmental orientation will assume responsibility for assisting others to understand its orientation and mission. Hence, the teacher will communicate actively with parents, as well as with administrators and other educational personnel. When the school system and curriculum personnel impose expectations contrary to the developmental perspective, the teacher avoids antagonistic and destructive polarization and provides the best approximation of the developmental model possible within the constraints of the situation. The child's well-being should always remain central in decision-making about competing political and philosophical views.

The next part of this book continues discussion of cognition, particularly as it relates to the nurturance of creativity.

Part Two: Questions for Discussion

1. Describe each of the three educational orientations, as set forth by Kohlberg and Mayer. What distinguishes them from one another? How does each view the teacher's role?
2. What specifically distinguishes the romantic point of view from the cognitive-developmental one?
3. Describe the four categories that define the critical qualities of the teacher in a cognitive-developmental classroom. In your own words, identify some of the essential features that describe such a teacher.
4. Why is the process of observing and recording children's behavior and academic progress important to the developmental teacher? What techniques and strategies are helpful in documenting children's performance?
5. Some people think that teachers who are interested in developmental education are indifferent to teaching skills and using worksheets. Discuss.

PART

3 STIMULATING CREATIVE THINKING

Creativity is valued highly. Every attempt is made to capitalize on children's imaginative, expressive thinking.

Valuing creativity as an important aspect of children's intellectual, social, and emotional growth is an essential characteristic of a developmentally appropriate program. Most young children are born with a capacity for creative thinking. The environment in which they grow can either nurture or stifle this capacity. Since a basic goal of early childhood education is to enable children to take responsibility for their own learning, and since children attending school today will be faced with a variety of problems that their elders cannot even imagine, schools have a duty to help children maximize their creative thinking and problem-solving abilities. To carry out this responsibility, teachers need to understand the meaning of creativity and to consider thoughtfully all its ramifications.

Consider the following example. Paul, age four, is in the early representational stage of drawing and takes great pleasure in producing animals of various shapes and sizes. These animals almost always have a large, circular form that designates the eye. One day while drawing on a pad of notepaper that had a hole at the top for hanging it on the wall, Paul created one of his fantastic, imaginative animals, using the hole in the paper to represent the eye of the animal. (See Figure 1.) The drawing, although crude and elementary, represents an important aspect of Paul's intellectual development: the process of creative thinking—of establishing new

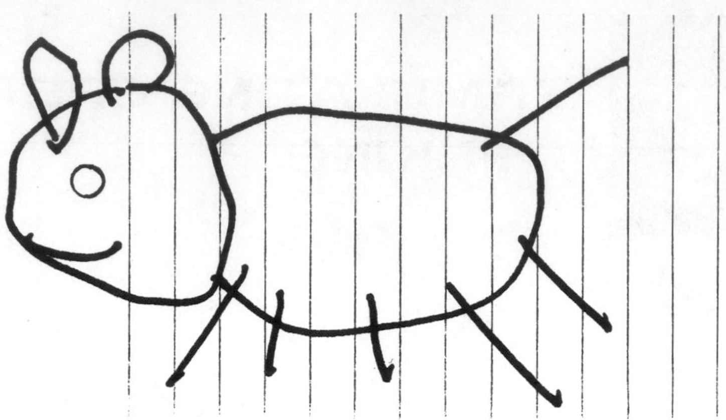

FIGURE 1

Paul's animal

relationships and trusting one's own impulses and ideas enough to invent a new and idiosyncratic product. What Paul did was to join two elements, previously unrelated, into a new conceptual whole that was uniquely his. He was able to imagine the hole in the paper, which had been intended for an entirely different purpose, as an eye and to join it with one of his representations of an animal. Paul's small act is of tremendous importance in helping us understand how young children naturally learn and integrate new information. This example stimulates our thinking about the nature of young children's creative ingenuity and how we can best guide it.

Defining creativity is a difficult task. What do we really mean when we speak of creativity and young children? Was Paul's act a genuinely creative act—or simply the naive meanderings of a small child stumbling upon possibilities that are new for him, though not for others? Is it appropriate to label young children's spontaneous or even planned productions as creative acts when the "novel" thinking that these products reveal has often been engaged in already by other children who are manipulating similar materials and ideas? How do we define creativity, and what are its components?

CHAPTER 6 CREATIVITY: WHAT IT IS AND WHY IT IS IMPORTANT

Building on Maslow's (1963) concept of primary and secondary creativity, this chapter differentiates between the creative capacity all people have (**primary creativity**) and the special capability (**secondary creativity**) that one often associates with those who are highly creative in a particular domain. This distinction is important because it makes apparent the necessity for teachers to view creativity as an essential part of the cognitive development of all children, not just something for the talented few. The chapter also makes the distinction between creativity—that is, the capacity to invent, transform, and reorganize—and expressivity—the capacity to give tangible form to one's feelings. In nurturing both creativity and expressivity, the teacher plays a pivotal role.

This chapter explains the term *creativity* and highlights developmental stages through which the child's creative capacity evolves. It provides examples of how creativity is manifested in the classroom and how it can pervade the entire curriculum of the preschool, kindergarten, and primary grades. For the teacher looking for ideas to use with children, for the program coordinator interested in the process of formative evaluation, and for the educator seeking convincing arguments to explain the value of creativity to other educators, parents, and the community, this chapter is a valuable resource.

Toward a Definition of Creativity

Friedrich Froebel, known as the father of the kindergarten, compared the child's creative work with that of an artist. In his enlightened treatise on education, he emphasized that the child's spirit is reflected in what the child creates and suggested that true education must nurture creativity (Froebel, 1987). Creativity is generally defined as the capacity to bring something new into existence, or the ability to relate ideas or materials that were previously unrelated. The notion of finding new relationships among elements that were previously unrelated is central to the concept. However, various theorists have attempted to define the term in different ways. The following additional characteristics of creativity are generally identified as (Barron & Harrington, 1981; Renzulli, Ford, Smith, & Renzulli, 1976):

- the tendency to provide unique responses
- the capacity to generate multiple solutions to problems (fluency)
- the ability to think metaphorically or analogically, as well as logically, and to make numerous and unusual associations
- independence of thought and action; judgments are often unconventional or even outlandish
- attraction to complexity; rejection of common solutions
- uninhibited expressiveness and spontaneity
- tolerance for ambiguity
- willingness to take risks

Creativity is the capacity for divergent thinking—thinking that is open-ended, fluid, and unexpected, as contrasted with convergent thinking, which is more linear, predictable, and governed by established precepts (Guilford, 1967). Both convergent and divergent thinking are important. Indeed, the argument is often made that divergent thinking is dependent upon convergent thinking—that they are two complementary processes, in that one cannot invent without having a knowledge base on which to build.

Sternberg (1985) maintains that intelligence is fundamental to the creative process, although it is not a "sufficient condition for creativity." He maintains that creativity is

> due largely to the insightful use of knowledge-acquisition components and to extremely sensitive feedback between the various kinds of [intellectual] components. . . . Thus, for creativity to be shown, a high level of functioning

FIGURE 6-1

Douglas's picture reveals how much the eight-year-old knows about his subject. To launch the rocket that appears on the upper left, scientists are using computers, tape recorders, and other electronic equipment to coordinate their efforts. The picture reveals Douglas' understanding of how various categories of workers join efforts on behalf of a collective accomplishment. The man in the upper right corner is being tested for heat endurance! Douglas's picture demonstrates how divergent thinking (creative thought) is dependent on convergent thinking (knowledge about a particular set of events). Collection of Sylvia G. Feinburg

> in the knowledge-acquisition components would seem to be necessary. These high levels of functioning are not in themselves sufficient for creativity to occur, however, since a sophisticated knowledge base does not guarantee that the knowledge base will be used with sophisticated feedback between kinds of components. (pp. 125–126)

This suggests that the expression of creative thinking depends on the individual's general intelligence and knowledge and that the capacity to function creatively does not operate in a vacuum. On the other hand, high intelligence and accumulated knowledge do not in and of themselves guarantee high levels of creative functioning.

The distinction between imagination and creativity is important. Imagination consists of fantasizing and inventing in one's mind, of considering new or old possibilities. But until these mental meanderings are translated into tangible products that can be seen, touched, heard, or tasted, they cannot be thought of as creative acts. Creativity involves actualizing images, ideas, and mental ruminations in some form, leaving a concrete product for another to experience. The product may take the form of a story, an artwork, an experiment, or a creative solution to a problem either personal or interpersonal in nature. The following is one interesting perspective on defining creativity:

> Thinking cannot be made clear till it has had expression. We must write, or speak, or act our thoughts, or they will remain in half torpid form. Our feelings must have expression, or they will be as clouds, which, till they descend in rain, will never bring up fruit or flower. So it is with all the inward feelings; expression gives them development. Thought is the blossom; language the opening bud; action the fruit behind it. (Edwards, 1955, quoting H. W. Beecher)

Primary and Secondary Creativity

Some would argue that children are incapable of producing genuinely creative products, that this is only possible for a few gifted, highly proficient adults who possess extensive knowledge within a given domain, and that unless one is able to transcend the accumulated knowledge of this domain, creativity is not truly being demonstrated. However, Paul's act of creating an animal, described in the beginning of this part of the text, is compelling, demanding that we acknowledge the innovative thinking it represents. Maslow (1963) attempted to illuminate the task of defining creativity by identifying two forms: primary and secondary creativity. Primary creativity is involved in acts such as Paul's, when an individual uncovers new relationships that represent novel thinking for the producer, even though such acts may not appear unique to others. Secondary creativity identifies acts that represent a high level of sophistication within a given field and transcend what already exists; secondary creativity breaks the bounds of the culture's accumulated knowledge and represents genuine innovation.

This distinction is helpful, since it enables us to put aside those theoretical arguments that rely on the product's inherent uniqueness as a basis for defining creativity (secondary creativity), allowing us to focus on the more basic and central issue of primary creativity. Children use primary creativity to organize, invent, and express ideas in their own unique ways in order to increase their understanding of the world in which they live and to give expressive form to key experiences. It is primary creativity that concerns us when we consider the endeavors of the young child.

People tend to dichotomize creativity—to think of it as something either present or absent in a given child. This is a limited view of a particular dimension of intelligence, which exists on a continuum. All of us possess the ability to function creatively in some manner. How well we utilize and develop this capacity is, like everything else, a function of basic genetic endowment interacting with environmental circumstances. An environment that values and nourishes creative potential is critical, not just for gifted children, but for all children. The capacities to invent, reorganize, consider alternatives, and raise questions are competencies that are fundamental to all intellectual and educational objectives.

Creativity Throughout the Curriculum

Some people tend to associate the term *creativity* with the arts, using it to identify children who are particularly gifted in drawing and painting, music, dramatic arts, or dance. People commonly associate the creative process with the arts, which make particular use of imagination and expressivity. However, this view is a limited one, since it relates a fundamental cognitive capacity to its expression within a given domain. Many artists are not necessarily highly creative; they are simply skillful in a given medium. Conversely, many people who are not artistic are nevertheless highly original and inventive in much of what they undertake. Although an individual may be able to express him- or herself in a particular medium better than another individual can, creativity can reveal itself across a wide range of activities, whether mathematical, verbal, literary, scientific, or even interpersonal in nature. The capacity to function creatively transcends a given means of expression and applies to every area of human endeavor.

For very young children, however, creative activity is closely associated with play, since process and product are often so inextricably intertwined. The three- or four-year-old child, for example, does not always set about the task of making something tangible that will have significance beyond the time of its creation. Spontaneous inventions of props for dramatic play, drawings and paintings that become the field for exploring certain ideas, and stories that are generated to involve others in social events are all examples of the way actions and products may become fused. Young children pay only cursory attention to products as ends in and of themselves; the major function of products is to symbolize and represent elements that are part of fantasy play, thereby making those elements more real. Hendrick (1988) makes the point that young children express their creativity through two dominant mechanisms: (1) the unusual use of familiar materials and equipment, and (2) role-playing and imaginative play.

As children move into the kindergarten and primary grades, the product increases in importance, and they are able to appreciate its integrity as a separate and independent entity. However, the appreciation that the four-year-old feels toward a product—for instance, a typewriter made out of household junk—is on an entirely different level from that of the seven-year-old. The younger child may

For young children creativity may be expressed through role playing and imaginative play. Ideas are transformed into expressive events.
© Elizabeth Crews

take pleasure in the object, but only as an extension of him- or herself and as clear evidence of having produced something that adults may admire and value. The older child, however, can distinguish process from product and appreciate the object as a separate, tangible thing, worthy of reflection and evaluation.

Three Ways Creativity is Expressed

Creativity may be expressed in any of three ways in young children.

1. *Novel for the individual:* A child may express an idea or create a product that represents a creative leap for him or her, even though others around might be readily able to do the same thing with ease. The accomplishment is thus new to the maker.

FIGURE 6-2

This extraordinary drawing executed by Valerie, a kindergarten child, is an example of a child demonstrating unusual intellectual and creative ability in a particular domain—art. Valerie's picture, entitled "The Battle Between the Wolves and the Poodle Dogs," engaged her in rich fantasy play. The picture illustrates Valerie's outstanding ability to represent reality, capture motion and detail, and integrate many complex elements into a coherent spatial whole. Valerie also reveals great sensitivity for line, shape, and bilateral symmetry. Courtesy of Valerie A. Gruber

2. *Originality within the expected developmental stage:* A child may generate an idea or product that is not necessarily developmentally unusual in terms of skill or cognitive level, but reflects originality and freshness of vision that transcends what is typical of other children. The child's response is unique, unpredictable.

3. *Extraordinary competence within a domain:* A child may demonstrate extraordinary competence and originality in a given domain that enables him or her to go well beyond what is typical of the child's age group. Giftedness is then unambiguously present. (See Figure 6.2.)

The Importance of Creativity

Intellectual Development

Creativity is a critical component in children's intellectual development. In her seminal article "The Having of Wonderful Ideas," Eleanor Duckworth (1987) strengthened the argument for the importance of teachers encouraging children's creativity. Duckworth argued persuasively that teachers should respect the notion of creativity as a central objective in education, maintaining that creativity is, in fact, the cornerstone of all intellectual activity. Through the process of raising hypotheses, wondering "what would happen if . . . ," and building on hunches, children are best able to examine and come to grips with new and confounding information, whatever the particular subject matter.

Duckworth suggests that the ideas that children come up with when they are at work and play—the questions they ask, the creations that they construct, the problems that they pose for themselves—are the crucial basis on which children construct knowledge. Without this kind of meaningful activity in school, we run the risk of teaching children isolated skills and information that are not internalized in any significant way. Developmental education by its very nature demands that we value and facilitate the child's creative impulses, for creativity is one of our most powerful learning instruments.

The relationship between creativity and learning is difficult to perceive without understanding how thinking develops in young children. Children in the preoperational stage of cognitive development (usually ages two to six years) are egocentric in their thinking. When we speak of young children as being cognitively egocentric, we do not mean that they are selfish and unconcerned with others; rather, we mean that they are unable to think about things from another person's vantage point. Young children are highly subjective in processing experiences and ideas and consider information in terms of how it impacts upon them personally. Their play, drawings, dictated stories, block constructions, and other invented products are clear attempts not only to concretize concepts, but also to establish connections among disparate events. Sutton-Smith (1971) maintained that play increases the child's "repertoire of responses" and provides opportunities to produce more than one answer to a problem. When a child reaches for two sticks and other salvage scraps to fashion himself an airplane, this attempt goes beyond artistic production in the narrow sense of the word. The act is an effort to integrate what is known about planes and what they need to fly and to symbolize these abstract ideas in a direct and personally meaningful way.

"I still don't have all the answers, but I'm beginning to ask the right questions."

Drawing by Lorenz; copyright ©1989 New Yorker Magazine, Inc.

Classrooms that offer children ample opportunities for creative expression in a wide variety of media are offering them the tools they need to clarify understanding of fundamental concepts. Creative activity enhances intellectual development.

Self-Esteem and Personal Power

When teachers value children's ideas, and children are made to feel that their suggestions and the products they create are valued and respected, there is the important dividend of strengthening children's self-esteem and confidence. Children see school as relevant and meaningful, a place where their insights and interests are reinforced and made central to the learning situation. When children's contributions are given support and recognition, the dividends are compounded exponentially. Ideas that are reinforced build confidence—and confidence builds more ideas. (See Figure 6.3.)

No greater contribution to children's self-esteem can be made than to enable them to feel that the issues they choose to address, and the ways they seek to address those issues, are both valued and facilitated by key adults. Consider the child who is having difficulty with fine motor skills and feels hampered by how

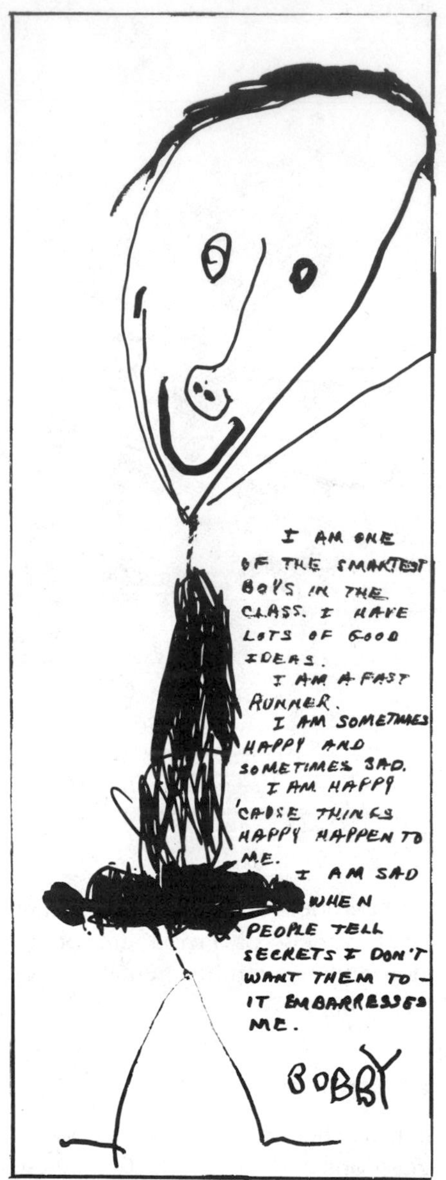

FIGURE 6-3

Bobby, a kindergarten child, responds to his teacher's request to "make a picture of yourself and share what kind of a person you are; tell about those things that make you special." Bobby is a gifted child intellectually but has some problems socially. He reveals how much he understands about himself and how much he values his own creative ability.

slowly he is able to write when creating a story about which he is very excited and has many ideas to communicate. If the teacher suggests that he talks the story into a tape recorder and then have help getting it transcribed into print at a later time, she is letting him know that she values his active participation in his own learning. The teacher exercises a powerful instructional technique when she trusts the learner to identify the methods by which he or she can most optimally learn.

Expressivity and Affective Development

Self-esteem is highly influential in shaping affective development. In affective development, as in cognitive development, expressivity plays an important role. Young children struggle to find meaning in experiences not only from an intellectual vantage point, but from a social-emotional vantage point as well. The world is complex. It places many demands on the child, all of which must be examined and processed in concrete ways. Children need to address such crucial feelings as love, anger, jealousy, power, fear, and aspirations for the future. Children spontaneously attempt to deal with these issues in their play—when, for example, they pretend to "punish the baby" in the doll corner, become the "boss" on the jungle gym and decide who can come and go, squish play dough into monsterlike forms and try to scare a friend, or create a mock birthday party and decide who is invited and who is uninvited. Children who function creatively are in a better position to see more possibilities in terms of human interactions. Hence, they are in a better position to gain an understanding of their own behavior, as well as that of others.

However, there is much that teachers can do to enhance expressivity and affective development. Teachers can present motivations that help children to identify and express their feelings about key dynamic issues. These activities can be integrated into the curriculum in an interdisciplinary way.

The following are examples of different kinds of lessons valuable for children from kindergarten through the primary grades. The examples presented here involve art and language arts, but the same themes could be addressed in dramatics, music, dance, or social studies.

- *Dreams:* "What is a dream? Is it real? Does it really happen? Can you remember a particular dream? What are the images that you recall? How did the dream make you feel?" (Children may use paint and large paper, written narratives—see Figure 6.4.)

For example, in one lesson a kindergarten teacher elicited a discussion about dreams and recorded children's perceptions of what dreams are. The following statements are direct quotes from individual children. Note the children's struggle to separate reality from fantasy and to use language that clarifies this complex idea.

> "Something you think about, then you see pictures in your head."
> "It all happens at night."
> "If it's a horse it doesn't come to you."
> "It's something you think when you're asleep."
> "Some dreams are dangerous especially when they come true."
> "Sometimes I dream of food and I wake up and try to grab it."

FIGURE 6-4

During activity time small groups of children were encouraged to paint about dreams. One kindergarten child painted this vibrant menacing monster and dictated this story: "There is a big lion trying to come into the house. If he catches me he'll take me home and eat me for dinner. First, he'll chop off my head, so I won't know he's going to eat me for dinner." Collection of Sylvia G. Feinburg

"When you're sleeping you imagine in the night and it really isn't happening, you just think about it in the night."
"You have to watch it."
"Sometimes it is a nightmare."
"Sometimes I cry 'cause a monster chases me."
"Once I saw a TV on the wall, but I couldn't hear anything."
"Sometimes I don't go to sleep . . . a dream comes . . . oh yes, a daydream."
"Boy, I've had daymares—they're worse!"

◗ *Anger:* "What does it mean to be angry? What do you do when you get angry? What do other people do? What are good ways to express anger? Ways that aren't too good? Tell us about a time when you were angry." (Children may use chalk, paint, large paper, written narrative.)

◗ *Power and authority:* Children are given small foil sheriff badges, paste, large paper, and crayons. "You can put this badge anywhere you want on your paper and use it as part of your picture. What does it make you think about? What idea does it suggest? You can change its shape if you want." Most children will create sheriffs in various authority-based situations.

Lessons such as these require that children exercise their creative capabilities in order to address important social-emotional issues. Creativity and self-expression are inextricably intertwined, each one enhancing the other. Children exercise their creativity when they give form to images and words that have personal significance. Genuine self-expression by definition involves creativity. Children who exercise their creative capacities to express meaningful social-emotional ideas are empowered to direct their own intellectual growth.

To sum up the reasons creative activity is important for young children:

1. Since play and other concrete activities are the means children use to clarify concepts and assimilate disparate information, creative activity is central to concept formation and intellectual development.
2. Children gain self-confidence and self-esteem when the products they create are given validity by significant adults. Hence, creative activity empowers children.
3. Creative activities offer children an important avenue for expressing social and emotional issues. Expression is enhanced when the child has the opportunity to deal with issues that are personally meaningful.
4. When creativity is a central part of the school curriculum, children learn that knowledge and intellectual power are the result of raising key questions, taking risks, being innovative, and solving problems.
5. The potential for success in a given undertaking is enhanced when creativity is involved, since imagination contributes to the quality of a given piece of work. Products that are original and expressive are more apt to achieve aesthetic and conceptual success, as contrasted with those that are trite, banal, and repetitive.

Developmental and Educational Issues

People commonly admire the creative products of preschool and kindergarten children. All kinds of positive qualities are attributed to their work. The work is often characterized as fresh, imaginative, independent, and free of stereotypic thinking. Teachers and parents alike extol the creative power and products of the very young, commending the personal vitality that they represent.

By contrast, we are less responsive to the work of first-, second-, and third-grade children. Their work is often described as hackneyed, lacking in expressive zeal, repetitious, and highly conforming. Teachers and parents often lament the apparent diminishing creative capacities of elementary school children. One hears them say about a child, "She used to be so imaginative and had so many interesting, original ideas, and now she just makes the same trite things over and over again. I can't figure out what happened!"

This is particularly the case in the area of art. Artist and educator alike acknowledge that the artistic work of preschool and kindergarten children is far more powerful than that of the older child. This phenomenon of apparently diminishing creativity is in fact occurring in all the child's pursuits. In the case of art it is made more readily apparent because drawings and paintings provide us with direct, concrete evidence of the nature of the child's thought. Furthermore, since these products may be saved over time, we are able to make comparisons and see the changes that are taking place—something more difficult to do in areas such as language, spontaneous play, and block building, where the products are more elusive and less permanent. Not only is a drawing clear documentation of how the child organizes his or her thinking; but since it is readily preserved, it can substantiate adults' perceptions of changes in a child.

A number of issues, both educational and developmental in nature, contribute to this shift in children's work. Schooling changes as the child grows older. Skills and competencies of a universal nature are of key importance on the elementary level, in contrast to preschool and kindergarten, where the spontaneous, the unique, and fantasy play are highly valued. Preschool teachers value and expect different things from children than elementary school teachers do. Creativity, individuality, and self-expression are more apt to be honored in most preschools than in most elementary schools. Teachers of the early elementary grades feel heavy pressure to teach basic skills in narrow ways, and teacher performance is often evaluated in terms of how well children master certain expectations. Consequently, many teachers tend to use repetitive worksheets and copy work, allocating little time for imaginative, expressive activities. This significant shift in many classrooms has tremendous negative impact on the older child's confidence to produce original, creative work across the curriculum.

On the other hand, it is naive to see changes in a child's work as simply a consequence of schooling, without also addressing the crucial issue of development. The cognitive shift in thinking that occurs as children move from preschool into the elementary school years is also highly influential. Cognition and the culture of school instruction are interacting in a significant way.

Children's art—like all their products—changes as children grow older, because children's thinking is changing. The productions of three-, four-, and five-year-olds, which appear fresh, direct, whimsical, and original, are in fact the repercussions of preoperational thinking. Preoperational thinking is characterized by such qualities as egocentrism, an inability to assume another's point of view, and difficulty in considering multiple aspects of a situation at a given moment. These cognitive limitations, coupled with the child's limited motoric skills and inability to control the media, result in products that we may find compelling but that are, in the final analysis, the result of intellectual naiveté. This is not to suggest that preschoolers are incapable of producing original, expressive work, but rather that their work by its very nature is more readily predisposed toward these qualities.

As children move into their elementary school years and toward what Piaget refers to as "the period of concrete operations," they become more rational and logical and better able to classify, categorize, and deal with rule systems. The capacity to engage in **perspective taking**—to consider a given problem or situation in terms of how others might view it—emerges. These developing capabilities represent new power and potential for children and render them more capable and receptive to a wide range of learnings. On the other hand, as children become less egocentric and better able to internalize procedures and systems that are part of the culture, they are more vulnerable to influence. Second- or third-grade children are far more concerned with other children's work, how they express ideas and solve problems, than preschool children, who pursue their own reactions to a given situation in relative intellectual isolation. Older children are more eager to imitate, copy, and demonstrate their understanding of "the right way" to accomplish a given task; the right way, more often than not, is the way everyone else is doing it!

It is a limited view, however, that sees the elementary school child's predisposition toward imitation and conformity as a fixed negative consequence of intellectual growth. The challenge for us is to help the child to utilize these new capabilities, to observe and learn from others in convergent ways and at the same time retain the capacity to function divergently and be in charge of his or her own creative powers. How children are guided through the transition from egocentrism to more objective thought is of crucial importance and demands tremendous sensitivity and skill on the part of the teacher.

Developmental Stages and Art

Children's artistic expression is a powerful tool to examine the expression of creativity on a developmental continuum. For that reason, we are specifically identifying the domain of art for documentation. It is an important area for teachers to be aware of, since art is a common means through which children initially approach creative expression and contributes to their perceptions of themselves as creative thinkers. Understanding the progression that children move through in art, and its accompanying pedagogical implications, is of key importance for the teacher of young children and is generalizable to many aspects of the curriculum. Note in the discussion of stages that follows these three points:

1. The age levels identified here are presented as a guide only. Individual differences are often significant.
2. Discussion centers on two-dimensional work. Three-dimensional work follows a similar progression.
3. The move toward representationalism is being emphasized, primarily because it assumes particular importance for the child and should be understood by the adult. This is not to suggest, however, that nonobjective and fantasy-related work is not also important to the child.

Stage One: Eighteen Months to Three Years, Eight Months

During this period, children's sensorimotor activity in art results in scribbling, initially quite randomly and then with increasing control. What the adult may think is nothing of great importance is in fact the child's vigorous campaign to achieve power over markmaking and the use of tools. In scribbling, as in much of the toddler's activity, the child finds out the repercussions of certain actions, testing what happens if he or she does one thing as opposed to another.

Crude, ambiguous strokes eventually give way to the emergence of the circle, radial and sun forms, and other simple linear configurations. Rhoda Kellogg (1969) exhaustively documented these forms, providing a meaningful way for educators to examine the natural progression through which all children move in building a vocabulary of nonobjective visual forms.

As development progresses, the child's increased capacity to function symbolically joins with form-making ability. The three-year-old begins to name lines and forms, first somewhat arbitrarily and later with deference to their visual relationship to ideas. This process leads to deliberate representational work. The mean age for the tadpole man, so readily associated with the preschool child, is three years, ten months (Kellogg, 1969). Children continue to work both nonobjectively and representationally throughout the third and early part of the fourth year, since both processes—constructing forms and identifying ideas—are of major importance.

Stage Two: Three Years, Six Months to Six Years

By the early part of their fourth year, most children who have been given the opportunity to work with art materials are able to make forms that are symbolic in nature. Common subject matter includes things near and dear in daily life—mommy, daddy, babies, houses, animals, cars and trucks, and trees—and are clearly related to the nonobjective forms children have been busy gaining control over during preceding months. Early representational drawing reflects preoperational thinking and reveals qualities generally associated with that stage of development. Hence, egocentrism, the inability to deal with multiple aspects of a situation simultaneously, a preoccupation with before-the-eye reality, and other comparable cognitive functions are readily apparent.

This stage of development manifests itself in artwork in the following ways:

1. The ways basic concepts, such as people, houses, and cars, are represented are subject to considerable variation. The child does not rigidly repeat a given formula for representing an idea; a good deal of flexibility is revealed.

2. What adults might consider basic is often omitted. The child may, for example, leave hair, ears, and hands out of a drawing of a person. Children include the parts that are central to their thinking at the moment and are unable to include everything that they know. Omissions, exaggerations of size and shape, and economy of expression all prevail. It is not uncommon, for example, for a person to be drawn larger than a house, or for one person in a picture to have a pair of ears and a full head of hair, while another has neither.

3. The notion that color is used to depict reality is not of paramount importance. The child may flirt with the idea, but is more apt to use color for aesthetic and emotional purposes.

4. Sun forms, mandalas, and other basic configurations are still the foundation upon which reality is constructed.

5. Representation of space is highly subjective. Elements float randomly across the picture field, with little objective relationship to one another. Gradually, the child begins to utilize the baseline at the bottom of the paper and aligns the various elements on a horizontal-vertical grid. By late kindergarten, most children show evidence of this kind of thinking.

6. The narrative is a significant aspect of production. The child may engage in labeling and storytelling while in the process of making art, or do so after the

FIGURE 6-5

Katja, age four, makes four figures and labels them: children, daddy, mommy, children. Notice that some have mouths; some do not. Details and consistency are not important. After having completed the figures Katja wraps a line around them, at first perhaps as an aesthetic act, trying to relate them visually. Once they are enclosed, she fabricates a rich story, which the teacher records: "They're in a cage 'cause they're bad people. They push people down. The bad people put them in. The nice people put them in jail, but he forgot he mustn't put them in jail." Collection of Sylvia G. Feinburg

picture has been completed. Thoughts are translated into both symbol systems—language and art—in a collaborative, interactive way. Telling about a picture to a teacher who will write down what the child has to say becomes a joyful process, which helps confirm the importance of graphic communication.

Changes in the capacity to produce representational work are dramatic during this brief period. A kindergarten-aged child's work is for the most part comprehensible to the adult and reflects a more predictable systematic approach to working than a four-year-old's work does.

Teachers commonly ask children to draw a person, using the product as a basis for evaluating intellectual and academic competence. This process of using a single drawing can be very misleading, since during the preoperational period there is much variation from drawing to drawing. Although cognition is reflected in the way children create pictures, many variables are at work, including how comfortable the child feels at the task, how much experience he or she has had with drawing and the media involved, and the flexible nature of drawing at this stage of development. Teachers who want to use art products as an evaluation tool are advised to collect a number of drawings over a two- to three-week period and to make their inferences on this basis.

Stage Three: Six to Eight Years

After age six, most children are better able to apply rule systems and logical thinking to their representational work. The child's growing ability to classify, categorize, and consider simple mathematical relationships reveals itself in drawings that are more reality-bound.

Children's artwork at this stage manifests the following characteristics:

1. Children are more apt to be consistent in the way they construct basic forms, such as people, trees, and houses. Their artwork shows less variability and change than the work of younger children. Gross distortions of size and shape are less apparent; work is more "correct." Color-object relationships assume greater importance.

2. Spatial challenges are more standardized at this stage. Although children have not yet discovered the plane, the horizontal-vertical grid is well respected. First- and second-graders' work reflects notions of what is up high (the sky or the ceiling), and what is down low (the grass or the floor). Elements are lined up with some degree of respect for the relationships between larger and smaller things, what is inside as opposed to outside, and so on. More complex spatial challenges are being addressed as well, including occlusion (overlapping of elements), the use of double baselines to imply depth, turning a corner, and circularity.

3. Children are more predisposed to filling in the whole picture. Children respect completeness and appreciate fine motor skills, sometimes demonstrated by the willingness to work long and hard to finish and make a piece of work orderly.

4. Children this age are better able to "take the perspective of the other" (Piaget). They are thus concerned with how other people create and view things and are more likely to make drawings that others understand. Socially acceptable ways of producing common elements are held in high regard. The child takes great pleasure in the universality of symbol-making—not hard to understand when one considers the emphasis during this period on mastering symbols in other contexts, during particularly reading and writing.

The movement toward reality is complex and difficult; all these representational challenges are far from mastered during the initial stage of concrete operations. During this stage children do, however, become better able to recognize and produce more reality-bound pictures; children struggle to increase this capacity. During the early elementary school years, children give great importance to representing reality in clear and unambiguous ways; color accuracy, size relationships, and attention to detail are all considerations. Creative drive is often focused in this direction of artwork, but certainly not exclusively.

FIGURE 6-6

"The Twins' Christmas," a crayon drawing produced by a second-grade girl, illustrates well the nature of thought at this stage of development—the early stage of concrete operational thought. She has established a set of rules for representing key ideas and reveals a concern for logic and clear interrelatedness of the many elements involved. The twins, both the same size, stand next to mother and the brother (who stands on the chair) and are placed with concern for correct size relationships. Key ideas are placed on the bottom of the page; windows and wall decorations are placed above. Part of the fireplace and other people are to the left and right sides, showing the child's understanding of continuity beyond the paper edges.
Collection of Sylvia G. Feinburg

The Teacher's Role

Determiner of Classroom Climate

The teacher is a critical figure in designing a classroom that fosters a high level of creative activity in children. What the teacher says and does, the ways he or she praises and reinforces some behaviors and attempts to extinguish others, are naturally central to children's growing perceptions of what is valued in the area of work and productivity. The adult must be deliberate in letting children know that imaginative, independent thinking will be reinforced in the classroom. Every mechanism should be used to develop an appreciation of this important competence.

Children learn quickly whether adults take actions on behalf of what they support in words. In addition to communicating the importance of creative activity verbally, when teachers follow up on their support—by getting additional materials, making small shifts in the environment, or remembering at a later date that particular class members had suggested certain ideas—children learn in concrete ways that words are not hollow. It is unrealistic to expect that a teacher can always build on the many contributions children make within a busy and active classroom. The teacher must be selective and discriminating in choosing what to extend.

Many teachers believe that the way to enable creativity to take place is to simply provide a rich environment and basic materials and let children determine for themselves what will transpire. This is a common misconception. The teacher is not merely a passive observer who is casually supportive and laissez-faire in approach. Of course, with very young children, teachers may often take this approach, since bold exploration is a natural part of early development; but this is not to suggest that the teacher's role is a minimal one—far from it! The teacher is an active agent, the catalyst who sets the stage for what Duckworth (1987) called "the having of wonderful ideas": "When children are afforded the occasions to be intellectually creative, by being offered subject matter to be concerned about intellectually and by having their ideas accepted, then not only do they learn about the world, but their general intellectual ability is stimulated as well." Children need the teacher to be strategically aware of the many environmental and motivational techniques that enhance and stimulate creative activity.

Creative Force

These functions require that the adult is able to operate creatively, that he or she remains flexible, aware, and open to alternative strategies in teaching children. The teacher who approaches divergent tasks with ease obviously is in a better position to encourage this kind of thinking in the classroom than the teacher who is narrowly bound to established procedures. Like all intellectual undertakings, however, creativity can grow and develop when we make a firm commitment to it as an important objective.

At the same time that we recognize that the teacher's creativity is central to the process of stimulating it in others, we must be aware of the distinction between the teacher exercising his or her own creativity, as opposed to stimulating creativity in children. For example, a teacher who comes up with an interesting and novel way of designing a worksheet or art activity that demands that the children imitate it in a convergent way, may be demonstrating his or her own creativity, but not encouraging it in children. If, on the other hand, the adult utilizes his or her own creativity on behalf of generating dynamic opportunities for children to exercise their imaginative, expressive capabilities, then something very important is occurring.

The central role for the adult is to stimulate children themselves to think and perform in original and personally meaningful ways. The teacher will exercise his or her own creativity on behalf of helping children to arrive at responses that represent their own independent thinking. The teacher may guide and limit the range of options in terms of the media and the nature of the task, and provide specific motivational input, but it is the child who must ultimately determine the specific form that the product takes.

To review, the teacher's role involves fulfilling the following functions:

1. The teacher observes and records individual and group behavior to determine cognitive and social-emotional factors that are influencing performance and interest levels, and uses this information to design learning activities. Observing individual children with sufficient depth to determine what objectives they are establishing for themselves is also important. What children set out to do in pursuit of creative undertakings is not always crystal clear to the adult.

2. The teacher shapes the physical environment in order to stimulate and facilitate innovative pursuit. This includes collecting and organizing a wide range of materials and equipment and making them available in an orderly and systematic manner. The teacher must see the potential in materials for helping children to deal with a range of concepts.

3. The teacher provides a psychological environment that communicates clearly and unambiguously the positive value of asking questions, generating hypotheses, taking risks, and introducing original and personally meaningful products and responses.

4. The teacher finds the balance between leaving children free to pursue their ideas in some situations and taking clear initiative in other cases by directly provoking thinking—by suggesting simple alternatives, asking provocative questions, and guiding the child's thinking in decisive ways. The adult must recognize that knowledge and information feed creative pursuit and should not be reluctant to deliver these elements when the circumstances so dictate.

5. The teacher recognizes that creative opportunities must be made available across the full range of the curriculum, not reserved solely for the expressive arts. The teacher will want to find opportunities across all curriculum domains for encouraging original thought.

Summary

In summary, the enhancement of creativity is a key characteristic of the cognitive-developmental model. This chapter has presented the theoretical background for understanding what creativity is, how it is demonstrated naturally, and how it can be nurtured in all areas of the curriculum. The chapter has provided insight into the definition of creativity, Maslow's concepts of primary and secondary creativity, Guilford's emphasis on divergence, and Sternberg's clarification of the relationship between intelligence and creative thought. Learning how creativity is expressed enhances one's ability to observe in the creative domain. This delineation of the teacher's role in fostering creative development sets the stage for the operational characteristics that form the basis for the next chapter.

CHAPTER 7

PROMOTING CREATIVE DEVELOPMENT: OPERATIONAL CHARACTERISTICS

- *The Teacher Reinforces Creativity*
- *The Teacher Organizes the Physical Environment to Promote Creativity*
- *The Teacher Designs the Curriculum and Motivates Children to Extend Creative Thinking*
- *Deterrents to Fostering Creativity*
- *Summary*

This chapter elaborates on the many ways creativity manifests itself in the early childhood classroom.* The subtleties of teacher behavior and leadership that contribute to the development of creativity in children are described, that is, the characteristics of teaching behaviors that reinforce creativity, setting up the physical environment, and designing curriculum experiences that motivate and extend creative thinking. Each characteristic is amplified and operationalized in order to make vivid how they are expressed across the developmental continuum. Also identified are teaching behaviors that serve as deterrents to the creative process.

The Teacher Reinforces Creativity

Acknowledging Children's Contributions

The teacher is alert for situations in which to acknowledge an individual child's contribution for a particular idea or product. The teacher validates the unique—and sometimes even the outrageous—in responding to children's contributions, in order to let them know that it is all right to move beyond the common and predictable. (Occasionally, children will suggest things that are socially unacceptable or in poor taste; obviously, the teacher must exercise judgment in setting limits.) Examples of situations in which the teacher reinforces creativity by acknowledging individual contributions follow.

- A kindergarten teacher reinforces a child's novel juxtaposition of two unrelated materials: "Using that old telephone cord as part of the pulley that you and Jeannie are making was an interesting solution. Good for you."
- A three-year-old uses a boot as a puppet by turning it upside down, putting her hand inside it to simulate an animal head. The teacher encourages her to share it at group time.
- A first grader insists at show-and-tell that dinosaurs are still alive and that he thinks one lives in the center of town. Children begin to tease and ridicule him. The teacher takes the statement seriously and initiates discussion about whether or not it is possible. She seeks both confirming and contradictory feedback.
- During an art lesson in which children are drawing and writing about imaginative creatures, the teacher makes the following comments to individuals: "You seem to be unstuck; the ideas are just flowing." "You have this amazing way of phrasing things; you put it so clearly and beautifully. It opens up the whole scene for me." "Do you want to tell me what your thought was?" "I enjoy those little details over here."

Learning from Mistakes

The teacher helps children understand that mistakes and small accidents connected with one's work can be capitalized on and turned to advantage. Examples follow.

* The classroom evaluation guide, Form D, in Chapter 11 relates to this chapter.

◗ A kindergartner's painting is drying, and another painting placed on top becomes attached to it. When they are separated, several small scraps of construction paper adhere to the painting. The child becomes upset. The teacher explains that the child has the option of painting those scraps into the painting or removing them, and says that unexpected things often provide us with new opportunities.

◗ A third-grade teacher explains the benefits of understanding errors. In math, she encourages children to look at their own and others' mistakes and to study and analyze what produced these errors, and what can be learned from them.

◗ A kindergartner is painting at an easel and attempts to paint eyes on a face with too much paint on the brush. Eyes drip down the paper, ruining the child's objective; she becomes frustrated. The teacher explains the potential to turn the painting into something else entirely at the same time that she demonstrates a brush technique that will help the child gain control over the problem. The teacher talks about how painters have many options.

Communicating Respect for Differences

The teacher communicates that a child's work that deviates or is different in some way from what is typical is not to be demeaned or ridiculed. This principle applies to work that is less advanced, more advanced, or discrepant because it represents a somehow altered perspective. Respect for differences is continuously reinforced. Examples follow.

◗ A first grader who is making a book and illustrating it has poor fine motor skills and has difficulty maintaining the horizontal when writing words and drawing pictures. Elements float all over the pages, crudely organized, but rich in content; the book appears disorderly. When other children begin to tease him for being messy, the teacher addresses the matter directly, pointing out that there are differences in fine motor ability, as there are in all abilities, and reinforcing the notion that the child's ideas and thinking are the important thing.

◗ A second-grade boy makes a war picture that contains lots of soldiers, bombing, and shooting. One girl in the class announces that it's bad to make such pictures and ridicules the boy. The teacher emphasizes that in expressive work, people can decide for themselves what subject matter they want to address—that this is the boy's prerogative. The teacher reassures the girl about the controversial issue of the subject of war and suggests that they all talk about the matter in a group time.

Following Up on Children's Suggestions

When a child makes a viable contribution about something that can be done in the classroom, the teacher follows up on it, making certain the opportunity arises either immediately or in the near future. The teacher may need to gather specific equipment and materials.

◗ A four-year-old mentions that it would be good to be able to use the blocks outdoors in connection with a construction project in the sandbox. The teacher reinforces the child for thinking of the idea and solicits other children's opinions on how blocks could be moved outdoors in an efficient and orderly manner.

◗ When doing a mathematics game that involves rolling dice along with plus and minus cubes, a kindergartner recommends coding colored squares of flannel to represent subtraction and addition problems. The teacher follows up.

Encouraging Cooperative and Interactive Thinking

The teacher models how other people's ideas can strengthen one's own and encourages children to build on one another's thinking.

◗ After individual first graders share personal news during circle time, other children are invited to give feedback to specific individuals about something that interested them in their presentations.

◗ A small group of first graders are working on a project in the science area and share their concerns about how to move water from one location to another and how to make a siphon work. The teacher asks for ideas from the class about how to solve this problem.

◗ Three four-year-olds are upset because the toy telephone is missing from the dramatic play area. The group discusses what they could use to represent a telephone until the original one is found.

Sensitivity to Children's Ideas

The teacher is sensitive to the child's intentions and ownership of a particular set of ideas and does not impose a solution for achieving the child's objective. For example, suggestions about ways to solve a problem are offered as options, not as expectations to be fulfilled. Children are encouraged to value their own ideas.

◗ A third grader has written a vibrant story about dangerous circumstances, but does not know how to extricate the hero from his plight. He is determined to arrive at a superior solution and asks the teacher what it should be. The teacher avoids giving him a single answer and emphasizes the possible ways of thinking about the problem: Should it be based on fantasy or reality? Should it have to do with psychological or physical power? These categories help the child to think of a number of original possibilities.

◗ Second graders are doing bookkeeping on the profits and losses that have occurred in conjunction with a cookie-baking business they have set up in the school. One girl has a plan for a recordkeeping system that the teacher finds cumbersome but the group heartily supports. The teacher shares her own ideas, but allows the children to disagree and pursue their preference.

Destroying and Rebuilding as Part of the Creative Process

The teacher recognizes that destroying something is often done on behalf of rebuilding and reorganizing ideas. Examples of such positive uses of destruction follow.

- A kindergartner who is struggling with an unstable block structure breaks it in order to begin again. The teacher reinforces her for persevering and raises simple questions about how to achieve greater stability.
- Kindergarten boys are involved in constructing a village with papier-mâché and modeling clay. They have worked for a long time in making hills, valleys, caves, and forts. Eventually their play becomes combative, and they begin to attack the village with plasticene balls, simulating bombing by planes. They destroy a good part of the village and afterward set about the task of rebuilding it.

Valuing Process and Product

The teacher recognizes that the process can be as important as the product. The teacher occasionally accepts messiness, abandoned attempts, crude workmanship, and the like when they appear to be natural consequences of creative thinking.

- A second grader is trying to understand how football is played, including the notions of downs, yard lines, and so on. He creates a picture of a field with yard lines on a large piece of paper; makes a paper ball he can move across the field; plays the game on the surface, penetrating the paper to represent where a ball has been thrown or kicked; and draws crude circles to identify the movement of the players. When he is finished, the paper is torn and unattractive; but the activity was powerful in terms of helping him to understand the complex ideas of time and space involved.

Flexibility in Scheduling

The teacher is flexible in terms of time and schedule in order to enable certain meaningful pursuits to continue. The teacher adapts the program to be responsive to children's productivity.

- A kindergarten girl who has been making paper cutouts of houses has just discovered how to make them stand up without falling over. She is very excited, but it is the end of activity time. The teacher allows the child to continue experimenting with paper while group time begins. The girl joins the group later, when she feels finished.
- Kindergarten and first-grade children have been painting outdoors and become deeply involved in painting around each other's shadows, exploring changing sizes and shapes, and measuring the shadows. The teacher cancels the next scheduled activity and allows the painting to continue. An interdisciplinary unit grows out of this initial experimentation and goes on for a few weeks.

The Teacher Organizes the Physical Environment to Promote Creativity

Displaying Children's Original Work

Many examples of children's work are evident throughout the room, reflecting unique individual interpretations. The work on display represents a range of activities, not just the visual arts.

◗ Second graders' paintings and written descriptions of how a recent hurricane affected their houses is on a large bulletin board. Related objects, such as a broken shingle and an old drain spout, are displayed beneath the board.

◗ An elaborate block structure kindergartners have made is left standing and labeled to show the names of the designers.

◗ Books kindergarten and first-grade children have written are on shelves or tables for others to share. Children can "check out" books their classmates have made.

◗ A scientific contraption two four-year-olds have designed out of wire, styrofoam, and small hardware items is displayed on a countertop where other children can do "experiments."

Avoiding Adult Commercial Work Displays

Adult work of a commercial nature does not dominate bulletin boards and room decorations. Children's products are respectfully presented in instructional and decorative displays.

◗ Kindergartners have made suns, clouds, and rain for a weather chart used during group time. Four children create the chart alone after a lengthy discussion about what will work best.

◗ Second graders arrange autumn-related items they have found outside into a decorative display. Included are dried grasses and leaves, parts of old birds' nests, and twigs.

◗ The teacher mats and hangs four-year-olds' colorful paintings in an organized and respectful manner.

◗ Many graphs that kindergartners have created are displayed around the room. The graphs communicate information about such topics as how many people children have in their families, what color hair children have, and when their birthdays are. Child-made drawings and writing are combined with teacher-made graphs.

Availability of Materials

Basic art and construction materials are visible and readily accessible for children to use spontaneously, as well as in conjunction with teacher-initiated activities. Materials include crayons and markers, glue, rulers, scissors, collage scraps, paper punches, staplers, colored stickers and dots, and miscellaneous papers and cardboards of different sizes and shapes.

◗ First graders make math cards out of small pieces of cardboard and gummed dots as part of a teacher-initiated lesson in which they have to find ways to help a friend do subtraction.

◗ Kindergartners and first graders spontaneously make rainbow pictures with Magic Markers on tissue paper and delight in the bleeding quality that results. The teacher encourages them to experiment and a few days later introduces watercolors.

◗ When third graders are told that they can add anything to their science folders on microscopy, there is a spontaneous burst of interest in making large representations of three-dimensional microscopic animals that live in pond water and are not visible except under high magnification. Each child is provided with heavy paper, a microscope, depression slides, and pond water. The children observe, discuss detail and movement, then create what they see. The products are very large and quite realistic; some had moving parts.

Novel Materials

Novel items are introduced periodically and placed in close proximity to basic materials. Such items include buttons, corks, styrofoam scraps, miscellaneous kitchen salvage, beads, springs, mobile hardware, pipe cleaners, and industrial salvage. Children may use these items spontaneously or in conjunction with a particular activity that the teacher presents.

◗ A four-year-old spontaneously makes a mock telephone to include in dramatic play corner.

◗ As an outgrowth of reading, discussion, and science experiments about owls, second graders make props for a child-initiated play, including owl wings and face, a camera, and a clapper.

◗ In early February, doilies, heart stickers, and pink, red, black, and purple paper are added to the paper box in a first-grade classroom to stimulate valentine-making, which will later be joined with a poem-writing activity about "special friends."

◗ A first grader uses a piece of reflective foil to represent a pond in a book he is writing and illustrating.

◗ A kindergartner who is infatuated with the teacher's guitar-playing ability makes a guitar out of old cardboard boxes and remnants, and staples wire to represent strings. This activity becomes the basis for other children's making musical instruments out of salvage material. A band is created.

Making Particular Materials Available

The teacher acquires and makes available particular materials that are necessary for a project that children have initiated. This may occur spontaneously, or may be planned for a subsequent time.

◗ A four-year-old finds a wild flower in the woods and is intensely interested. She brings it into the classroom and continues to ask questions about it. During the

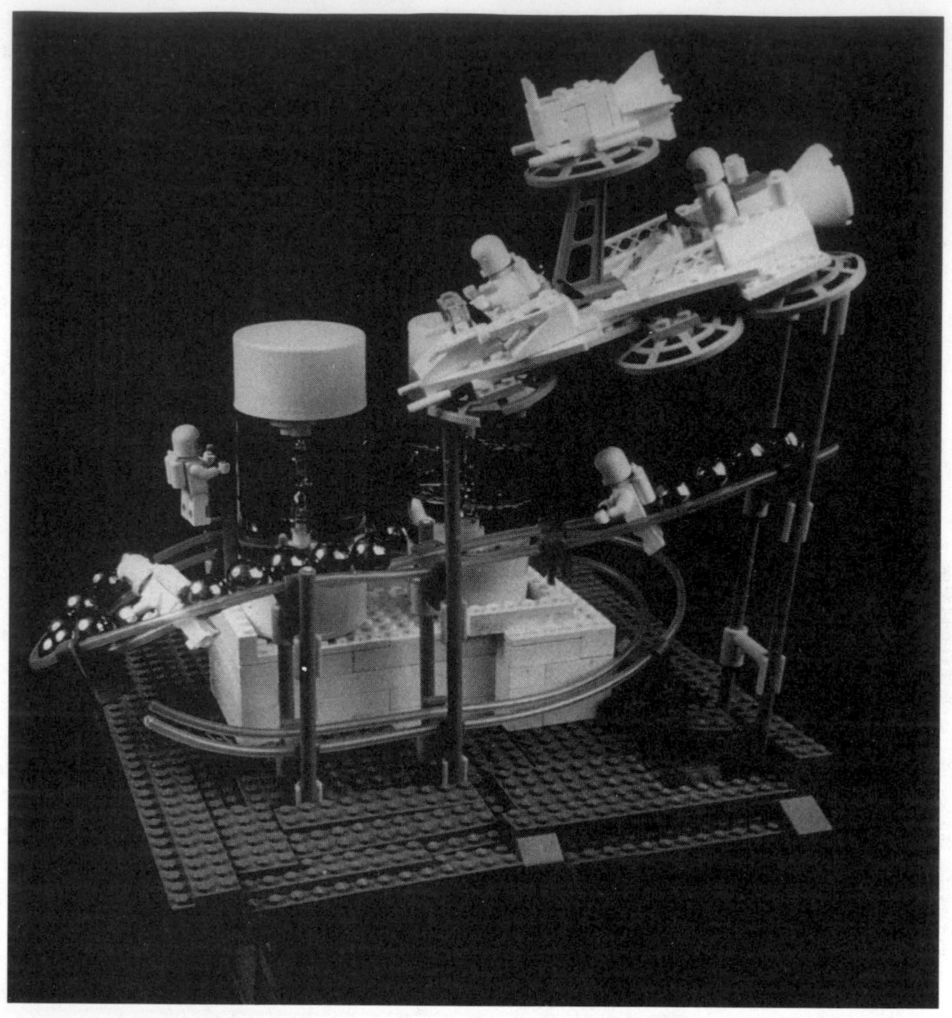

Imagination is stimulated when materials are made available that suggest new possibilities. This delightful example of a construction by a nine-year-old boy uses small figures, marbles, and basic Lego components. Michael calls his construction a Lego space ship.
Courtesy of Leslie Margolis

next few days, the teacher collects other kinds of unusual wild flowers, assembles relevant books and a magnifying glass, and sets up a small area for the child to continue to examine and study the wild flowers. Other children join the project, and rich observation and analysis takes place.

◗ A third-grade math class wants to make three-dimensional tetrahedrons. The teacher obtains cardboard scraps from a paper supplier. Together, teacher and class work out a way to make the one-dimensional form from the math book into a three-dimensional one.

Allowing Novel Uses of Materials

Children are not restricted from using objects and equipment in ways different from their intended uses, except as safety requires and when damaging an object would be of serious consequence. Limitations are established for particularly vulnerable materials such as math sets and fragile objects.

▸ Kindergarten boys turn two chairs upside down and combine them with rope and other materials to make an "arrow machine to kill the girls." Arrows are made out of Tinkertoys and are inserted in the holes of a radiator cover. The teacher sets limits for the boys' aggressive behavior toward the girls, but encourages the children's inventiveness in having made the machine. Rich dramatic play continues.

▸ A roll of shelf paper is extended half the length of the classroom floor to provide a surface for first graders to use vegetable-printing to make aggregates—an activity that relates to what the children are learning in mathematics.

▸ A second grader makes a marble-rolling machine out of an adult exercise board, cuisenaire rods, miscellaneous desk equipment (a tape container, an old book, and so on). Marbles roll through a channel and land in a cardboard bucket.

Moving Materials from One Place to Another

Children are allowed to move some materials from one area of the room to another, when they seem to be in pursuit of a legitimate objective. Limitations are established for potentially dangerous or inappropriate ideas.

▸ In a child-initiated idea, puzzle pieces are borrowed temporarily from the manipulative area for tracing at the art table after a kindergarten lesson on shapes.

▸ A three-year-old takes a fake fur piece from the dress-up area to use as an animal in a block structure that represents a zoo.

▸ Four-year-olds want to float a set of delicate, hand-painted wooden animals brought in by one child for show-and-tell. The teacher forbids this plan, explaining why it is not a good idea. She substitutes salvage wood forms.

Varying Presentation of Materials

The teacher places materials in different and unlikely places, or presents them in an altered way, to invite children to see the materials anew or in conjunction with other stimuli.

▸ An ant farm, placed on a table at children's eye level, is surrounded with drawing and writing materials (thin markers, paper of various sizes, and so on). Two first graders sit in front of the farm observing and discussing the ants and then spontaneously produce clear, observational drawings of the ants without teacher intervention. Later, children write stories.

▸ Paint cans with brushes in them, which had been at the easel, are placed inside an empty water table, along with paper. Four-year olds paint inside the table with renewed interest.

◗ Clay, which is usually placed in small mounds for individual children at a round table, is arranged in a large single mass on the center of the table. Sticks, straws, and small circular plastic forms have been plunged randomly into the clay to invite investigation by three-year-olds.

◗ A painting activity focused on "how you look different from other people" is arranged on counter space beneath the windows of a kindergarten classroom. A large, horizontal mirror is propped along the base of the window to enable children to view their faces while they are painting.

◗ Scissors are eliminated from an activity in which first graders are making a construction paper mural related to a social studies project. The children are forced to tear shapes to achieve their objectives.

The Role of Order

Although a certain amount of disorder is a natural part of creation in children's activities, the teacher recognizes that organization and order in the environment are absolutely critical to facilitating creativity.

◗ Materials for drawing, painting, and constructing are stored in a systematic, orderly way. Bins, sturdy boxes, and containers provide clarity. Children know where things belong and are responsible for returning staples and leftovers to appropriate places.

◗ When tables are set up with enticing materials for small groups of children, attention is given to arranging things in a way that defines where one works, how materials are handled, and how many can be at a given location.

◗ Materials are treated with respect and care. Limits are set on children's abusive use of tools and equipment (such as leaving tops off markers, not washing paintbrushes, and leaving glue on tabletops).

◗ Children are involved in the process of collecting and maintaining materials. They are encouraged to find and bring in appropriate salvage, equipment, and usable objects. This process of considering the potential in what has been discarded is an important lesson.

The Role of the Unexpected

The teacher understands the importance of the unexpected in the physical environment and sees to it that the room is periodically charged with provocative, interesting objects, pictures, and apparatus.

◗ A display of discarded things is exhibited on a large table in a kindergarten classroom. Included are such things as an old disposal cover, a clock, a torn shoe, a mechanical toy, and games with missing parts. These objects are introduced as part of a unit on the idea of recycling, but are also available for children to investigate as they choose.

◗ A collection of balls of all sizes and shapes are gathered and displayed. Second graders examine the physical properties of the balls, classify them in various ways, and write imaginative stories about where they have been and who has played with them.

◗ Photographs of teenagers are arranged on the bulletin board. Children at all early levels are encouraged to think of activities they might pursue related to this age group. First graders discuss the definition of a teenager, how you can tell a teenager from an adult, clothes that teenagers wear, and so on. Stories and pictures are generated.

The Teacher Designs a Curriculum and Motivates Children to Extend Creative Thinking

Intervening Selectively in Children's Activities

The teacher uses appropriate judgment in determining when to intervene in children's play or in their use of materials. In many situations, children benefit from a minimum of direct teacher intervention—particularly when materials are new or presented in an especially challenging way, or when children have ideas that they are interested in pursuing on their own. In these situations, adult intervention can be counterproductive to children's efforts to work through a problem or pursue an unusual or highly personal piece of expression. We have all seen instances in which well-intended teacher questioning and redirection has confused or extinguished a child's original intention and even terminated involvement. Conversely, in other instances, the teacher's contributions can be of crucial importance in helping the child to clarify objectives and discover new areas of pursuit. Sensitive adults are alert to when and how they should step in to influence thinking, and they recognize that very young children are less apt to benefit from extensive verbalization than are older children.

In the case of creative activity, it is of particular importance that adults be discriminating in the way they intervene, since children's intentions may not be immediately apparent. Adults will want to observe carefully in order to find a balance between, on the one hand, leaving children free to pursue ideas on their own and, on the other hand, shaping thinking in strategic ways. A well-posed question or statement, and even the delivery of specific information, can be of major importance in extending productivity. Knowledge and information feed creative pursuit. Adults should not be reluctant to deliver these essential ingredients when the circumstances so dictate. (See the example in Figure 7-1.)

Awareness of Cognitive Developmental Factors

The teacher is aware of developmental factors that influence children's responsiveness to lessons from a cognitive vantage point. Hence, the teacher designs activities that are congruent with children's abilities to accommodate the expectations involved.

◗ In working with children who have not yet reached the symbolic stage in drawing, the teacher does not expect them to participate in art lessons that demand that they produce symbolic pictures. Three- and four-year-olds are not expected to make turkeys, Christmas trees, or butterflies in order to please parents and teachers.

FIGURE 7-1

The trite picture of a house, cloud, and person was created by Amy in her kindergarten classroom where there was little stimulation and the paints were thin, lacking color and aesthetic vitality. Little changed at the easel from day to day and Amy's painting reflected the lack of stimulation. Amy also painted the vigorous representation of a tree and park bench at home during the same period of time. The richness of detail was the result of Amy overhearing a group of adults discussing trees in some detail while observing them. This simple stimulation provided Amy with important information which she integrated into her work.
Collection of Sylvia G. Feinburg

Instead, lessons are planned for them in which scribbling and form-making are respected and are motivated by the way materials are arranged and presented—without expectations for representationalism. In an example of an inappropriate model, an art teacher drew a portrait for a class of first graders, explaining how to start with an oval, divide it into quarters, and then place the features in their respective places. (See Figure 7-2.) The teacher demonstrated exactly how to use the materials and stressed the importance of mathematically analyzing the size relationships of the head and face. Then he asked the children to make a portrait. Douglas (age six), drew a picture of his father on a sunny day, with a tree, and then remembered it was supposed to have been a portrait. To solve the problem, he drew a square around the head and dismissed the task.

The teacher's expectations of the children were developmentally inappropriate, and Douglas responded by denying the motivation. The children might have benefited more from a simple discussion about faces. To make it easier for the children to identify with the task and to analyze the face in a more personally significant manner, the teacher could ask questions like, "What is larger, the nose or the ears?" "What is the shape of the nose?" "Does the person have lots of hair, or just a little?"

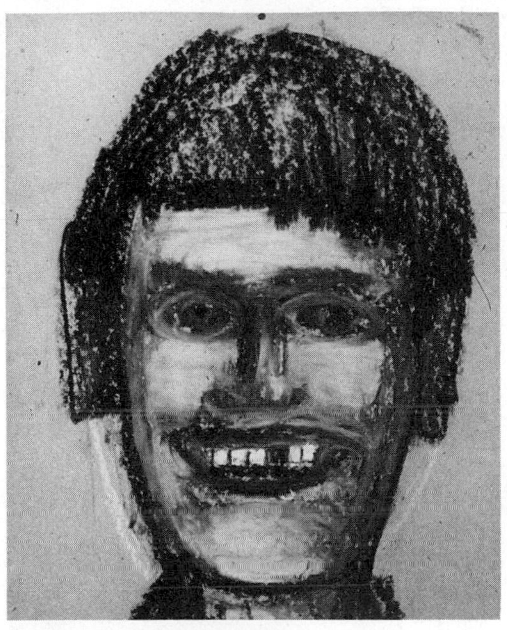

FIGURE 7-2

The teacher's model of a portrait is at left. Douglas's response to this inappropriate lesson that ignores developmental factors is shown. Collection of Sylvia G. Feinburg

Recognizing Children's Important Issues

The teacher is aware of developmental factors that influence children's responsiveness to imaginative challenges. The teacher recognizes that certain issues are central to young children, and he or she addresses these issues when planning the curriculum.

- Four-year-olds are interested in power figures and superheroes. The teacher reads stories about robbers and starts a discussion about what stealing is, who steals, and why. Children's high level of response leads to an ongoing unit on good and evil; this theme is expressed in dramatic play, art, and literacy. Children produce many expressive products about good and bad people.
- Many first-grade girls are involved in drawing rainbows as part of their preoccupation with prettiness. These are usually repetitive, hackneyed drawings with little imaginative content. The teacher stimulates a watercolor and Magic Marker lesson on rainbows, emphasizing such notions as repetition, symmetry, color mixing, and reflection. Simple scientific concepts are presented. Mirrors are used to stimulate color repetitions. Results are powerful and complex.

Alertness to Children's Interests and Cultural Orientations

The teacher remains alert to children's interests and concerns by listening to what children talk about and share with one another. When they bring in things from home, the teacher watches carefully to determine which objects are of particular significance. The teacher is sensitive to cultural differences and designs the curriculum with deference to children's interests, as opposed to the teacher's.

◗ Refer to Vivian Paley's books *Wally's Stories* (1981) or *You Can't Say You Can't Play* (1992). Paley is expert at observing and listening to children's conversations and extracting the critical issues involved, with the focus on preschool and kindergarten children.

◗ At group time, one kindergartner shares a broken disposal cover she has brought from home. Children become very involved in discussing it, and the teacher becomes aware of how important the notion of brokenness is to the group. The teacher initiates a unit on the subject, and individual children bring in a wide assortment of broken things from home. These objects are displayed, observed, examined, and classified. Much experimentation and creative activity follows.

The teacher plans lessons that have creativity and self-expression as central objectives. These lessons are not confined to the arts but are embedded within the entire curriculum, including reading, mathematics, and social studies.

◗ In math, simple graphing is being introduced. First graders are asked to design a picture of a single object to be placed in one graph, then to duplicate it twice, making it larger each successive time.

◗ In conjunction with a unit on emotions, the issue of jealousy is identified for study. Third graders explore ideas such as what makes them and other people feel jealous; why people feel jealous; and positive and negative ways of dealing with such feelings. This material is used in conjunction with writing and art, and a set of illustrated picture books is produced.

◗ Christy's "Pencilphone" is a response to a teacher-motivated lesson about inventing a new tool to help with a job that one needs to have done. The children were asked to draw their idea, and then to write about it. (See Figure 7-3.)

FIGURE 7-3

Christy, age 6 and a half years, drew her "pencilphone" in response to a teacher-motivated lesson about inventing a new tool to help you with a job you need done. The children were asked to draw their idea, and then to write about it.

◗ A kindergarten teacher makes worksheets on the computer as homework for her children. The teacher is interested in collaboration between parent and child and in helping parents understand the importance of children's originality in drawing and writing. One worksheet reads, "Draw a picture of your favorite place to play on the playground," and leaves a space for children to fill in. Then the worksheet states, "Now ask your mom or dad to help you write what you like to play in your favorite playground place." In response, the parent takes dictation from the child, thus providing a collaborative homework assignment that promotes creativity in both drawing and storytelling. Another worksheet provides space for creating two drawings, with key words written on the sides for parents to read to the child. The key words stimulate thinking about the possible elements that can be included.

Maintaining Enthusiasm and Vitality

The teacher demonstrates enthusiasm and vitality in the way he or she stimulates children. The teacher models an appreciation of the unique and unexpected, and is not afraid to employ fantasy and humor in interactions with children.

◗ A kindergarten teacher begins circle time by spontaneously saying to children, "I have a moon in my pocket! Who else has something in his or her pocket to tell the group about?" The teacher continues to elicit children's "pretend" imaginative responses, leading to dramatic storytelling and picture-book-making.

◗ A second-grade teacher wears an outrageous homemade hat made out of kitchen salvage while leading a discussion about recycling.

◗ In a classroom for four-year-olds, one day is designated "Backwards Day," and the daily schedule is reversed, beginning with activities that usually end the day and ending with free play and morning meeting time.

◗ Third graders are encouraged to write original stories for a bulletin board display called "Unlikely Events." Mock awards are given weekly for the event least likely to happen.

Using Motivational Strategies

The teacher uses a range of motivational strategies to stimulate children's imaginative thinking, such as slides and film, music and sound, stories, poems, direct observation and field trips, and smells. Speech is not the only way the teacher stimulates children. The teacher understands that heightened affect is central to creative expression.

◗ A second-grade teacher uses a record of thunder and pounding rain to stimulate an art lesson about rainy weather. Umbrellas are opened, and rubbers and boots are present as well. Children simulate walking in the rain.

◗ A discussion of dreams takes place in conjunction with a lesson on fantasy versus reality. Music of different moods is used to stimulate first graders to share dream imagery. These images are then incorporated into writing and illustrating a group book.

◗ During a lesson on valentines for kindergartners and first graders, one table is set up to encourage children to make hearts out of any color but red, using origami paper. The teacher shows Matisse prints to encourage them to think about how exciting it is to put colors together in novel ways.

Modeling a Scientific Approach to Problem Solving

The teacher models the scientific approach to problem solving by asking questions such as these: "What would happen if . . . ?"; "If we did this, how would it affect that . . . ?"; "How many ways can you think of to . . . ?" By framing comments strategically, the teacher helps children raise questions and experiment for themselves.

◗ A kindergarten teacher tears small pieces of paper in front of a group and asks, "How many different ways are there to join paper?" At first children provide conventional responses—Scotch tape, paper clips, glue. The teacher gets each child to demonstrate. After they exhaust these ways, the teacher continues; and children begin to model more unusual methods, such as twisting, tearing and folding, and using plasticene and toothpicks.

◗ A toy falls behind radiator in the classroom and is stuck. Three-year-olds are unable to get it out and ask the teacher to help. She asks them to think of all the possible ways it could be retrieved. Many answers are suggested, and one boy uses a yard stick to dislodge it and ease it out.

◗ During a discussion about pumpkins, kindergartners realize that pumpkins can be both green and orange. Many contributions are made; one child asks, "How did it get off the vine?" The teacher asks, "Does it need to remain on the vine to turn orange? How could we find out?"

Using Metaphors and Analogies

The teacher uses metaphors and analogies to strengthen children's imaginative capacities. The teacher is aware of the power of analyzing similarities and differences and making comparisons when discussing ideas.

◗ Third graders are tapping a maple tree for sap, which is being caught in a bucket. They notice the rhythm of the sap dropping into the bucket, and a discussion ensues about how the sap moves through the entire tree, nourishing it. One child mentions that "It's just like blood pumping through my body." The teacher reinforces the idea and asks whether they can think of other examples.

◗ The teacher is explaining to second graders about what psychotherapy means and how sometimes it is valuable for people to examine unpleasant things that have happened in the past in order to understand why they feel and act the way they do. She suggests that doing this is sometimes painful and uncomfortable, but as time goes by important benefits come from having been involved in the process. She asks whether they understand what she means. One boy responds, "When a tree is having trouble, maybe like it's planted in the wrong place, if you dig it up and move it to a better place, it may struggle and not do so well. But eventually it grows stronger and better." The teacher explains that he has created a metaphor and applauds his contribution.

Modeling Skills and Techniques

The teacher models skills and techniques in ways that instruct children and stimulate mastery. The teacher understands how learning a process or technique differs from imitating adult-conceived products. The teacher recognizes, as well, that looking at others' work can be a constructive way to challenge thinking and help build concepts, as long as children are not asked to imitate that work mechanistically.

◗ A kindergarten child is having difficulty painting eyes on a large painting of a face; they keep running down the paper and destroying the image. The teacher gets another piece of paper and demonstrates how to wipe the paintbrush carefully on the edge of the container in order to control the amount of paint. She simulates making eyes by creating a serious of random dots. The child imitates the process on scrap paper and then returns to do the face picture with full control over the brush.

◗ A four-year-old is sawing wood in a random manner and has no control over what is happening. The teacher demonstrates two or three ways of using the saw and asks the child to decide which approach works best and why.

Discussing how the skills/creativity challenge is addressed by the schools for young children in Reggio Emilia, in northern Italy—where innovative integrated curriculum with a strong focus on the arts takes place—George Forman (1990) emphasizes the relationship between cognition and creativity. His statement regarding this issue, quoted in Chapter 4 (p. 122) of this book, highlights an important consideration in encouraging cognitive development. Reggio Emilia teachers find the balance between direct instruction and self-regulated learning, and that is one characteristic of the Reggio Emilia approach that attracts the interest of educators throughout the world. The approach heightens children's sensory awareness, provides instruction in new skills as needed, and leaves the child to create his or her own renderings of the experience. The schools in Reggio Emilia place a strong emphasis on documenting experiences and on providing a social context in which conversations about the documentations are of key importance (Forman, 1990).

Flexibility of Focus

The teacher shifts focus when motivating a particular lesson or discussion and children seem unresponsive or are drawn to an alternative direction that has merit and relevance. Examples follow.

◗ Four-year-olds are pasting sponges down on construction paper. One child suggests that "you can print with sponges" and indicates a desire to do so; other children concur. Teacher reinforces the suggestion and makes it possible to accomplish the child's goal, instead of responding, "That's not the way we do it."

◗ Teacher is cooking with children and introduces the garlic press as a way to get "tiny pieces of garlic." A three-year-old responds, "I think it would work better to mash it with the hammer on a wooden block." The teacher encourages her to try it out and see how it works.

Encouraging and Guiding Emerging Ideas

The teacher encourages the development of an idea that is emerging, particularly when it is difficult for a particular child to follow through. Examples follow.

◗ A teacher of four-year-olds says, "Tell me more about what you will need to make that cake out of styrofoam. It is going to be a birthday cake, or a regular cake?"

◗ During creative writing time, a first grader is growing impatient because she can't think of a way to develop a story about which she had initially been very excited. The teacher says, "Close your eyes, take a deep breath, and let your mind go. Just concentrate and use your imagination. Let the idea play there in your mind for a little while; it's okay to take your time thinking."

Watching for the Right Moment

The teacher observes carefully for the right moment to pose a question or dilemma, watching for signals from the child that suggest that he or she would benefit from intervention. The teacher watches for cues that provide information about the child's intentions.

◗ A kindergartner is making bridge out of construction paper, and it keeps collapsing on the table. The teacher watches as the child tries various alternatives and begins to get frustrated. She intervenes and says, "What could you use to make the paper stronger? Maybe you could find something over there in the box that would keep it from slipping." The child begins experimenting anew.

Balancing Teacher- and Child-Initiated Activities

The teacher provides a balance between activities in which he or she is central and opportunities for children to work relatively independently. The teacher recognizes that materials and environmental setups are forms of teacher stimulation. Speech is not the only way in which the teacher stimulates creative thinking.

◗ During activity time, children may select from four different options. Three do not require active teacher involvement: (1) block play; (2) drawing and writing in journals, which are worked on daily; (3) painting at the easel; and (4) working with Cuisenaire rods and completing a related worksheet. A science activity requires a good deal of the teacher's involvement; she works closely with a small group of children while monitoring the other four groups from a distance.

◗ A tape recorder is available during activity time for second graders to listen to a tape that deals with mathematical concepts. The teacher has made the tape so that children can practice certain concepts independently. An example from the tape is the following: "Find two things in the room, one of which is larger than an orange, the other, smaller, which weigh the same amount; use the scale. Record on your worksheet what you have found and how much they weigh."

Recognizing the Importance of Contrast

The teacher recognizes that contrast stimulates creative thinking. Hence, in art, for example, the teacher considers such variables as size (working on small or large surfaces), spontaneity and control (working with precision versus working loosely), and simplicity or complexity. Lessons are planned that address these variables.

◗ Kindergartners have the opportunity to design a deck of cards using magic markers, small labels, and gummed dots. They must make at least six pairs within their deck, each of which must be identical. An alternative activity within the room during the same period of time is using rollers and large pans of black paint to make roads on a long roll of shelf paper. When dry, road paintings are used for driving cars.

◗ The teacher introduces the two words *simple* and *complex*. Second graders define the words with help from the teacher. The teacher shows the children slides of paintings, which illustrate each of the two qualities; a discussion of pattern and texture emerges, as well. Follow-up activity requires that the children make two paintings of the same subject—one simple, the other complex.

Using Constraints to Stimulate

The teacher recognizes that constraints and the elimination of certain expectations are ways to stimulate and challenge thinking. Examples follow.

◗ During a math lesson on estimating and measuring objects in a first-grade classroom (tables, windows, books, and so on), rulers and tape measures are eliminated. Children must find other solutions to use: for example, using their handbreadth, the length of their shoes, sticks, and so on. Issues of variation of size from one person to another are discussed.

◗ When making a mural of fall trees with colored paper, second graders must tear the shapes of the trees and their foliage instead of cutting them. The elimination of scissors is challenging to fine motor skills and creates more interesting, unexpected shapes.

Deterrents to Fostering Creativity

When creativity abounds in a classroom, a joie de vivre permeates the atmosphere. Teachers seem to have an extra sense of energy, and children seem to be in control of their own learning. Unfortunately, in some situations, the value of creativity is not fully appreciated, and practices take hold that act as deterrents to the development of creativity. These deterrents should be recognized in order to make a conscious attempt to eliminate them and replace them with more developmentally appropriate practices.

Patterns and Follow-the-Directions Lessons

Lessons that do not allow children to determine the specific form of an idea or product are counterproductive to creative thinking, since they rob the child of the most important part of creation—determining the form that the concept will take. Hence, teachers should avoid lessons that demand that the child replicate or complete adult-conceived products. These include the following:

- stereotypic art activities that produce lookalike products through the use of ditto forms, stencils, follow-the-directions assemblage, and narrow copying of a model; activities that often result in such things as trite Indian hats, spring flowers, jack-o'-lanterns, and holiday symbols
- worksheets with stereotyped forms for coloring in or connecting dots, used in conjunction with teaching basic skills, including reading, writing, and arithmetic

The issue of modeling for children is complex. The teacher's modeling how to use a tool or a technique, or perhaps sharing what an adult artist or another child has made, differs in important ways from asking children to imitate slavishly what someone else has created. On the other hand, there is value in the teacher's extracting principles and concepts from other people's work, and then encouraging children to translate these concepts in their own way. This can be a rich and meaningful kind of stimulation.

Disparaging Comments

Some types of comments need no explanation.

- "You know that's not the way I wanted it done! I want you to do it just like mine; leave your ideas out of it."
- "That's interesting, Paul, but it isn't very neat or pretty!"
- "Where'd you get that idea? It certainly is a silly one!"
- "I can't draw a straight line with a ruler. Don't expect any help from me!"
- "I didn't say anything about cutting it out!"
- "He needs me to show him how because he's not really very creative."

Rather than explain such comments, the important thing is to recognize when they are used and the impact they have on children's self-concepts, and identify ways such comments can be avoided.

Heavy Emphasis on Reality-Based Ideas

It is natural for adults to want to reinforce children's developmental progression from being impulsive and egocentric to becoming more logical and rational in their thinking. Six- and seven-year-olds, for example, are proud of their capacities to classify and order ideas and symbols, and are often contemptuous of the naive inventiveness of the younger child. But at the same time that we help them to acquire these new cognitive capabilities, it is important that we help them understand the importance of fantasy, imagination, and the power to create the unique. Older children often appear less creative than younger ones because they are more logical thinkers; children who are helped to value both kinds of thinking have the fullest expressive options.

Preoccupation with Neatness and Orderliness in Work

When too much attention is placed on fine motor skills and being neat and orderly, children may feel that these qualities are of higher importance than the ideas that they generate. Teachers can find ways to support children's motivation to increase their motor skills without extinguishing creative impulses. Sometimes a highly creative child is motorically immature. It is crucial in this situation to help children to see the distinction between the two kinds of achievement. (See the example in Figure 7-4.)

FIGURE 7-4

Roger, a first grader, produced this fascinating picture of himself having his hair cut at the barber shop in response to the teacher's motivation about the subject. Although Roger's motor skills are crude, his ability to express a complex idea is strong. On the right Roger sits on the barber's chair with the barber standing to the right. Above Roger is a calendar on the wall, a clock, and a light fixture high on the ceiling. A large mirror is in the middle of the picture, above drawers and cabinets. Both Roger and the barber are reflected in the mirror, as well as the clock, a portion of the chandelier, and the various bottles sitting on the countertop. It is important for adults to distinguish between children's ability to conceptualize and their motor skills. Collection of Sylvia G. Feinburg

Excessive Order and Control in the Physical Environment

As we have seen, clarity and order in the physical environment are necessary ingredients in establishing a climate that allows creative thinking to flourish. Excessive preoccupation with where things go, how the table is laid out, and where you can and cannot work, however, can be stultifying. The child who is all excited about "making a long snake" out of tissue paper and drops to the floor to work in order to be unencumbered by a small tabletop, needs to feel that it is all right. Having established a basically orderly environment within which to work, the adult must be flexible and open-ended about the many minor disorderly acts that accompany the creative process.

Inappropriate Focus on Competition

As in every other aspect of performance, children show a wide range of capabilities in demonstrating creativity. For some children, being original and inventive will reveal itself across a range of subject areas; for other children, creative abilities will be most apparent in a given domain—in writing, drawing, expressing themselves verbally or physically, for example. Others will have difficulty in feeling accomplished, regardless of the particular area of focus. When teachers exaggerate these natural differences in ability by excessive praise and reinforcement to some, to the neglect of others, or by giving out awards, stickers, or stars, feelings of inadequacy and superiority are bound to emerge.

The adult must strive to help children compete with themselves and to grow and improve as individuals, as contrasted with continuously comparing themselves with peers. Children can learn to respect and value the notion that people have different levels of competence and can be satisfied with a realistic picture of their own capabilities, if the adults who guide them reduce competition and base evaluation on individual growth. Respect for someone else's competence is more apt to flourish in an environment where the notion of individual differences is genuinely accepted.

Part Three: Questions for Discussion

1. Define creativity and explain why it is an important part of intellectual development. Is creativity something that pertains to the arts only? Explain.
2. Identify a few key behaviors on the part of the teacher that reinforce children's creativity. Give particular attention to those that represent a different point of view from what seems customary.
3. In what ways does room organization and decoration contribute toward either supporting or extinguishing children's creative vitality? Explain.
4. Some people may think that in order to encourage children's creativity adults should assume a passive role and accept whatever children choose to produce as valuable. Discuss.
5. In what ways can teachers thwart children's creativity? Identify a number of teaching techniques and behaviors that stifle children's independent and original thinking.

PART 4 A COGNITIVE APPROACH TO SOCIAL-EMOTIONAL ISSUES

In the cognitive-developmental classroom, social-emotional issues are an important part of intellectual development and are integrated into both the curriculum and classroom management.

When one enters an early childhood classroom—whether it be a program serving three-year-olds or eight-year-olds—one almost immediately gets a feeling for how the people in that environment are relating to one another. In some classrooms, teachers give orders, and children follow directions. If a child has difficulty following directions, the emphasis is on the task, not on how the child is feeling or reacting to the task. In this type of classroom, the teacher either ignores children's interactions with one another or redirects them so that the children focus on what they are "supposed to be doing"—which is usually prescribed by the teacher.

In contrast, in some classrooms, obvious attention is paid to social-emotional issues. These issues are brought to the forefront and constitute a key component of the program. Teachers help children identify and talk about their feelings and apply problem-solving strategies to social interactions. These programs recognize that young children can and should use their intellectual and creative abilities to deal with social-emotional issues. *Social cognition* is the term used to describe this process, which is a key component of developmentally appropriate programs.

The rationale is clear. In this rapidly changing world, the ability to use one's thinking powers in all types of situations is a valuable asset. Changes are occurring in family structure, in occupational opportunities, in modes of communication, and in scientific developments that affect the environment. These changes impinge on children's lives and require flexible coping strategies. The rapidity of change increases children's stress levels as well as adults'. For this reason, it is increasingly important that individuals acquire an ability to recognize and contend with their own emotional needs and be in control of their relationships with others. Children who have pent-up emotions and those who express emotions in ways that are inappropriate for the social setting often are unable to focus on a task. Their ability to make friends is affected, and their ability to learn is often diminished. Social cognition not only increases children's understanding of feelings and emotions but also augments children's ability to control their own social-emotional behavior.

Previous sections of this text focused on the cognitive and creative domains in early childhood education. This section links these earlier discussions with the social-emotional aspects of the program, highlighting the need for a cognitive approach to social-emotional issues in both curriculum and classroom management. Chapter 8 presents an extended discussion of the theory underlying social cognition—why social cognition is important and the various factors that influence the process. This chapter also discusses how children acquire social skills and the relationship of self-concept, cultural identity, and gender to the variations in skill development. The purpose is to provide a theoretical framework for incorporating social cognition into the early childhood program and to clearly delineate the teacher's role in this process.

Chapter 9 highlights the operational characteristics of this approach. The chapter includes suggestions for encouraging prosocial behaviors and links the establishment of a positive classroom atmosphere with a curriculum that incorporates social-emotional issues and a classroom management style that builds upon a cognitive perspective. The discussion of curriculum includes sample lesson plans for helping children understand and deal with feelings, appreciate similarities and differences, and develop friendship-making skills. Accompanying the plans are detailed discussions to help the teacher acquire a basis for further planning and for observing developmentally appropriate practices. The classroom management component considers children's involvement in the formulation of rules, their engagement in thinking about appropriate and inappropriate behavior, and their use of problem-solving techniques. The examples are drawn from preschool, kindergarten, and primary grade classrooms in order to highlight the similarities and differences in approach that teachers use in working in the area of social cognition with three-year-olds, six-year-olds, and eight-year-olds.

CHAPTER

8 SOCIAL COGNITION: WHAT IT MEANS AND WHAT IT ENCOMPASSES

In the cognitive-developmental model, cognition pervades all aspects of the program—including the academic, creative, and social-emotional domains. The linking of cognitive and social-emotional development is referred to as social cognition. Within the field of developmental psychology, social cognition is a specialized area of study. This chapter explains the term *social cognition,* shows why it is important to incorporate social cognition into classroom practice, and describes various factors that influence its development. The chapter also describes specific approaches for facilitating children's acquisition of social skills. It concludes with a succinct recapitulation of some underlying principles of social cognition, with roots in Piagetian and Vygotskian theory, and an overview of the teacher's role in translating this theory into classroom practice.

Since the 1970s, a growing body of research has developed that links social and cognitive development (Kohlberg, 1969; Damon, 1977; Shure & Spivack, 1978a). This research builds on Piaget's theory of morality, with its constructivist orientation, and considers how the child develops concepts about the self, about friendship, and about right and wrong (Berk, 1991). Highlighted in this chapter are aspects of social-cognitive theory with implications for the early childhood teacher.

Social Cognition Defined

Social cognition is the process of thinking about emotions, feelings, and how people interact with one another. It is a developmental process that plays a critical role in the acquisition of social skills, ability to engage in interpersonal problem solving, and development of an inner **locus of control.** Locus of control concerns the belief about one's ability to influence the outcomes of one's own actions (Fogel & Melson, 1988). People who have an inner locus of control believe that they are in charge of their own lives, that they can decide how to act, and that these decisions make a difference in how they feel and how they interact with others. This inner locus of control is in contrast to the belief that whatever one does makes no difference in one's achievements or social relationships—that achievements and relationships are controlled by some outer force (often thought of as luck) or by somebody other than oneself. Without an inner locus of control, the individual believes that whatever happens is beyond his or her personal sphere of influence.

Children are born with the capacity to develop an inner locus of control, which may be nurtured by life experience or may be continually chipped away and eventually eroded. Social cognition encourages the development of an inner locus of control: the belief that how one manages emotions, feelings, and interactions does make a difference in one's own life and in one's interactions with others.

Social Cognition and Developmental Psychology

Social cognition is a specialized area of study in the field of developmental psychology. Its roots lie in a basic principle of development: namely, that all areas of growth are interrelated, and what happens to a child as the child grows socially and emotionally influences development in the cognitive area. Similarly, experiences in the cognitive area affect social and emotional development (Gilligan &

Bower, 1984; Kostelnik, Soderman, & Whiren, 1993). Social cognition embraces this principle and many additional concepts as well.

Social cognition is an integral part of cognitive-developmental theory and as such supports the idea that the basic growth-producing force for all areas of development, including the social-emotional, lies within the individual. Through the interaction of this inner force with factors operating in the family and cultural milieu in which one lives, the individual constructs his or her own knowledge about the physical and social world. This perspective is consistent with the constructivist view of development, the perspective that pervades the discussion of cognition and creativity in previous parts of this book.

The Cognitive-Developmental and Cultural Transmission Orientations Contrasted

To better understand the constructivist aspects approach of social cognition, it is useful to contrast it with an antithetical approach: cultural transmission, with its roots in behaviorism or social learning theory. This latter approach usually relies on directly telling the child how to behave, and it incorporates extrinsic rewards and punishments as a way of helping children learn behaviors appropriate in particular setting.

To clarify the difference between the two approaches, consider the following incident, which occurred in a first-grade class. The teacher was working with a small group of children, while the rest of the class was engaged in various projects. Tomo was concentrating on some math problems and was using unifix cubes to verify his calculations. In front of him on a table he had an array of configurations. Uma walked by carrying a large sheet of newsprint. The newsprint accidentally swept across the table on which Tomo was working. Several of the unifix cubes fell to the floor, and most of the work Tomo had done was disrupted. "You get out of here!" spouted Tomo through clenched teeth, and he gave Uma a strong punch in the back. Uma retaliated with a kick: "Leave me alone!" This type of interaction is common among children. In a classroom in which the developmental perspective does not prevail the teacher would tend to reprimand the children for creating a disturbance, order the children to remain in their seats, and threaten to keep them in at recess as a punishment for inappropriate behavior.

In contrast, the constructivist teacher might use the incident between Tomo and Uma as the basis for helping these two children engage in problem-solving. The teacher, in a private conversation with the two children, might ask each child to reflect on the incident and to relate what happened as he or she perceived it. This step would help the children improve their perspective-taking ability. Each would gain an enhanced view of how the other viewed the situation. The teacher would then direct the children's attention to generating a list of alternative ways of acting if such a situation occurred again. The teacher might also engage them in a discussion of their actions (Shure, 1992; Seigle, 1990–1991). The experience becomes a socially cognitive one, as the teacher helps the children think about their actions and identify other ways they could handle a similar incident.

The teacher might decide to extend the learning from this incident to the entire class. Some teachers reserve twenty minutes at the end of the day for group processing of situations that occurred during the day. On this particular day, the teacher describes for the group the incident that took place with Tomo and Uma. He identifies the danger inherent in this type of action and asks the children to identify other ways Tomo and Uma could have reacted. The focus is on developing alternative solutions. This social problem requires thought on the children's part. The teacher's role is to stimulate thinking and encourage the children to identify various alternative behaviors. The teacher whose aim is to develop social cognition sees social-emotional issues—clearly evident in the Tomo and Uma's interaction—as an important part of intellectual development and integrates these issues into curriculum and classroom management.

Teachers who consider themselves constructivist may sometimes behave in a nonconstructivist way. It is often appropriate for the teacher to do this. Even in a classroom where the developmental perspective prevails, there are occasions when the time or the nature of the situation does not warrant a more elaborate consideration of a particular incident—when the most effective thing a teacher could do is to react expediently and pragmatically. Skilled teachers use behaviors appropriate to the situation. Even though one's ultimate goal may be to stimulate social cognition, it is important to be firm, establish and enforce limits, and act so as to extinguish or reinforce particular behaviors. Social cognition is effective in situations in which clear limits have been established. The teacher needs to make a distinction between using direct techniques as a way of moving toward social cognition and using such techniques as ends in themselves. When children come to school with firmly established inner controls, teachers can more readily engage them in social problem solving. Children with fewer internal controls may, in the beginning, require a more mechanistic approach to alter their behavior. The goal with these children is to stop inappropriate actions and at the same time remain committed to and deeply involved in moving these children toward an intellectual understanding of their own and others' behavior.

In the constructivist approach, the adult's role is to help the child direct his or her own behavior and recognize the consequences of his or her actions (the external as well as the internal rewards and punishments). As the child grows in understanding self and others, the constructivist teacher provides experiences that encourage the child to look more carefully at various facets of emotional experiences and social relationships: "What do I do when I feel angry?" "How can I get a person to be my friend?" "What can I do when my friends and I disagree?" "How can I tell my friends that I am angry without hurting their feelings?" Children are very interested in these questions and appreciate having them discussed openly.

Learning in the cognitive-developmental model employs the same cognitive processes in the social as in the academic realm. Children categorize other children's attributes, classify emotional reactions, and use the scientific problem-solving method to generate solutions to social problems, much as they do to figure out problems in any other area of the curriculum. Yet many educators and parents, although they adhere to a constructivist view when considering academic problems, take on a behaviors view when dealing with social issues. Social cognition represents an attempt to bring together cognitive and social learning in a consistent manner.

The Importance of Social Cognition

Issues related to social-emotional development have always been important in programs for young children. In recent years, as developmental psychologists have expanded our understanding of social-emotional growth, they have clearly made the connection between social-emotional behavior and cognition (Kohlberg, 1966; Shure & Spivack, 1978a; Damon, 1977).

Why does social cognition deserve our attention? The answer to this question relates to three important dimensions of human activity: first, successful learning at school; second, coping with life's stresses; and third, effectively adapting as an individual to society's changing demands.

Impact on Learning

Teachers committed to improving children's academic skill recognize the relationship between social cognition and school success: matters of self-esteem and social relationships impact children's ability to acquire and improve their writing, reading, and mathematics skills. Some consider the school's role to be limited to teaching academic skills and helping children gain knowledge. This notion provides the framework for the "back to basics" movement and is also at the heart of many school reform programs. Children do need to learn how to read, write, and compute. They need to know basic information about science and history; and they need to be exposed to great works of literature, art, and music. The school's role is to further this type of learning—basically, learning in the intellectual domain.

The real question is whether it is possible to achieve these goals without taking into consideration the learner's mental health. Learners' feelings about themselves and their ability to cope with frustration, get along with peers, and function effectively in the school setting are important factors in children's interest in and ability to master school subjects. Developmental education places a strong emphasis on the role of mental health in learning. Feelings about oneself and others are thought to be of critical importance in how a child learns (Currie, 1988; Kupersmidt, 1983).

Ability to Cope with Stress

Social cognition also helps children identify ways of coping with stress, a key factor in mental health. For many children, growing up in today's world presents situations that evoke strong negative feelings. Parents are often under economic or interpersonal stress. Frequently they are required to change jobs and move the family's residence. In many families, parents divorce; some enter into other relationships, some remarry, and some maintain single-parent households. Accompanying each of these situations is a period of transition, which is usually associated with increased stress. In addition, the number of reported child abuse cases is increasing, and the use of alcohol and drugs is becoming more widespread. Rapid changes in societal values affect attitudes toward school, home, and church. These rapid changes, with their accompanying lack of stability, increase the number of children who bring to school deep-seated feelings of fear and hostility.

Teachers report an increase in the number of children who are aggressive, who act out, who have difficulty getting along in school. They also report an increase in the number of children who are listless, apathetic, and disinterested in learning. The conditions under which these children live often provide little opportunity for healthy expression of emotions, and thus children are learning inadequate coping strategies. Stress per se is not the problem. Stress is a fact of life. What is important is the way individuals learn to cope with stress. This learning is complex; the ability to reflect on one's behavior and to use problem-solving strategies to bring about desired results is valuable in helping children gain control over their lives.

Learning how to deal with stress in a problem-solving way is as important a curricular goal in a day care program for three-year-olds as it is in a second-grade classroom with seven-year-olds. Some children's social-emotional problems are so complicated that teachers feel the problems are beyond the children's ability to deal with them, and other interventions are recommended.

Consider Vasily, in a second-grade classroom. She exhibits aggressive behavior on the playground, comes late to school every day, and refuses to engage in any written tasks the teacher provides. Vasily's teacher thinks this behavior is related to a parental attitude toward school. The teacher has tried to influence the parental attitude. She has repeatedly explained to the parent the difficulty arriving late is causing for Vasily. Vasily misses periods of initial instruction. By the time she joins the group, the children have already settled in for the day. They have already established social interaction patterns—deciding whom to talk with, and with whom to work. Vasily, when she arrives late, feels left out and has a difficult time becoming a member of the group. Following teacher conversations with the parent, Vasily usually arrives at school on time two out of five days of the week. This pattern rapidly regresses, and Vasily again is coming late every day.

The principal intercedes and informs the child's parent that if the child does not arrive at school on time, the child would not be allowed to enter. The child would be considered absent and might need to repeat the grade. Once again the school arrival pattern improved, but once in school Vasily continued to show a defiant attitude: "I won't do this work and you can't make me." Vasily's defiance could lead her in one or more different directions. She could continue to resist school expectations and eventually drop out of school; or she might develop a pattern of **learned helplessness,** and just give up on learning and eventually on life.

Many teachers who work with young children report that an increasing number of children suffer from learned helplessness, which is gaining increased attention in the psychological literature and seems to be on the increase in young children. The term refers to a behavior pattern in which a child experiencing any type of difficulty tends to give up rather than put forth effort to try to solve the problem (Fincham & Cain, 1985).

The term was coined by two animal researchers, Seligman and Maier (1967), who noticed that after rats had been subjected to a number of uncontrollable electric shocks, they tended to give up seeking exits even when exits were available. This process resembles what happens to children who, because they are not helped to maintain a feeling of control over their own behavior, seem to learn a pattern of action that makes them feel that they lack control. They come to believe that they can do nothing about what happens to them. If other children will not play with them, if a school task is too difficult, if the teacher says something they do not understand, these children blame themselves: "I'm no good at making friends. I'm not smart in school" (Fogel & Melson, 1988, p. 408). One of the most important goals of social cognition is to enable children to avoid learned helplessness and to develop an inner locus of control.

Vasily's case may require taking some pragmatic steps to reverse the pattern in as short a time as possible. These steps may or may not be consistent with the constructivist perspective. However, the long-term goal should be to stimulate this child and parent to think about and analyze the situations in which they find themselves, and to develop problem solving strategies that will enable Vasily to take charge of her own learning in the personal-social realm as well as in all aspects of behavior. These steps need to be taken before Vasily's defiance turns into an attitude of giving up on school.

In a complex world that changes rapidly where children, as they grow older, will need to make decisions about AIDS, drugs, health, driving patterns, caring for the environment, about almost everything, and where the number of alternatives is great—children must acquire the problem-solving skills necessary to cope.

Children need to learn patterns of coping with stress early in life, and the patterns they learn need to be ones that will be useful throughout life. Much of the literature on coping strategies places heavy emphasis on helping children tackle their problems in a cognitive way (Brenner, 1984; Shure, 1982; Kostelnik, Stein, Whiren, & Soderman, 1993). Children who learn to make thoughtful decisions are more apt to behave in socially appropriate ways than are children who act on impulse. Both children and society benefit.

Adjustment to Changing Societal Demands

The third aspect of the answer to the question why thinking about behavior is important has to do with the individual's ability to respond to the changing demands of society. Understanding how people behave is essential to all personal and work-related affairs. In our information age society, it's not only what you know that's important, but also your ability to use what you know in a constructive way in interactions with others. Education is limiting when it narrowly emphasizes or is preoccupied with the acquisition of knowledge without also creating an understanding of how to use that knowledge in relations with others. In contrast, education that values both the acquisition of knowledge and the social-emotional issues important to the learner—education that respects children's capacity to deal with these issues in a thoughtful, problem-solving way—is much better suited to the current needs of our society.

Up to this point, we have considered macro issues: how social cognition affects learning, coping skills, and society's workforce. It is also important to consider the micro perspective: the effect of social cognition on understanding oneself, understanding others, and acquiring friendship-making skills.

Understanding Oneself and Getting Along with Others

Self-understanding involves issues of motivation; self-esteem; and ability to use personal and social resources, to surmount obstacles, to extract the best from oneself, to learn, to interact with others, to overcome temperamental limitations, and to deal with strong feelings—feelings of fear, being alone, being abandoned, anger or jealousy, exuberance, love.

Consider the following scenario. Sam is four years old. This is his first year in preschool. His mother and father both work. Up to this time Sam has been cared for by a motherly babysitter who took care only of Sam in her home. The arrangement has worked out well. However, the mother felt that by four years of age, Sam would benefit from the regular stimulation of children his own age. The school staff encouraged parents to help children make a gradual transition to school. This meant that the mother, whose professional status allowed her time, accompanied Sam to school the first week and gradually reduced the length of time she spent in the classroom. During this time things seemed to be going very well for Sam.

At the beginning of the second week, Sam's mother drove him to school. She pulled up to the school gate to greet the teacher and prepared to leave. Sam protested his mother's leaving. The teacher reported that he did manage to gain control of himself during the school morning. Each day however—as he got into the car to go to school, as his mother (or father, or babysitter) tried to get him to leave the car to go into the building, as the teacher tried to acknowledge the mother's leaving and divert Sam's attention—his protests became more forceful. This daily battle continued well into the school year. Sam's emotions were very strong, and he expressed them very vociferously as he watched his mother drive off.

For the mother, the situation was embarrassing and unsettling. For the teacher, the situation was difficult, at least for the first twenty minutes of each day. As for Sam, simply by watching the behavior one could not say what he was feeling.

The teacher noted that the mother seemed quite concerned about car safety. For one thing, she insisted that Sam, who was quite a sturdy four-year-old, always ride in his car seat. The seat belt alone was not sufficient. In fact, Sam himself seemed to have an attachment to the car seat. On several occasions the teacher made time to talk with the mother. She learned that when Sam was almost three, he and his parents were in a serious automobile accident. Sam was removed from the car by a total stranger and taken to the hospital. He suffered minor knee injuries and was released in the care of his grandparents. His father was hospitalized for a week and returned home on crutches. His mother required surgery and was hospitalized for eight weeks. Although Sam was occasionally permitted to visit his mother during this time, she was in such a weakened condition that these visits were not always the most pleasant. Nine months later his mother was still recovering. She required a second surgery. During this period she wanted to bring Sam close to her, but it was very difficult for her to cuddle this very active little boy. After about three months following the second surgery Sam's mother began feeling more like herself. She had been pretty well recovered for about six months prior to Sam's enrollment in nursery school.

This information shed new light on Sam's behavior. The teacher observed Sam at play in the preschool and noticed that he was particularly attracted to the cars and to people getting in and out of them. She accepted Sam's apparent perseveration with this theme and at appropriate times reflected the feelings he demonstrated in his words and his actions. Within this structure Sam did all the manipulating of the materials. The teacher listened and supported the play. Gradually Sam's protests about leaving the car when he came to school in the morning lessened. He showed marked improvement in the freedom and spirit with which he engaged in school activities. Some of this improvement was due to Sam's increasing trust in the teachers, his greater comfort level in the school environment, and his increasing maturity. Another factor was that the free play at school afforded Sam a mode for thinking about his behavior. As Sam's worries and concerns became more tangible and more manageable, Sam's ability to make friends improved.

This example illustrates the energy children expend in dealing with their emotions and trying to understand them. When children deny their emotions—deep-seated as Sam's or of a less traumatic origin—they gain expression either through inappropriate overt or covert behavior. One could even look at such expression as desirable: unless a child finds a way to express feelings, the complex structure of the relationships between feelings and behavior becomes so strong that, like a constructed bird's nest, it becomes difficult to pull apart. Unexpressed feelings will interfere with an individual's ability to function, learn, and interact with others. Expressing feelings in inappropriate ways also causes many other problems.

Rationale for the Cognitive Approach

The discussion thus far has centered on the rationale for including social-emotional issues in the curriculum and the important role social-emotional issues play in learning and development. Why is it valuable to help children develop a thinking approach to their social-emotional concerns? Why not use a behavioral approach, and let the teacher tell the child what the rules are in the classroom and how one needs to behave in order to get along with others and then just expect that children will learn and will behave appropriately? Or why not use a play prevention approach, and let children express their feelings in play? Give children a chance to interact freely with materials and to be with peers, and they will soon learn how to get along. Neither of these approaches is consistent with the developmental framework. The behavioral approach, reflecting the cultural transmission orientation, provides for responsibility to rest with the authority figure rather than with the child. The play prevention approach reflects a romantic orientation. It does provide opportunity through play for children to express and master overwhelming emotions and to work out social-emotional issues. However, play prevention often does not go far enough in articulating the role of the adult in guiding children's play and stimulating the use of other techniques for social problem-solving.

Social cognition, as a part of the cognitive-developmental model, is broader in its emphasis and encourages generalization. It helps individuals feel in charge and responsible for their own behavior and enables individuals to learn from their own actions and from interactions with the environment. Social cognition, or the process of thinking about one's feelings and interactions with others, is useful not only in helping children cope with strong feelings and redirect their socially inappropriate behavior, but also in other areas of human functioning. Teaching children to think about their own behavior can help them be more productive, work more efficiently, achieve more for themselves, and become empowered, for they will not be owned by obstacles that stand in the way of their taking control of themselves. Teachers can engage children in thinking about questions such as: "What will help you get started on your project?" "Where will it be easy for you to work?" "If you are near Marlene, will it help you or not?" Children can also be encouraged to think about making transitions, improving work habits, identifying the supports they need, countering distraction or impulsivity, and taking joy and pleasure for themselves.

Factors Influencing Development of Social Cognition

In discussing social cognition, we identified several reasons it is important to incorporate social-emotional issues into the curriculum and classroom management and emphasized the value of the social-cognitive approach in this process.

At this point we need to explore in greater detail exactly what is involved in acquiring competence in this approach. The goal of this section is to identify specific factors that influence the process. Understanding these factors is important for the teacher who is attempting to implement this approach in the classroom or evaluate aspects of it that are already in place. The factors include the following:

- cognitive stage of development: egocentricity and the process of decentering
- children's construction of social knowledge: understanding rules; right and wrong; friendship patterns
- factors influencing the acquisition of social skills: self-concept; cultural identity; gender
- approaches to social skill training: thought-provoking motivation; problem-solving techniques

Cognitive Stage of Development

What developmental stages do children go through as they acquire social knowledge? Of what type of thinking are they capable at different ages? Piaget's work on cognitive development provides the groundwork for answering these questions. Piaget applied stage theory to children's **moral reasoning** as well as to their thinking about aspects of the physical world. According to Piagetian theory, one important change that occurs between the preoperational and the concrete operational stages is a shift from egocentric thinking—viewing experiences from one's own point of view—to an ability to decenter, or take another's perspective.

To gain an understanding of how egocentric thinking manifests itself in social behavior, consider the following incident. A three-year-old picks up a pencil, uses it for a while on a piece of paper, and then decides to find out, in a sensorimotor fashion, all the things a sharp pointed pencil can do. He takes the pencil and walks around the room, apparently looking for another piece of paper. He spies the teacher's foam-cushioned chair, raises his arm and with great force and great glee, punches a hole right through the seat. From the adult's perspective, this behavior is inappropriate. It represents a destruction of property, and it cannot and should not be continued. However, the ability to consider the child's point of view influences in what tone this message is conveyed.

The child in a preoperational stage of thinking can keep in mind only one idea at a time. The idea in the preoperational thinker is usually an egocentric one—that is, based on the child's perception of the situation rather than on how this egocentric idea, namely the pleasure of experimenting with the pushing tool, might impinge on the rights of others. At the particular moment of punching the hole in the seat, the child was engrossed in the idea of finding a new way to use a sharp pointed pencil. If this is the nature of the child's thinking, then how can we expect socially appropriate behavior at this age? The fact that thrusting the pencil could cause damage to the seat was beyond the child's comprehension at the moment that he was engaged in the pencil thrust. In situations such as these, the adult's instinctive reaction is to reprimand or punish the child. However, this response ignores the fact that the child, because he is an egocentric thinker, cannot fully comprehend why he is being punished. In a situation like this, the child is most apt to conclude that his or her ideas are not good and are not valued. Young children cannot differentiate their ideas from themselves. Thus, the experience leaves the child feeling, "I am no good."

The implication here is not that the adult should ignore socially inappropriate behavior from a child in an egocentric stage of development. Rather, the idea is to understand the child's perspective and use this understanding as a basis for setting up the environment and interacting with the child so that socially inappropriate behavior does not occur. For a young child, being made to feel no good—whatever the reason—is a very devastating experience. It is less likely to occur in a classroom where the teacher is sensitive to children's egocentric thinking and uses this understanding to prevent inappropriate behavior from occurring.

One way that adults can take young children's egocentricity into account is to lay the foundation for expected behaviors in clearly expressed terms. Through the use of positive statements, adults can guide behavior and channel egocentrism into positive channels: "Use the pencil on the paper. Keep the paper on the table when you are writing." Sometimes when children fail to adhere to the expected behavior, it is because the adult has failed to clearly state the expectations and thus has allowed children's egocentrism to get played out in inappropriate ways.

Because the term *egocentricity* has a double meaning, it is often misunderstood and viewed negatively. When we talk about a person being egocentric, we frequently mean that the person thinks only about him- or herself. Often, the behavior that results from such thinking is described as selfishness. Putting this interpretation on children's thinking—or on any thinking for that matter—results in a gross misinterpretation of development. Hillel, the famous biblical philosopher, wrote: "If I am not for myself, who will be for me? And if I am only for myself, what am I? If not now, when?" (Platt, 1969), This often-quoted statement epitomizes social-emotional development.

Piaget helped us recognize that egocentric thought is characteristic of a particular stage of development. Although Piaget himself stated that there is no direct relationship between age and stage and that an individual progresses from one stage to another according to his or her own developmental rate, egocentrism, as indicative of preoperational thought, is most often associated with children ages two to seven. If young children cannot view a situation from another's perspective, then how can we expect them to engage in the processes of thinking about social situations, in which perspective-taking is of critical importance? At what age can children take another person's perspective? At what age can we expect a child to think before using a pencil to punch a hole through a seat cover, to think about the damage to property, the implications of this damage, and the effect that this action will have on others? Or to put it in Piagetian terms, at what point can we expect a child to decenter; to behave less egocentrically; and to be able to engage in perspective-taking, the capacity to understand how others feel and think?

Piagetian research describes children as being egocentric until the age of six or seven. More recent studies, however, have indicated that egocentricity as manifested in being able to take the perspective of others appears "at dramatically different ages—at eighteen months, at two and a half years, at four or even ten years—according to the task and the setting" (Dunn, 1988, p. 3; Flavell, 1985b). Some people use these findings to cast doubt on the efficacy of Piagetian theory. Others, like Dunn, view these new findings as building upon Piagetian ideas. Piaget may not have been totally accurate in his description of stages. Or perhaps he limited his study only to specific aspects of the child's behavior: how children acquire an understanding of rules, and ideas about what is fair and unfair. Despite some of the new findings that are interpreted as weakening Piaget's theory, Piaget did highlight the importance of cognitive development and did relate cognition to the moral domain. Current research is refining this area of study.

Children's Construction of Social Knowledge

A second factor influencing the process of social cognition is the way children construct **social knowledge**: ideas about rules, right and wrong, and friendship patterns. Judy Dunn (1988), a researcher who studied children's development of social understanding, acknowledged the Piagetian contribution: "I take it for granted that cognitive changes are involved in the dramatic developments in a child's ability to reflect on others and the social world, but the growth of this understanding involves more than an unfolding of cognitive abilities" (p. 176). Also operating, according to Dunn, is the child's drive to understand self and others, a drive linked to "the nature of the child's relationships within the family," particularly those relationships involving the child's social effectiveness within the family—opportunities the child has for organizing play, engaging in conversation, and sharing jokes. Also contributing are affective experiences within the family. These may be related to socialization practices involving experiences of guilt, anxiety, or fear and the affective tension in relationships between siblings and between parent and child. This tension "provides an important impetus for understanding the social world" (Dunn, 1988, p. 181). In this sense, conflicts between children and between adult and child are considered to be growth-producing.

For example, in play with others, and sometimes as a way to test adults, children often engage in a type of humor that focuses on socially inappropriate bathroom talk and that many adults find very annoying. This type of behavior usually occurs as children are beginning to be aware of the prevailing social attitude toward this topic of conversation and are trying to understand it. Once they recognize that bathroom talk is not socially acceptable in certain situations, they test out its inappropriateness through humor. Appreciating that this type of humor is the child's way of constructing understanding influences adults' reactions to it.

From the reactions generated in these types of situations, the child constructs social knowledge. According to Piaget, individuals gain social knowledge through the process of arguing, justifying, and negotiating aspects of interactions with others. However, the force that impels children toward greater understanding of the social world is not solely a cognitive one. Vygotsky's and others' work has helped us appreciate that cognition alone does not result in understanding. Rather, cognition is combined with affective experiences of a sociocultural nature.

Ideas About Rules

When a four-year-old changes the rules of the checker game while the game is in progress to suit her own ends, this behavior probably results from the way she thinks about rules. Four-year-olds can repeat the rules as stated—but try to explain to a four-year-old why she can only move from one black square to another adjacent black square! Frequently, the child becomes irritated with the explanation. According to four-year-old thinking, rules can be made, broken, or ignored to serve the child's own purpose. To insist that the rules be followed is futile and will undoubtedly result in a tirade of angry feelings. To call the child a cheater can be damaging to her self-concept and also does not reflect understanding of development. Most four-year-olds, on their own volition, have difficulty adhering to rules.

The seven-year-old, on the other hand, is usually rule-bound. If the rule is that we take turns carrying the ball out to recess, then a great deal of energy is expended in verifying whose turn it is. Angry feelings are generated anytime differences of opinion arise about how the rules are being followed.

Children's understanding of rules, according to stage theories of moral development, progresses in a clearly defined sequence and is related to cognitive development. As they mature, children construct their own understanding of rules. They do this through their interactions with peers (Piaget, 1932/1965; Kohlberg, 1976). Just as the child experiments with pulleys and levers and discovers for herself how these things work, so, too, the child experiments with what is often called cheating. The child organizes experiences related to the behavior and arrives at his or her own guidelines for future action. When is it okay not to play by the rules? Is cheating ever acceptable? These kinds of judgments come from a process of moral reasoning. Note that although the words *cheating, lying,* and *stealing* have a negative connotation, those who work with children recognize that the behaviors they describe are a part of most children's repertoire, particularly at certain stages of development.

Issues of Right and Wrong

Lying, stealing, and being a tattletale are behaviors that are not considered appropriate in the school culture but are exhibited by many children in the primary grades. These behaviors are often related to children's stage of development.

Consider, for example, young children's tendency to distort the truth, which is often related to an inability to distinguish between fantasy and reality. This tendency explains the extreme fear younger children experience when someone they know dresses up in a spooky Halloween costume or puts on a scary mask. Between the ages of two and seven, children frequently have difficulty distinguishing between reality and fantasy. They make up stories that they put forth as true. Usually these stories have some similarity to the child's actual experience. However, in the spirit of creative thinking—an important intellectual process that the child becomes capable of during the preschool years—the stories usually combine facts from a variety of different experiences; added to this combination is a bit of imaginative or symbolic thinking. Thus, the child who becomes afraid to go to school because there is a big dog in the playground may be describing in hyperbolic terms a small chihuahua, or may be describing a German shepherd he saw at the playground while visiting his grandmother in another state.

When this storytelling tendency results in a child's coming home at the beginning of the first grade and telling her mother that she doesn't want to go to school anymore, that she has a bad teacher who yells a lot, doesn't let children go out for recess, and makes them sit in their seats all day—a story that, based on adult experience, sounds plausible—the parent is almost ready to go up to the school to see what is going on. However, usually the parent has heard many other stories, part true and part imagined, and tries first to question the child about the reality. "Now, Eve, tell me the truth. What actually happened?" And Eve repeats the story adding a few more gory details. The parent may begin to worry: "What type of a child is this? A born liar? What should I do?" At this point suffice to say that we understand what causes this behavior: the child's budding sense of initiative combined with the intellectual ability to create in the mind symbolic images and an inability sometimes to distinguish between fact and fantasy.

Older children, those between the ages of five and ten, worry about being able to do what is expected in terms of schoolwork or in terms of athletics. Frequently they resort to telling tall tales or to tattletale behavior. The first-grade child who wants to become a good reader, the second-grade child who wants the praise of the adults as much as the attention of peers, the child who shows industriousness as she struggles to become good at jumping rope—these children are experiencing a continuous tug between industry and inferiority (an Eriksonian concept). As children experience setbacks in striving to achieve competence, they often resort to compensatory behaviors such as stealing and lying.

The constructivist teacher believes that learning comes from within the child and that the child needs to participate actively in the learning process. Just as children need to experiment with magnets and discover magnetic properties for themselves, so, too, children need to experiment with what is often called cheating, lying, or stealing in order to determine for themselves when they should play by the rules and when the rules need to be adapted to fit the situation. Children also need the opportunity to engage in problem-solving discussions about this behavior. Only experience can help an individual know under what circumstances it is better to tell a white lie than to proclaim the truth. This development occurs as a result of maturation and interactions in the environment.

Friendship Patterns

Children's relationships with others constitute another area in which developmental forces, both cognitive and emotional, are reflected and combined with children's construction of the idea of friendship (Damon, 1977; Kohlberg, 1969; Edwards, 1986). The four-year-old's patterns of friendship are very different from those of the six- or eight-year-old. Carolyn Edwards (1986) made this point very clearly in describing children's friendship patterns at different ages. The younger child refers to other children as friends, but generally *friend* means someone with whom one plays. When young children proclaim to one another, "You are not my friend," they usually mean "I do not want to play with you right now." This developmental stage has classroom implications: when engaging children in discussion about friends it is important to recognize their conception of friendship. In redirecting behavior of young children, focusing on the physical aspects of the situation ("Pushing hurts—use words") is usually more effective than using expressions such as "Be nice to her—she is your friend."

Children do not have enduring concepts of friendship and thus do not generally comprehend the latter message. This same principle holds true in trying to build a sense of community in classrooms of younger children. As Edwards (1986) explains, expressions such as "We are all friends in this classroom" are usually meaningless to young children. Children respond more readily to situations in which they share experiences, such as mealtimes and music or movement activities. Most children progress very rapidly in their friendship-making skills. By age seven or eight, friendships are more long term and are based on mutual trust. Good friends in this age group share "feelings, secrets, and promises" (Edwards, 1986, p. 118).

This rapid progression in friendship making skills can be seen in the contrast between the four-year-old who enters a new environment where there are other children clutching a favorite teddy bear or a blanket and the six-year old who also experiences anxiety at the beginning of the school year and takes comfort in forming alliances with the other children.

This point is dramatically illustrated in a short story by William Saroyan, "The First Day of School." The story reveals how Jim Davies expresses his anger and his fear as his caretaker takes him off to school on the first day and how these feelings of anger and fear become dissipated as the day goes on. The story shows how children align themselves with other children and how far removed they are—even in first grade—from the influences of the teacher. When Hannah Winter is reprimanded for chewing gum, Jim Davies has as his one main goal to get some gum so that he too can be reprimanded. It is obvious from the story that Jim wants to be like Hannah—a part of the group. This is a primary motive for his behavior.

As children are engaged in constructing their own notion of friendship, they frequently show behavior that can be troublesome to teachers. Consider the following typical peer interaction among seven-year-olds:

> Skipper, a seven-year-old boy, is sitting on a bean bag in the reading corner of his first-grade classroom. His eyes are focused on the book he is reading. Occasionally he glances around the room to see what other children are doing. He makes eye contact with Louisa, who decides that she too would like to read

Children construct an understanding of friendship through repeated encounters with others. This understanding is influenced by normative growth patterns, children's unique qualities, and their daily experiences. © 1992 by Jeffrey High/Image Productions

> a book. In her words, as she explained the incident to the teacher, "I needed to get a book, so I crept into the reading corner. There wasn't much room so I slid in between the book shelves and the bean bag so that I could find the book that I wanted. As I slipped through, Skipper became all excited and started to call me names: 'You ugly jerk. You're such a smelly skunk! Get out of here.'"

This was only one of many incidents that occurred throughout the day. In some, Skipper and Louisa were the principal participants: "Just because a picture fell off the wall, he said that I did it." "He just keeps following me around. He says everyone hates me." In other incidents, other children were involved—for example, Louisa and Adrian: "Adrian keeps licking herself and rubbing it on my back. When I tell her to stop it, she just adds one more thing."

What prompts children to act in this manner? Commonly, children's behavior toward one another is explained as resulting from their family background. Try analyzing the above situations in terms of family background. Did Adrian ever see her parents or other adults in her environment try to make friends by licking fingers and rubbing the fingers on the potential friend (or potential enemy, since friends and enemies are often on two ends of the same continuum)? Most likely not. It is also most unlikely that Louisa's interactions with Skipper resulted from their imitating adult behavior or from their upbringing. This type of behavior occurs in many children as they attempt to work through patterns of social interaction. Perhaps the children's sex or a clash between their temperaments has something to do with it. How teachers react to this type of behavior and how they help children understand and deal with it can be of critical importance in children's development.

Acquisition of Social Skills

Children's developing intellect, along with their emotional and social experiences in their families and communities, contributes to the development of social skills. Social skills can be grouped in two categories: skills related to **prosocial behavior,** which include being cooperative, helpful, and willing to share with others; and friendship-making skills, which include making contact, establishing positive relationships, and being able to engage in conflict resolution.

Influential Factors

Underlying skill development in both of these categories are individuals' feelings about themselves, as well as factors associated with culture and gender.

Self-Concept

Developing a positive **self-concept** is critical to the development of social skills. Kostelnik, Stein, Whiren, and Soderman (1993) make this point very graphically. These authors describe two children, each reacting to the same comment from a teacher: "I'm sorry. There will not be time to hear everyone's ideas." One child said that he felt that the teacher did not see that he had his hand up from the very beginning, so she did not call on him. Another child indicated that the teacher deliberately ignored him because nothing he had to say would have been important. This type of reasoning is related both to self-concept and to **attribution theory,** which Berk (1991) described as "common everyday speculations about the causes of behavior" (p. 441). Attribution theory is often related to achievement motivation. An individual with a positive self-concept tends to attribute success to personal effort; those with lower self-concepts tend to feel that whether they meet with failure or success is a matter of luck and has nothing to do with their efforts. It takes only a little imagination to figure out how these different perceptions would play out in individual children's social interactions. Self-concept is related to self-esteem. People with high self-esteem believe they have the power to make a difference that is satisfying to themselves and valued by those they care about. (Note the link between attribution theory and the locus of control concept.)

"Self-concept refers to individuals' overall perception of their abilities, behavior, and personality" (Santrock & Yussen, 1992, p. 68). Carl Rogers, the founder of humanistic psychology, stressed the importance of three factors in adult attempts to help children develop positive self-concepts. The first is unconditional positive regard: accepting, valuing, and being positive toward another person regardless of that person's behavior. According to Rogerian psychology, it is important that the adult let the child know how the adult feels about a particular behavior and at the same time convey a feeling of positive regard for the child him- or herself. The second and third factors for adults to remember as they try to help children develop a positive self-concept are empathy, which involves being a sensitive listener, and genuineness, which means being open about one's feelings. Genuineness involves providing clear feedback—praise that is specific and clearly indicates why praise is justified. These techniques, which help individuals feel good about themselves, also help the individual get along with others (Santrock & Yussen, 1992, p. 68; Rogers, 1974).

Self-concept begins to develop at birth. It is influenced by children's "experiences with their bodies, experience with their social environments, and their cognitive developmental stage" (Derman-Sparks & A.B.C. Task Force, 1989, p. 2). Children begin to form concepts about racial and gender identity between the ages of two and six (Katz, 1982; Kohlberg, 1966). They develop attitudes toward children with disabilities during this same period (Froschl & Sprung, 1983). As a result, early childhood teachers need to be particularly aware of the curriculum to which children are exposed. The books children read, the reactions children have toward one another, and the stereotypes children reflect in their play need to be addressed through a social cognitive approach if the concepts embodied in these different activities are to have a positive impact on children's self-concepts.

Being able to identify with aspects of the school environment influences self-concept and is an important factor in children's willingness to take risks associated with learning. For this reason, teachers need to assess their environments thoughtfully. If all the pictures of families presented in the classroom show a mother, a father, and children, the child with a different family structure will have difficulty identifying with the school environment. Similarly children who are native American, Asian, or African American will have difficulty feeling valued in an environment where they see no pictures or objects reflecting their images or cultures.

Cultural Identity

Social skills are culturally linked; they represent particular value systems or survival patterns. Before teachers can attempt to engage children in a particular set of value-laden social skills—through preaching, through reward and punishment, or through a constructivist approach—teachers need to take into account parents' values regarding their children's behavior, including ideas about aggression, rules, and methods of enforcement. For example, teachers who punish are looked on positively by some cultural groups and rejected by others. Similarly, teachers who use a constructivist approach will meet with favor from some parents and disapproval from others. As cultural groups come into greater contact with one another, it is important that the tension brought about by conflicting values be addressed.

In addition, schools should help children form attitudes about cultural diversity. The aim is to help children appreciate and value differences, to have opportunities that will aid them in refining overgeneralizations and stereotypes (Edwards, 1986). Edwards pointed out that overgeneralizing is a common tendency in young children and is usually due to limited experience. As an example of an overgeneralization, she quoted a white child, four years and seven months old:

The children are learning about African culture as they watch and participate in this demonstration of turban wrapping. © Gail Meese/Meese Photo Research

"Chinese people eat in restaurants." When the teacher asked, "All the time or some of the time?" the child responded, "All of the time!" For an interesting discussion of this characteristic of children's thinking, as well as activities consistent with the social cognitive approach, that are designed to clarify this thinking, see Carolyn Edwards' *Promoting Social and Moral Development in Young Children: Creative Approaches for the Classroom* (1986).

Gender

A number of studies have emphasized that despite major similarities in the way the sexes interact and approach social situations, there are some significant differences (Feinburg, 1977; Gilligan, 1982; Pitcher & Schultz, 1983). Boys are more concerned with objects, materials, and events of an impersonal nature, whereas girls are more personal in their orientation. "Boys . . . often orient toward individualism and 'separateness' from others," whereas "girls often acquire a morality of care because from infancy on they orient towards attachment and 'connectedness' with others" (Damon, 1988, quoting Gilligan, 1982, p. 97). A key question that research is attempting to answer is how these different orientations relate to childrearing practice.

The differences manifest themselves in a wide assortment of ways—in the nature of children's play, in the toys and equipment children find compelling, and in the way they interact socially. Girls are more interested in individual relationships; boys, in groups, gangs, and teams (Feinburg, 1977). Many female teachers identify easily with girls, whose "care" orientation provides a basis for understanding feelings other than one's own. Often female teachers experience difficulty relating to boys, whose orientation is more individualistic.

These generalizations are helpful in guiding teachers' understanding of the common orientation for each of the genders; however, individual differences persist, and many children challenge these stereotypes. Nonetheless, an understanding of certain proclivities of boys and girls will assist the teacher in designing social experiences that foster attributes and attitudes in synch with the child's orientation.

Approaches to Social Skills Training

Some people believe that children take on the social patterns of interaction that they observe in the adults with whom they interact: parents or teachers. Certainly some behaviors are learned through imitation, with several factors influencing the process, including the temperament of the child and of the adult, the child's physical state, and the cultural milieu in which the child spends out-of-school hours.

When we talk about social skills in this chapter, we are not talking about skills that adults try to teach children by preaching. Nor are we referring to social behavior that children learn through imitation and modeling. The term *social skills* in the developmental framework refers to children's ability to think about and be in control of their own social behavior; this sense of the term is consistent with the constructivist view of development, which postulates that the forces for growth and development come from within the child and from the child's interaction with the environment.

In an earlier chapter, we talked about the common belief that children learn social skills by having an adult tell them how to behave—a cultural transmission orientation: "If you don't share your toys, the other children will not play with you." "Grabbing things from other people is not nice. If you do that, nobody will want to be your friend." The cognitive-developmentalists believe that children learn very little from this type of preaching. Cognitive-developmentalists point out that preoperational thinkers, who can keep in mind only one idea at a time, probably will hear "other children will not play with you" and act on that premise or will focus on the power phrase, "grabbing things," fail to pay attention to the "not nice" part of the statement, and grab things even more intently. If you would like to test out this postulation, you need only observe interactions between children and adults. Listen for preaching statements, and watch how children respond to them. Or you, yourself, can try directing behavior using these kinds of statements and see what happens.

The challenge to the developmental teacher is to increase children's understanding and at the same time find ways to enhance their natural development. The key is to identify strategies that help children to be in control of their own learning. Obviously, the assumption here is that as children develop, they will want to act in ways that society considers appropriate. (In some circumstances, this assumption does not hold true—for example, in the case of delinquent or criminal behavior when an individual thinks about his or her behavior and decides to act in totally inappropriate ways. However, even in such cases there is evidence that children whose behavior is socially inappropriate often do not think about their actions or indeed know how to think about them [Spivack & Levine, 1963].) Children are social beings; for the most part, when children feel in control of their own behavior, and a particular situation does not conflict with their developmental needs at the time, children can be trusted and expected to act appropriately.

The Interpersonal Cognitive Problem-Solving Program

Some of the early work in social cognition was carried out by Shure and Spivack in 1974. Working at the Hahnemann Medical College and Hospital in Philadelphia, they developed a program called "A Cognitive Approach to Solving Interpersonal Problems: A Mental Health Program for Kindergarten Children" (revised in 1978, and again in 1992 with forms for preschool and kindergarten through primary grades). One interesting aspect of this work was its focus on the thought processes children use in making decisions about how to act in interpersonal situations, rather than on specific behaviors such as hitting or taking toys away from others.

The research carried out on this program (later referred to as the Interpersonal Cognitive Problem Solving Curriculum, or ICPS) is also interesting. The social skills training based on this program seemed to be equally valuable to children with a wide range of IQs (70–120 and up). When such training was provided in nursery school, it seemed to act as a preventive measure. After three months of using the ICPS curriculum, teachers and the researchers noted changes in the children's behavior. As compared with a control group, significantly fewer children who showed problem behavior in nursery school and who received the ICPS training demonstrated problem behavior in kindergarten (Shure & Spivack, 1978a).

Shure and Spivack also related the children's acquisition of ICPS skills with their mothers' childrearing practices. They contrasted mothers who told their children how to behave in social situations (for example, "Hit back," or "Tell the teacher") with mothers who help their children think about problems and generate solutions on their own. When parents tell children what to do, the children may either worry about how to carry out that advice or act impulsively and carry out the advice in inappropriate situations.

Shure told the story of a child who was standing in front of the slide with her back turned toward the slide. The child was accidentally bumped on the shoulder by a child who came down the slide, and she turned and hit that child. When asked why she hit the child, she replied, "My mommy told me to hit." She seemed totally oblivious to the reason she was bumped in the first place and to the fact that her impulsive action could cause more hitting and other problems. She simply did what she was told to do.

When Shure and her associates provided training in ICPS skills for mothers and children—both sons and daughters—together, teachers who were unaware of the home training noted improved ICPS skills in the school setting. Teachers noted these results only three months after home training. Teachers saw the improvement in boys as well as girls, possibly because the training encouraged providing children with the opportunity to think for themselves, thus reducing the boys' resistance to guidance (Shure & Spivack, 1978a).

A Cognitive-Social Learning Model of Social Skills Training

Another model of social skills training for preschool children was developed by Mize and Ladd (1990). The preschool program was developed as an intervention for children identified as neglected or rejected through sociometric techniques and classroom observation. The researchers were prompted to develop a program specifically for preschool children because (1) they recognized "the potential current and long-term consequences of peer rejection in childhood" (Mize & Ladd, 1990), and (2) they identified specific aspects of social behavior in preschoolers that made preschool an optimal time to introduce social skills training. Aspects of preschoolers' social behavior include the important role peers play in young children's development (Hartup, 1983; Mize, Ladd, & Price, 1985), and the fact that differences in social competence and peer acceptance appear to remain somewhat stable over time (Ladd & Price, 1987; Waldrup & Halverson, 1975).

The Mize and Ladd (1990) model focuses on target skills:

- prosocial leading: making positive suggestions (in a somewhat directed but not a bossy way) as a way to initiate, direct, elaborate, and maintain joint play themes
- asking questions in a friendly or neutral tone
- commenting and identifying the play theme (for example, "We're putting out the fire! We're putting out the fire!")
- supporting (making explicitly positive statements to peers, giving peers help, or showing affection)

This social skills training program was carried out in the context of sociodramatic play. The materials included "blocks, stuffed animals and medical equipment (for a pretend veterinary hospital); a toy pickup truck with trailer, boat driver and passenger; Legos; a Sesame Street railroad set; and small animals, people and vehicles" (Mize & Ladd, 1990, pp. 345–346). These researchers used puppets "to present both didactic and modeled concept information" (p. 348) and videotape playback of children's interactions in specific training sessions in order to help children perceive the effect of their behaviors on others.

The researchers "observed changes in the children's use of the targeted skills in classroom interaction and noted improvements in social knowledge and sociometric scores" (p. 355). The researchers pointed out, however, that their conclusions were tentative as a result of the timing of the follow-up study. On the basis of their experiences, they identified several areas in which further research was needed, highlighting questions about the age at which interventions can be most effective, the type of intervention best suited for children with differing patterns of social interaction, the specific social skills that should be included in the program, and the best methods for providing the training.

In their discussion of possible training methods, the researchers recommended looking at "the principles and practices that characterize intervention research in other domains, such as cognitive skills training. They referred specifically to the "zone of proximal development," a concept used in reading comprehension training (Palinscar & Brown, 1984) in which the "instructor first attempts to teach the child at a level only slightly higher than his or her current level of competence. . . . Operating in the child's zone of proximal development involves an adult and a child collaborating on solving a problem" (Campione, Brown, Ferrara, & Bryant, 1984). Mize and Ladd concluded that "prior social skills interventions may have succeeded partly because the child was involved in a joint venture with an adult who began at his or her developmental level and nurtured more advanced conceptions of social interaction, more proficient performance, and more mature monitoring of the social environment" (1990, p. 357). (Note how Vygotskian theory is influencing all aspects of curriculum planning.)

Two basic approaches to social skills training the authors have identified follow. One is related to raising awareness, asking thought-provoking questions, and engaging in discussion. The second is based on a problem-solving approach.

Providing Thought-Provoking Motivation

Consider the following example: A teacher decides that the children in the group need to learn to act more kindly to one another and presents the task: "Make a picture of yourself doing something kind." This represents a romantic approach to curriculum, in which the teacher does not extend or clarify the children's understanding of the concept. The constructivist teacher encourages children to do more than pay lip service to the concept of kindness. The constructivist teacher encourages them to deal with the subject in substantive ways. For example, the teacher recognizes that asking children to make pictures of themselves may provide the opportunity for some personal exploration, but without additional input from the adult, this activity does not expand children's concept of kindness. A more meaningful motivation for this experience would be for the teacher to raise issues such as the following:

- "Do you ever feel like being kind? Let's talk about it."
- "What makes people want to be kind to others?"
- "Are you ever not kind? Why do you think that's the case?"
- "Think of some way that you could be kind to a friend, something that you don't usually do."
- "When is it hard to be kind—when you want to be kind, but you feel it's very difficult?"
- "Think of a time when someone was kind to you. How did it make you feel?"

Questions such as these stimulate discussion of issues and increase children's understanding of abstract concepts such as kindness. Adults are frequently not tuned into teasing apart concepts like kindness, fear, jealousy, and sharing and identifying the potential cognitive conflict embedded within them. In order to develop understanding of these ideas, the teacher needs to identify the concepts involved and help children understand them. This step is essential if one is to engage children in the process of social cognition.

Some children naturally engage in a reflective approach to thinking about behavior. Others find it more difficult. Some children may or may not be able to think about the consequences of their actions or to state the cause of their own or another person's behavior. They may or may not be able to see a situation from the other person's point of view. Others seem to have no difficulty acquiring these skills. If you watch a group of young children at play or work and focus on the child who seems to be the most well-adjusted socially, you will see many examples of these skills.

In the following example, a child wards off potential problems by generating nonforceful ways to get what she wants. Janel and Yolanda are working side by side at a table using a variety of objects to make prints in play dough. Janel wants to use the spool that Yolanda has been using. "Can I use that spool?" she asks. Yolanda replies, "No, I'm using it." A few moments later Janel says, "Let's see if we can make 100 spool circles. You make all you can on your dough. Then I'll make more on mine." Contrast this type of behavior to either grabbing the spool from the other other child (who would then proceed to struggle to get it back) or else whining, "Teacher, Yolanda won't give me a turn with the spool."

All children are interested in and benefit from discussions of social-emotional issues. For those who for a variety of possible reasons do not acquire skills in this area, a program that focuses specifically on these skills can be a great benefit to mental health, to interpersonal relations, and to cognitive development.

The Problem-Solving Approach

In addition to providing thought-provoking motivation and observing and discussing prosocial behaviors children exhibit, the cognitive-developmental teacher also finds problem-solving techniques particularly useful for developing interpersonal skills. Research has indicated that helping children become better social problem solvers "improves their relationships and reduces the risk of maladjustment among children from distressed family backgrounds" (Berk, 1991; Downey & Walker, 1989; Pettit, Dodge, & Brown, 1988). Spivack and Shure (1974) found that "after applying a specific problem solving program with low income inner city children at risk for adjustment difficulties, trained pupils, in contrast to untrained controls, improved in both social reasoning and teacher-rated social adjustment. These gains were still evident a year after completion of training" (Berk, 1991, p. 467; Spivack & Shure, 1974; Shure, 1981).

The ability to solve problems is a skill that children need to learn and that can be applied to cognitive problems as well as to social-emotional ones. The problem-solving approach is fairly well known. It is a thoughtful approach that, if internalized early, can be exceptionally useful. It involves five basic steps:

1. identifying the problem
2. brainstorming possible solutions
3. selecting one solution
4. trying out the solution
5. evaluating the results

The problem-solving paradigm is useful in all curriculum areas and in all walks of life. It is particularly appropriate in the social arena.

The first step is to define the problem clearly. When people first begin to talk about a problem, their descriptions are usually quite global. In the case of Uma and Tomo described earlier in this chapter, the problem as Tomo saw it was that Uma had messed up all his work. Uma, however, wondered, "Couldn't Tomo see that this was just an accident? He didn't need to punch me." In fact, many related issues make up this problem—issues related to the traffic pattern, the way materials are obtained and carried, the appropriate way to act when someone is aggressive, the attitude one should assume when one accidentally causes damage to someone else's property, the way one reacts to an accidental damage, how unifix cubes are arranged on the desk. As one identifies all the issues, it becomes clearer what the real problem is.

Once one identifies the real problem—in this case how one reacts when someone damages or upsets your work—the second step is to brainstorm other possible solutions. One cardinal rule of brainstorming is not to pass judgment on other people's ideas. All ideas are accepted, no matter how far-fetched or humorous. In fact, in brainstorming in business think tanks, one often hears a great deal of laughter as people suggest outlandish ideas. From these outlandish ideas usually stems a very useful and creative solution. Here are some possible solutions to the Tomo-Uma problem—solutions that were actually generated by the children themselves:

- "Count to ten before speaking."
- "Force Tomo to go to the wall and beat his brains out."
- "Tell the teacher so that he will have to stay after school."
- "Let Tomo do all of Uma's math work for one week."
- "Ask Uma to help re-create the patterns."

The third step involves selecting one solution that is worth trying out—the solution that has been evaluated as the most likely to succeed. Evaluation requires some criteria: for example, it might be decided that the solution should not physically harm anyone or hurt anyone's feelings, and be likely to really work. Which of all the alternative solutions suggested above best meets these criteria?

The fourth step involves trying out the solution, and step #5 involves deciding whether or not the solution actually worked. In this case the children decided to re-create the situation. The solution they tried was to have Uma help Tomo arrange the unifix cubes exactly as they were before the accident. It was interesting to watch the friendship bonds being cemented and the minds at work on this problem.

Teachers, particularly those working with three- and four-year-olds, may find it useful to isolate the skills of this model and focus only on one aspect—for example, brainstorming alternatives or observing means-end relationships. This approach framed the research studies Spivack and Shure (1974) conducted.

Some Basic Underlying Principles

This section reviews the basic underlying principles of social cognition: the constructivist perspective on moral development, the difference between arbitrary social knowledge and moral reasoning, the role of autonomy in constructivist theory, and the dissimilarity in adult and child perspectives.

The Constructivist Perspective on Moral Development

Piaget helped us to understand the developmental issues that underscore children's thinking about moral issues. Before Piaget's ideas became popular, people used to think that moral development was the "internalization" of social values and rules. These people—parents, teachers, grandparents—believed that they could teach children not to cheat, take things that do not belong to them, or tell lies. The idea was that children would identify with the significant adults in their environment, and through identification and conscience building, the adults could ensure that the child would adhere to the adult's moral values. In a similar fashion, people believed that children could be taught to share, take turns, and be thoughtful of other people, and in this way children would make friends and become involved in appropriate social situations. Certainly, identification and modeling are important processes in determining moral values, moral behavior, and more specifically how people act with each other, but they are only a part of a much larger set of the child's personal objectives.

Piaget's work helped us to recognize that each individual constructs his or her own moral values and is in control of the way he or she behaves in social-emotional situations. Piaget showed us that moral development is a process of construction from within. In Piaget's words, "Adult behaviors which attempt to restrain the child do not promote moral development because they prevent the development of autonomy [internal control]. External rules become the child's own only when he adapts them or constructs them of his own free will" (source unknown). In Piaget's view, the child doesn't come to understand the complexities of an idea until the child has experienced, manipulated, examined, and explored it in many ways over time. An idea cannot, as Piaget maintains, be comprehended as a result of a single verbal intervention by an adult. Genuine understanding comes from repeated encounters in which the child is an active participant in making sense of the information. Vygotsky added to this perspective culture's influence on this process.

The Difference Between Arbitrary Social Knowledge and Moral Reasoning

Piaget distinguished arbitrary social knowledge from social-emotional development and moral reasoning. Arbitrary social knowledge comes from the information we receive from people in our environment. Examples of social knowledge include the following: December 25 is Christmas; there is no school on Saturdays and Sundays; people eat meat and vegetables before they eat dessert. These are arbitrary rules. So, too, is the rule that jumping on tables is not acceptable behavior. How children feel about rules, and whether or not they abide by rules, are in the realm of social-emotional and moral development. This kind of knowledge is very different from the kind of knowledge that individuals need to construct for themselves: how to make and keep friends, what causes problems in friendship situations, when to tell a white lie. One kind of knowledge involves transmission of information; the other involves construction of understanding.

The Role of Autonomy in Constructivist Theory

Autonomy is the opposite of **heteronomy.** Autonomy means being self-governed; heteronomy means allowing oneself to be governed by others. Heteronomous thinkers feel that an individual needs to be taught and guided by others. Also implicit in the concept of heteronomy is the notion that individuals will naturally follow others and that this natural tendency should be fostered. Autonomy, on the other hand, assumes that the individual can, does, and should take responsibility for his or her own behavior. It assumes that others in the individual's environment respect this innate human capacity for making decisions about one's own actions. Autonomy does not imply complete freedom, but freedom bounded by the rights of others. Earlier in this chapter, we established the rationale for the idea that the world needs autonomous thinkers.

Piaget's support for the idea of autonomy is based in part on his attitude toward apparent errors in children's thinking. These errors, according to Piaget, are important. As Carolyn Edwards (1986) explains, they are

> necessary and valuable because they create the mental tension that motivates growth and change. Because the "right" kind of errors and uncertainties are essential to development, the teacher's role should not be to try to root out and correct children's errors, but rather to implement learning encounters that let children work on the problems that naturally interest them. This perspective challenges one of the most common assumptions of teachers—that they should try to "correct" children's errors right away. Instead, teachers should create learning encounters that amplify problems and uncertainties in children's own thinking. These encounters will capture children's interest

> because they correspond to the issues on which children themselves are spontaneously working at their stage of development. (p. 9)

Children will be "confused by a teaching method that seeks to correct their errors and replace their ideas with isolated bits of adult wisdom" (Edwards, 1986, p. 12). Kamii and DeVries (1978) stated that "such teaching confuses the child because it is in opposition to his spontaneous beliefs, and it thus contributes to the development of attitudes that stifle the construction of knowledge" (p. 36).

When children are governed by adult precept, they behave in order to achieve praise and appreciation or to avoid punishment. When they are allowed to act voluntarily and autonomously, their reasons for sharing and telling the truth are different. As the children act autonomously, they become willing to sacrifice immediate benefits for the benefit of mutual relationships. Thus, they construct their own moral rules rather than merely internalizing a ready-made adult rule. For example, the individual who acts autonomously comes to feel an inner need to be truthful, because deceitfulness destroys mutual trust.

Dissimilarity of Adult and Child Perspectives

Social cognition spans three areas of development: emotional, social, and cognitive. In order to facilitate children's understanding of their own feelings and behavior as well as the feelings and behavior of others, teachers need to take into account a developmental perspective on issues in each of these areas. People tend to look at children's social-emotional behavior from an adult perspective—understandably, since children and adults experience many of the same emotions. What is different, though, is the cognitive stage of development and the accompanying ability that children and adults are able to bring to bear on their social-emotional interactions. Emotional reactions that on the surface may look very familiar to adults may be experienced by children in a totally different way because children do not have the same ability to think about or process these feelings. For example, both adults and children experience a sense of threat in the face of possible abandonment by loved ones. However, when a loved one says that he or she will return in a week, the adult has a sufficient understanding of time to temper his or her feelings, at least until the week is up. A three-year-old's sense of time is very different. The idea of one week or one hour has very little meaning for a three-year-old. Thus, any attempt to comfort a child who is distressed by the parent leaving him at school by explaining that the parent will return in an hour is relatively meaningless.

Many Piagetian ideas have become embedded in the constructivist perspective. However, recent research has questioned some specific aspects of his theory. One of these is his emphasis on stages of cognitive development. Children do show inconsistencies in their perspective-taking ability, suggesting that other factors may also be operating. Consider, for example, the inconsistencies children show in their ability to take another's point of view. At times, preschool children will totally ignore or refuse to accept an adult suggestion that they share a toy. If asked, "How would you feel if you were . . . ?" the child often responds with a blank stare. One possible reason for this lack of response is the child's inability to consider another person's point of view. Under some conditions, however, the child is willing to share. How does one explain the inconsistency? Frequently, this inconsistency leads to adults' misperception of children's ability to understand.

Some critics of Piagetian stage theory argue that it does not sufficiently take into account the social context in which learning is taking place. As appreciation for the role of culture in development has become more widespread, Vygotskian theory—particularly his concept of the zone of proximal development, described earlier as an important concept in children's cognitive growth—also operates in the area of social development. This notion has had widespread application in cognitive-developmental programs, as teachers identify strategies to engage a child at the potential level of understanding, including the pairing of a child with a more socially skilled peer:

> For example, a teacher may pair a child with low social skills with a more sociable peer in the hope that each will learn from the experience. The child who has difficulty in social situations may be challenged and encouraged to interact more adeptly in his encounters with his sociable model. The latter, on the other hand, may find that trying to interact with his less skilled partner challenges him to be more conscious of another's perspective and to develop new approaches to engage this child. Both children are extending their skills and are functioning in the zone of proximal development. (Ramsey, 1991, p. 16)

The Teacher's Role

All teachers are concerned with managing children's behavior and implementing meaningful curriculum. A commitment to social cognition is of critical importance in both areas. When social cognition is considered as a crucial aspect of the learning environment, it influences how the teacher carries out management and curriculum planning responsibilities. For example, it influences who the children consider to be the authority. Do the children see the teacher as an authority figure who tells them what to do, lays down the rules, and helps them settle disputes? Or do the children experience the teacher as a person who encourages them to think for themselves, value their own ability to produce ideas, and solve their own problems? The teacher needs to find the balance between assertively maintaining the authoritative role and enabling children to assume authority in situations that call for it. The teacher needs to plan times and seize opportunities to help children themselves solve interpersonal problems. The teacher can help children to identify and reflect upon their own feelings in particular situations, to become autonomous in their ability to solve interpersonal problems, and to grow in their ability to identify alternative coping strategies. These strategies are consistent with the intimate connection between social-emotional factors and cognition.

The task of learning to assume authority in the learning environment is quite complex, and the teacher's role in that task is subtle. The challenge is to allow children, at least in some circumstances, to take responsibility for their own actions and to have faith in their own capacity for self-directed learning. At the same time, the teacher needs to establish an environment in which the child feels comfortable and safe and is willing to take the risks related to problem-solving in interpersonal situations as well as with materials. The constructivist environment is characterized by opportunities for children to be active so that they have many chances to co-operate with peers and adults.

The challenge for teachers is to stimulate co-operation in the Piagetian sense and to be able, in interactions with children, to distinguish between co-operation, which means operating in relationship to another person or considering one's own ideas in relationship to others, and cooperating, which implies just getting along or giving in (Kamii, 1982). Co-operation stimulates thought processes and provides direction for children's autonomous growth. It frequently leads to cooperating—that is, getting along comfortably with others, being willing to share and to give in—but the process through which this behavior takes shape is very different from the moralistic or lecturing way adults try to impose their values on children. Certainly it is valuable at times for children to cooperate, to get along comfortably with others, to be willing to share and give in. However, if children come to this awareness through their own interactions, the value becomes their own and the conviction that surrounds the value is much greater. The challenge for the teacher is to be certain that children have both types of experiences—that they are exposed to adults valuing cooperation and that they also have many opportunities to develop this value for themselves.

In order to meet this challenge, teachers need to view themselves as carrying out four complementary roles: observer/evaluator, planner/stimulator, mentor/collaborator, and philosopher/researcher. By assuming each of these roles the teacher can make thoughtful decisions about the who, what, where, when, and how of incorporating an intellectual component into the social-emotional aspects of curriculum and classroom management.

The Teacher as Observer and Evaluator

A major responsibility for the teacher is to observe and continually evaluate what is going on in the classroom. Deciding whom to observe, when to observe, what to observe, and how to record observations are important professional decisions. Experience indicates that those teachers who make systematic observations of children, develop instructional strategies designed to meet specific goals, and continually monitor the effectiveness of these strategies are those who really make a difference in the lives of children. Certainly it is not possible, nor is it desirable, for the teacher at all times with all children to be observing and evaluating. Nor is it possible for a teacher at all times to be fostering the constructivist view of development. What is important is that teachers work toward helping children to manage themselves so that they can have time to devote to observation and evaluation.

Initially, the teacher should focus observations on a child who seems to possess strong interpersonal and intrapersonal skills—the child to whom other children gravitate, who seems to have many ideas for enriching play, who is a good negotiator in times of conflict, who is able to make peace when relationships are strained, who seems to be in touch with his or her own feelings, and who finds it easy to make friends. By watching the child who possesses these skills, the teacher gains an appreciation for unique qualities in children, for their power of self-direction, and for the developmental limitations that children experience.

Observing the child who functions effectively is a good place to start. It places the focus on the positive. It helps the teacher to articulate the desired behaviors, and it strengthens the teacher's ability to help children improve their observational skills. Also, observing children whose social-emotional abilities are strong provides a basis for internalizing what behavior is age-appropriate and starts the teacher on the process of constructing his or her own information regarding the range of normative behavior for children of a specific chronological age. The teacher can then use observation skills to gain a grasp of each child in the classroom and each child's way of operating.

The value of observation becomes clearly apparent when one considers the following example. Marc, a four-year-old, was physically the largest child in the Head Start class. He frequently bullied other children. He talked to teachers and to other adults in disrespectful ways, and much of his language, particularly when he was angry, was inappropriate for the classroom. His typical pattern of behavior was to enter the room and to run around wildly, knocking over or ripping down anything and knocking down anybody in his path. On the days when Marc was absent, the teachers breathed a sigh of relief. The lead teacher in this classroom was effective; and the classroom, except for Marc's disruptions, was a comfortable, warm, and stimulating environment for the children.

Analysis of written observations indicated that no one ever said anything positive to Marc. The records were full of comments like these: "Stop that." "Marc, if you don't sit down right now, you will . . ." "Don't hit." "Marc, leave Joanie alone."

Also described were several incidents in which Marc was particularly resourceful (although this word did not appear in the notes). On one occasion the children had lined up to go up a few steps and then run down an inclined plane. Marc entered into this activity with gusto. He figured out that by crawling underneath the steps he could come up at the front of the line twice as often as any of the other children. Also included as part of the running record were bits and pieces of information Marc shouted out as he bolted around the classroom indicating that he was imagining himself to be on a boat. In fact, he seemed to know quite a bit about boats.

From these observations, three hypotheses emerged that had not occurred either to the teacher or to the student teacher before they read the running records. First, teacher attempts to redirect Marc's behavior in an authoritative manner were ineffective. Second, the negative comments that Marc received were becoming a part of his self-image and were reinforcing rather than redirecting his inappropriate behavior. Third, Marc's intellectual abilities could be channeled so that he could begin to generate ideas about alternative ways to interact in the school and in other environments.

Important to observe are the characteristics that make each child unique. It is important to note differences in temperament, facility with the use of language, and preferences for specific activities. Does the child function best with a particular child, in a particular setting, at a particular time of day? What emotional issues are important to this child at this time? How does the child express emotion and deal with frustration?

Observation is useful not only in management issues, but also in helping the teacher understand what children are experiencing and how they are feeling about their experiences. With the information the teacher gains from observation, he or she can provide curriculum experiences that give children an opportunity to share, discuss, and think about their feelings. Mr. Moore, a second-grade teacher, was a master of this type of observation. When he noticed a child who looked sad, he shared his observation with the child: "Jamie, you look sad today . . ." The teacher made time to talk with the child about the feeling and encouraged the child to consider the topic "What makes me feel sad" as a possibility for his journal entry.

Observation is closely linked to evaluation. Observation data provide the basis for planning and the criteria for evaluating children's progress. On the basis of the observation, the teacher determines the next steps in evaluation and planning. Let's return to Marc's case. Marc's school experience was dramatically altered based on data gained from observation. In team planning meetings, staff discussed ways they could interact with Marc—ways that would provide not only positive direction, but also problem-solving challenges. It was decided to build upon Marc's interest in boats. As the group engaged in a construction of a sailboat (using hollow blocks and other collage material in the classroom), there were many opportunities for making decisions related to materials and to interpersonal relationships. The boat project took place over several weeks and involved a trip to the river to see the boats, contacting the boating company to make it possible for a small group of children to go on the boat, and many types of literature, music, and art experiences. Marc's progress in the area of social-emotional development did not go smoothly. There were many periods of regression, and in Piagetian terms many valuable intellectual errors. Nonetheless, the observations provided concrete evidence of Marc's progress and also provided ongoing direction for planning.

The Teacher as Planner and Stimulator

Effective teachers incorporate aspects of constructivist psychology into their programs. They plan for discussion of social-emotional issues or problems that occur in the classroom. Sometimes these discussions occur in the group as a whole, in small groups, or between teacher and child. As teachers identify social-emotional issues that are of concern to children—issues such as fears, dreams, shyness, insecurity, friends, birthdays, illness, death, divorce—they can provide experiences that allow the children to process the information and the feelings they have about these subjects. Group discussions, role-plays, and creation of class lists or graphs are some strategies that can be useful in this area. However, planning the strategies themselves is not sufficient. The teacher needs to think in advance of the opener to use that would stimulate the problem solving, for example: "What do you do when you are afraid?" "How do you decide what to give your friend for a birthday present?"

In addition to discussions about social-emotional topics, teachers also need to find ways for children to express their ideas: making a book, drawing a picture, or engaging in dramatic play. In each of these experiences, children need a degree of freedom to express their own ideas. Children also need adults and peers with whom they can become intellectually engaged in thinking about their work. (See Figure 8.1.)

Planning for the teacher in the constructivist mode also includes identifying strategies to help individual children improve their friendship-making skills. These

Informal discussions that encourage interaction among members of the group provide an opportunity for sharing experiences and building espirit de corps. © Elizabeth Crews/ The Image Works

strategies involve helping children become more effective observers, supporters, and adapters. It involves helping children use words to describe what others are doing—words that are supportive rather than antagonistic. It involves helping children generate alternative solutions to problems and a willingness to try out these alternatives.

The Teacher as Mentor and Collaborator

Piaget has identified the aim of education "not just to furnish the mind, but to help form its reasoning power" (DeVries & Kohlberg, 1990, p. 41). To help form children's reasoning power, teachers need to step down from the authoritarian role and to get away from developing heteronomous relationships with children. In heteronomous relationships, children come to depend on the teacher to tell them how to behave, rather than depending on their own resources.

Teachers cannot and should not always interact with children in the mentoring or collaborating mode. There are times when it is essential for teachers to exercise authority and to set firm limits. In some matters pertaining to health and safety, school rules, and behavioral expectations that help children feel physically and

psychologically secure in the environment, an authoritative position does need to be a part of the teacher's repertoire of behaviors. At times, the teacher needs to stop a particular behavior at the moment it occurs. The teacher sometimes needs to revisit with children to make sure they understand the parameters. Occasionally, particular children are overloaded—receiving more stimulation than they are able to process. At times, children's home patterns are in conflict with the patterns of behavior the teacher is expecting (Delpit, 1988). Teachers need to consider all these factors as they determine whether to use an approach that is clear and brief ("You need to put the crayons in the box," "You need to sit here") or one that involves more talking and elaboration ("How can you tell if working next to Colin is helping you do your work?").

As a mentor, the teacher identifies resources both in the planning and implementation phases of the curriculum and engages children in this process. The resources may take the form of material things—finding props for a role-play, for example—or they may take the form of soliciting ideas for solving a particular problem from other members of the group.

In the collaboration aspect of the teacher's role, the teacher needs to work with children at times as a co-worker rather than as a person in authority. DeVries and Kohlberg (1990), in *Constructivist Early Education: Overview and Comparison with Other Programs,* discussed several principles of teaching that allow a teacher to assume the collaborator role using group games. (Paraphrases of the original appear in brackets in the following.)

> Reduce the Use of Adult Authority, and Encourage Children to Regulate the Game . . . .
>
> 1. Present rules as coming from authority beyond the teacher. [Refer to written rules.]
> 2. Participate as a player. [Talk aloud about play and model feelings about losing. The teacher may protest when rules are not followed and initiate discussions of what is fair.]
> 3. When conflicts arise, support and help children discuss rules and reach mutual agreement about how to play and what is fair. . . . Conflicts should not be smoothed over to get back to the game. They deserve time and effort because it is in such situations that children learn

FIGURE 8-1

(on facing page) In this kindergarten lesson the teacher motivated children to think about birthday parties. As part of the discussion they talked about the clothes that are worn to parties and how they differ from everyday clothes. Afterward, the children were asked to paint themselves without clothes on a large sheet of paper and then dress the pictures in party clothes using tissue paper, doilies, pieces of shiny paper, wallpaper, and so on. This was demanding because they had to alter the shapes and sizes of the scrap materials. Stacia created herself in a three dimensional tissue paper dress, replete with doilies and stated: "I'm hot in party dresses! My pink dress has two layers. I'm going to Carolyn's party. I'm bringing her a present." Sylvia G. Feinburg

methods of cooperating: negotiating, compromising, and proposing new rules to get everyone's agreement how to play.

4. When children ask the teacher what to do, refrain from telling and turn the decision making back to children. . . . "That is a problem. What can we do?" [If the children do not have any ideas, the teacher may suggest a solution, but always ask the children whether or not the solution is acceptable to them.]
5. Encourage children to invent games. [Involved in this process would be a discussion of the rules and a recording of the rules upon which the children agree.]

Modify the Game in Terms of How Children Think, So They Have Something They Want to Try to Figure Out

1. Let the children play according to their understanding of the rules. [For example, the teacher in an aiming game may restate a rule that she thinks the children may have missed: "Stand behind the line before you throw." If the children do not stand behind the line and nobody objects, do not insist on the rule. The teacher may restate the rule when it is her turn: "I'm going to stand behind the line because it is more fun to try when it's kind of hard. The rule said to stand behind the line."] When a child breaks the rule, the teacher may try to help the child become conscious of it by remarking, "Josh decided not to stand behind the line" or "Do you want to keep that rule." If other children protest, engage them in discussion. Collaborate with them in making a decision about what to do. Children experience correction by other children differently than correction by the teacher. The decision as to when to insist on the rules and when to refrain from insisting is a matter of considering what is going on in the mind of an individual child.
2. Do not insist on competition. . . . For young children, it is often enough to figure out how to follow the rules that say what to do. [Competition is not developmentally appropriate until children can take into account the opponent's intentions.]
3. Evaluate a game in terms of how mentally active children are. "Figure out what is going on in children's minds from moment to moment." . . . This includes observing the sense children make of the rules, assessing whether or not they have a competitive attitude, and observing the strategies or lack of strategies they invent." [Refer to Kamii and DeVries (1980) for other principles of teaching group games.] (DeVries & Kohlberg, 1990, pp. 140–142)

As a mentor and as a collaborator, the teacher needs to be aware of children's thinking at the moment and provide the stimulation that supports and challenges that thinking. This is one of the most difficult roles of the constructivist teacher. It requires a great deal of practice, considerable mentoring of the teacher, and an ongoing interest in what the child is thinking. When a teacher succeeds in "engaging children's minds" (Katz & Chard, 1989), the resulting sense of excitement and satisfaction is difficult to duplicate.

The Teacher as Philosopher and Researcher

From this discussion of the teacher's role, it is clear that an understanding of a single philosophical approach to early childhood education is not sufficient. Teachers need to understand the three basic orientations: romanticism, cultural transmission, and cognitive developmental. They need to be able to identify in their own behavior evidence of each of these orientations as it occurs. When children are left on their own to play without teacher intervention, the romanticist view is operating. When teachers provide direct instruction or attempt to control behavior by extrinsic reward or praise, they are showing evidence of a belief in the cultural transmission view. When teachers engage children in thinking about their own behavior or their own actions, teachers are using the constructivist approach.

Being an eclectic teacher and using all of these approaches makes sense in a culture as diverse as that of the United States. In cultures that are more homogeneous, such as the Japanese culture, the way teachers interact with children seems to be more clear-cut:

> The Japanese teacher delegates more authority to children than we find in American schools; intervenes less quickly in arguments; has lower expectations for the control of noise generated by the class; gives fewer verbal cues; organizes more structured large-group activities, such as morning exercise; and finally makes more use of peer-group approval and control and less of teacher's direct influence. (White, 1987, p. 68)

In Japan, children learn patterns of interaction from their mothers. All children learn the same patterns; the school reinforces these patterns. Teachers in the United States need to make many more decisions about how to interact with children and need to be particularly cognizant of how these interactions are related to teaching goals and to the values and goals of the children's home environment.

Summary

Social cognition is the process of thinking about emotions, feelings, and the ways people interact with one another. It is a specialized field within developmental psychology that links cognition and social-emotional behavior. The theory is that individuals themselves construct an understanding of feelings such as kindness, happiness, anger, and fear, and they make sense out of rules that govern play and social relationships. Because individuals construct their own meanings, they are empowered to control their own behavior. Consideration of social-emotional issues within the educational program also impacts the children's learning in all areas of the curriculum, their ability to cope with stress of a personal or environmental nature, and their understanding of self and others.

Several factors influence the development of social cognition. The first of these is the child's stage of cognitive development. As children move from being preoperational to concrete operational thinkers, their ability to think about themselves and others also changes. A key factor is the child's emerging ability to take another's perspective. In addition, children strive to construct their own social knowledge; they test out their increasing level of understanding in play and through humor. In this process, their ideas about rules, what they understand to be right and wrong, and their concepts of friendship also change.

Children's acquisition of social skills is also influenced by factors such as self-concept and their perceptions of cultural identity and gender. These factors contribute to the variations in social skill development. Two approaches have been identified through which adults can stimulate children's cognitive acquisition of social skills. One approach motivates thinking through questions and discussion; the other uses the problem-solving paradigm. In each of these approaches, emphasis is on developing autonomy and fostering the child's reasoning capacity. The teacher's role in this process is to act as observer/evaluator, planner/stimulator, mentor/collaborator, and philosopher/researcher.

The next chapter elaborates the operational characteristics required to implement the social-cognitive approach in classrooms for young children. A discussion of ways teachers establish a positive classroom atmosphere, introduce social cognition into the curriculum, and incorporate it into classroom management is included. In effect, atmosphere and curriculum are key components of effective classroom management. Separating these creates an artificial dichotomy, useful only as a means of highlighting each of the three closely related components.

CHAPTER

9 ESTABLISHING A POSITIVE CLASSROOM ATMOSPHERE: OPERATIONAL CHARACTERISTICS

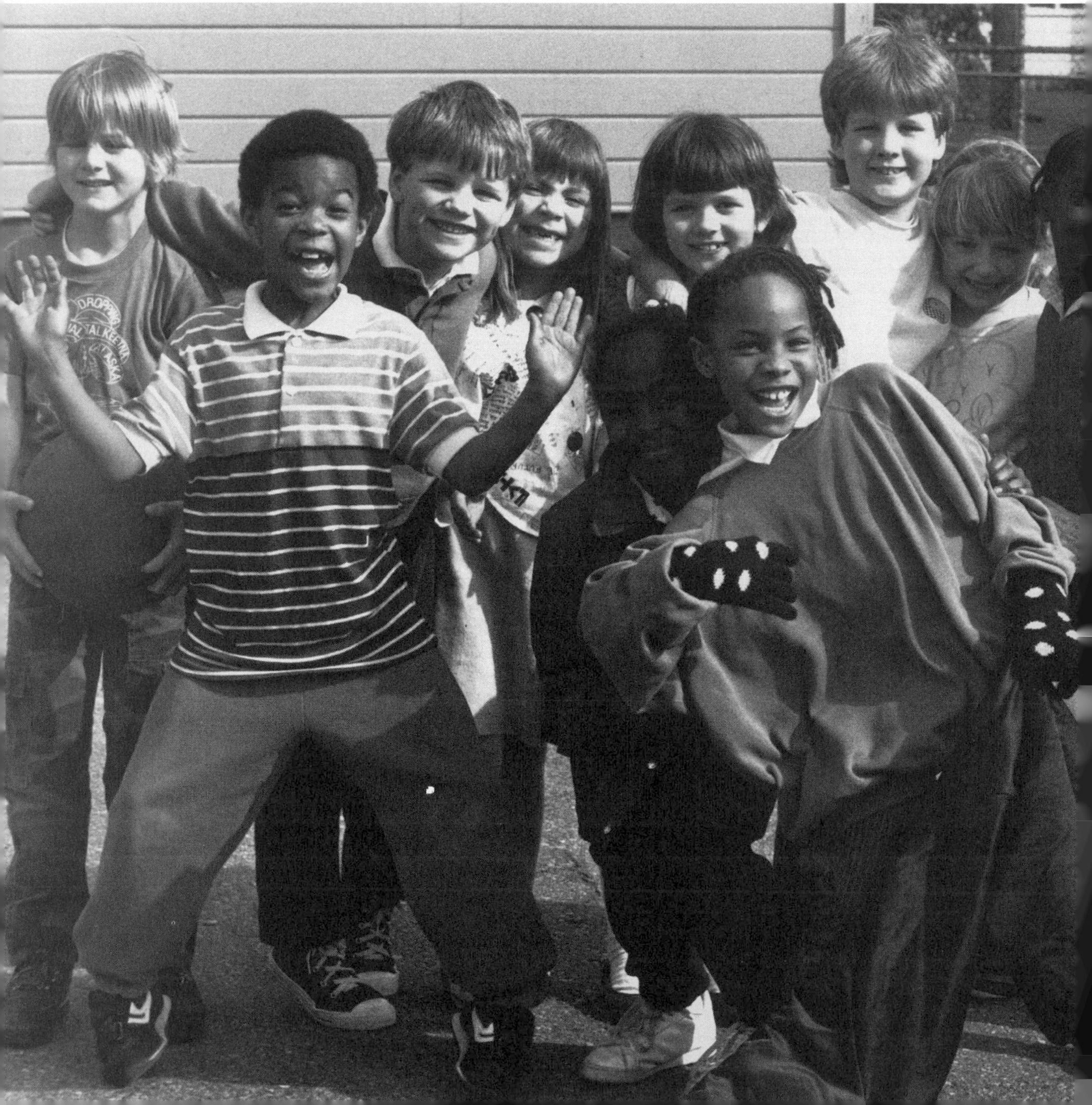

- *Elements of Classroom Atmosphere*
- *Establishing a Positive Classroom Atmosphere: Operational Characteristics*
- *Social-Emotional Issues as Curriculum for Young Children*
- *Social-Emotional Issues in Curriculum: Operational Characteristics*
- *Classroom Management from a Cognitive Perspective*
- *Classroom Management: Operational Characteristics*
- *Establishing a Positive Classroom Atmosphere: A Summary*

One of the key characteristics of cognitive-developmental programs is that social-emotional issues are incorporated into curriculum and classroom management. The theory from which the practice emanates was discussed in Chapter 8. This chapter identifies the operational characteristics through which teachers can implement these ideas.*

A primary consideration is the establishment of a productive work/play environment in which the principles of social cognition can be effectively implemented. The three operational characteristics related to establishing this type of an environment are as follows: modeling and encouraging mutually respectful behaviors, eliciting caring and respectful behaviors from children, and understanding how prosocial behavior contributes to work and productivity. Each of these is discussed fully with many examples of classroom interactions.

The section on curriculum begins with a discussion of special considerations: identifying relevant and important issues, considering developmental stages, identifying feelings of universal concern, and addressing sensitive issues. The operational characteristics include dealing with feelings, understanding similarities and differences, and the development of friendship-making skills. For each of these characteristics, several sample lessons are presented as a basis for further planning and observation of developmentally appropriate practice.

Classroom management focuses on the following operational characteristics: involving children in the formulation of rules, thinking about appropriate and inappropriate behaviors, and using problem-solving techniques. For each of these characteristics, detailed discussions and descriptions of classroom interactions clarify the general principles.

Elements of Classroom Atmosphere

The atmosphere in a classroom is a key factor in determining how social-emotional issues are incorporated into the program. Most teachers recognize that how children feel about themselves is a critical component of how they function intellectually and academically. Children who are secure, relate well to others, have a strong sense of self-worth and productive capabilities, and feel valued by others are better able to engage in the work of the classroom. Conversely, children who are insecure, have difficulty establishing relationships, and do not see themselves as capable, productive, or valued have difficulty bringing their full potential to the learning process. Hence, a fundamental educational objective is to create a classroom atmosphere that nourishes each child's self-esteem and facilitates his or her capacity to work and play efficiently with others. Social-emotional development is not a peripheral factor in learning; it must be embedded in the very identity of the educational process.

Teachers must recognize that they play a critical role in establishing basic values for the human relationships in the classroom. The way teachers deal with individual children, children's interactions with one another, and the working process in general communicates to the children a powerful message about what is appropriate and inappropriate behavior in the classroom.

*The classroom evaluation guide, Form E, in Chapter 11 relates to this chapter.

Rationale

A classroom is a group of individuals who share some common goals. Developing a sense of community in the classroom is important in helping children distinguish between their personal needs, the needs of other individuals, and the needs of the larger group. Although young children have limitations in their abilities to identify with others, they can begin to see that they are part of some dyadic relationships (a brother, a friend), small units (family, groups of friends), and a larger unit (classroom, school). Making children aware of the different needs of the individual and the group, and helping them to understand that a group can do things that individuals cannot do alone, provides the impetus for important transitions in development.

In addition, promoting a sense of community teaches children that it is important to care for others, not only to achieve goals but also to promote a shared sense of humanity. Children need to learn that people must depend on one another both emotionally and functionally, and that a society works well when cooperation and care are shared goals. Young children must be helped to understand the reasons to be concerned about others, beyond what they themselves will receive. Seeing themselves within the context of a group and learning to appreciate the needs of individuals within the group are steps in learning to care for and about others.

Many small communities exist within each classroom—such as a group of children working together on a project, or three children reading the same book. Each of these groups has an identity that is greater than the sum of individuals within that group. The teacher's role is to facilitate behaviors and introduce activities that help children recognize the identity and needs of that community. The teacher balances the needs of the individual with those of the group and engages children in the establishment of a productive work/play environment.

Setting up and maintaining this type of environment involves specific behaviors on the part of the teacher. These behaviors can be grouped into the following categories:

1. modeling and encouraging mutually respectful behaviors
2. eliciting caring and respectful behavior from children
3. helping children understand how prosocial behavior contributes to work and productivity

These categories are described as operational characteristics essential for establishing a positive classroom atmosphere—a climate that results in a respectful and supportive learning environment.

Establishing a Positive Classroom Atmosphere: Operational Characteristics

Described in this category are fundamental teacher behaviors that build self-esteem and a positive sense of community. The behaviors and the examples illustrate how the teacher makes caring and respect explicitly important elements in the classroom.

Encouraging Mutually Respectful Behaviors

The teacher models and encourages mutually respectful behavior.

- "Thank you for reminding me that it is time to get ready for gym. It's just terrific when everybody is helping to make things run smoothly."
- "You let me know whether you want to keep this section in your book report. It's your report, and it's important that you make the decision for yourself."
- "Oh, I can see you're really involved in sawing that big piece of wood. Tanja and Pedro will work over here so they won't get in your way."
- "Let me know when you feel ready for me to take your dictation. After all, you're the best judge."

Another way the teacher models respectful behavior is to recognize for the total classroom community the progress made by individual members.

- "Alyssa has been working really hard in group time on trying not to push and bump into people when we're all sitting on the steps. Remember how Rosa told us that it is hard for her to find a place on the steps without pushing or bumping into other people who are already seated. I think we should all give her a big hand because she did so beautifully today."
- A four-year-old is navigating a wheelchair up a ramp. The teacher comments: "Look how much faster Melanie is able to get her wheelchair up that ramp. Melanie, the children have been telling me how impressed they are with the way you are able to move your wheelchair so smoothly." And to Katie, who made the observation, the teacher says, "You're absolutely right that Melanie has learned to make the wheelchair move smoothly. Why don't you tell her how impressed you are!"

Note in the following examples how the teacher helps children understand that all people need support and caring from others. The teacher helps children understand the importance of their contributions in these areas.

- "Thank you for sharing with the children in the block corner how much you liked the parking garage that they made. It feels good when people let you know they appreciate your work."
- "Jim needs a lot of help from us today because he's worried about his little brother who is in the hospital. Let's think of some things we can do to let him know we care about him."

The next example illustrates how a teacher models respect for children's special qualities, unique limitations, or particular strengths. In this way the teacher helps children understand themselves and value their own unique qualities.

- "Remember, Hannah, that one of the reasons that Paolo and Cecil continue to tease you is because they have real trouble with how talented you are. They make fun of your original ideas." (Hannah is a first grader who has many creative ideas and is constantly being ridiculed for her high level of originality. She needs to learn to make decisions for herself regarding when to defend her ideas and when to defer to the group norm. In either case the way she accomplishes her goal will be critical in determining her self-esteem and her acceptance by peers.)

It is important that the teacher identify children's strengths and make them apparent to others. The teacher helps children understand that all people have both strengths and weaknesses. The teacher makes it all right not to be equally competent in all areas. To do so, however, requires a degree of sensitivity, because there are many times when teachers need to reduce the attention paid to problem areas.

◗ The teacher talks privately to a first grader: "I understand that you are feeling embarrassed because you had an accident. I'll help you find something to change into. I know that you don't want the others to know."

In the following examples the teacher models respect for individual differences. The teacher helps children to understand, through his or her own behavior, that likes and dislikes are a matter of individual preference.

◗ "I really liked the snake in the Science Museum. Jorge thought that the owl was more interesting."

◗ Second graders are engaged in the creative drawing of teddy bears. Megan draws a fanciful bear. Jodi, a child who is attracted to literal interpretations, comments, "What a stupid picture! Who has ever seen a teddy bear that looks like that?" The teacher points out that unique solutions should be valued and makes a mental note to try to find a story or create one that would help the children appreciate the value of diverse responses. In discussing the story, the teacher helps individual children gain courage to defend their own ideas or convictions. There is value in helping children appreciate that there are times when they are independent of the group and the group's evaluation: "If Jodi doesn't like the way that you drew your teddy bear, he can give you his reasons and you can listen to them; but what matters is that you are satisfied with it."

Of key importance is that teachers deal with each child in the classroom with full and complete respect, that they treat each child with sensitivity and appreciation of how the child functions as an individual and the circumstances that contribute to who the child is and how he or she interacts. These circumstances include differences in personality and temperament, cultural and family background, prior school and group experience, differences in speech, and differences in levels of understanding. All of these influence how a child deals with the school experience. This focus does not mitigate the need to establish firm limits.

◗ At lunchtime, a kindergarten teacher hears the following from Benji: "Ugh, you have a peanut butter and mayonnaise sandwich? I don't like those two together. I only like marshmallow with peanut butter. Eek, Danny's eating seaweed!" The teacher responds: "Benji, when you say that to Danny, it upsets him. In his house people like that kind of a sandwich. It is okay if you don't like it, but you cannot make fun of what other people like to eat."

Although it is important to consider children as individuals, children are also members of a total group. Self-esteem is intimately connected to how one feels and functions within the group. In the following examples, the teachers show that they understand the child's individual need and at the same time help the child to defer to the needs of others.

◗ "Yes, I know that you want my attention, and I want to be able to give it to you; but I can't listen right now because I'm listening to Zenaida read." (Contrast this statement with "Don't interrupt. I'm listening to Zenaida read now.")

◗ "I know that you want to make your own Lego structure today, Mike. But if you do, Katie, Max, and Cesar won't have enough pieces to complete this big castle they've been working on together. So you can either work with them on their castle, or wait until tomorrow to make your own building."

Showing respect is an attitude as well as a behavior. In order to become pervasive, respect needs to be demonstrated in all interpersonal relations.

◗ While a student teacher and a classroom teacher were supervising the playground, the student teacher started to talk about a three-year-old child's family. She commented on how much money the family had and the effect on the child. The teacher responded, "I know you are interested in Jerry's family, but it's not appropriate for us to be discussing it now. Jerry could overhear our discussion."

Eliciting Caring and Respectful Behaviors

The teacher elicits caring and respectful behavior from children. As children interact with each other, the teacher observes and comments on how individuals talk to one another.

◗ A first-grade teacher explains to Michael, "When you tell André to get out of the chair because it's your turn and you tell him that way, it doesn't make him feel like doing it. How can you let him know that it's your turn in a nicer way?"

◗ "Get Rebecca over here to see what you've discovered about the butterfly. She is always interested in nature things."

The teacher helps children understand that different people may hold different values about the same thing. The teacher strengthens understandings of the influence of culture and special circumstances in arriving at a particular decision or opinion.

◗ The children were discussing the upcoming election: "My father says that anyone who doesn't vote yes is a dumbbell," said one child, in a manner that indicates that he is mimicking what he has heard at home. Other children indicate that their families are expressing an opposite point of view. The teacher asks, "Do you know why your father is in favor of voting yes on that question? In voting people often have different opinions. That's why we vote, to see how many people say yes and how many say no."

Respect includes articulating the fact that people hold different beliefs.

◗ When Harmony's grandmother died, her kindergarten class talked about grandmothers and how sad it was when someone you loved died. In the discussion, Alex tried to be helpful by explaining that when someone who has done good things dies, that person goes to heaven. This statement prompted William to blurt out what he had heard on this subject: "There is no such thing as heaven." The teacher replied, "Different people have different ideas about that. You may want to talk to your parents and see how they feel."

◗ Jade, who was in the first grade when she lost her first tooth, was proud to announce that the tooth fairy had come and left a dollar bill under her pillow. "There's no such thing as a tooth fairy!" blurted Margo. "Yes, there is," Jade asserted. "I'll show you the dollar she left for me." As often happens in this kind of discussion, children reflect biases they hear at home. To Jade's mother, her child's belief in the good fairy is important, because it stirs the six-year old's imagination. As children share family customs, they reflect upon the idea that not everyone has the same understanding and the same experiences. They turn to the teacher to reaffirm their own beliefs. The teacher's role is to help the child understand that families are not all alike, that they often differ in what they believe and the way they do things. The teacher emphasizes the importance of listening to others, hearing contradictory information, and then coming to one's own decision. The teacher avoids presenting her view in a didactic manner. "People seem to have different ideas about the tooth fairy. Each of us has to make up our own mind about this."

The teacher helps children understand that emotions affect the way people behave. When the child is feeling sad, lonely, or frightened, the child may behave differently from the way he or she usually does.

◗ "Cole, we want you to be a part of this class, but you are being scary and frightening to the group. Get a book to look at alone for a few minutes. When you are feeling better, you can join us. I want you to be with us, Cole, but I can't let you frighten other people."

The teacher helps children understand that all people need support and caring from others. The teacher helps children understand the importance of their contributions in these areas.

◗ "I think it's important that you let Dominic know that his suggestion was helpful. Maybe during the break you'll have a few minutes to talk to him."

◗ "Stephan is new in our class. Franz, you know a lot about how we do things here. Would you be Stephan's special buddy and help him get used to our room and our school? You can show him where the materials are kept, where the bathroom is, how we line up for lunch, and what we do if there is a fire drill."

◗ "Rebecca noticed that there wasn't enough room to sit down between Monica and Nikki, so she found another place without stepping on anyone."

◗ On the playground, Ben, a four-year-old, is running around and chanting, "You can't catch me. I'm as fast as a bee." Sam, who seems to be unengaged, is

Children are encouraged to help other children and also to value positive behavior.

watching Ben. The teacher comments, "Ben, is that a rhyme you made up to help you feel safe outside?" She verbalizes what Ben is doing loud enough so that Sam can hear it and encourages Sam to find a way that he can help himself feel safe outside. Individual differences will prevail in children's capacities to analyze and interpret their own and others' social behavior. The teacher recognizes these differences and has different expectations for performance. She knows that Sam has a slow-to-warm-up temperament and that it will take him a while to feel comfortable enough to make up and share rhymes and to run with such abandonment around the playground. Through her interaction she acknowledges Sam's interest in Ben, she identifies and verbalizes the feeling element which Ben is expressing through his rhyme and leaves the children to take the next steps in their own way.

The teacher provides a balance between independent activities, partner work, and cooperative learning teams.

◗ "Rachel was sick yesterday and I saw Elena helping her with her mobile so that Rachel would be able to hang it with the others on our big classroom mobile.

Doesn't it look great when each person's mobile joins together to make a great big class mobile!"

Helping Children Understand the Value of Prosocial Behavior

The teacher helps children understand how prosocial behavior contributes to work and productivity. People's behavior toward one another in every arena affects their ability to be productive in their endeavors. This is as true in school as it is in the home and in the workplace. For this reason, it is important that the teacher helps children understand that adults, as well as children, have strong feelings and emotional needs.

◗ Corrine, a kindergartner, a second time deliberately disturbed the order in which the math materials were stored. She wildly began to throw the containers of sorted materials onto the floor so that all the materials became intermingled and needed to be sorted over again. The teacher with whom she was working held her arms firmly and said, "I don't want to be the kind of a teacher, Corrine, who forces you to do things. I want to be a friendly teacher who helps you to learn. You are making it hard for me to be this kind of teacher. I want to be the best teacher I can. You make it hard for me to do my job."

◗ When Sarah hastily completes an entry in her journal and then finds reason to start running around the room, her second-grade teacher reminds her that this is writing time and that she needs to find a way to be sure that in her journal entry she tells everything that she can about this topic. The teacher works continuously to help children demand the best from themselves.

◗ A first-grade teacher is reminding Alexander to write his name and the date in his journal. Alexander says to the teacher in a taunting voice. "I can't do it. I *c-a-n-'t* do it. I can't." The teacher says, "That's the voice people use to tease. I think you're teasing me. Maybe that's because you don't think you can do this work; but I've watched you. I know you can do it. You don't need to tease. I'll help you."

Development of effective work habits contributes to learning and productivity. The teacher helps children acquire habits early in their school careers that will contribute to their current learning and stay with them throughout their lives.

◗ Jamila, a three-year-old, sits herself down at the small table where the teacher has put a teacher-made board game. On her lap is a stuffed animal Jamila has carried with her from the doll corner. She spies Jared and invites him to play. Jared is carrying a small toy car, which he plunks down on one corner of the game board. As the children begin the game, the teacher notices that they are having trouble working effectively because the toys are distracting them. She helps the children to realize this by commenting, "It would be easier to move the pieces around if the car went back to the garage and the teddy bear found a place to rest in the doll corner." The children remove the toys and come back and enjoy the game.

Appropriately setting up the work/play space adds a great deal to the enjoyment of an activity. The removal of unnecessary objects prevents accidents and other disruptions. It helps children focus their concentration.

◗ "The reason why José was able to get so much done today was because he found a place to work where he wouldn't be distracted."

◗ John, a kindergartner, went with his father to a stationery supply store to buy some supplies. John reported that his father let him select a folder in which to keep his work. He selected one with three pockets. In this way he could keep the papers that he wanted to hand in separate from those the teacher handed back, and he would have a third pocket for his personal things. When John shared this experience with the children at group time, the teacher commented on how important it was to organize one's work. She engaged the children in a discussion of how the work spaces were organized in the classroom and encouraged their discussion of the organization which they observed in their homes.

◗ The teacher talked with the children about the writing she was doing at home. She commented on how important it was to her to set up her work space before she began to work. "I get my papers all lined up. I fix my lamp so that it will shine on my work." Sharing this kind of information with children helps them to recognize that there are systems to everything that one deals with and that each individual has the power to establish his or her own system.

The teacher provides feedback on children's work that helps them to develop criteria for evaluation.

◗ Luis, a second grader, shows the teacher the painting he has just completed. The teacher comments on the fact that he has chosen colors that feel wintry. She talks with him about how the colors one chooses can help one to feel a particular way. She talks about how winter colors are different from fall colors. The criterion she is helping the child to assimilate is the importance of choice of colors in planning and evaluating a painting.

◗ Chelsea is working on some math problems and is recording her answers in her math journal. Her first-grade teacher comments on the process Chelsea is using: she records her first answer, and then finds two different ways to be sure that her answer is correct. As she records each answer, she checks it with the first to be sure that it is the same. The teacher commends Chelsea for checking her answers and being so thoughtful and reflective about her own work.

◗ Freddie, who is in nursery school, is working at the easel. As he finishes using one color, he carefully looks to find the appropriate container in which to replace the brush. He does this because he wants to be sure that he keeps his colors pure. At meeting time the teacher brings the paint containers to the meeting and talks with the children about how rich the colors are. "Freddie wanted to be sure that he had true colors to work with so he carefully wiped his brush before he dipped it into a new color container. Because Freddie was so careful, we all have true colors to work with. Thank you, Freddie."

The teacher helps the children to develop standards for their performance.

◗ Following a discussion of problems kindergarten and first-grade children were experiencing in the block area, the teacher led a discussion in which children came up with three criteria for block-building: sturdy, safe, and beautiful. The teacher recorded the children's ideas on a sign posted in the block area (from

Marion Reynolds' classroom at the Eliot-Pearson Children's School, Tufts University, Medford, Massachusetts):

> Sturdy means balanced, strong, will not fall down.
> Safe means I have control of my body when I build.
> Beautiful means using lots of shapes and putting them together in different ways, and having a plan and putting blocks where I plan.

◗ The following end-of-day statement by one teacher summarizes the results of the group's attention to the building of a respectful and supportive environment. "I want to give you people a compliment: great day, great cleanup. You took care of yourself and each other. You took care of our room."

Although educators would agree on the importance of establishing a respectful and supportive environment, they often do not pay attention to specific behaviors for achieving this goal. The following summarizes the behaviors teachers use to achieve this end. The behaviors are grouped into three main categories.

1. The teacher models and encourages mutually respectful behavior by
   a. making caring and respect an explicitly important element in the classroom
   b. recognizing for the total classroom community the progress made by individual members
   c. helping children understand that all people need support and caring from others; helping them understand the importance of their contributions in these areas
   d. modeling respect for a child's special qualities, unique limitations, or particular strengths
   e. identifying children's strengths and making these apparent to others
   f. modeling respect for individual differences
   g. pointing out that unique solutions should be valued
   h. helping children gain courage to defend their own ideas or convictions
   i. dealing with each child with full and complete respect; treating each child with sensitivity and appreciation of how the child functions as an individual and the circumstances that contribute to who the child is and how he or she interacts
   j. showing understanding for the child's individual need while helping the child defer to the needs of others
   k. maintaining a respectful attitude in all interpersonal relations
2. The teacher elicits caring and respectful behavior from children by
   a. observing and commenting on how individuals talk to one another
   b. helping children understand that different people may hold different values about the same thing; strengthening understanding of the influence of culture and special circumstances in arriving at a particular decision or opinion
   c. helping children understand that emotions affect the way people behave
   d. helping children understand that all people need support and caring from others and the importance of their contributions in these areas

e. recognizing individual differences and having different expectations for performance
f. providing a balance between independent activities, partner work, and cooperative learning teams
3. The teacher helps children understand how prosocial behavior contributes to work and productivity by
a. helping children understand that adults as well as children have strong feelings and emotional needs
b. helping children demand the best from themselves
c. helping children acquire habits early in their school careers that will contribute to their current learning and will stay with them throughout their lives
d. providing feedback on children's work that helps them develop criteria for evaluation
e. helping children develop standards for their performance

Each of these teacher behaviors contributes to the establishment of a respectful and supportive environment. Together they provide the scaffolding for consideration of social-emotional issues in the curriculum and in classroom management.

Social-Emotional Issues as Curriculum for Young Children

Historically we have always looked at the study of human behavior as a topic adults study, not children. Yet, the psychology of behavior is relevant for children to address. It is social science content and belongs in the social science curriculum along with topics like studying the community or identifying the sources of the food that we eat. What makes people jealous? Why do people cry? What is the importance of crying? Should people cry? Is crying a good or bad thing? Is it natural to be frightened? Do just some people get frightened or does everybody get frightened? Do people have to work hard in order to learn new things? Have grownups always known what they know? Questions such as these are a part of the study of psychology. They deal with issues that are important for children to examine, and they provide a way to increase children's understanding of how people function as human beings. No subject is more crucial in all of life.

Rationale

Young children are capable and interested in studying how people behave, why they behave as they do, and how they feel in certain situations. They are also interested in studying some of the causes and effects of human behavior. Much of this studying occurs coincidentally as certain situations emerge in the classroom—for example, situations that involve such things as sharing and fighting. In these kinds of situations, teachers frequently explain human behavior extemporaneously. They help children identify the reasons the behavior occurred, how each of the children involved is feeling about the incident, and the effects the specific behavior has on their relationship and on their productivity.

Responding to events that occur spontaneously as a result of daily interactions is obviously a necessary step every teacher must take to maintain classroom harmony. The effective teacher uses these interactions as a way to increase children's understanding of behavior. Usually in these spontaneous situations, emotions are high and affect is a strong motivator. The learning that occurs can be enormously valuable.

There is also great value in dealing with affective issues when emotions are not charged and do not interfere with the children's cognitive ability to process information. Such learning opportunities should be planned in a deliberate, comprehensive way. They should involve lessons and activities with explicit objectives related to the understanding of behavior, and should take place independently of the here and now. They should constitute a significant aspect of the curriculum and, wherever feasible, should be integrated into other subject areas.

Identifying Relevant and Important Issues

How does the teacher identify social-emotional issues that should be addressed in the curriculum?

Careful Observations

One way to identify issues is through careful observation. As children interact with one another, minor provocations often occur. For example, children may disagree about who was first in line or whose turn it was to use the computer. Observations may reveal that the group is continually rebuffing a child, or that one child is refusing to participate in group efforts to maintain a sense of order in the classroom. The teacher needs to help children deal with these situations as they occur; but the teacher also should note the central psychological issues with which the children are dealing, so that these issues can be addressed at a later time in a planned and thoughtful way.

The following example highlights how a teacher listens to children's conversations, identifies the emotional content, and uses the curriculum to help children deal with their feelings. At a time when the news was full of stories about war, a child approached the teacher with a question: "Why does that ruler want that little country? It's so little. He already has a big country." The teacher's first response was at a cognitive level: "There is a lot of oil in the little country. He wants the oil." The child responded: "Why is he fighting over it? Why doesn't he just ask for it?" As the teacher thought about this conversation, as she listened to the child's tone of voice, she recognized that the emotion the child was expressing was one of intense concern about what motivates aggression, that the cognitive questioning was the child's attempt to allay this concern. The teacher noted also that this concern about aggression and what motivates it had reoccurred in children's interactions with each other, in their play and in their conversations. In their play children had several times referred to the idea that big people were taking advantage of little people. The key questions centered around fairness: What is fair? What is unfair? The children seemed concerned about the issue of people who were taking advantage of other people. On the

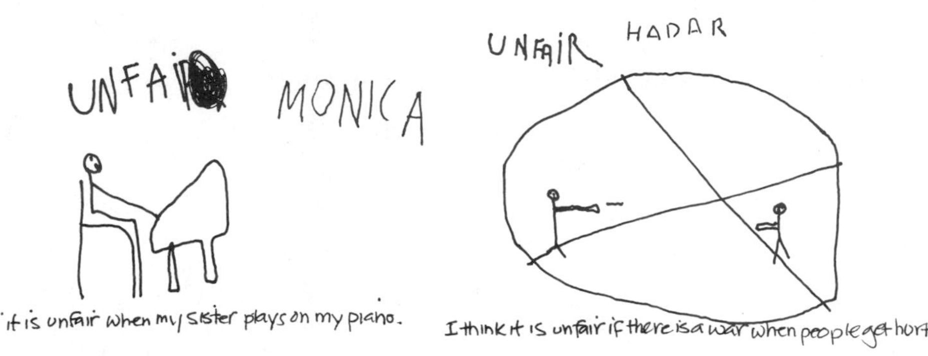

FIGURE 9-1

What is fair? What is unfair? Kindergarten children's responses
(teacher Jennifer McGuinn, Tufts University)

basis of these observations the teacher decided to plan ways that children could deal with these questions in the curriculum: in journal writing, role-playing, art. Figure 9.1 represents children's responses as expressed through art.

Considering Developmental Stages

Central to the identification of psychological topics to include in the curriculum is consideration of developmental stage. Certain kinds of understandings about behavior are critical at particular stages of development. For example, the teacher knows that for all children, sharing and turn-taking are issues. So, too, is being considerate of other people's needs. These issues are important at every age but have particular significance during the early childhood years. The developmental stage within which children are operating also influences the way the teacher handles a particular topic and the responses the teacher expects from the children. Thus, the teacher plans less elaborate and less complex discussions with four-year-olds than with older children but still addresses the issue.

As an example, consider the poignant story told in the book *Love You Forever,* by Robert Munsch (1986). This book describes a mother's devotion to her son from infancy through adulthood. Regardless of his age or how he behaves, the mother remains devoted to him and repeats over and over:

> I'll love you forever,
> I'll like you for always,
> As long as I'm living
> my baby you'll be.

As the son grows older, the mother grows older. The mother becomes frail and the son cares for her. He repeats the verse to her that she has shared with him time and time again. When the son has a child of his own, he uses the same verse to convey his love. The story shows how love is carried over from one generation to the next.

Love You Forever is relevant to every age, with emotional power that appeals to four-year-olds, seven-year-olds, and adults. The teacher interested in expanding on children's experience with this book would focus on very different aspects of the story with four-year-olds than with seven-year-olds. With the four-year-olds, the teacher would keep the discussion simple—the main concept being that a mother always loves her child no matter what the child does. If the child is naughty, if the child forgets and does things that he or she is not supposed to do, still the mother will always love the child. With the seven-year-olds, the discussion can be more complex. Discussion can center on why these feelings of love and acceptance are so strong. Discussion can open up the idea that over time relationships change: as children grow older and develop and as parents grow older, the love between parent and child remains strong, but the nature of the interactions changes.

Identifying Feelings of Universal Concern

Many emotions are of enduring importance. People are faced with these emotions when they are young and return to them over and over throughout life. The feeling of love is one of these emotions.

Robert Munsch's book *Love You Forever* also provides a wonderful opportunity to consider the nature of love and how it is revealed. A book that is powerful usually relates to concepts about basic human emotions. The teacher, as part of planning, needs to take time to identify the key concepts in the story and think through how to engage children in a discussion or activities related to the story:

- Simple concepts: mothers care about their children; children sometimes do things that make mothers and fathers angry.
- Intermediate concepts: why do people rock babies? how does rocking make you feel? why did the mother feel she wanted to sell her son to the zoo?
- Did she really mean it?
- Higher-level concepts: children grow and change, and so do adults; you can still love a person even if you get angry at what the person does.

Another topic that is of universal and timeless interest is the concept that people change over time in what they know, what they can do, and what they understand. This topic has particular significance for young children. Children enjoy looking at pictures they made when they were in nursery school and talking about the way a person's drawings change as he or she grows. Children can understand that what

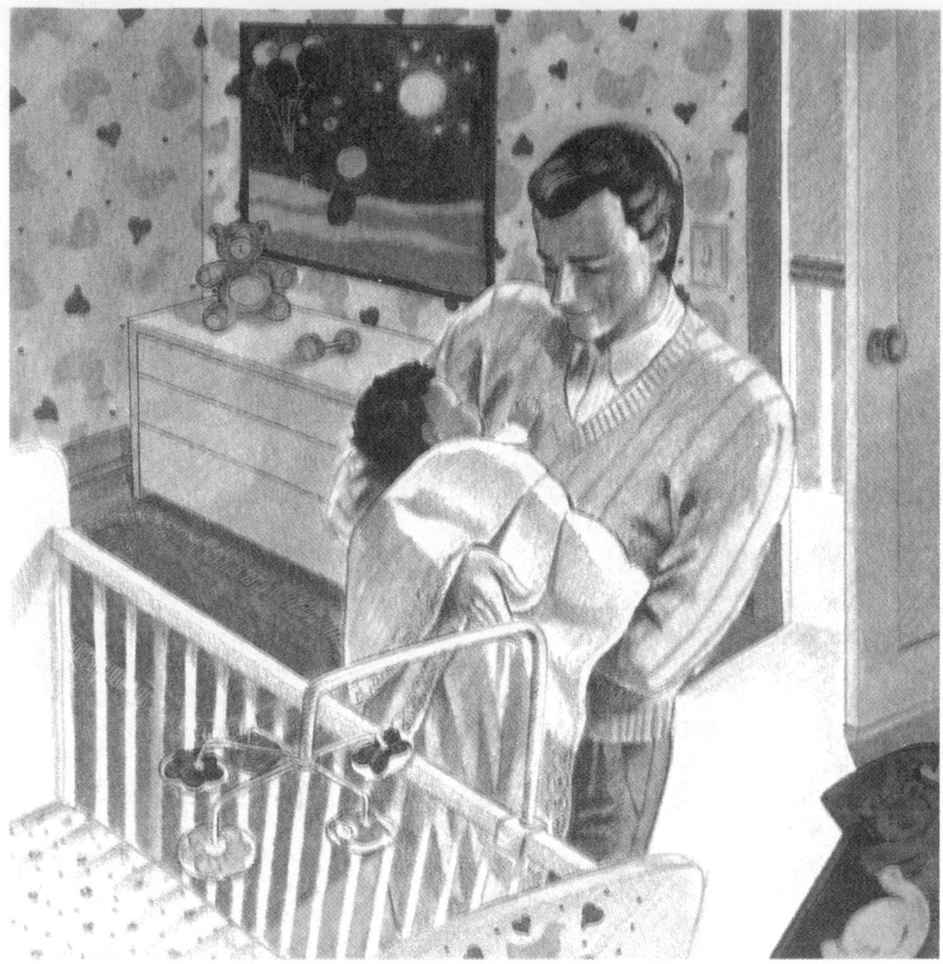

FIGURE 9-2

Illustration from Love You Forever Illustration by S. McGraw, 1986. In *Love You Forever* by R. Munsch. Copyright © 1986 by Robert Munsch. Reprinted by permission of Firefly Books Ltd.

people are able to do is related to developing abilities as well as to work and practice. Introduction to the idea that effort and perserverance are the basis for achievement is crucial. As the concept becomes strengthened, it will impact the child's attitude toward learning throughout life.

Feelings of love occur at all ages for all human beings, as can feelings of fear and frustration, and issues related to making and keeping friends. These issues are predictable; everyone experiences them over and over. So, too, are the ways people show kindness, how people feel when they are left out, what people do when they are angry; these will always be central in interpersonal relations and important in the learning situation as well. They occur and recur in different ways with every group. Therefore, they also constitute a basis on which to build curriculum experiences.

Following is an illustration of how a second-grade teacher integrated the subject of fear into the curriculum. A child reported during group meeting time: "A lady in my neighborhood got her pocketbook taken away." "When did it happen?" asked the teacher. "It happened in the morning when she was going to the bakery. He just grabbed her pocketbook and ran away." "Did the lady tell the police?" "I don't know. I don't know if I can go to the ball field anymore. I'm afraid to walk by the bakery. The man might be there waiting." "That is a scary thought, Timmy." The teacher recognized that this incident was not unlike two or three other incidents that had come up. As a pre-writing activity several days later, the teacher engaged the group in brainstorming topics for journal writing—The subject, "things that make me feel afraid."

A kindergarten teacher shared a similar emotional incident that came up in her class. Kim came into kindergarten looking unusually tense. "Is something bothering you, Kim?" the teacher asked. After some conversation, one of the children who walked to school with Kim told the story: "A big dog was on the sidewalk where Kim needed to walk. The dog had a great big tail and he kept swishing it back and forth, back and forth, and it hit Kim on the leg." "That must have been scary to have a big dog right in your path" was the teacher's comment. The kindergarten and the second-grade teacher handled the child's expression of fear in a similar way. Both teachers helped the child to identify and label the emotion. Both encouraged children to express their emotion by drawing pictures or writing stories about their experiences. The stories the children wrote reflected their individual levels of maturity.

Addressing Sensitive Issues

Sometimes teachers avoid planning experiences related to helping children understand behavior because they are uncomfortable bringing up issues that are difficult to discuss. These include topics about which people have intense personal feelings. Consider, for example, the topic of death. The topic of death comes up frequently in classrooms in which there are plants or animals. Talking about death is never easy. Even teachers who can routinely respond to children's questions about why the fish died can sometimes be faced with emotionally laden responses from a parent. For example, in *The Moral Child* (1988), William Damon described an incident in a first-grade classroom in which children asked many questions:

> What will happen to the fish now that it is dead? Would it come back to life somewhere, would it still be happy, would it remember the little girl who cared for it? The teacher immediately recognized the religious implications of these questions. She simply reassured the child that the fish was in no pain and that they could bury it outside in the school yard. She told the girl that they would never see the fish alive again and suggested that she raise a new one. (p. 9)

The child in relaying the experience to her parents, as children are wont to do, embellished the story a bit. She included details about the fish going to heaven. The parents became very irate and "objected to their daughter's learning in school that fish could have an afterlife."

Teachers who are not reluctant to talk with children about death when a plant or a goldfish dies may experience great anxiety about how to discuss the fact that a classmate or a teacher has died. Should the teacher plan to provide experiences that help children cope with their feelings surrounding this experience? The answer is a definite yes. The way to carry out this discussion and the activities to involve children in, however, need to be thought through carefully.

Another kind of discussion teachers tend to avoid involves children's self-perceptions, such as being smaller than other children or not as strong. Teachers often are sensitive to children's feelings about being unique or in some way different from the others in the group. The teacher often thinks that discussing how a child differs from others in the group might make the child uncomfortable and particularly vulnerable. Yet the alternative—not to deal with the subject at all—is not necessarily appropriate.

Some teachers find it difficult to discuss situations that reflect newly emerging changes in lifestyles occurring within the culture. In one first-grade classroom, the teacher had planned a math graphing experience to provide visual documentation of the size of the children's families. As the children began to talk about their families, two children got into a heated argument: "He says he's got two mothers and no fathers. You can't have two mothers." "I do," said the second boy tentatively.

There was high interest in this conversation. The teacher helped the children identify many different family structures. At the end of the discussion the child who was earlier convinced that having two mothers was not possible articulated his new insight: "Oh, you mean they're gay." For many teachers, such a discussion would cause a great deal of discomfort. The children involved, however, once they understood the situation, accepted it matter-of-factly.

Teachers might avoid helping children to understand delicate issues for many reasons. Sometimes teachers feel uncomfortable about bringing up subjects of an interpersonal nature because they are respectful of family issues and do not want to infringe on people's private lives. Other times teachers are not sure where to go when discussing a topic that is emotionally laden, especially when the discussion relates to the child or to the child's family life. It is easy to talk about anger, fear, and love in a general way; but it is infinitely more difficult to talk about these issues in terms of children's lives within their families. When children bring up things that happen at home—arguments, physical violence, drug or alcohol abuse—the discussion can evoke strong and deep-seated feelings, which the teacher may think will cause the child embarrassment. Teachers fear that they may overstep the boundaries of educator and move into the role of counselor or therapist, a role for which they do not feel prepared. Sensitive teachers are able to take children's spontaneous contributions to a discussion of a difficult situation, identify general concepts, and neutralize children's personal vulnerability. Such teachers are able to guide discussions into general concepts that place less attention on a single individual and enable children to grapple with the issues within a more generalized framework.

Some issues are sensitive ones for a particular group of people at a particular time. These issues, too, need to be addressed in substantive ways. For example, in one community, location of a waste disposal site was consuming citizen attention. In another community, labor disputes were going on, and children were exposed to picket lines and strikes.

In a first-grade classroom a child announced to his teacher, "My father says that teachers shouldn't go on strike." The teacher was active in the union and the newspaper had been filled with stories of the deadlock on negotiation issues. Situations such as this are difficult. Tempting though it may be to push her own point of view, it is the adult's responsibility to help children understand that grownups, too, disagree, and there are often competing issues. The teacher needs to help children recognize that people do have different points of view about issues, that these points of view each need to be considered and respected, and that each point of view may be accompanied by deep-seated feelings. Parents who value education or may be faced with trying to find child care if the impending strike materializes may become worried, concerned, and possibly angry. Teachers have feelings about not being able to come to school because community groups cannot agree on a particular issue. The message here is that the teacher needs to plan for children's consideration of human behavior in light of the experiences that are a part of daily life.

Helping children use their cognitive abilities in the interest of mental health and the development of social competence is a key aspect of the educator's role. Not to help children deal with these issues is an abdication of a very important role teachers play in today's society. Teachers need to help children recognize that feelings and emotions are an important part of life and that coping with one's feelings and emotions constitutes an important skill. In addition, children need to understand that when emotions are not recognized and expressed, they can wreak havoc with one's ability to learn. The child who is particularly small for his age, the child whose classmate has died, the child who witnesses violence—for each of these children, the opportunity to express emotion and to continue to be accepted once the emotion is expressed is vitally important.

Guidelines for Addressing Sensitive Issues

Encourage the expression of feelings First is the need to generate the expression of feelings, to encourage children to vent their emotions and to articulate them. Expression may take the form of body movement, drawing, or sculpting. Articulation involves putting into words how one feels. The teacher needs to help the children find an appropriate forum for the expression of feelings without exposing children and leaving them powerless. The objective is not to encourage a raw expression of feelings without any opportunity to give form to these feelings.

The raw expression of feelings—without processing the feelings in a cognitive manner—reflects a limited perspective and is encouraged sometimes by those who adhere to a romantic view of learning. It is of limited value to encourage children to tell stories that are full of emotion or that express jealousy and fear, or to draw pictures that tackle issues like power and anger, without also helping children to understand these complex emotions. The romanticists consider the catharsis that occurs to be valuable in and of itself. In the romantic classroom, children often do not go beyond the pure expression of feelings.

The cognitive-developmentalist also encourages catharsis, or the expression of feelings. The emphasis from the cognitive-developmentalist (or constructivist) perspective, however, is on the sharing of emotions on behalf of building greater understanding. The key in the cognitive developmental model is to identify concepts that facilitate children's taking charge of themselves and functioning effectively with others. To do so requires understanding one's own behavior as well as the behavior of others. In order to achieve this understanding, it is necessary to consider a wide range of feelings, reactions, and viewpoints about a particular issue and to examine the causes for certain behaviors.

Elicit many different points of view A second guideline is that the teacher should elicit many different ideas about a particular topic. For example, some children may express fear when they talk about seeing adults fighting; others may react to the excitement. The teacher needs to help children understand that people feel differently about certain things—that there is a range of responses.

Consider a discussion of a classmate's death. Some children may express the idea that the child has gone to heaven. Others talk about burial, in a box under the ground. Others may have heard about being cremated. The teacher's role is to help children recognize that death is something that people have different ideas about and that having different ideas is okay. Unless the teacher establishes the acceptance of different ideas, children will not feel comfortable in settings in which their ideas differ from those expressed by the majority of the group.

Use professional judgment in sharing one's own point of view When should teachers share their views about controversial issues? A third guideline emphasizes the need for teachers to provide objective information, not to judge the information or to get involved in a discussion of values. If teachers do decide to express their own views, they should exercise caution. They should express their own views only after they are certain that a wide range of views have been expressed by the group. Teachers also need to be respectful of parental preferences and the children's developmental level. These two factors must be considered in determining when to expand on an idea and when such expansion is inappropriate.

In one classroom of three-year-olds, children were making jello with fruit. One child was holding a bunch of grapes in his hand and offered some to the teacher. The teacher refused, saying, "No, I don't eat grapes because they don't pay the grape pickers enough money." This teacher shared her own viewpoint about labor and labor unions with a three-year-old who was developmentally unable to comprehend the issue. The child replied, "My mommy eats grapes and so do I." Little was accomplished by the teacher asserting her point of view about an issue far beyond the child's level of comprehension.

Provide factual information consistent with children's developmental level and need at a particular time Sometimes children hear frightening accounts of hostility on television and in adult conversations. When this happens, three- and four-year-olds need continual reassurance both through words and through extra physical cuddling that they will be safe. The seven-year-old also needs reassurance about being safe. Developmentally, however, the child of seven can begin to work through some of the competing values.

Perhaps a child heard a news broadcast that was frightening or overheard an argument between his parents that disturbed him. These experiences may indirectly become a part of the child's conversation or be reflected in his behavior. In some cases the child may share the experience directly with the teacher. The teacher listens to the child as the child expresses his concern. She provides a caring ear and often reflects the child's feelings. This listening response is often more helpful and more instructive than any information the teacher could provide at the time. What children need when they spontaneously bring up emotionally laden situations—for example, situations that are frightening or puzzling—is the reassurance that they will be safe and well cared for. At a later time they can deal on a cognitive level with the universality of emotion, the idea that all people experience fear at some time and that people have found different ways to cope with this feeling.

Sometimes teachers can expose children to information and allow children to return to the information as experience and interest dictates. One effective way to do this is through literature. The book *Love You Forever* referred to earlier in this section, is a clear example of a story through which children can take in information about aging and the life cycle in an informal and comfortable manner.

As teachers develop skill in handling sensitive issues, as their competence increases, their fears diminish. They become increasingly more comfortable taking on for discussion potentially embarrassing situations. They sense which issues should be temporarily ignored and which should be reframed and dealt with in a more neutral discussion. They can lead children sensitively through potentially difficult discussions. They help children gain not only the sense of relief that comes from the expression of feelings, but also increased insight, understanding, and skill.

Social-Emotional Issues in Curriculum: Operational Characteristics

By planning and implementing curriculum experiences that focus on children's feelings, teachers can empower children to take responsibility for their own behavior. They can identify specific curriculum content by listening to and observing children, understanding developmental issues, and considering the universality of emotions. Generally this content will fall into three major areas: (1) helping children deal with feelings, (2) helping children understand similarities and differences among people, and (3) helping children understand and develop friendship-making skills.

Each of these areas is content-related. Each focuses on specific information or the acquisition of specific skills. In each, the emphasis is on helping children think about feelings, and each involves specific teacher behaviors. In the next section, these teacher behaviors are described as operational characteristics, and they are embedded in classroom examples. The examples extend some concepts and approaches proven successful with young children. The examples are intended to stimulate the reader to adapt, extend, revise, or invent new strategies for deliberate planning of experiences that will help children begin to unravel the complexities of human behavior. First, let's consider ways teachers help children deal with feelings.

Helping Children Deal with Feelings

The teacher plans opportunities for helping children deal with their own feelings and the feelings of others. Included is the full range of feelings: the hostile, negative feelings related to fear, jealousy, anger, frustration, and aggression; and the positive feelings that have to do with love, affection, exhilaration, work and productivity, competence, and high self-esteem.

Teachers encourage children to express their ideas about affective issues in a variety of ways. At group time, they identify excellent opportunities for discussion. They stimulate journal writing and book-making and use these activities to help children work through significant emotional issues. They engage children in the expressive arts—play, drama, poetry, puppetry, movement, dance, music, and the visual arts—as natural avenues for the imagination to focus on reasons for behavior and the expression of feelings. They build on children's experiences with books (published and teacher-created) so that stories become a form of bibliotherapy,* and they incorporate the study of human behavior into math, science, and social studies. They plan in advance to engage children in thinking about behavior because they know how important this subject is to young children. They appreciate the attention to detail required to maximize these learning opportunities.

The range of subjects related to understanding emotionally laden experiences appropriate for young children to examine is vast: "Do you ever get angry? What makes you angry? What do you do when you're angry? Do grownups get angry?" "Did you ever wish for something and have it come true? What was it and what made it come true?" "What does it mean to be disappointed? Were you ever disappointed? What made you feel that way? What did you do about it?" "Did you ever think that you couldn't do something and then discover that you could? How did you feel before you did it? How did you feel afterwards?" The possibilities are endless and exciting to explore. The sensitive teacher will select those issues pertinent to the particular group of children and develop meaningful activities that expand understanding of key concepts generalizable to other comparable events. Those concepts include the following:

- People can talk about things that they feel, and it is important to do so because it helps them to understand what is involved.
- Most feelings that you have are not unusual; other people have comparable feelings.
- There are reasons behind the way you behave.
- There are reasons behind how other people behave.
- When you understand the reasons for behavior, you can sometimes do something about the matter. People have options in responding to their feelings.

* Bibliotherapy, in the third edition of *Webster's New International Dictionary,* is defined as "guidance in the solution of personal problems through directed reading." The Phi Delta Kappan Fastback, *Bibliotherapy: The Right Book at the Right Time,* Cornett (1980) defined bibliotherapy as "a basically simple idea: the use of books to help people."

FIGURE 9-3

This haunting painting by a third-grade girl was created after a classroom discussion about angry feelings. Faces and hands are interspersed abstractly to render an intensely emotional product. The teacher helped the children understand how strong feelings can be expressed in visual as well as verbal ways. Collection of Sylvia G. Feinburg

Examples of Lessons Designed Around Feelings

Feelings on the first day of school: A group time experience From the first day of school, a second-grade teacher lets it be known that feelings are an important part of the curriculum.

She has put up a large poster on the wall. The poster, "How Do You Feel on the First Day of School?" has five columns.

How Do You Feel on the First Day of School?				
excited	nervous	sad	happy	scared
Liana	Charmaine		Michael	Sean
Peter			Costanza	Maddie
				Rachel

The teacher gave each child a paper square. Children each identified how they were feeling, drew a picture to illustrate the feeling, and put their names on it. The children in turn then put their square in the appropriate column. The result was a class graph, a valuable mathematical experience (counting, one-to-one correspondence), and a real awareness of the shared feelings about the first day of school.

"Being left out": a group time experience In one first-grade classroom, the teacher, Jennifer Morrison, planned a group discussion to focus children's attention on the issue of personal rejection. In a number of incidents, children had been insensitive to other children's feelings about being included or excluded, and the teacher wanted to expand their understanding of this important realm of human behavior. During group time, she raised the following issues for discussion: "Have you ever been left out? Not been allowed to participate when others were involved in something really exciting and fun? How did it make you feel?"

Children were quick to respond and had a range of reactions and incidents to share. The teacher encouraged their elaboration. After the discussion had gone on a while, she asked them to summarize the way that people tend to feel when they are left out of a given situation. Children responded that they felt: sad, bad, dumb, stupid, like a loser, mad, ready to fight; "I felt like I had lost a friend." The teacher accepted all the children's comments. She encouraged the children to listen to one another and with them reviewed the list of feelings they had shared. She left the list posted in the room for a few days. Children requested the opportunity to add some ideas to the list: "angry," "irritated," and "very mad." At another group meeting time, the teacher reviewed the list and expanded on the experience. "What did you do when you were left out?" she asked the children. She recorded their responses on another chart.

What Did You Do When You Were Left Out?
Went to my room
Would watch them
Played tricks on them
Thinking to myself, "It's not that great a game"
Kicked the table, ran to my room
Put a water balloon on my sister
Played by myself
Hide and think to myself
Said, "I don't care" and did something myself
Try some more
Did something without asking

A few days later, the discussion continued, and the class prepared another chart.

What's the Best Thing You Can Do When You Are Left Out?

Play with someone else

Play alone

Ignore them

Watch T.V.

Tell the parent or the teacher

Throw something

Ask someone else to do something with me

Look for another group of kids

Just walk away

Tell them they can't exclude you

Think "it's not the end of the world"

Through this discussion the teacher helped the children recognize the inevitability of everyone being left out at some time or other. She also conveyed the belief that each child had the power to develop his or her own coping mechanisms when confronted with other people's negative behavior. Of central importance in this experience is children coming to understand that all people, regardless of who they are and how old they are, experience being left out and must struggle to deal with the intense feelings of being rejected.

Obviously, this subject could be continued and developed in more elaborated, complex ways. The teacher might have chosen to deal with questions such as the following: Why do children reject other children? Can someone be your friend and still be unkind? Do you ever reject people? Why do you think you do? To what extent the teacher decides to develop the subject is a function of the children's age and capabilities, as well as how interested and involved children become as the matter is addressed.

Joining hands: a social studies experience In another class (K–1, multi-age), the issue of inclusion and exclusion, taking part and not taking part, took a different direction. The children had engaged in a long-term project in which each child in turn laid down on a heavy piece of butcher paper while two other children traced around the body shape. Each child painted on his or her own shape facial features and clothing. The child-sized portraits were then mounted on the wall in such a way that they all appeared to be holding hands with each other. Two girls who tended to be shy and reticent did not want to be traced and thus were not included on the mural. The teacher did not push the issue. She allowed the girls to decline the chance to be included in this activity. She also made a mental note that she needed to plan a discussion of feelings about not wanting to participate in something.

During group time one of the children called attention to the fact that Brenda and Angelica were missing. "They're not up there. They're in our group and they were scared to be traced. They didn't want to be traced. They didn't want to, and they're not up there so we don't have the whole class."

Children started asking Brenda and Angelica why they didn't want to be included. Brenda squirmed, and Angelica looked down. The teacher deflected the attention from the two girls by beginning a more neutral discussion: "Sometimes people don't want to be included; sometimes they do. Can you think of a time when you didn't want to do something that the other people around you wanted you to do? Who has an example? All of us have times when we would just feel better about not being a part of what's going to happen."

One child reported: "When everyone was going to kiss great-grandpa Harry at his ninetieth birthday party. He's got a big beard. My aunts and mother and grandma and cousins all did it—but, ick, not me. I don't kiss hairy men."

Another child, Amy, told about the following incident. "I didn't want to go to Marissa's birthday party. I just didn't wanna go, and I didn't want to call her either. My mother kept saying, 'Why don't you want to go? You'll have a good time. If you don't go, you'll hurt Marissa's feelings and she won't want to play with you anymore. How would you feel if no one came to your birthday party?' But I wasn't going—I just wasn't going—and that's that." The teacher remembers her objective, to encourage children to express their feelings about being included and excluded, and so does not fall into a trap that would be quite natural—namely, to take a detour in the discussion and try to find out the child's reason for not wanting to go to the party. What the teacher is really aiming to do is to generate several different examples that would lead Brenda and Angelica, as well as the other children in the class, to the appreciation of the commonality of their experiences. Her purpose is to gather several examples so that they become part of a pattern of how people behave. In this way the teacher establishes the fact that all human beings are capable of this behavior.

The teacher is cognizant of the fact that her objective is not to find out why Amy did not want to go to Marissa's party. Her aim is to help children recognize the importance of feelings in making decisions. She continues to gather more examples from the group and to stimulate children's thinking about the issue: "Do you think it is important to do what people want you to do? Should you always have to do it in this kind of situation?" She tries to get the children to weigh the pros and cons. She doesn't want to leave them with the message that it's okay to refuse to participate, and that's that. She wants them to realize that sometimes people have strong feelings that make it difficult for them to participate when other people want them to and they don't want to. They are encouraged to think about the situation and think of the reasons they don't want to participate and think of the reasons other people want them to be included. They need to try to do the thing that makes the most sense at the time. "Sometimes if you push yourself a little bit, you're glad; and sometimes it's better not to be included."

The teacher engages the children in hypothetical decision making: "Do you think Amy should go to the party when she doesn't want to? How does a person decide a dilemma like that? Her mother wants her to go, but she doesn't want to. How does she decide?"

The degree to which the teacher decides to pursue a discussion such as this is influenced by many factors: comfort of the group, the vulnerability of individuals within the group, and children's involvement in the issue at the particular time. In some cases the concept will not be developed further. In other situations, the teacher will sense that the issue is of central concern and will develop other curriculum experiences around it. The teacher will encourage children to write or draw about their experiences. At journal writing time the next day, the teacher might remind the children: "Remember we were talking about that yesterday? That may be something that you want to write about in your journal." In addition to providing writing experience for children, journals also afford the teacher key opportunities to get to know children's personal concerns. Through responses to children's writing or drawing, the teacher can encourage a real sharing of feelings. Books provide another avenue for developing curriculum. The teacher may encourage a particular child to consult with the librarian to find a book that deals with the subject. (Libraries have many resource books that list books by topics and provide annotations, and librarians themselves are excellent resources.)

The important message for the reader is not to be frightened by awkward topics, but rather to feel comfortable taking on for discussion potentially embarrassing situations. On the rare occasion when someone is willing to raise a subject that is potentially difficult for us to discuss, we as adults are often relieved. Notice in the example just given the teacher's skill in ignoring the two girls on whom the attention was originally focused. She identified the central issue and made it okay for the whole group to develop it. The five- to seven-year-old child is in a developmental period when he or she may not want to be the focus of attention. For the child of this age it is very important to recognize that he is not alone in this feeling.

As it turned out, in the discussion Brenda did reveal her reason for not wanting to be drawn around. She was afraid that she would get marker ink on her clothes. The incident illustrates another important point. Teachers need to be careful not to label children's behavior. What originally seemed to be evidence of shyness was in reality a demonstration of a legitimate concern.

Feeling angry or afraid: any expressive media In the same way, the teacher helps children identify feelings associated with other emotionally laden experiences. What do you do when you are angry? What makes you afraid?

For example, in conjunction with an animal unit, the teacher poses the following questions: Are cats and dogs ever afraid? How do cats show you when they are afraid? When they are frightened of people? When they are angry at what people have done? The teacher points out that knowledge is sometimes a potent way of understanding and alleviating fear. Children verbalize their responses and illustrate or write a story about them. In the drawings or in the stories, children often share what other people or other animals do when they are angry or things that make other people or animals afraid.

A house for animals: block building Children often reveal their feelings through dramatic play. The expression of feelings is in itself valuable. Sometimes, however, the teacher picks up on the feeling clues provided by the children as they engage in regular classroom activities. Teachers who are keen observers can pick up on these clues and use them as the basis for planned curriculum experiences.

Danny, a four-year-old, is playing with blocks. He calls the teacher to show her his construction. "This is a house where animals stay. This is the door that they go in," he says as he points to the opening. He picks up the plastic animals and exclaims, "These animals are wild. That's why they go to jail." The teacher senses the fear in Danny's voice and in his body actions and detects the bravado that Danny is displaying as a way of coping with the fear. The teacher asks, "What do they do in jail?" "They don't die. They just can't be wild. See, each of the animals has a separate cage, and there's bars so that they can't get out." Danny is agitated as he provides this explanation and his actions become increasingly more violent as he manipulates the animals in and out of the cages. This play together with the teacher's reflections of the behavior and the feelings was in and of itself a valuable way of expressing and coping with fear. As the teacher found out later, Danny's father was in the hospital with a serious illness. He could not come home to see Danny. The dramatic play was one way of Danny trying to make sense out of what he was feeling.

Showing that you care: an art experience The focus is not only on emotions that evoke negative responses. Helping children to appreciate kindness and to experience the joy of love and caring are also addressed. For Valentine's Day, the teacher developed the following lesson plan:

- *Objective:* Use Valentine's Day as an opportunity to extend children's understandings of how to express love and appreciation of other people, as well as to explore activities with paper, such as cutting, curling, slotting, and penetrating.
- *Materials:* Many sizes and shapes of white and colored paper, small gummed letters, rubber stamps of letters, magazine picture scraps, magic markers, and scissors.
- *Motivation:* "All of us know people whom we care about, people with whom we live or play, family members or friends. Valentine's Day is a wonderful opportunity to let those people know why they are important to us—what we like and appreciate about them. Think about somebody that you're very glad you know. It could be a friend or a relative; it could be someone here at school. What does that person do that makes you care about them? Do they share things with you? Do they listen to you when you want to tell about something? Do they come to your place to visit? Why are they important to you?" The teacher encourages the sharing of this kind of information and reinforces children's pertinent comments. The teacher also relates this discussion to prior lessons on using paper in two- and three-dimensional ways.
- *Procedures:* The teacher provides many kinds, sizes, and shapes of paper and introduces the notion that paper can be manipulated in a wide assortment of ways—tearing, folding, curling, slotting, penetrating. The teacher encourages the children to write words themselves and to use the gummed letters, rubber stamps, or letters that they tear out of magazines.
- *Evaluation:* When the children share their Valentine's Day cards, the focus of the discussion is on the message of kindness and caring the card conveys as well as the techniques for using paper in a variety of different ways to express an idea.

Note in the plan the teacher's thoughtful attention to the discussion starters she uses to stimulate children's ideas. This step is critical in stimulating children's thinking.

Halloween science/social studies: a group time experience Another holiday example extended kindergartners' experiences related to Halloween.

Many teachers as part of their science program at Halloween encourage children to observe an aging pumpkin or, as they talk about planting, have children suspend a potato and watch it sprout and eventually wither as it ages. One teacher who was particularly sensitive to subjects in which children had real interest began a mini-unit talking about how old people are different from young people. She asked the children to give definitions of old and young. One child's definition of old: "when you live in an apartment."

Helping Children Understand Similarities and Differences

The teacher helps children understand similarities and differences among people. Similarities and differences are revealed in many ways: in race, gender, age, physical and mental capabilities, family patterns, and cultural backgrounds. People like one another in one of these ways have some things in common and are also different from each other in many ways. All people need to be respected and valued. For children to become respectful and to grow in appreciation of differences as well as similarities, teachers need to take a proactive stance in building this understanding. It is not sufficient to sit back and wait for a negative incident to occur. Teachers need to model respectful and positive behavior directly, and they need to provide experiences for children through which this growth can take place.

According to Louise Derman-Sparks (1989), early childhood is a critical time to lay the groundwork for children's acceptance and appreciation of differences in people. The reasons are threefold: (1) developmentally, children are beginning to acquire a sense of their own identity (gender, race, religion); (2) are also very susceptible to social experiences; and (3) are developing increasing cognitive capacities.

Children's increasing cognitive capacity to classify is a part of their normal development and is reflected in their responses to differences. Children make comments about facial features, skin color, or any other physical attribute that they notice as unlike their own. Children's initial responses to what they see as different or discrepant from what they are accustomed to seeing often appear to adults to be prejudicial, hurtful, or lacking in tact. In actuality, the comments children make are the basis on which they are building their understanding of similarities and differences. Their comments about differences are usually neither negative nor positive, but almost always are neutral. Since children during the early childhood years are naturally engaged in seeing differences and acknowledging them, these years represent a critical time for determining whether children are going to embrace differences and accept them as positive, or reject differences and treat them as something to be avoided.

An action research study carried out by a student from Lesley College (Verruso, 1990) demonstrated that as children move from kindergarten through the elementary school, they become increasingly more aware of ways in which they are similar and dissimilar from their classmates. This aspect of cognitive development leads to many inclusionary and exclusionary practices among children.

In the study, twenty children from a rural area of Vermont in which the population was totally homogeneous in terms of race (all were Caucasian), the children were asked to select from paper dolls of different races and genders "the child they would like to play with at school, at home, which child they would invite to their birthday party, which child they would invite to a sleep-over." The Caucasian kindergarten children, many of whom had never seen a person of a different race, were not at all hesitant to choose an African American doll. None of the kindergarten children put the dolls together according to race. With the first-grade children the situation was quite different. "All of the children put the paper dolls together according to race and none of the children chose the African American doll nor would they choose the African American person in the pictures when asked who they would invite to their party or to their sleep-over."

This comparison of kindergarten and first-grade children reflects, to a large degree, the nature of normal development. Although this study was carried out with a small number of children and lacked sophistication in control of variables, it does provide first-hand corroboration of other studies (Katz, 1976, 1983; Williams & Morland, 1976) that indicate "by the age of three or four, young children can identify, label, and match people according to different racial characteristics" (Ramsey, 1986). Ramsey also reports that same-race preference often emerges when children are asked to select dolls, puppets, or photographs that represent potential friends. Teachers need to observe and listen to the children in their classrooms in order to determine how they are organizing information about differences, help them acknowledge the differences as well as the similarities that exist among people, and use their developing capacities to enrich rather than restrict their experiences.

Following are some ways teachers can build this understanding.

- deliberately plan experiences that call attention to differences as well as to similarities
- set up an environment in which children can discover and raise issues about similarities and differences
- integrate into all aspects of the curriculum a focus on ways that people are alike and different
- continually expand their own understanding about different groups of people (and about individuals within the groups) and share this understanding with children in a variety of ways

Examples of Lessons Designed Around Differences and Similarities

Our class wall hanging: a work period activity continued for several days The goal of this experience, observed in Janice Danielson and Andrea Doane's kindergarten class at Devotion School in Brookline, Massachusetts, was to stimulate discussion about similarities and differences. The class was multiethnic. Children came from a variety of racial, cultural, and geographic backgrounds. The teacher put out at one of the workstations a large white sheet she had divided into squares. At five of the squares, she placed a mirror, markers, chalk, and cosmetics. She began the project by orienting a small group of children. She instructed each child to draw his or her own facial portrait. The children were asked to look in the mirror and note the shape of their heads, their eyes, their nose, and their mouth. They observed and talked about differences in shape of facial features, in skin color, in color of eyes, and in color of hair. Then the children proceeded to draw their own facial portraits, each in a designated square. Each day a different group of children engaged in the observations, the discussion, and the drawing. The end result was a magnificent class mural that was hung on the wall. The similarities and differences were clearly apparent.

A visitor comes to class: a group time experience Differences that are obviously seen as negative are often threatening and frightening to children. Unfamiliarity and lack of experience increases children's vulnerability to difference. When the unusual becomes more common, acceptance is likely to take place.

One teacher in a school had received a special needs awareness grant. In an experience shared by Ruth Japinga, a student in Lesley College's CCDA (Continuing Career Development for Adults) program, the teacher invited Cindy, a prospective teacher who was also a parent of a child with special needs, to come to the classroom and talk with the children. Both Cindy and her son, Pete, came into the classroom in wheelchairs. Cindy waved to the children and said hello to them in sign language. The children took a little while to get accustomed to their visitors. However, soon most of them felt comfortable waving back.

Cindy then used her voice to help the children reflect upon the experience. She asked the children what she had said to them in sign language. At first the children were unable to answer this question; but when Cindy explained that she was sure they had understood because they had answered her by waving back, the children realized that without using her mouth Cindy had said "Hi" to them; and they, without using their mouths, were able to respond. In the discussion the children revealed some familiarity with sign language since they had seen it used on television.

Cindy asked the children to walk forward, backward, and in a circle, which they did easily. She then tried to do the same thing in the wheelchair. The children saw that this was much more difficult. Then Cindy got up from the chair and demonstrated that she could use her legs to walk. "Let's see if Pete can get up from the chair and use his legs." The children observed that Pete's legs did not work, and he could not get up from the chair. This led to a discussion of why Pete needed the wheelchair to help him get around.

Cindy engaged the children in a discussion of feelings. "If you come home from school and your mother gives you some hot chocolate and your favorite kind of cookie, how does this make you feel?" Several of the children volunteered answers. They agreed that this would make them feel happy. Cindy pointed out that when Pete comes home from school and she gives him hot chocolate and his favorite kind of cookie, he, too, feels happy. "If you fall down and scrape your knee, how do you feel?" The children responded, "sad," "hurt." "When Pete gets a scrape or a cut, he, too, feels sad or hurt." Pete was a severely handicapped child. He was blind. His eyes looked crossed. He had very poor gross and fine motor coordination. Nonetheless, the children were building an appreciation of some of the similarities they shared with Pete. Cindy reiterated the notion that although Pete was different from them in many ways, they could still be friends with him.

Cindy and Pete came to the class another day. This time Cindy brought a blindfold. She invited the children to take turns putting on the blindfold and trying to find a friend by listening to the direction from which the friend was calling. The children were very eager to take turns in this activity. The activity was followed by a discussion about how people whose eyes did not work use their ears to help them "see." Then Cindy demonstrated how she fed Pete. She let the children help her by pushing food into the tube. "That's like a short cut to his stomach," one child observed.

The teacher in the classroom, on Cindy's suggestion, had sent home a note to parents asking them to send a big winter hat to school. On the third visit Cindy took out paper, scissors, and crayons. She had the children put their hat on the hand with which they write. She then asked them to try to pick up a crayon and write their names. One child found this so difficult that she started crying and, of course, took off the hat. Another responded by taunting: "Aw. This is going to be so-o-o easy." What Cindy was demonstrating was that some people's hands don't work well, and it's very hard for them to pick up scissors and cut out a circle or pick up a crayon and write their name. Cindy encouraged the children to draw a picture of things they could do with a handicapped friend.

Having Cindy and Pete visit this classroom generated discussion between the children and their parents and between the teacher and the parents. The message here for adults is that they need to accept children's statement about differences as normal. They should not be embarrassed by such statements nor should they consider them negative. Cindy encouraged the teacher to share with the parents that they do not need to pull their child away from a handicapped person. She indicated that it is okay for children to look and to ask. They need a simple explanation: "This is Pete. He's blind. That's why his eyes look funny." When children ask, "How come he sits like that?" the answer is direct: "His muscles aren't working right, and he can't sit up straight." Children, as they perceive these differences, may or may not need help in recognizing ways that handicapped children are like themselves and in thinking of ways that they can play together.

An environment that stimulates appreciation of diversity The classroom is made up of both a physical and a human environment. In terms of the physical aspects of the classroom, the teacher needs to be sure that the pictures on the walls, the dolls, the books, the puzzles, and other materials are multiethnic and nonsexist and represent people of a variety of ages, abilities, and disabilities in a variety of roles. Books provide one source of stimulating children's discovery of differences. They provide an excellent avenue for stimulating discussion about diversity.

In terms of the human aspects of the environment, children benefit from having contact with people who are like themselves. They also benefit from having contact with as many aspects of human diversity as is possible. The **inclusionary philosophy** is a deep commitment to the integration of children with special needs into regular educational programs. When integration is accomplished, all children benefit.

Children with visible physical limitations may arouse fear and resentment in other children. The teacher needs to guard against these reactions by sharing routinely factual information that can be helpful. For example, in a classroom with one blind member, the teacher can help the children recognize how they can be helpful in their interactions.

- "Why don't you let Susan feel the paint so she can know how exciting it is?" "Susan, have a feel."
- "Susan, do you want Jamie to help you find the circles or do you want to find them yourself?"
- When Susan, who was unable to see what she was doing, pushed several markers on to Maria's picture, the teacher noticed that this bothered Maria: "Maria, tell Susan how it makes you feel when she doesn't stop to figure out where you are working."

Diversity also occurs in classrooms in terms of the values particular families hold or in terms of the family structure within which children live.

- When the class celebrated birthdays, this represented a conflict for one child whose religion did not permit birthday celebrations. The teacher discussed this conflict with the parents, and together they made a plan for what the child would do during any birthday celebration. This information was shared directly with the child and with the class.
- The class was making Mother's Day cards. One child did not have a mother; he had two fathers. Most of the children did have mothers. They were aware that in this way Stephen was different from them. In a routine conversation Stephen announced that his fathers were very special to him and that he was going to make cards for them.
- In one class, the teacher's expectation for the children differed from that of the parents. The teacher wanted the kindergarten children to be able to identify written letters. The parent wanted to be sure that the child was not being pushed into reading too early, so she convinced the child that he was not ready to read and that he should refuse to read until his mother told him he was ready. The teacher accepted this and encouraged the child's participation in ways that did not conflict with the parent's value system. It was interesting to note that at the time of the eye screening test, the child's mother did not tell him that reading would be involved. The child had no difficulty describing the letters on the chart.

An integrated diversity curriculum The teacher can take many steps in working proactively to help children recognize and appreciate diversity. She can select books that broaden children's awareness of cultures different than their own.

For example, the book *The Day of Ahmed's Secret* (Heide & Gilliland, 1990) takes place in Cairo, Egypt. It is a story of a boy who is growing up and taking on more responsibility. As he sets about delivering the butagaz (the fuel for the stoves), he keeps in his head the secret that he can now write his name. At the end of the story he proudly shares his secret. The reader not only feels great empathy with the main character, but also coincidentally learns a great deal about life in Egypt.

Different cultural traditions are reflected in the way stories are told. English stories are linear. They provide particulars and build up to the main point. Japanese have a different pattern of telling stories. They tend to omit certain things and encourage inferences. Teachers should expose children to these differences and, as appropriate, help children identify the similarities and the differences.

Interwoven with the music experiences offered to children should be an appreciation of some of the distinct cultural characteristics reflected in music. Children should be given information that would help them to appreciate the differences. For example, Chinese music is often played on black keys. Most music with which children living in America are familiar is played primarily on the white keys. The musical scales are also different. Parents in all cultural groups sing songs and lullabies to their children. The songs tend to emphasize the values of the culture. For example, native American parents and grandparents sing songs and lullabies "that carry messages of hope and aspiration, [and] reflect appreciation of beauty, sharing and physical strength" (Burgess, 1986). Lullabies sound differently in different homes. Children enjoy listening to and singing songs in other languages.

In the dramatic play area, children often reveal aspects of their background. When the play reflects sex stereotypes, the teacher has an opportunity to reflect a nonsexist view. He or she needs to do this in a way that shows respect for the child's background and at the same time establishes the nonsexist viewpoint.

◗ A group of three-year-olds were playing in the housekeeping corner. In the class were some white children, some black children, and some children who had recently come to the United States from Puerto Rico. When the telephone in the dramatic play area rang, Leila asked Juan to answer it. Juan refused, saying, "I'm a father. Fathers don't answer the telephone. Only mothers do."

◗ In the same class Pedro, another three-year-old, refused to sweep up the crumbs he had spilled on the floor. Here again the child referred to the fact that men in his house don't sweep the floors. The teacher made a point of telling Pedro and Juan, as well as the other children involved in the play, that in school it was different. Both boys and girls were responsible for helping to clean up the room, and in some homes both mothers and fathers answer the telephone when it rings. This bit of cultural conflict is not easy for children or for their parents. In Pedro's case, his mother was a single parent interested in becoming acculturated to the American way. She did not complain about the difference in role expectations between the two cultures.

Expanding cultural understanding Children who come into schools in which the dominant culture is different from their own often feel uncomfortable. This feeling may be due to differences in mores. For example, in some cultures, children have utmost respect for teachers. Children are expected to defer to adults, not initiate conversation with them, and not to speak up unless the adult addresses a question directly to the child. When the mores in the class are different, the situation can be very intimidating to a child.

◗ In one first-grade class, the teacher valued creativity. She tended to respond to children who were uninhibited. As she grew in her cultural competence, she recognized the cultural differences, acknowledged these to herself and to the children, and adapted her expectations to take into account the cultural diversity within the class.

◗ In a second-grade class, the teacher repeatedly emphasized the need for children to work carefully, to avoid making mistakes. One child who came from a native American background seemed very resistant. As the teacher came to appreciate that in native American culture "artifacts (baskets, rugs, pottery, etc.) are made with purposeful imperfections as a lesson to children that no one is perfect; we all make mistakes," (Burgess, 1986), she experienced a changed attitude toward the child, and toward all children, and a greater appreciation of cultural differences. As the teacher found ways to integrate this new awareness into the curriculum, she and the children were enriched.

Encouraging Friendship-Making Skills

The teacher encourages the development of friendship-making skills. Some children are naturally skilled in the area of interpersonal relations. They seem to possess a high degree of what Howard Gardner calls "interpersonal intelligence." They naturally know how to negotiate what they want, they have many interesting ideas, and other children gravitate toward them. Some children who are naturally less skilled develop proficiency in interpersonal relationships through frequent opportunities they have to interact with other children. However, there are many children who seem to have real difficulty making friends. "Children without friends are lonely and they are more likely than children with friends to have serious problems later in life . . . dropping out of school, [engaging] in criminal behavior, and [having] mental health problems" (Asher & Williams, 1987, p. 5).

The implications of this data for curriculum building are significant. Teachers need to include, in their curriculum, planned experiences that help children develop friendship-making skills. Some practice in these skill areas should be planned to take place on a one-to-one basis; at other times, the experiences should include a small group or the total class. The teacher who is planning to include friendship making skills in the curriculum will find it particularly helpful to observe children who seem naturally to possess a high degree of these skills. These observations will provide useful information in structuring experiences that can be helpful to others.

Friendship-making skills include the following:

1. listening to others and being able to read others' behaviors
2. gaining entrance into ongoing peer activities
3. getting along with others, and being able to negotiate conflict so that one's ego is intact and others feel good about themselves and want to continue the activity
4. initiating contact
5. handling rejection
6. sustaining a relationship: expressing empathy, giving feedback, providing ideas or building on the ideas of others (Kostelnik et al., 1993)

Examples of Lessons Designed Around Friendship-Making Skills

Roger and the guinea pig: an individual experience for a four-year-old As an example of planning for an individual child, the teacher notices that Roger, a preschooler, seems to need help in developing empathy. She has noticed that he seems to be totally oblivious to others' feelings. He enjoys playing with the guinea pig, but most of his interactions result in his taking pleasure in squeezing the pig too hard and watching its reactions or pouncing on another child and watching the child cry. As a first step, the teacher makes clear the fact that she will not allow Roger to hurt animals or people. She plans time to be alone with Roger and the guinea pig and works explicitly on the development of empathy: "See how happy the guinea pig is when she smells the food." "The guinea pig is having so much fun racing around the block maze that we made for her." The teacher plans similar times to stay with Roger as he interacts with other children.

Let's be friends: A group time experience At group time, the teacher engages first graders in a role-play: "Let's pretend that two people are playing together. Alex and Marc, will you come up and be the two people who are playing? What will you pretend you are playing? Now let's suppose that Danielle wants to play, too, but that you don't want her to play with you right now. Show us, Danielle, what you would do." The teacher observes, labels, comments, discusses, records, and repeats descriptions of behaviors that are socially appropriate and that reflect feelings of empathy.

The teacher engages children in a discussion of specific skills: What do you do when you want to play with someone? When someone won't let you take a turn? When someone calls you names? When you and your friend get into an argument? Sometimes the teacher relates a specific incident the children have experienced in their interactions with one another. The teacher recounts the incident and lets the children role-play alternative solutions. Changing the names of the children involved is an effective distancing technique. As children come to a realization of who the players really are, they also develop insight into the problem.

What should Nikki do? A discussion group experience A second-grade teacher presented the following problem to the class: "Andrea brought her jump rope to school. She said that Nikki could use it at recess time. Then at recess she didn't let Nikki have a turn. Nikki stood around and watched as Andrea and Charly twirled the rope, skipped over it a few times, and then made a game of seeing how many times each person could skip over it without landing on the rope. Nikki asked when it would be her turn. Andrea and Charly ignored her. What should Nikki do?" One child answered, "The best thing that Nikki could do would be to find something else to do. This would be hard because she really wanted to play jump rope. She could tell Andrea that she can't trust her to keep her promise." "But," another child interrupted, "if she does tell Andrea that she can't trust her, Andrea might get mad." "Nikki should just ignore Andrea." More important than the alternative suggestions is the children's realization that this is a difficult problem, that real feelings are involved, and that there are many ways of reacting.

"Reading" behavior: a language arts experience The teacher used the book *Mean Maxine* by Barbara Bottner as a way of helping kindergarten children build skills for "reading other people's behavior." In the story Ralph is upset because Maxine keeps calling him names. After Ralph figures out a way to cope with this name-calling, Maxine reveals the fact that she was just looking for a friend. That's why she kept calling him names. The teacher tells and retells this story. She engages children in summarizing the story and in identifying the main characters and the problems they face. The teacher discusses with the children how the characters felt at the beginning and at the end of the story, and how and why their feelings changed. She encourages children to relate themselves to the characters, to evaluate their own actions, and to draw conclusions. This is the process of bibliotherapy: "the right book at the right time" (Cornett & Cornett, 1980), accompanied with the right questions, can provide a powerful growth experience. The following is the teacher's plan.

- *Goal:* To improve children's ability to "read" the behavior of others
- *Concept:* To develop an appreciation of the fact that people try to make friends in many different ways; some are helpful ways, and others are not.
- *Objective:* Children will be able to relate their own experiences to those of characters in the story *Mean Maxine.* They will be able to describe one reason why some children show bullying behavior and make suggestions for protecting themselves and helping the bully.
- *Materials: Mean Maxine* by Barbara Bottner.
- *Procedures:*

1. Read the story to the children.
2. Reread the story (probably at a different time).
3. Ask children to retell the story.
4. Ask: What was Ralph's problem?
5. Ask: What happened to Ralph? How do you think Ralph felt? What happened to Maxine? How do you think Maxine felt?
6. Ask: What did Ralph do? How did he change what he did? What did Maxine do? How did she change?
7. Ask: What would you have done if you were Maxine? if you were Ralph? Has anything like this ever happened to you? How could you change that situation?
8. Ask: Now what do you think this story is about?

- *Evaluation:* Consider the responses of individual children in terms of the insight that the responses show regarding causes of bullying behavior and how they can take steps to change this behavior in themselves and in others.

Another teacher engaged children in picture study. The teacher had collected pictures of people who were angry, happy, frightened, and sad. The children talked about the pictures. They identified the clues that told them about the feelings that were being expressed. They also related their own experiences to the feelings related in the pictures.

Ollie Owl, the class puppet The teacher had a puppet she used to help children learn about friendship-making skills. The children had named this puppet

Ollie Owl. Ollie Owl was a regular visitor to the classroom. On this particular day he was witnessing a simulation of a game that the children frequently played outside. His job was to demonstrate unsuccessful behaviors for gaining entry into a group activity and to elicit from the children suggestions of ways in which he could be more successful.

The children are playing "Down, Down Baby," a game that depends on building up a group rhythm and engaging in simultaneous actions. The children stand in a circle and chant:

1. Down, down baby,
   Down, down the roller coaster.
   Sweet, sweet baby,
   I'll never let you go.
2. Chimey, chimey cocoa pop.
   Chimey, chimey pow.
   Chimey, chimey cocoa pop.
   Chimey, chimey pow.
3. Grandma, grandma sick in bed
   Call the doctor
   And the doctor said
4. Let's get the rhythm of the head—
   ding dong.
   (Repeat)
   Let's get the rhythm of the hands—
   clap clap.
   (Repeat)
   Let's get the rhythm of the feet—
   stomp stomp.
   (Repeat)
   Hey dog.
5. Put 'em all together and what do you get? Ding dong, clap, clap, stomp, stomp, hey dog.
   (Repeat)
   Put 'em all backwards and what do you get? Stomp, stomp, clap, clap, ding dong, hey dog.
   (Repeat)

The children get through the first verse and Ollie Owl interrupts. "Hey guys, can I play? One child answers, "No, you'll spoil the game." This situation is quite familiar to the children, and the teacher has seen it occur on several occasions. This happens a few times. The teacher interrupts: "Ollie Owl really wants to play. What should he do?"

The conversation that followed was very interesting. "He already spoiled the game." "He does that all the time." "Tell him to get lost." "He should tap someone on the shoulder and see if that person would move over so he could get in without interrupting the game." "He could wait 'til the next game." Children need opportunities such as these to think about ways to get along with other people. Learning how to help people whose behavior is not acceptable is also a valuable learning experience. Ollie Owl provides a very good model. He demonstrates giving positive feedback, listening to and extending other people's ideas, ways of handling rejection and how to sustain a relationship. It is amazing how engaged young children become in the Ollie Owl activities.

How to negotiate When it comes to teaching negotiating skills, one teacher prefers a direct approach. She has a negotiating chart on the wall, and the class refers to it often.

What We Do When We Disagree

1. Each person tells what happened.
2. Each person describes the problem.
3. Each person tries to think up at least three alternative plans to resolve the disagreement.
4. The people agree to try one plan.
5. The people agree to evaluate the plan. Did it resolve the problem? Are both people satisfied?

The authors interviewed several children regarding friendship-related issues. Children described situations similar to the following: "At lunch David put food on Angelica's head." "In the bus line Shaun tried to put mud on me. I screamed and I told him not to do it. He laughed and got more mud on his fingers. He's weird. I ran away." "Someone was teasing Allison. She got upset. I told her to tell him he's cute. Maybe he'd like her better." "I made a club with my friends. People have to ask me or one of my friends if they can come in. I was going to stop with five. Then so many people asked me. I said they could come in." "One time some kids were playing Red Rover. When I asked to play, they said no because there's already too many people. If it gets too long, it takes all day."

The teacher can do a great deal to encourage the development of friendship-making skills. However, it is important to remember that a great deal of growth that takes place in this area happens through children's spontaneous interactions. Children have the capacity to alter their behavior in response to the reactions they receive. Teachers, in their zest to help children learn, need to be sure that they do not interfere with natural growth processes.

To summarize operational characteristics related to curriculum, three main features of teacher behavior have been discussed. First, the teacher plans experiences that help children deal with their own feelings and the feelings of others by

- encouraging children to express their ideas about affective issues
- focusing children's attention on negative as well as positive feelings
- accepting children's comments
- encouraging children to listen to one another
- recording children's reactions
- developing plans that elicit children's expression of feelings
- observing and listening to children's spontaneous comments
- structuring neutral discussions; deflecting attention from particular children
- helping children generate many alternative suggestions
- helping children recognize the importance of feelings in making decisions
- engaging children in hypothetical decision making
- providing opportunities for children to label and express feelings

Second, the teacher helps children understand the similarities and differences among people by

- deliberately planning experiences that call attention to differences as well as to similarities among people
- setting up an environment in which children can discover and raise issues about similarities and differences
- integrating into all aspects of the curriculum a focus on ways that people are alike and different
- continually expanding their own understanding about different groups of people and about differences within the group and sharing this understanding with children in a variety of ways

Third, the teacher encourages the development of friendship-making skills by helping children learn to

- listen to and observe others
- be able to read the behavior of others
- know how to gain entrance into an ongoing activity
- be able to negotiate conflict
- initiate contact
- handle rejections
- sustain a relationship
- express empathy
- give feedback
- provide ideas or build on the ideas of others
- engage in discussion of specific behaviors and social skills

Classroom Management from a Cognitive Perspective

Many teachers consider themselves to be constructivist teachers. They engage children in problem solving in curriculum areas. They value the hands-on approach to learning. They allow children to make their own discoveries when building with blocks, going on a nature walk, or making a big book based on a story; but when it comes to classroom management, many of these same teachers assume an authoritarian, highly directed, teacher-in-control stance. This authoritarian management style is sometimes indicative of what the teacher values. Other times it reflects the teacher's previous school experiences, what school was like when the teacher was growing up, or the ideas the teacher took on while preparing his or her career.

Thoughtful reflection on one's management style is critical. The way teachers manage a classroom demonstrates to children what they value and their expectations regarding the development and exercise of self-control and the handling of impulsivity. The ways a teacher maintains authority and control reveal to children in a vivid manner the teacher's stance toward the importance of the individual's assuming responsibility for his or her own behavior.

A teacher who constantly uses mechanistic and behavioral strategies in handling interactions to some extent weakens the effect of constructivist approaches used in curriculum activities. How management is handled cannot be separated from the rest of the curriculum. A constructivist teacher aims toward the constructivist approach in management as well as in curriculum. To say this is not to negate what we have mentioned before, the idea that teachers will and should use a range of strategies in handling behavior. Although at a given moment teachers may use a succinct or didactic method to deal with a situation, the larger objective is to help children understand and have control over their own behavior. The way behavior is handled in the classroom influences the way children learn.

When one talks about classroom atmosphere and a curriculum that fosters understanding and respect, one is actually talking about classroom management. In a well-managed classroom, one hardly notices what the teacher is doing that makes things go so smoothly. Often, an observer thinks, "It's just a great group of kids." Frequently, though, a closer look reveals a teacher who has carefully incorporated thinking about feelings into the climate and the curriculum, and who deals with negative behavior in cognitive ways.

This chapter addresses aspects of management that focus on children's behaviors. It is further limited to discussion of those responses in which the teacher uses cognitive strategies as a way of helping children take control of their own behavior and appreciate their ability to influence the behavior of others. Although the teachers described in these situations use cognitive strategies whenever feasible, they also rely on other strategies, such as providing direct positive statements, using clear verbal and body language, and sometimes demonstrating a willingness to overlook behavior that should be discontinued. These teachers use such strategies whenever the situation does not warrant a cognitive approach, and they are able to make clear judgments in deciding at the moment which approach is most appropriate. Like all teachers, and others who work in fields involving human interaction, sometimes these teachers make decisions that are right on the mark; other times, as they reflect on their teaching behaviors in particular situations, they assess the possible effectiveness of alternative approaches.

In a classroom in which children and teachers respect and support each other, a classroom in which the importance of feelings, friendships, and similarities and differences is acknowledged and appreciated, management issues become a positive part of daily living. The inappropriate behaviors children sometimes show in school are kept to a minimum. When inappropriate behaviors do occur, if the time and the conditions are right, the teacher helps the children use their thinking capabilities in order to redirect their energies. How does the constructivist teacher help children manage their own behavior?

Management strategies considered here relate to three categories:

1. formulating rules
2. modifying inappropriate behavior
3. engaging children in the use of problem-solving techniques

Classroom Management: Operational Characteristics

The teacher behaviors described in this section support the premise that classroom management issues can be viewed as part of intellectual development. Engaging children in thinking about these issues can result in a smoothly functioning group and can provide children with skills that will be useful to them throughout their lives.

Involving Children in Establishing Rules

The teacher involves children in the formulation of rules.

◗ For example, the teacher might say, "It is important that we agree on some rules if we are going to live and work together. What rules do you think we should have in this classroom?" Children generate several rules: "Clean up your own mess." "Talk softly." Note how the teacher provides the rule structure. "How can we tell whether or not a rule is a really important rule, one that we should always remember?" The children agree that rules regarding safety meet this criterion. Also valued are rules related to showing thoughtfulness to others and those enabling people to work more productively.

Giving Examples

The teacher gives examples of situations in which rules are important. Children learn through senses. An example that stimulates a sensory response usually helps children to put themselves into the situation.

◗ "One time there was a group of children playing with table blocks. They wanted to see how high they could stack the blocks. They put on five, six, seven, eight blocks and all of a sudden the blocks tumbled down. One of the blocks fell off of the table and hit a child hard on his foot."

◗ "Sometimes when I am trying to have a writing conference with someone, I have a hard time hearing what that person is telling me about his or her writing." The teacher pauses. One child picks up the clue and responds, "That's because some children working at their desks are talking too loudly."

Focusing on Reasons

The teacher helps children focus on the reason for having rules and the areas in which rules are necessary. The key here is to encourage children to share what they know and feel about the rules, to have children talk together in groups so that they can influence and be influenced by what others are thinking.

◗ In one first-grade classroom, rules are posted strategically throughout the room. In the block area the rule chart says: "Block Rules: Blocks can't be stacked too high. Buildings can't be crashed." The children in the classroom when asked about the rules stated that the rules had been there since the first day of school. They referred to the rules as "our rules" and explained that on the first day of school the teacher clipped a large piece of paper to the display board. She invited each child who had a rule to raise his or her hand. These children felt a sense of ownership of these rules. It was with great animation that they described all the terrible things that could happen if one child did not follow them.

Reinforcing Rules

The teacher recognizes that rules need to be reinforced. The teacher needs to repeatedly call children's attention to the rules, to talk about why the rule is important, and to assess how carefully the children are following the rules. Much of this can be done in a group evaluation session. Often the teacher can genuinely commend a whole group of children for the care they are taking in following the rules. On some occasions, the teacher can talk individually with a child for whom there is a goal to stimulate increased understanding of the rule.

When a child breaks a rule, the teacher has three options. The first option is for the teacher to let the children take over the leadership role, much as teachers do in Japan. In Japan, the children themselves remind others about the rules. Lewis (1984) reported the following incident observed in a Japanese nursery school.

> Two boys had a fight which progressed from sand throwing to hair pulling and hitting. The teacher ignored the fight. . . . When asked by a child why the two boys were fighting, the teacher said, "You'd better ask the fighters." The teacher encouraged two bystanders to report what they had learned. After eliciting the reports, the teacher said, "You're the caretakers, so you should decide what to do" and turned her back. The caretakers tried to get each fighter to apologize but failed. The caretakers then became frustrated and abandoned their mediation efforts. The fighting resumed, and the teacher asked a girl watching the fight to help the two fighters make up. At the same time, the teacher said, "I am washing my hands of this" and walked away. The girl and a second nearby girl each began to question the fighters, saying, "Are you mad? If no, say you are sorry." Meanwhile, the teacher drew a circle around the fighters and children solving the fight and asked the rest of the children to start cleaning up to go home. The two girls succeeded in getting the fighters to apologize to each other. Each girl held hands with one fighter and brushed the sand off him, and then the two girls joined hands, forming a chain with the two fighters. From a distance, the teacher said, "Great! The problem has been solved, due to the two girls."

In American schools one can observe occurrences that are similar in some respects. As children attempt to internalize rules, they frequently appear to be imitating an adult. As one three-year-old child says to another, "Jamie, blocks cannot be stacked. It's a rule."

As a second option, the teacher can bring up the subject of rules in a total class discussion period. This approach is useful when the breaking of the rules has been a problem for many children in the group. Ben, a teacher, gathers the group together. He holds up his hand, spreading all five fingers. He reminds the children that "this is a special teacher signal for stop. It means, 'Please don't talk to me now because I'm talking to someone else.' Now if you see this signal, you can either ask a friend for help, ask another teacher, or wait until that teacher is done talking. So, when the teacher does this [again he models the hand signal], it's because he is talking to another child." Note in this example how effectively the teacher engages children in the concretization of rules.*

A third option is to talk privately with the child who is having difficulty adhering to a particular rule. Austin, a four-year-old, smashes a potato masher to the floor. Ben, the teacher, gives a reason for following the rule: "Austin, please pick that up so no one steps on it and gets hurt. Is there a reason why you threw it?" "Yes, I'm mad," Austin says, emphasizing the last word. "Okay, you need to come sit on my lap and talk about it. I have a spot on my lap for an angry dog." Austin climbs up. "Why are you angry?" "No paper," replies Austin. "What kind of paper are you looking for?" Austin says he is looking for paper to draw on, and Ben asks him where he thinks he could look to find it. Austin recalls where it is and skips off to get it. In this instance the teacher reinforces the rule regarding how anger can be expressed in this classroom: "Remember, the rule here is use your words."*

Helping Children Think About Appropriate Behavior

The teacher engages children in thinking about appropriate and inappropriate behavior.

Labeling and Describing Appropriate Behavior

The teacher labels and describes appropriate behavior. This is not as easy to do as it sounds. Very often, we do not think about what is appropriate behavior until inappropriate behavior occurs. When one child bites another child, labeling the inappropriate behavior is easy: "Don't bite." When a child goes to the reading mat and starts to wrestle with another child who is quietly reading, the almost automatic response is "Stop wrestling." Neither of these responses tells the child what to do. Young children are action-oriented and have difficulty processing the negative aspect of a statement.

Contrast these negative statements with verbalizations such as the following: "Use your words. Tell him you do not want him to take your car." "Get a book and sit on the mat." In classrooms in which the teacher engages children in thinking about appropriate behavior, the first step she takes is to verbalize the expectation for the children.

Helping Children Take Responsibility

The teacher helps children take responsibility for acting appropriately. When the teacher describes the behavior, she links it to the reason that the behavior is desirable: "People are staying in line. That helps us go through the corridors without disturbing any other classes." This is very different from saying, "I like the way Johnny is standing in line. I like the way Susan is standing in line." This latter response is more consistent with the romanticist or cultural transmission philosophy.

Some teachers do preface their descriptions of desirable behaviors with the "I like" phrase and, through using this phrase, are very effective in gaining young

* From a student paper by Margaret Consalvi, Tufts University, 1990.

children's cooperation (especially in the presence of the adult who uses the phrase). Children, though, need to gain experience in acting autonomously. They need to take control of their own behavior. They need to stand in line because they understand why this behavior is helpful to the group.

Talking About Why Behavior Is Appropriate

The teacher talks with children about why a particular behavior is appropriate. In these discussions, the key is to elicit from children as many of their ideas as possible: "It helps children in other classes concentrate on their work." "No one will get thrown down." "Nobody will get lost." It is also important to use as many different strategies as possible to help the children associate action with words. One time it may be making a book about "Why We Walk in Line." Another time it could be a class mural or a dramatization of walking in line.

Developing the Concept

The teacher helps children develop the concept of appropriate behavior. A concept is a group of related facts. Many specific bits of information go into the formation of a concept, but once a person has grouped related facts together, that concept becomes much more internalized and much more useful in guiding one's own behavior. A concept is not static. It can continually have facts or bits of information added to it or taken away from it. In order to understand the concept of appropriate behavior, one needs to distinguish appropriate from inappropriate behavior. The moral dilemma approach can be useful.

The teacher can create during meeting times a story in which the main character of the story is faced with a dilemma. The character needs to decide which course of action to take and why one course of action is better than another. The dilemma could be one based on an actual incident that occurred in the classroom or it could be one that the teacher (and later the children) create: "At today's meeting I'm going to tell you a story. It's a story that happens a great deal in first-grade classrooms."

"Michael had finished his work. He went to the reading shelf, found a book that interested him, and sat down and began to read. Shortly after that Colin, who hadn't quite finished his work, decided that he, too, wanted to read. So he got up out of his seat, went directly to the reading mat, and pounced on Michael. What should Michael do? Please help me finish this story." The children can explain their ideas in words or act them out. The important thing is that the children generate a variety of different endings and that they talk at length about the effects of each of the imagined endings. They also, of course, could reconstruct the story. The goal in using this approach is to encourage all ideas and to engage children in thinking about each other's ideas. The teacher should be prepared to accept all the suggestions without placing a value judgment on them. It is the peer interaction that encourages growth in judgment-making abilities.

Reinforcing Understanding

The teacher helps children at periodic intervals to reinforce their understanding of appropriate behavior. Many competing developmental and environmental factors influence children's understanding.

For example, a physiological need to change one's position or to come into physical contact with another person could easily become the dominant need at any particular time and thus overshadow the child's perception about the reading rug rule, where one sits quietly on the rug with a book.

The younger the child is developmentally, the more likely that egocentric drives will obstruct the demonstration of appropriate behavior. Three-year-olds are helped by having the rule reiterated in exactly the same language. Five-year-olds are able to discuss alternatives, but they have a rather fluid conception of rules: "We always go through the corridor in line, but I really needed a drink of water." Six through eight is a rule-bound age. The rule is the rule; children are happy to talk about what the rule means and how it can be enforced. Whatever the age, continuously reinforcing a child's own identification of appropriate behavior is necessary to strengthen the concept so it becomes part of the child's autonomous repertoire. This reinforcement needs to be responsive to the child's developmental level and should engage the child in thinking about the behavior.

"I find there's a lot of pressure to be good."

Drawing by Weber; copyright © 1989 New Yorker Magazine, Inc.

Reinforcement in a cognitive sense should be differentiated from reinforcement used in a behavioral sense. A teacher who adheres to a behaviorist philosophy may reward appropriate behavior either verbally or with more tangible evidence such as stars, stickers, positive reports to parents, and special awards. This type of behavioral reinforcement, when it is successful, leads to children's dependency on extrinsic reward. The behavior may be generalized to other situations in which there is an expectation of reward. However, this approach does not meet the goal of helping children become skilled in mediating their own behavior and taking responsibility for their own decisions.

Setting Limits

The teacher sets limits regarding appropriate and inappropriate behavior. Of utmost importance to children are the responses they receive from their peers. Often, children's responses to one another are of a negative or injurious nature. The teacher does not tolerate this kind of behavior. The teacher does not tolerate insults, scapegoating, or the diminishing of others. When this behavior occurs, the teacher provides a prosocial alternative.

◗ In the block area, first graders are in the process of building a block garage. One child passes by and shouts: "What a stupid building. No car could ever get up on that roof. That's not the way to make the garage good. You guys don't know how to build." The teacher responds: "If you have some ideas on how they could make the garage better, it is important that you share them with the garage builders; but it is not helpful when you just tell them it isn't any good."

◗ Romeo, a second grader, is teasing Juanita. "You can't play with us. You smell." In this case, Romeo is making an accurate observation. The teacher needs to help Romeo recognize that his remarks are hurting Juanita. At the same time the teacher needs to take into account that these remarks, although they are hurtful, may be the only way that Romeo knows how to communicate his perceptions. The teacher finds an appropriate time and talks privately to Juanita: "I'd like to talk to you about something that Romeo said to you today. He said that he didn't want to play with you because you smell." Often this is a complicated and complex problem. The important things here are honesty and openness. The teacher lets the child know that she understands how the child feels and that she is going to try to help correct the situation, possibly by talking to the parents or the school nurse (whichever is appropriate in the situation). Just to ignore the incident is not helpful to Juanita or to Romeo.

Considering Others' Opinions

In other situations, the taunting reflects children's preferences or the materialism in society. The teacher helps children understand the importance of listening to and considering other people's points of view. The teacher encourages active listening and respect for diversity of opinion.

◗ "Those sneakers are no good. The kind you have to have are Bo Jackson's. They're the neatest!" The teacher's response deals with the preference aspect. "Oh, it's interesting that you prefer Bo Jackson sneakers. During group time tomorrow, let's have a discussion about sneakers." The teacher invites first graders to put one of their sneakers into the center. The group examines and charts the similarities and differences. This process reinforces the notion that one's choice of brand of sneaker is a matter of individual preference. The teacher encourages children to share their opinions and in the final analysis acknowledges that it is important to investigate and decide for yourself whether you like a particular brand of sneakers. The teacher also helps children to recognize that it is important to listen to other people's opinions because it gives you more information to make your own judgment. It is not helpful if someone just tells you what he or she thinks is best. That person needs to give you a reason. In this way the idea of children as consumers becomes important, and children become energized about the process of making thoughtful choices.

The teacher strengthens children's understanding of social behavior by identifying certain situations that transpire and clarifying what is taking place. The teacher helps children to see the importance of cause and effect in people's behavior.

- "I know you want to use the scissors badly by the way that you're stamping your foot; but we're not using them until the afternoon."
- "Mari, you need to figure out how to keep your body still so people aren't irritated when you sit next to them."
- One kindergarten youngster had been trying many different ways to make friends—antagonizing, bribing, bartering—and was not meeting with success. The teacher felt it was time to help the child to understand that there was a logic to people's behavior. "Bobby, the reason that Katie doesn't want to have you as a partner is that you always take all the rods and she needs to wait a long time for a turn."

Engaging Children in Problem-Solving Techniques

The teacher engages children in the use of problem-solving techniques. Following is an example of a kindergarten teacher who was moving toward incorporating a more developmental approach into her program. The teacher had established a rule that only four people could work in the block corner at a time. She had established this rule based on past experience. More than four children in the block area detracted from constructive play and usually resulted in chaos.

In mid-October, the teacher noticed that usually more than four children were eager to work in the block area during a given time. Many children were disappointed, and they carried on all kinds of discussions about who worked in the block area yesterday and the day before yesterday and the day before that, and whose turn it was to work with the blocks on a given day. In fact, the identification of block area participants became a turn-taking discussion rather than resulting in children working in the block area because they had a particular project they wanted to carry out. The four-person rule also limited the opportunities children could have to leave their constructions standing so that they could continue to work on them the next day. She decided that this was a good time to engage children in problem solving.

At the morning meeting, she pointed out her observation. There always seemed to be some children who wanted to work in the block area and who were unable to do so because more than four children had requested this area. What did the children think about this situation? The children began to tell about their experiences with the blocks and about the constructions they had made and had to take down before they were finished with them. They also got into a heated discussion about whose turn it was and how many turns each child had had in the block area.

"Is there a way that we can keep a record of the number of children who want blocks as their first choice?" With this question, the teacher was framing the problem. One child suggested—with quite a bit of agreement for this idea from the group—that the teacher write down each day the names of all the children who wanted to work with the blocks. Up to this time, the teacher had the first four children put their name tags on a planning chart. Now they were going to have everyone's name who wanted to play with the blocks, and these names were going to be written on the planning calendar. This is what they found.

Planning on Monday

Painting	Housekeeping	Blocks	Making Books	Table Activities
Joe	Patty	Susan	Jody	Aaron
Marie	Brian	Peter	Lorraine	Judy
Carmen	Ariel	Ethan	Nathan	
Brad		Marty	Patty	
		Liz		
		David		

This same pattern occurred every day and the children began to comment on the fact that a lot of children chose blocks, more than four children every day. One child made the observation, "That looks like a graph." With that as stimulation, the class agreed to make a "blocks as first choice" graph for one week. The children engaged in a discussion of what the graph showed. The teacher presented the problem: "What could we do to make it possible for more people who want to work with blocks on a certain day to be able to do that?" The children generated many suggestions, and the teacher recorded these suggestions on a large piece of newsprint.

At the next class meeting, the teacher called the children's attention to the suggestions they had made for solving the problem of having too many children who wanted to work with blocks. The class decided that one of the best ways of solving the problem was to set up two block areas—and that's what they did. Children separated the hollow blocks from the unit blocks, put these in two separate but adjacent areas, and changed the four-person rule. Now eight people could choose blocks, and anybody who wanted to keep up a building to work on it the next day would be allowed to do that. This system worked well for a while, until one group of children decided that they needed both hollow and unit blocks for their train station; this became the basis for another problem-solving experience.

The basic steps in the problem-solving model were described in Chapter 8. They are as follows:

1. identification of the problem
2. brainstorming alternative solutions
3. selecting one alternative to try
4. trying the alternative
5. evaluating how well the alternative works

The model is very similar to the one described for negotiating disagreements between friends described in the theoretical chapter. The same procedures are involved in helping children solve problems related to the formulation and implementation of rules, in redirecting inappropriate behavior, and in solving problems that arise because of the physical setup of the room. The more often the steps of the model are articulated and the more often children are guided in following this procedure, the greater will become both their skill in using it as a tool for managing their own behavior; children will become more autonomous. The principle involved here is the same as the one involved in the Chinese saying: "If you give a man a fish, you give him food for a day. If you teach him how to fish, you give him food for a lifetime." If you give children a solution to a problem, you help them for the minute. If you teach them how to solve problems, you are helping them acquire a skill that will be useful throughout their lives.

◗ Let's consider the case of Michael and Colin, the two children who are wrestling on the reading rug. The teacher intervenes and gets the two boys separated. She sits down on the rug with them. "Michael, what's going on here? What is the problem?" "I was sitting on the rug, minding my own business when all of a sudden Colin jumped on me and started to wrestle." "Colin, what do you see as the problem?" "I was just walking by and Michael tripped me. I fell on top of him and he started to wrestle."

The teacher reframes the problem using as many of the children's words as possible. "The problem seems to be that you boys need to decide what to do to get yourself out of a wrestling match when it is time to be looking at books. Do either of you have any ideas about how you could do that?" Colin responds, "You could wrestle over to the bookshelf and take a book." Teacher: "That's one idea. What else could you do?" This process continues until the boys have generated several alternatives. The teacher repeats or records the alternatives and engages the children in selecting the one approach they agree to try the next time they get involved in wrestling at the wrong time.

The teacher needs to be alert to when the boys need to be reminded of this discussion and the alternative plan they had derived for redirecting their own behavior. Once the plan is implemented, time is necessary to talk about how well the plan worked. Is this the solution that the boys agree to continue to use because it is effective in bringing about the desired results? Or do the boys need to explore another alternative?

▶ Another example of the problem-solving approach in action took place in a second-grade class. The children were preparing a seashore mural. The group that was working on the shoreline wanted to put the mural up on the wall before it was finished. This, they thought, would help them decide how to take the next steps. In order to put up the mural, one child had to stand on a table. She got up on the science materials table, which had on it a collection of shells. There was only a small space for her foot. As she tried to get onto the edge of the table, the table tipped, the shells went to the floor, and the child managed to land on two feet without suffering any personal injury. The teacher who wanted to maximize the learning potential of this situation engaged the child in a discussion about what happened. The teacher assisted the child in framing the problem: "What would we have to do so that you could put up the mural and take it down without hurting yourself and disturbing our exhibit?" Thus, a situation that could have embarrassed the child ended up helping her feel empowered to make decisions that would avoid accidents.

This problem-solving process takes a considerable amount of teacher time. It requires time to engage children in thinking about, formulating, and evaluating their own solutions to problems. The children need to be able to work independently so that the teacher can deal cognitively with classroom management issues.

Teachers can explore a variety of creative ways for involving children in the formulation of rules, engaging them in looking at appropriate and inappropriate behavior, and suggesting ways to make inappropriate behavior more appropriate. Teachers can identify many different strategies to help children develop the cognitive skill necessary for resolving conflicts, making friends, and considering the needs of others in the group. Teachers can help children take responsibility for maintaining a classroom environment that is warm, supportive, and conducive to learning. The approach is powerful.

To summarize the operational characteristics related to classroom management, first, the teacher involves children in the formulation of rules by

- providing the rule structure
- giving examples of situations in which rules are important
- helping children focus on the reason for having rules
- recognizing that rules need to be reinforced
- taking action when a rule is violated

Second, the teacher engages children in thinking about appropriate and inappropriate behavior by

- labeling and describing appropriate behavior
- helping children take responsibility for acting appropriately
- talking with children about why a particular behavior is appropriate

- helping children develop the concept of appropriate behavior
- reinforcing children's understanding of appropriate behavior
- setting limits regarding appropriate and inappropriate behavior
- providing prosocial alternatives to inappropriate behavior
- helping children listen to and consider other people's point of view
- clarifying what is taking place in social situations

Third, the teacher engages children in the use of problem-solving techniques by

- helping children to identify the problem
- encouraging children to generate alternatives for solving the problem
- aiding children in the selection of one alternative to try
- implementing the alternative
- evaluating the solution

Establishing a Positive Classroom Atmosphere: A Summary

In classrooms that seem to be going well, children are usually respectful of each other and engaged in productive activities. The areas of the classroom seem well organized. Yet, it is not easy to identify what the teacher is doing that establishes and maintains this type of classroom environment. This chapter identifies the operational characteristics that are indicative of a positive classroom climate. The teaching behaviors are clustered in three categories:

1. modeling and encouraging mutually respectful behaviors
2. eliciting caring and respectful behaviors from children
3. helping children understand how prosocial behavior contributes to work and productivity

The examples provided illustrate the specific steps the teacher takes in order to achieve these broad objectives.

Contributing to classroom atmosphere is how the teacher integrates social-emotional issues into curriculum and classroom management. The chapter provides sample lessons for helping children deal with feelings, understand similarities and differences, and develop friendship-making skills. The sample lessons lend themselves to integration with the other aspects of curriculum.

The chapter also considers classroom management from a cognitive perspective and highlights involving children in the formulation of rules, engaging children in thinking about appropriate and inappropriate behavior, and using problem-solving techniques. The classroom climate reflects this approach to curriculum and classroom management.

In order to implement these characteristics, teachers need to become skilled observers. Through careful observation, teachers can discern issues of concern to children, how children are reasoning, and misconceptions they are acquiring. Classroom observation and assessment provide the focus of the final section of this text.

Part Four: Questions for Discussion

1. Explain the value of incorporating principles of social cognition into curriculum and classroom management.
2. Describe the changes that take place in the age range from three through eight, in terms of children's understanding of rules, their ideas about right and wrong, and their understanding of friendship.
3. Using the cognitive-developmental approach described in this chapter, explain how a teacher could help children deal with feelings of loneliness or fear.
4. Assume that you are visiting a classroom in which children are getting out of control. They are not productively engaged in activities. Contrast the responses of a teacher with a constructivist orientation and one who adheres to the philosophy of cultural transmission.

PART 5 OBSERVATION AND ASSESSMENT

To look is one thing.
To see what you look at is another.
To understand what you see is a third.
To learn from what you understand is still something else.
But to act upon what you learn is all that really matters.
(source unknown)

Since the developmental approach is dynamic in nature, the process of observing, recording, and analyzing the educational process must be a well-defined part of the adult's responsibilities. This part is devoted to helping teachers increase their skills in observing and making judgments about what takes place in classrooms—whether the classroom is their own, that of a colleague, or one taught by an unknown person in an entirely different school environment. This part of the book differs from the section on observation in the cognitive chapter, where the focus is on observing and recording the progress of individual children. The emphasis here is on strengthening understanding of the teaching process as a totality.

Chapter 10 explains the importance of observation, provides a brief overview of what is involved in becoming an astute observer of children and classroom dynamics, and identifies a number of methods for collecting and analyzing data.

Observation is viewed from a comprehensive vantage point, including observing all of the following:

- one's own classroom
- other teachers' classrooms
- children
- teachers working in a range of curriculum areas
- the physical environment
- certain dynamic issues—gender, aggression, friendships, and shyness

Chapter 11 is a collection of forms that may be used to strengthen understanding and to evaluate the various characteristics already presented. One major tool in the compendium is the form "Characteristics of a Developmentally Based Early Childhood Program." This form is presented in two versions: Form A-1, a comprehensive form useful in arriving at a clear definition of what is developmental education; and Form A-2, an abbreviated version that lends itself to classroom observation. These two forms enable an observer to review a given classroom in depth in order to determine to what extent it can legitimately be identified as developmental in nature. These forms can also be used as self-evaluation tools to help in determining the area of the program to which attention should be directed.

In addition, in Chapter 11 are Forms B, C, D, and E, each corresponding to one of the operational chapters within the text. Forms B and C are thus related to challenging children intellectually, including the critical qualities of the teacher and aspects of the curriculum. Form D pertains to stimulating creativity, and Form E to social-emotional issues in curriculum and classroom management. All the forms are a distillation of the material presented in this book. They provide a succint, efficient way to capture some basic concepts of the developmental model.

CHAPTER 10

THE OBSERVATIONAL PROCESS IN THE DEVELOPMENTAL CLASSROOM

- *Observing as a Tool for Improving Teacher Effectiveness*
- *Important Things to Consider About the Observational Process*
- *Systematic Techniques for Recording Classroom Behavior*
- *Optimizing Classroom Observing*
- *Summary*

This book is based on the premise that observation is critical in implementing and maintaining developmentally appropriate programs. The operational characteristics that appear throughout this book provide guidelines for what to observe. This chapter focuses on the observation process itself, describing what teachers can learn from observing their own and other teachers' classrooms, and identifying important considerations in the observation process. The chapter also highlights several systematic techniques for recording what goes on in classrooms and provides suggestions for optimizing classroom observing. Emphasized is the need to identify a focus and to determine a set of objectives. A variety of examples are provided to illustrate the many possible foci for observation. The chapter concludes with a summary of important things to remember about observation.

Recently, when a summer institute on developmental education was held at the Department of Child Study at Tufts University, a group of teachers, administrators, and other school personnel had the opportunity to observe three demonstration laboratory classrooms for young children on a regular basis. The physical situation enabled teachers to observe through a screened booth the length of a classroom, where they could both see and hear what was happening without being readily visible or obtrusive to the children and teachers. Particularly powerful was the opportunity for group observation of the same situation, followed by discussion afterward, when people's reactions could be shared and they could engage in enthusiastic debate. Occasionally the teachers working in the demonstration situation would join the discussion groups, providing important insights and general information about children and prior events that would inform the dialogue. The observing teachers were enormously enthusiastic about this experience and were impressed by how much they learned.

Many of the institute participants found the experience of observing and analyzing another classroom to be unique—not just observing demonstration classrooms, but observing any classroom, in their own school or elsewhere. The teachers said that even though many of them had taught for a long period of time, they had never had the opportunity to sit back, completely free of responsibilities, and objectively observe another teaching situation. Whatever exposure to another classroom had occurred was usually a somewhat haphazard event, standing in a doorway between two rooms, watching something spontaneously, or when groups of classes got together for a combined experience and one teacher could sit back and watch another. Most of them agreed that the notion of objective observation, the serious studying of classrooms, was not a regular part of their professional experience.

Observing as a Tool for Improving Teacher Effectiveness

As institute participants began to discuss this issue in greater depth, they identified a number of important issues that created obstacles to observation.

Impeding Factors

Not only was it not customary for teachers to observe each others' classrooms, or other schools, participants realized that only a few of them engaged in the process of observing their own classrooms, free of teaching responsibility, with or without another professional with whom they could share reactions. Certainly, teachers instinctively watched what was happening in their own rooms. But they watched randomly, usually pressured with other matters, and without a clear focus or in a way that allowed them to see things contextually and comprehensively.

The teachers also recognized how unusual it was for them to engage in dialogue and debate around classroom practices. One morning, the institute participants were given a head teacher's lesson plan in advance to read, observed her teaching the lesson, and then gathered to analyze how it had gone, with the teacher present. She elicited their feedback as fully as she could, encouraging them to speak freely and openly about what they had observed, and how the children had responded: "Did any of you happen to notice how Shabatu responded to the lesson? I'm really curious for that feedback." "Do you think the motivation was too long? How might I have done it differently?" As the observers began to discuss these and other questions, and as the teacher encouraged their open responsiveness, people became relaxed and were eager to participate. When the session was over and they were reflecting upon the morning, one administrator shared his feelings: "I couldn't get over how willing this young teacher was to engage in a conversation about her own teaching; it was so terrific to feel that she was open to people's insights without feeling threatened. She maintained such a warm, accepting disposition, and she seemed so genuinely interested in what people had to share. I couldn't believe the whole thing."

Others agreed, and as discussion continued the participants spoke about how in most schools there is an unspoken understanding that teachers don't talk about one another's teaching for fear of being seen as critical or judgmental. Many felt that it was inappropriate to talk about teaching in any substantive way, and that teachers are frequently socialized to work in isolation from one another, without significant communication. The teachers recognized that there is little in pre- and inservice teacher education that encourages the process of peer observation and discussion—or even real sharing of how particular lessons and teaching approaches turn out. Most agreed that the organization, scheduling, and the ethos of schools makes it extremely difficult for teachers to learn from one another.

The implications of this difficulty are profound. Unfortunately, the majority of teachers are cut off from one of the most powerful mechanisms for strengthening understanding about teaching—the way others function in the classroom and solve problems common to everyone. Most teachers work in relative isolation, engaged in the same task, yet separated from one another in terms of feedback and stimulation. Teachers have much to learn from and to give to one another. The reasons for teachers' isolation are embedded in a number of issues familiar to most of us: historical patterns, the economics of release time, scheduling constraints, and so on. But in large part, these problems remain unresolved, because historically teaching has been viewed as an individual pursuit. Systematic observation of another's classroom is frequently associated only with periodic administrative evaluation, not with constructive give-and-take of a collegial nature. Even in situations where administrators are supportive and enthusiastic about providing opportunities for interactions among staff, or where some teachers want to become involved, they are often met with resistance from others who do not see the relevance of encouraging observation and interaction among teachers.

What Teachers Learn

From observing and documenting what goes on in their own and other teachers' classrooms, teachers can learn a great deal. Here are some comments made by teachers who are not accustomed to thinking about observation as a learning instrument. When you consider how infrequently the process is used, particularly for in-service training, it's not difficult to understand their reactions.

"The principal wants me to sign up for observation of another teacher's classroom. I guess that must mean that she doesn't have a lot of faith in the way I do things." An administrator who encourages her staff of teachers to observe one another is not necessarily passing judgment on a given teacher's teaching skills. The principal probably recognizes that it is important for teachers to share, learn from one another, and engage in professional exchange. Knowledgeable people recognize that teaching, like all professions, demands ongoing analysis and stimulation. Teachers who are defensive about sharing with others limit their own opportunities for growth and development. In a climate of mutual support, teachers can learn to feel more comfortable about the experience, since everyone stands to gain.

"I barely have time to accomplish all the things I'm expected to do; do you really think I have the time to sit back, uninvolved, and just watch?" Teachers may feel that if they are not engaged in direct teaching, they are not making a contribution to the learning process. Children learn an enormous amount working on their own, not just from the teacher. When teachers step back, record what is happening, and then reflect on this information, they learn much that will influence how they spend their time and how they handle individual children. The teacher must be a diagnostician in order to be effective. Objective observation is a basic tool for improving teacher effectiveness. It allows one to become aware of such things as how a quiet, relatively passive child can be the provocateur in an aggressive exchange between two children; how the presence or absence of certain materials influences a given activity center; how a troubled child is occupied during a forty-five-minute group time; how one child becomes energized or disinterested in a given task; and how a teacher's persistent questioning becomes tedious over time. Preceding or pivotal events that impact on a given teaching situation become much clearer when one is able to remain a passive, critical observer. Consider the following:

◗ A teacher observed a small group of children doing worksheets and discovered that one child continuously broke her pencil tip and went to sharpen it, over and over again, never quite mastering the sharpening process. She eventually became frustrated and scribbled on her paper. Later, the teacher took the time to redirect the way the child was holding the pencil and built upon the experience by doing a brief lesson on pencil sharpening that was of great interest to many.

- A teacher observed her student teacher leading their usual forty-five-minute early morning group time, as she had modeled for her. As she watched closely and took notes on what was occurring, she realized how much time was being wasted on doing the calendar and early morning exercises. She discussed her observations with the student teacher later in a nonjudgmental way, asking her how she thought they could improve things. Together they came up with a method to make things more concise and interesting, shortening the group time to twenty minutes.

"I already know how a kindergarten is supposed to be run; why should I take time to go see another one? It's not as if I'm a beginner." No matter how much one knows about teaching, one can always strengthen one's understandings and competence. The skillful teacher is a reflective practitioner, who recognizes that improving one's skills is a never-ending process; a good teacher does not remain static. Observing another teacher's classroom provides the opportunity to examine such important issues as the physical environment and how it functions; how the other teacher motivates and engages interest; what children talk about and consider important; the nature of the reading or social studies program; transitions and how they are handled. There are endless things to address. Consider the following:

- A third-grade teacher visited a kindergarten classroom and was impressed with how the teacher asked children to give feedback to one another when they presented during show-and-tell. The observer found the approach fascinating and thought of how her own class could benefit from this process. She introduced the technique when the children had "news time." She extended the activity by having her children write a personal reaction paper to share with the presenting person. The news person got to read and respond briefly to classmates' written reactions.
- A kindergarten teacher felt comfortable with the way she was providing children with art materials in a completely open-ended manner. While visiting another kindergarten teacher she watched a brief art motivation on "dressing up in party clothes." She was astonished at the children's involvement and interest spans, and the complexity of their final products. Afterwards, she began to provide occasional motivations for her own children and was impressed by how much richer their productivity was. She got in touch with the teacher she had observed, and together they discussed what they both felt was most effective in motivating this age group.

"I like observing classrooms, but the ones we get to see are always so ideal and unrealistic; the teachers have so many more materials to work with than I do. And sometimes there are two or three assistants in the classroom. It doesn't have much to do with what I have to deal with." It is sometimes frustrating to visit a classroom in which materials and teaching assistance are in such full supply. But regardless of the match between one's own classroom and the one being observed, the astute teacher can find valuable things to stretch her thinking. Of particular importance is finding a focus and being analytical about what is transpiring. It is important to raise questions for oneself, to help to make the observational situation most meaningful. Consider the following:

◗ A teacher was interested in improving her language when speaking to children; she had listened to herself on tape and realized that she asked long strings of questions without giving children an opportunity to respond. She selected a teacher for observation whom she had been told was strong in this respect. She recorded as much of the teacher's speech as she could during group time and activity time. She paid particular attention to questioning skills, vocabulary, and to the way the teacher listened carefully to children when they were speaking. She analyzed this data carefully and began the process of change.

◗ While visiting a first and second grade, where there were a number of student teachers and an aide, a visiting teacher was struck by the power of an early morning "read to each other" time. Teachers, paired with small groups of children, sat on the floor and read stories to one another. The involvement and sense of intimacy present was powerful. When she returned to her own classroom, the teacher decided to replicate the situation, using whatever resources she could muster. She created small "read to each other" groups without adults initially, eventually engaging a small group of parents who dropped their children off in the morning to remain for this experience. The idea caught on, and many parents were eager to participate throughout the year.

◗ A teacher of four-year-olds visited a university laboratory school where materials were plentiful. She focused her observation on the way art and construction materials were stored, and on how the children had been taught to get and return materials independently of adults. She made careful drawings of the storage and room arrangement in the area called "drawing and construction." She created a similar design in her own classroom by linking cardboard boxes together with sturdy tape and painting the boxes bright colors. Children and parents were encouraged to bring in salvage and other materials to keep them full. The group was stimulated by having ready access to styrofoam scraps, old zippers, buttons, sewing scraps, twigs, kitchen salvage, and so on, and creativity blossomed. As children maintained the bins, they learned how to organize and classify and to decide which scraps were worth saving and which were not.

◗ In another laboratory school situation, an observing teacher watched two tables set up with "beautiful junk" for children to make sculpture. The setup was identical at each table, but at one, a student teacher remained present all of the time, interacting with the children continuously. More children went to the table where the adult was present, but the observer recognized that although fewer children went to the other table, those who did produced more elaborate, complex work, and seemed more deeply involved in the task. The observing teacher decided to study this phenomenon further back in her own classroom.

"I'm expected to teach basic skills in my second grade; what can I learn from watching a four-year-old group messing about with sand tables and free play?"

◗ While observing four-year-olds involved in sand and water play at a large table, a second-grade teacher was struck by how involved the children became in containing water and making small puddles of various sizes. She realized that this media could be valuable for furthering a science project that her own children were involved in related to ponds, rivers, and lakes. She replicated the sand and water table with a child's plastic pool. Her second graders did extensive experiments related to their science project. The project stimulated children to define, classify, measure, and record the various concepts being explored.

◗ A second-grade teacher joined a guided observation of four-year-olds in the dramatic play area, where a play pizza shop was set up. The teacher was asked to record the children's verbal interactions, as well as to classify their behaviors along particular dimensions—namely, understanding roles and occupations, dealing with the exchange of money, and leadership and following behaviors. Later, when the teachers analyzed what they had observed, she was stunned to realize the complexity of what had occurred. The second-grade teacher gained new understanding of the power of four-year-old play, as well as how to structure an observation to make it more meaningful.

"So what's the point in sitting back and watching Paolo and George fighting yet one more time? I know what their problems are, and all the watching in the world isn't going to change things." Busy teachers are not always in a position to know what is really occurring between children who are having difficulty with each other. Even brief periods of sustained observation can provide important insights into the dynamics of behavior. Awareness of preceding and subsequent events can make a big difference in interpreting behavior.

◗ The teacher sits back as an objective observer during small group activity time to watch carefully children's interactions during a cooperative graph making exercise. Every time George, who is usually seen as highly aggressive, attempts to address the task, a girl says to Paolo, "He's going to wreck it; he can't measure and he doesn't know how to count." She continues to tell various members of the group that George is stupid and is hindering their achievement. Eventually, when George gets frustrated and begins to yell in self-defense, Paolo punches him. The teacher is fascinated to see how complex the situation really is, and how George's outbursts are due to incessant teasing and challenge to his self-esteem, not necessarily initiated by Paolo. Repeated observations reveal discernible patterns that the teacher is able to discuss with the special needs coordinator.

In summary, observation and data collection are valuable for the following reasons:

1. Children's behavior becomes easier to understand when it is observed and recorded objectively in context. When the teacher is actively involved in teaching and must respond to situations extemporaneously, it is sometimes difficult to recognize what is really occurring. By understanding the causes of behavior, it is easier for the adult to modify the circumstances that have contributed to a given problem.

2. Careful scrutiny of children across age levels—younger and older than the age one teaches—helps teachers to understand the developmental continuum. The range of behaviors and performances of individual children at a given age level thus becomes more understandable.

3. Observation is an important aspect of recordkeeping. Periodic stepping back and gathering data about children's achievement and working styles is central to the evaluation process. There are many ways to organize this data (see the section on observing children in Chapter 5).

4. Observation provokes teachers to consider new ways to teach and organize their classrooms. By observing classrooms that are both similar to, and different from, their own, teachers can extend their frames of reference and benefit from what other professionals have to share.

5. Analytical observation and writing contributes to the teacher's comprehensive understanding of the dynamics of teaching and provides a format for raising questions and hypotheses about issues that go beyond one's own classroom. It provides intellectual stimulation that makes teaching exciting and can stimulate writing and research.

6. Observation with a group of teachers and collecting data, followed by the opportunity to engage in dialogue about the experience, sharpens understanding of what is really occurring, and helps one to become more objective and skillful in drawing inferences about child and adult behavior. Although being observed may seem threatening initially, when the process is initiated on a regular basis in a supportive and collegial manner, the rewards are great.

Important Things to Consider About the Observational Process

Obvious though it may seem to state, it is important to observe another person's classroom with a seriousness of purpose and a high degree of professional behavior. Being observed puts a strain on teachers and classrooms, and the caring observer must be vigilant about making things go as smoothly as possible. Some classrooms have frequent observers, and the physical environment and behavior of both children and adults communicates this familiarity. Chairs may be placed around the room, and children and teachers ignore your presence, going about their business with little attention to the stray people who move in and out of the environment. This kind of a situation makes it easier for the observing adult to sit back in an impersonal manner, remaining silent and unobtrusive, focusing and gathering data without creating any undue pressure.

Maintaining a Professional Stance

In situations where teachers are unaccustomed to observers, however, your visit can be a more difficult undertaking and sensitive behavior can help to put the classroom at ease. Initially, it is usually appropriate to establish warm, appreciative contact and then to remain as inconspicuous as possible, refraining from interacting with children and adults. This is sometimes difficult, especially for people accustomed to being actively involved in classrooms, but it is important to learn to do. Subtle messages are communicated when the observer focuses in the beginning on the physical environment, small groups of children, and texts and other learning materials around the room, rather than on the teacher herself. This approach helps to put people at ease and sends the message that you are there to see the teaching process as a totality, not simply to watch how one person performs.

Most teachers appreciate observers who remain relatively passive and do not engage them in questions and conversation while they are teaching; to do so is not a part of the observational process. Particularly important is avoiding judgmental comments or behaviors; you are there to observe and record, not to question, evaluate, or inform. Sometimes, beginning students expect teachers who are being observed to engage in dialogue about what they are doing and why they have approached a situation in a particular way. This sort of dialogue is inappropriate, since any discussion that takes place should occur only in appropriate contexts, where it has been decided upon beforehand and is structured accordingly. Teachers who open their classrooms up to other professionals should not be placed in a position of having to translate and explain to others while they are teaching—or, for that matter, even later. The observer is a guest in the classroom and should remain as sensitive as possible to the primary responsibility of the teaching staff: dealing with the children.

It is also of tremendous importance that one confines all subsequent discussion and reactions of a given observation to appropriate professional contexts. Nothing is more destructive to the observational situation than gossip concerning what outsiders feel about what they have observed in a particular classroom. Notes, conversation in the teachers' room or even in a local coffee shop, and the like should be monitored strictly in order to ensure confidentiality. Remember that if a particular individual is not accustomed to being observed or is insecure about the process, everything that you say and do will have great impact on his or her continued receptivity to being observed. Professional behavior of the highest order is of great importance, not only for adults, but for children and families as well.

Maintaining Objectivity

In daily life, circumstances demand that we enter a given situation, observe quickly what is happening and make quick inferences in order to guide our behavior. In short, we observe and make judgments simultaneously. When we are observing and recording classroom behavior, however, we have a different set of objectives. In this case, the task is to move beyond our customary, quickly acquired responses in order to see with greater clarity and objectivity. To accomplish this, it is necessary to approach the observational process differently from what is customary in everyday life. The following competencies are important:

1. to be able to observe and record a given frame of classroom life in its objective state, capturing as much about it as possible
2. to be able to withhold one's judgments about what is occurring during the recording process
3. to raise questions and make inferences based on the data collected, rather than on one's biases and predispositions

Learning to observe effectively involves the process of separating what is being observed from what you think about what is happening, distinguishing between objective reality on the one hand and one's hunches and predispositions on the other. Impressions and reactions are of great importance, but only when they emerge from objective data, not predetermined biases, and when you have a working knowledge of yourself and the nature of the conclusions you are apt to form.

Effect of Personal Biases and Past Experiences

How do our own biases and past experiences affect the way we observe and form conclusions? We see selectively, based on what is personally relevant.

One day I was walking in a busy shopping area with a young friend, Anne, who was pregnant. It was a beautiful spring day, and activity was everywhere. Anne turned to me and said, "Isn't it incredible how many people are pregnant this year; everywhere I look, I see pregnant women!!" Long past childbearing age, I was taken aback. "Where?" I inquired. "Over there, across the street, there's a pregnant woman going into an ice cream shop, and down that alley near the bookstore, there's another one. And I noticed a third when we were crossing the street." I suspect no more pregnant women were around right then and there than usual, but Anne was cued to see them; I was not.

A year later the point was made once again. Her daughter, now almost a year old, was in a stroller (what was then called an "umbrella stroller"). We were again at a busy place, this time an outdoor art exhibition at a local museum. People of all sizes and shapes were everywhere. Anne remarked, "I can't get over how many umbrella strollers there are this year. Everyone has one." I laughed, since I had barely noticed the one in front of us. I was focusing on other things.

This tendency to see what is relevant to our own lives, and to ignore many things that are not, is important to be aware of. Certain issues and events become salient because of what is occurring, or because of what has already occurred, in our own personal lives. Two individuals exposed to a common set of events in which there is no single outstanding occurrence, will unconsciously sort what is there and identify the elements that have personal relevance. Obviously, it is necessary to select from the beehive of activity that surrounds us those things that are germane to our own concerns; this filtering process is important. But it can also cause us to see too myopically and obscure our awareness of other pertinent events that are occurring. A skillful observer strives to be aware of how personal selectivity influences not only the inferences that we draw, but even what we choose to focus on, as well.

When observing classrooms without a particular assigned focus, not only are observers predisposed to favor watching some events over other events, but they are more apt to choose particular kinds of children to focus on than others. We may be attracted to particular children because of certain physical characteristics (race, body type, facial qualities, or dress), as well as because of their behavior. Some of us are drawn to outgoing, interpersonally active children. For others, it is quite the reverse: the quiet, introverted child is immediately compelling. Some of us are more apt to focus on the child who seems aggressive, gifted, or involved in an area of the curriculum that we find interesting. In the same way as we may gravitate toward certain children more readily, we screen out other children and have difficulty seeing them at all. Once aware of this, many observers are fascinated to discover how they may tend to ignore certain kinds of children. It is important for each individual to be self-analytical and aware of their own tendencies to exercise bias in the way they observe.

Countering the Tendency to See Selectively

The following exercises can help counter the tendency to see selectively.

Observe a classroom you have never watched before.

- Make a list of all the events that immediately command your attention. Afterward, make a list of those events that you recognize are also occurring, but had not noticed as quickly. Compare the two.
- Make a list of parts of the classroom environment that emerge as being particularly interesting. Make another list of parts of the classroom that recede and do not command your attention. Pay particular attention to whether you are predisposed to watch certain activity areas frequently, or infrequently.
- Pretend that you have been asked to observe the classroom as a music consultant or a science consultant. Pick an area that you usually do not find yourself drawn to. Identify relevant things that you see present, looking through this particular lens. Consider both what is there and what is not.

Observe a group of children with whom you are unfamiliar.

- Identify two or three children who immediately attract your attention. Make notes about their physical descriptions, their behavior, their interactions with others, and so on. Analyze what it is about these children that has drawn your attention to them. Is it their body type? The way they are dressed? Their hair? Is there something about their behavior that has made them stand out? Are they talkative? Quiet? Active? Passive? Try to determine exactly what physical and behavioral qualities have attracted you to these children. Consider whether the children are like or unlike the way you remember yourself as having been as a child. Sometimes we choose children who seem similar to the way in which we remember ourselves; sometimes the opposite is true.
- Next, identify children in the group whom you have not felt particularly drawn to watching. Analyze these children, as well, along the same dimensions to determine what makes them less interesting. This information is important to consider. When you are observing groups of children afterwards, try to remain aware of your predisposition to watch some children attentively and to be less aware or interested in others. Keep notes.
- Make a list of the kinds clothing that children wear that you find appealing. Make a list of clothing that is not appealing to you. The way children are dressed influences us strongly, even though parental preference is apt to have influenced how children appear.
- Give consideration to how knowing a child's parents, and your feelings about them, influence how you view the children. We are prone to transferring feelings from parents to children.

Documenting Effectively in Writing

To those unfamiliar with documenting classroom events in written form, it may seem a laborious undertaking, but the rewards are great, and it is well worth the effort. Not only does writing things down dramatically influence the capacity to see what is occurring objectively and help us to understand the reasons behind certain events, but it provides important data that is useful for discussion purposes and for sharing with others. For example, an observer who carefully documents the dynamics of what occurs at a small group activity time where the teacher has provided initial motivation and then moved on, only to have things deteriorate quickly, may shed light how certain key factors have contributed to children's lack of involvement—namely, not enough working scissors, one child's aggressive behavior, lack of understanding of expectations, noise intrusion from nearby, and so on. Or a teacher who documents specific behaviors of a given child can use this material in writing reports for sharing with a special needs coordinator or a psychiatrist, or even for conferencing with parents. When evaluation is accompanied by data, it is far more meaningful to the person receiving the information.

Skillful observers work conscientiously to learn to record behavior and activity as it occurs in an incisive and accurate manner and to separate their spontaneous reactions from the recording process. **Objective recording** involves documenting what you are watching using one of a number of written recording techniques. Which technique you use depends on your particular objectives. Where it seems important to insert a simple hunch or hypothesis while recording objectively, it should be done parenthetically and separated from the recording process. Separating objective data from inferences about behavior is crucial: both are important, but they should be presented as two independent elements.

Systematic Techniques for Recording Classroom Behavior

The following is a distillation of information related to naturalistic observation gathered from many different sources, including books, pamphlets, and articles. It relies most heavily, however, on material contained in *Observational Strategies for Child Study* (Irwin & Bushnell, 1980), which is a most comprehensive overview of the entire subject of observation and recording.

Anecdotes or Snapshots

The first technique, the **anecdote** or snapshot, is a simple recording of an event in a collapsed form. It is usually executed after the fact, when some incident seems worth capturing. The technique is similar to what one does when explaining a brief event to someone after it has occurred (except that you remove any interpretive language you might use when talking informally). Anecdotes are usually written in the past tense. Irwin and Bushnell (1980) provided a delightful example:

> The four-year-old group had spent most of the afternoon outdoors and David had been in high gear the entire time. He was exhausted when his mother came to get him. Noticing this, she said, "You need something to help pick you up

The observer can learn to distinguish between developmental and nondevelopmental practices through careful scrutiny of classroom dynamics. © Bob Kalman/The Image Works

> when you get home. What would you like?" David's response was, "What I really need is a good stiff chocolate brownie." (p. 98)

Notice that in this form, specific, detailed information is not included, only the key information that renders the incident meaningful. The anecdote is in sharp contrast to the running record, which follows.

Running Records, Descriptive Narratives, and Specimen Descriptions

The second technique involves recording behavior exactly as it occurs, using incisive descriptive language in order to communicate clearly both the gross and finite actions involved. The task is one of approximating a video recorder—delivering to the reader a clear, nonsubjective recording. Although it is crucial to use descriptive, qualitative words in order to communicate the specific nature of behavior, judgmental, interpretive material should be eliminated. Attention should be given to body movements, facial expressions, voice, and so on, since these are important purveyors of what is happening. Either the present or past tense may be used, but once the decision has been made, it is important to remain consistent. Two types of recording may be used: (1) running (a linear depiction, or **running record,** of all activity, blow by blow) and (2) cumulative (more abbreviated than the running record, to accommodate situations where action is repetitive, rapid, or too complex to capture in its totality).

The language used in running records (and in anecdotal records, too) is important. Cohen and Stern (1978; rev. with Balaban, 1985) described the power of descriptive language, emphasizing the use of precise verbs that accurately describe the action.

> Some of us could think of a dozen synonyms for the word "walk" in a matter of seconds . . . amble, stroll, saunter, clomp, stomp, march, strut, ramble, etc. Others of us get paralyzed at the challenge. Yet the distinction between one child's actions or gross movements, and another's may depend on the correct synonym for the word "walk." (p. 20)

For the verb *say* these authors offer: "whisper, bellow, shout, scream, roar, lisp, whine, demand, tell, murmur" (p. 20). In discussing the use of adverbs and adverbial phrases, they emphasize the need to be objective, to refrain from passing judgment, and yet to describe the action fully: for example, "He tugged determinedly," or "He walked swinging his arms."

Compare the following two examples. The first one is too abbreviated. The second one seeks to capture the specific quality of the actions involved.

1. Tommy had taken a cookie. Mrs. A. said, "Put the cookie back." Tommy replied, "I want to eat it." Mrs. A. said, "Not now, you aren't," and she ushered him out of the room. She then sat down on her knees on the rug and began singing a song to a small group of children.

2. Tommy had taken a cookie from the juice table, glancing around the room from person to person with a tense look on his face. Mrs. A. noticed him from across the room, came over quickly and said with some agitation, "Put the cookie back!"

Tommy replied petulantly in a soft voice, dropping his head and looking up at her, "I want to eat it . . . eat it." Mrs. A. said, "Not now you aren't!" and she ushered him out of the room rapidly, with a firm grasp of the elbow. She reentered quickly and rejoined a small group of children on the rug, and in a buoyant fashion dropped to her knees and began singing a song exuberantly.

In the second example, we have a much clearer sense of not only what took place, but the quality of actions involved.

The following are examples of running records or specimens that include **subjective recordings** that intrude on the objectivity (these statements are in italic type).

1. Susan continues to push Margaret on the shoulder *(thinking about how much she dislikes her),* not vigorously, but with short, successive thrusts, sending her slightly off balance, and continues to chant in a sing-song voice, over and over again, "You're not to play with us; you're not going to play with us." *Susan is obviously spoiled and gives the impression of being a perpetual troublemaker.*
2. Paul keeps turning to look at the other children (apparently to see if anyone is watching). He *decides to take out his anger at the teacher* by squeezing the guinea pig with all his might. The teacher does not see him, since he is squatting behind a carton, and he continues *in this aggressive, hostile way, feeling great delight that nobody sees what he is doing.*

The subjective statements discuss motives and judgments; hence, they are inappropriate. In the first sentence of the second example, note that brief, qualified interjections can be included if they are contained within parentheses.

Verbal Vignettes

The third technique is gathering many small examples of speech or around a specific area of focus. These **verbal vignettes** may be compiled from what one individual person says or does or may be an accumulation of statements made by different individuals. These can be numbered for later reference.

For example, record all examples of a specific teacher's giving positive reinforcement to children verbally. Positive reinforcement is defined as any positive statement about a child, or his or her work, that suggests the teacher is pleased, not necessarily only praising comments such as the following:

- "That's good!"
- "Oh, you worked long and hard. You really stayed with it."
- "That's absolutely wonderful."
- "At the rate you're going with that, there's no end to what you can accomplish."
- "Nifty!"
- "Terrific!"
- "You've got the right approach."

These comments can be analyzed from many vantage points—namely, contrasting teachers, frequency of kinds of statements, gender, kind of activity involved, specific children, and so on.

Time Sampling

The fourth technique is the process of recording specific behaviors or events as they occur in particular time frames. The method of **time sampling** lends itself to coding, charting, and tabulating. For example, during a two-hour activity period, record how many children are present at each of the five major activity centers in the classroom at fifteen-minute intervals. Identify the sex of each child as well.

Event Sampling

The fifth technique is the process of compiling events that occur around a given focus, such as aggression, cooperative behavior, leaving an activity unfinished, and moving materials from one area of the room to another. **Event sampling** may or may not include time frames. For example, a teacher is interested in documenting events in which children are willing to help one another. Using the anecdotal approach, the teacher collects all incidents she can in which one child, not prodded by an adult, provides assistance to other children.

◗ Wayne is attempting to lace up his new sneakers and is obviously having difficulty. He keeps unlacing the laces over and over again. As he stamps his foot solidly on the floor and shouts, "I quit!" Leo says supportively, "Let me give you a hand, brother."

◗ Hilary and Manzoor are writing a poem together and are having a difference of opinion about how to end a rhyming sequence. Ramsey steps in uninvited and suggests, "Why don't you let me listen to the both of them, and help you decide which one works the best?"

After having collected a large number of these anecdotes the teacher realizes that they fall into a number of basic categories, such as helping with a personal need, helping solve an academic problem, helping with something requiring strength, or helping with an interpersonal problem. Over a number of weeks, the teacher tries to identify how this information relates to individual children.

Optimizing Classroom Observing

A classroom is a complex environment, replete with animate and inanimate things to examine. When an observer just sits down to watch the unfolding of random events without a clear set of objectives or observational foci, it is not always easy to make the most of the situation. There is value in occasionally observing without a given focus, especially when one is new to a particular situation. Unfocused observing also allows one to see what emerges—what seems particularly germane about a given classroom—and it provides the opportunity to establish relevant observational objectives. The most meaningful observation, however, is apt to occur when it is done with a predetermined set of objectives, such as wanting to learn more about how reading is taught, how certain problems in behavior are being addressed, or how a teacher is handling a special needs child who has needs similar to a child in the observer's own classroom.

When one enters the observational situation with a set of priorities and a clear focus, it is easier to observe in a more purposeful way and to see with greater clarity. Without a clear focus, one is vulnerable to responding intuitively to the morass of activity, rendering it vague and ambiguous. One tends to watch in a highly subjective way, responding to what is commanding attention visually, what is noisiest, what is nearest where one is seated in the room. Focused observation provides one with a mission and a sense of purpose; hence, it has the greatest power.

Establishing a Focus

A well-known aphorism states that if you aim at nothing in particular, you're bound to succeed. This aphorism suggests the importance of having a clear focus, which is particularly important in classroom observing. The following categories, individual focus and focus on a dynamic or topical issue, are helpful for determining the areas to target for examination and for identifying observational questions.

Individual Focus

Sometimes the focus is on a particular child or adult whom the observer wants to study. A particular set of issues may have provoked an interest in observation in order to problem-solve, such as the following examples.

- "Elizabeth seems to wander a lot. It's hard for her to settle down. I'd like to understand exactly how she spends her time during activity time and what her interactions with other children are really like."
- "Zachary has trouble making transitions. Once he's into something, it's next to impossible to get him to stop. He really becomes upset when a given time period is over."
- "Mrs. Lennon has really strong group control techniques. I always sense the children's involvement when she's in charge, but I'd like to find out exactly what it is that makes her compelling to the group."
- "The student teacher wants feedback on her speech with the children. We've been discussing her tendency to use a lot of slang and rhetorical questions. We thought there would be value in documenting exactly what she says to children."

A Dynamic or Topical Issue

A dynamic or topical issue may fall dominantly into one or more of three subcategories:

1. *Behavioral:* This category covers issues that involve behavior, but go beyond a single individual. For example, a teacher might want to understand more about children who are shy, aggressive, or slow-to-warm-up; or the teacher may

want to gain information about children who are leaders or followers, or to examine the nature of culture and its impact on friendships.

2. *Environmental:* This category covers certain features in the physical environment. For example, a teacher might want to gather data about how the reading area is set up; how dramatic play, blocks, or mathematics has been organized; or how storage and communication systems are presented in a particular classroom.

3. *Learning:* This category covers instructional and learning situations. It includes such things as presentation of a learning experience at an activity area; reading and mathematics instruction; music, art, social studies, curriculum; and the impact of a teacher's presence at a given activity. The category implies that a given lesson or learning experience is taking place that goes beyond setting up the physical environment alone.

After establishing a focus the next step is to design observational questions or a set of foci around which to gather data. This is an important process, since it provides a critical framework by which to focus one's thinking and observation. Furthermore, establishing a set of clear observational foci leads the observer quite naturally into determining exactly which form of data gathering is most logical and efficient for the objectives at hand.

The following guidelines may be kept in mind in framing observational questions and foci:

- Avoid yes or no questions; they are frequently too vague and general to be helpful and do not yield as much specificity as other questions do.
- Make certain that the questions are observable. You cannot observe an abstraction; you must observe specific behaviors or events that are concrete. For example, you cannot set about observing friendship; you must translate this concept into observable elements.
- Words such as *list, describe, cite examples of, how, observe how,* and *what appears to be* are helpful for creating observational questions; you may generate others.
- In instances in which objectivity is of particular importance, avoid the use of prejudicial language that suggests what you expect to find. Sometimes, there is value in designing questions that elicit both a positive and a negative response, making them both viable alternatives.
- Keep the language clear and precise. Would someone else be able to read your observational foci and understand them without an explanation? They must be broad enough to allow some flexibility, but specific enough to provide a clear focus.
- When looking at a single area in some depth, create a sequence of related questions, rather than one large unwieldy one.

Contrasting Examples

An observer is interested in determining whether or not a given teacher is sensitive to children emotionally. She wants to determine whether the classroom climate is one that recognizes and acknowledges children's feelings and emotional concerns.

Hence, she is interested in a behavioral issue with an individual focus—in this case, as it pertains to an adult. Compare the following observational questions.

1. "Is the teacher responsive to the children's needs emotionally?" "Does the teacher provide for children's emotional needs? Does the teacher care about the children's feelings?" These questions are not in observable form;they are too broad and elicit a yes or no answer. To determine whether the teacher is responding to children emotionally, we must determine what behaviors or attributes would reveal the presence or absence of emotional support.

2. The following questions are observable, more manageable, and do not elicit a yes or no answer: "Cite examples in which the teacher reveals sensitivity to children's feelings through the use of words." "Cite examples in which the teacher demonstrates sensitivity to children through her physical being, such as changes in location, posture, body language (stooping to be close and at eye level), or moving her position to interact in a more intimate manner." "Cite examples in which a teacher does not respond to a child's demonstrated emotional need. Give consideration to any related factors that might be occurring." This list could be elaborated to include a full profile of the teacher's relevant behaviors. It could be designed to examine how the teacher's general behaviors are influenced by individual children, as well as by other adults working in the classroom.

Let's assume that a group of observers interested in the subject of gender want to observe a particular classroom to determine how issues of bias and sex role behavior are being addressed. This topical issue may involve a wide number of variables, including the physical environment and teacher-teacher and teacher-child interactions. Together, the group members generate a set of questions that interest them; here are some examples extracted from that list that are in observable form, related to observing bias and sex role behavior:

- *Physical environment:* "Identify areas within the classroom that invite dramatic play. Describe the available equipment and props. Analyze those items in terms of gender relatedness, that is whether or not they include things that are associated traditionally with males, females, or both." "Examine the books in the reading area. Make a list of all of those that extend children's thinking about nontraditional occupations for each of the sexes."
- *Teacher behavior:* "Observe sharing time during group time. Record all of the teacher's responses to both boys' and girls' contributions. Analyze these along the following dimensions: frequency that boys and girls are called upon; contributions that are encouraged and elaborated upon; the level of enthusiasm that the teacher displays." "Record all of the teacher's praise and positive comments during art time. Analyze the comments that are made to boys and girls for similarities and differences."

This list could be extended to include a wide number of features, or the observational focus could be collapsed to address just one or two facets of the subject. All this depends, of course, on the objectives and concerns of the observers. What remains essential, however, is to design the questions with sufficient clarity and objectivity to elicit meaningful information.

Analyzing Data with Fairness and Objectivity

The process of analyzing data and attempting to make sense out of it is, in the final analysis, the most rewarding and valuable part of the observational undertaking. It is both challenging and gratifying to find connections among stray pieces of information and to draw inferences from them. But one must proceed with humility, recognizing that as clear and logical as certain conclusions may seem, we are not always in a position to form accurate opinions. Informal data analysis is an imperfect mission. The important task is to examine certain possibilities, compare new information with old, raise hypotheses, and share one's inferences with others.

One of the most valuable parts of a small group's observing the same situation is that professionals can compare their data and interpretations among themselves, testing their hunches and listening to other interpretations of the same material. Collective discussions help us to recognize how bias and limited information can influence the analytical process. For example, one observer who was watching a three-year-old girl, Rita, who had been identified as unusually shy and reticent, was stunned to find that teachers were ignoring the child completely while she sat at various activities by herself, making no contact with others. The data were clear. On at least five documented occasions, no teacher came to initiate any interactions with Rita; she seemed to be ignored. The observing adult came to what seemed to be a logical conclusion; the child was being neglected and needed more assistance socially from the teachers. The observer felt conviction about her recommendation.

At a later discussion, however, one of the head teachers was present, and further analysis of the situation revealed important information that the transient observer could not have known. A psychiatrist who was working with Rita and had monitored her behavior over a lengthy period of time—at home and at school—had come to the conclusion that she used her passivity as an attention-getting technique and that she was exercising considerable control of the situation. Teachers were encouraged to give her attention only when she initiated contact with adults, thereby reinforcing her attempts to make contact with others. The outside observer's interpretation of the data was obviously limited by not having this important information. This illustration helps to illuminate the wisdom of caution in thinking about what teachers should and should not do when one is not in a position to know the full circumstances.

Another thing to consider about forming conclusions is that we sometimes have a predisposition to look for the highly significant or the dramatic, as contrasted with the routine. Ordinary behavior is less exciting to the observer who is seeking psychological adventure. Hence, the tendency may arise to identify extremes—to see chaos in minor confusion; to see aggression when someone is simply standing up for his or her rights; to see a teacher as ineffectual when she is, in fact, just watching her classroom carefully. The wise adult must recognize the power of the typical and the predictable and find satisfaction in identifying these essential qualities. Furthermore, our understanding of the difficult child or the child with special needs is enhanced when we have a firm understanding of normal child development and classroom practice. Observers must keep their own emotional needs out of the analytical process.

In summary, important things to remember about observation include the following:

- the importance of observing children and classrooms objectively
- the need to allow sufficient observation time to enable a meaningful amount of data to be accumulated
- the importance of planning a focus
- the range of ways that one can record and gather data
- the need to analyze data with fairness and objectivity, and to suspend one's own biases when making interpretations

Summary

Classroom observation as a means of professional growth for teachers is a highly valuable but underutilized process. Most teachers do not make time to observe their own and other classrooms in systematic ways. They tend not to be able to free themselves from teaching responsibility and make sufficient time to stand back and take a focused view of what is going on in the classroom. Although teachers do observe in their classrooms, they usually do so in a random fashion, while attending to various other matters. Observing objectively is not a common professional activity. Even more rare is the opportunity to share observations with another professional. Teachers tend not to be relaxed with peer observations, and staff scheduling poses obstacles to providing this professional experience.

Yet experience has indicated that teachers can learn a great deal from observing and documenting what goes on in their own and others' classrooms. Through this process they become more effective diagnosticians, more responsive to individual needs. They engage in reflection about professional practice and adopt the attitude that improving teaching skill is an ongoing process. For example, a highly effective teacher might hypothesize that teacher's language influences the outcomes of a particular teaching approach and decide to focus on observing teacher language; or the teacher may be interested in changing the use of the physical space or incorporating different types of motivational strategies. Any of these areas may provide a focus for classroom observation. Teachers interested in augmenting their understanding of the developmental continuum may arrange to observe in classrooms for children of different age levels. By engaging in analytical observation, teachers gain a deeper understanding of the dynamics of teaching. They receive intellectual stimulation and experience teaching as an exciting profession.

Observing and documenting classroom practice involves considerable skill—including being able to observe objectively and unobtrusively, to maintain a professional stance when observing in the classroom of another teacher, and to recognize one's own biases so that they do not unconsciously affect the observation, the documentation, or the analysis. Documentation may take the form of anecdotes, running records, verbal vignettes, time sampling, or event sampling. Of critical importance is the need to establish a focus for the observation and to generate useful questions. Questions on which to focus observations need to be stated in observable form and in a manner that generates useful data. (See the example in this chapter related to studying gender issues.)

The final chapter of this book provides a compendium of instruments for classroom observation and assessment. Included are two general classroom observation forms and specific forms that relate to each of the operational characteristics sections of this text: the cognitive, the creative, and the social-emotional.

CHAPTER

11 A COMPENDIUM OF OBSERVATIONAL INSTRUMENTS

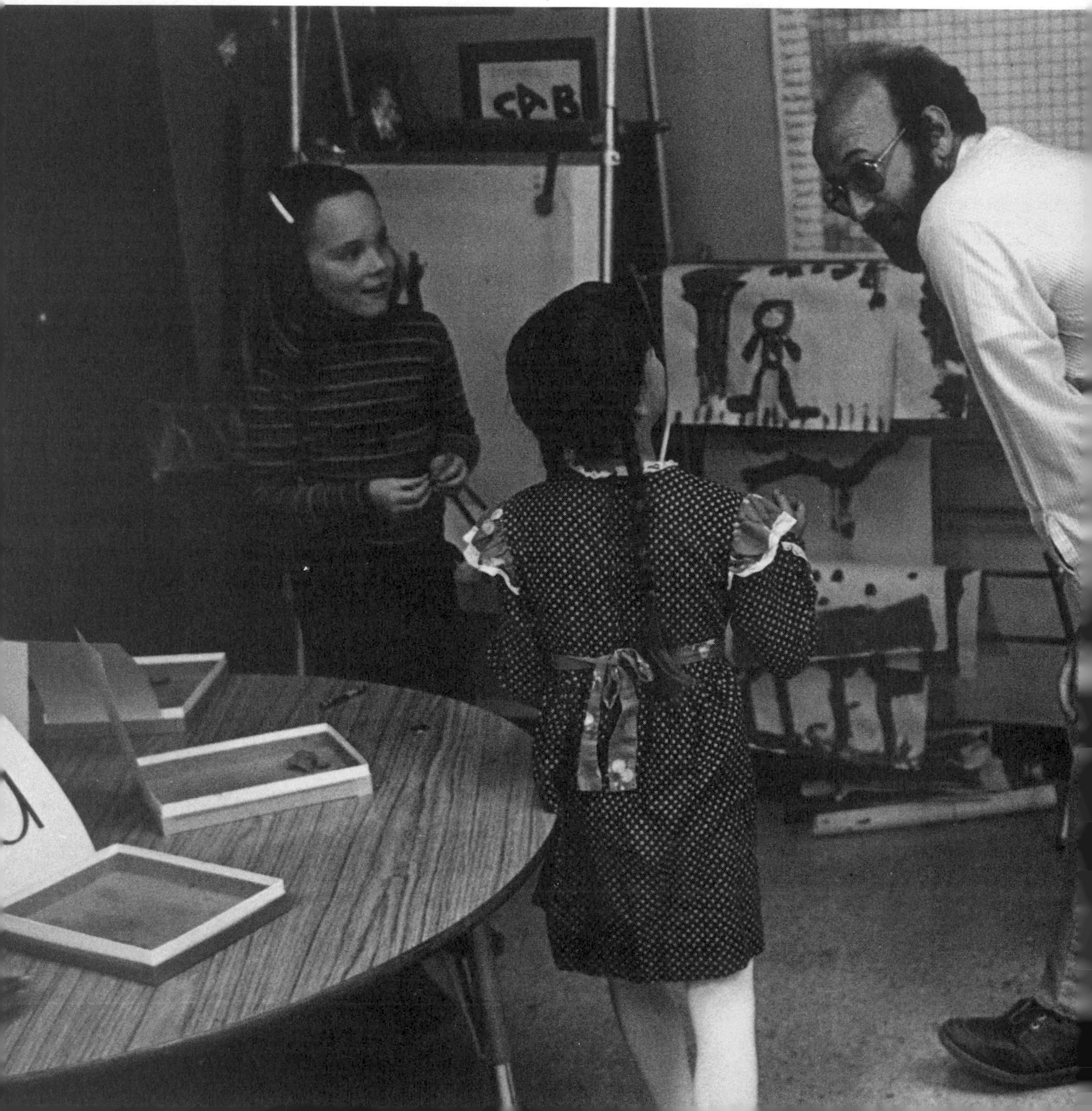

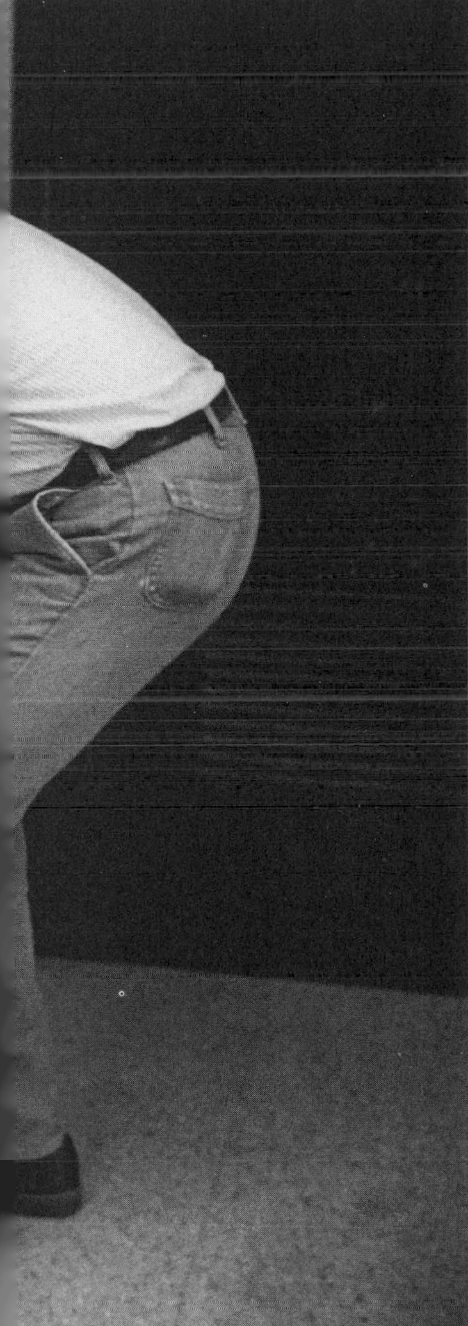

- *The Observation Forms and Their Function*
- *A Word About Gathering Data and Evaluation*
- *Form A-1: Characteristics of a Developmentally Based Early Childhood Program (Comprehensive Version)*
- *Form A-2: Characteristics of a Developmentally Based Early Childhood Program (Abbreviated Version)*
- *Form B: Critical Qualities of the Teacher*
- *Form C: Curriculum in the Dynamic Classroom*
- *Form D: Stimulating Creative Thinking*
- *Form E: Social-Emotional Issues*
- *Summary*

In Chapter 10, we discussed the observational process, described why it is important, and provided suggestions for developing skill in this area. This chapter extends the discussion of the observational process and invites the reader to engage in the process by using specific observation forms. These forms provide a way of gathering and evaluating data related to the various characteristics of developmentally appropriate programs. The forms guide the process of determining the degree to which a particular classroom meets the criteria of developmental appropriateness. When used in conjunction with the text, the forms provide a way for the reader to work toward augmenting the developmental appropriateness of a program in specific areas.

The form that pervades the entire process is "Characteristics of a Developmentally Based Early Childhood Program." It is presented in both a comprehensive and abbreviated format. The comprehensive format, Form A-1, encourages study, discussion, and clarification of each characteristic of a developmentally appropriate program. This form contains many examples to facilitate this understanding. The abbreviated form, Form A-2, lends itself more easily to being used in a setting in which observation is taking place. Also included are four forms that parallel the content of this text, covering the intellectual component (covering teacher qualities and curriculum characteristics), the creative component, and the social-emotional component.

In discussing the observation process in Chapter 10, we emphasized the need to observe with a specific focus and with identifiable questions to be answered. The forms provided in this chapter respond to this need. They focus on specific aspects of developmentally appropriate programs. Educators who have used the forms have reported on their value in clarifying the concept of developmental appropriateness, assessing the degree to which a given program is developmentally appropriate, and modifying or enriching their own programs.

The Observation Forms and Their Function

The observation forms in this chapter correspond to the material presented throughout the various sections of this book. The forms have two functions: (1) to enable the observer to strengthen understanding of the various characteristics set forth, and (2) to enable the observer to evaluate the extent to which a given classroom situation reflects the criteria set forth for a developmental classroom.

The following observation forms are included:

1. Form A-1: Characteristics of a Developmentally Based Early Childhood Program (comprehensive version)
2. Form A-2: Characteristics of a Developmentally Based Early Childhood Program (abbreviated version)
3. Form B: Critical Qualities of the Teacher
4. Form C: Curriculum in the Dynamic Classroom
5. Form D: Stimulating Creative Thinking
6. Form E: Social-Emotional Issues.

Although these forms include the essential information that is communicated throughout the various chapters, they vary in their format and may or may not correspond directly to the chapter layouts. For example, Forms B, C, and D each present in a concise manner all the operational characteristics described in Chapters 4 and 5 (challenging children intellectually), Chapter 7 (stimulating creative thinking), and Chapter 9 (incorporating social-emotional issues into curriculum and classroom management). This allows the forms to be used in an efficient way while observing a classroom. The abbreviated format allows the viewer to see the characteristics unencumbered by examples during the observational process. Forms A-1 and A-2, "Characteristics of a Developmentally Based Early Childhood Program" do not follow this format, since they are designed to stimulate a comprehensive look at a program. Form E summarizes the material dealing with social-emotional issues in Chapter 9.

A Word About Gathering Data and Evaluation

Chapter 10 emphasized the importance of learning to observe and record with sensitivity and care in order to increase one's understanding of what transpires in a classroom. The task of identifying and scrutinizing even the smallest of details is a powerful mechanism for developing an in-depth understanding of the teaching and learning process. The observer who collects and analyzes data systematically achieves a level of awareness that is qualitatively different from the observer who watches casually without a set of objectives. The observation forms are therefore designed to provide a clear focus for the viewer, reminding the viewer of specific criteria relevant to the particular area under consideration. The forms are built on the assumption that the reader has read and digested the theoretical and operational characteristics presented throughout the book. However, as the observer considers a specific aspect of a program, he or she may find it helpful to refer back to the sections of the text that elaborate and illustrate each of the characteristics.

The forms provide space for recording key information about the identified characteristics. The observer will want to gather specific teacher and child speech, small vignettes, information about the physical environment, recordkeeping, and other programmatic details as a means to sharpen understanding of how the characteristics reveal themselves. In some situations, the observer may be viewing a colleague's classroom or that of an unknown teacher; in other situations, looking at one's own classroom in order to gain information about children or a teaching partner. The observer may also be a parent interested in becoming involved in the child's education and in gaining increased understanding of developmental education or an administrator seeking to work with teachers in evaluating and improving educational programs. In any case, data may be used to provide feedback to others, as well as for one's own personal understanding.

In addition to gathering data, each form asks the viewer to rank the classroom situation along certain dimensions. Some people may feel resistance to this procedure, but without clear evaluation and assessment, it is difficult for growth to take place. Without a clear, unambiguous method to measure the presence or absence of certain features in a classroom, we run the risk of being oblivious to areas of the program that require attention and of labeling a classroom as developmental when, in fact, it is not.

The spirit of the evaluation process acknowledges that evaluation must be purposeful. We evaluate to determine strengths and weaknesses of a specific program or classroom, in order to help with the process of improving its quality. Under the best of circumstances, evaluation is not an isolated act, one in which judgments are made without the accompanying assistance that facilitates growth and change. It is hoped that whether an individual teacher or an administrator is undertaking observation, the forms will be used as a tool to identify areas for development—not as a narrow assessment instrument. Teachers can use these forms to identify specific areas for personal focus or for working collaboratively with other professionals and classroom helpers. There is particular value in small group observations, where insights and responses are shared and discussed.

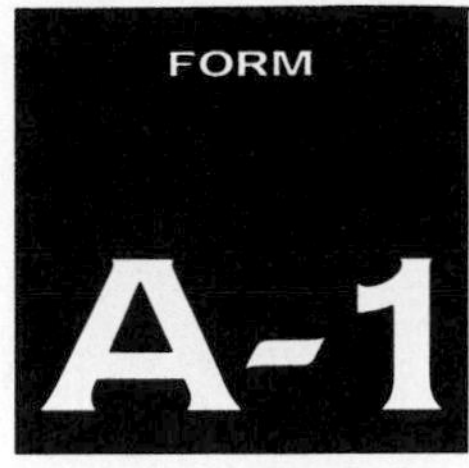

CHARACTERISTICS OF A DEVELOPMENTALLY BASED EARLY CHILDHOOD PROGRAM*

Name of teacher: ______________________ School/town: ______________________

Grade level: __________ Observer: ______________ Length of observation: ______________

Identified here are some major characteristics of a developmentally based early childhood program. Each characteristic is followed by three sets of observational guides designed to aid the observer in rating the degree to which a classroom is developmentally based in terms of the characteristics.

The observational guides are designated as low, medium, or high. Classrooms that are developmentally based in terms of the characteristic have a high rating. *Circle* the level that most closely corresponds for each characteristic.

A. THE PHYSICAL ENVIRONMENT IS DESIGNED TO OPTIMIZE CONCRETE LEARNING AND TO ENABLE CHILDREN TO EXPLORE A WIDE VARIETY OF OBJECTS AND MATERIALS.

Circle the level that most closely corresponds.

Low	Medium	High
Tables and chairs (or desks) dominate the classroom. Few objects, toys, or manipulatives are readily accessible. Those that do exist are often stored and used only when the teacher presents them in conjunction with a specific lesson. Worksheets and highly structured paper-and-pencil tasks are the central materials for instruction.	Room setup reveals basic equipment and media that are commonly accepted as being important for young children—such as books, blocks, manipulatives, puzzles, easels, crayons, markers and paper—but these remain relatively constant with little change or additional enrichment. These materials are used primarily during free play time, but are not usually integrated into the teacher's planned activities in any significant way.	The classroom reveals a wide variety of unique and unusual materials that children may observe, touch, or manipulate. Materials invite investigation and imaginative use and may be taken from shelves for spontaneous use: for example, measuring tools, mathematical rods, old typewriters, telephones, or other mechanical objects; outdoor materials (bark, pumpkins, reeds), animals, fish, ant colonies; cross-cultural dolls; books and charts with enlarged print; diverse art materials, both two- and three-dimensional.

Provide significant evidence supporting the level selected, including listing objects, materials, and the nature of tasks, as well as providing brief anecdotes and environmental descriptions. (Use a separate sheet, if necessary.)

Check those features in the physical environment that seem to apply.

Positives

_______ Organization communicates a sense of harmony and predictability; there is clarity and logic in storage (cubbies, bins, shelves are used to organize objects).
_______ There is sufficient flexibility and open-endedness in which to explore; appropriate messiness is accepted.
_______ Children help maintain the environment, know where things are stored, and how to get and return materials; they help in cleaning up.
_______ Consideration has been given to aesthetics, plants, and beautiful objects. Pictures are present. A rocking chair, pillows, or other inviting furnishings are present.

Negatives

_______ Messiness and disorganization are present.
_______ Too much attention is given to order and control in the environment; rigidity is communicated.
_______ Children do not make significant contribution to maintaining things; adults do most of the cleanup.
_______ Little attention is given to making the environment beautiful and inviting.

SUMMARY OF TOTAL PHYSICAL ENVIRONMENT
Circle the number that reflects an expression of this total characteristic.

1 2 3 4 5 6
Low Medium High

Qualifying comments:

B. THERE IS THE OPPORTUNITY FOR CHILDREN TO WORK ALONE, WITH ONE OR TWO OTHER CHILDREN, IN SMALL GROUPS, AND IN LARGE GROUP SITUATIONS. CHILDREN HAVE SOME OPTIONS IN CHOOSING LEARNING EXPERIENCES.

Circle the level that most closely corresponds.

Low	**Medium**	**High**
Except for free play time, children are organized primarily in large group experiences with everyone undertaking the same task at the same time. Activities are planned for the whole class, with little regard for differences in developmental capacities. Small, ability-related reading and math groups may exist.	Free play and choice time enable children to exercise options in how they spend their time; some small group instruction takes place, but large group experiences dominate. Central areas of the curriculum, such as language arts and mathematics, are taught primarily in large groups.	The teacher works in a range of ways with children, individually and in both small and large groups. The organization of children is related to individual interests as well as developmental capabilities. Since the importance of concrete activity is respected, many activities are taught in small groups, allowing the opportunity for direct manipulation of materials. Language arts and mathematics activities are not addressed exclusively in large groups.

Provide significant evidence supporting the level selected, including brief anecdotes, quotes, specific nature of groupings, and environmental descriptions. (Use a separate sheet, if necessary.)

SUMMARY OF ORGANIZATION OF CHILDREN
Circle the number that reflects an expression of this total characteristic.

1 2 3 4 5 6
Low Medium High

Qualifying comments: (identify any extenuating circumstances)

C. THE TEACHER OBSERVES, RECORDS, AND ASSESSES CHILD AND GROUP PROGRESS AND BASES INSTRUCTION ON THIS INFORMATION. CHILDREN'S SPECIAL TALENTS, AS WELL AS AREAS OF DIFFICULTY, ARE ADDRESSED.

Circle the level that most closely corresponds.

Low	Medium	High
Standardized achievement tests and paper-and-pencil tasks are the primary evaluation tools. Systematic observation and documentation of children's learning and behavior does not occur. Curriculum activities are not significantly differentiated across ability levels.	The teacher is aware of individual children's interests and ability through informal observation in play and open-ended activities, as well as through more structured tasks. Some activities are created to accommodate to differences, but emphasis is based primarily on group needs. Special talents are not emphasized, although remedial work may take place.	The teacher uses both informal and formal methods to document which activities children select and avoid, and is aware of special strengths and weaknesses. Children with exceptional capabilities, areas of concern, or special needs have activities planned specifically with them in mind. The teacher maintains files, portfolios, and other systems for reviewing work with children, parents, and other professionals. Evaluation is a multifaceted process.

Provide significant evidence supporting the level selected, including folders and portfolios, examples of planned activities for individuals, and teacher interviews. (Use a separate sheet, if necessary.)

SUMMARY OF OBSERVATION AND DOCUMENTATION
Circle the number that reflects an expression of this total characteristic.

1 2 3 4 5 6
Low Medium High

Qualifying comments:

D. THE TEACHER IS VIBRANT INTELLECTUALLY. THE TEACHER UNDERSTANDS THE IMPORTANCE OF MOTIVATIONAL STRATEGIES IN STIMULATING CHILDREN'S INTELLECTUAL AND EXPRESSIVE ACTIVITY AND IS ALERT TO THE ADULT'S ROLE IN SHAPING THE NATURE OF ACTIVITY. THE NOTION OF COGNITIVE CONFLICT* IS RESPECTED. THE ADULT SHARES INFORMATION, RAISES QUESTIONS, AND PROVOKES EXPERIMENTATION IN A WIDE VARIETY OF WAYS.

Circle the level that most closely corresponds.

Low	**Medium**	**High**
The teacher relies heavily on commercial texts and curriculum guides. Lessons are aimed at average ability levels, leaving some children with experiences that are too difficult or too easy. Activities offer little variety; they are static and repetitive. The teacher may stimulate by enticing children with such superficial statements as "We're going to do something special," rather than engaging children in substantive thought.	Some lessons are challenging and engage interest, but most teacher presentations are predictable in format; they rarely create "disequilibrium" in children's thinking. Challenge may come from the materials provided, but children are usually left to investigate the materials in an open-ended manner, without the adult's extending thinking. Some attention is paid to ability levels.	The teacher is dynamic and uses a variety of teaching strategies to stimulate interest. Lessons are designed thoughtfully, with clear learning objectives and an appreciation for differences in ability levels. A range of motivational teaching techniques are employed; the teacher asks questions, poses problems, and encourages critical thinking. Although materials are sometimes presented in an open-ended manner, the teacher balances these situations with activities where there are clear challenges to be addressed. The teacher uses language in a manner that extends intellectual growth.

Provide particularly significant evidence supporting the level selected, including brief anecdotes, exact quotes, motivational techniques, and specific lessons. (Use a separate sheet, if necessary.)

* Kohlberg and Mayer, (1972).

Comment on the teacher's use of language.

SUMMARY OF COGNITIVE CONFLICT
Circle the number that reflects an expression of this total characteristic.
1 2 3 4 5 6
Low Medium High

Qualifying comments:

E. THE ACADEMIC AREAS OF LANGUAGE ARTS AND MATHEMATICS ARE CRUCIAL ASPECTS OF THE CURRICULUM, BUT THEY ARE TAUGHT IN AN INTERDISCIPLINARY MANNER THAT MAKES THEM RELEVANT TO THE CHILD AND BUILDS RESPECT FOR THEIR IMPORTANCE.

Circle the level that most closely corresponds.

Low	Medium	High
Skills are taught in relative isolation with emphasis on workbooks, ditto sheets, and didactic paper-and-pencil tasks. Little individualization of the curriculum takes place, with children undertaking many of the same tasks, regardless of developmental level. Tutoring may take place with children who have learning difficulties. Phonics and programmed workbooks dominate the teaching of reading and writing.	Some opportunity exists for concrete experiences with drawing and writing, mathematical rods, and the like, but the teacher rarely uses these tasks to accomplish specific objectives. Structured workbook, paper-and-pencil tasks are the dominant approach; some individualization of the curriculum has been instituted. Phonics may be used in conjunction with other approaches to reading.	Academics are dealt with in a wide variety of ways, with skills incorporated into a number of ongoing activities. Individualization is central to instruction, with children working on a range of tasks, depending on developmental levels. Activities may allow children to count, measure, and compute while also drawing and writing. Interdisciplinary teaching occurs along with the direct teaching of skills. Skills are taught in context.

An eclectic approach to teaching language arts is present, including the following:

- A "whole language" philosophy predominates; "big books" are used.
- Phonics is an important resource.
- A drawing/writing center is provided for children to make books and journals; the process approach to reading and writing is taken; revisions and "publishing" are taught.
- Children's own phonetic writing (invented spelling) is accepted (Chomsky, 1971).
- An inviting reading/book area is set up with pillows and a rocking chair.
- The teacher reads to children and tells stories with frequency.

An eclectic approach to teaching mathematics is present, including such things as the following:

- Cuisenaire rods, Montessori mathematical equipment, miscellaneous measuring equipment (rulers, scales, and so on)
- commercial lesson plans that rely on concrete experiences, like *Math Their Way*

Provide significant evidence supporting the level selected, including the nature of learning centers, reading and mathematics materials, bulletin boards, journals and books written by children. (Use a separate sheet, if necessary.)

SUMMARY OF LANGUAGE ARTS AND MATHEMATICS
Circle the number that reflects an expression of this total characteristic.

1 2 3 4 5 6
Low Medium High

Qualifying comments:

F. CREATIVITY IS VALUED HIGHLY; HENCE, EVERY EFFORT IS MADE TO CAPITALIZE ON CHILDREN'S IMAGINATIVE, EXPRESSIVE THINKING AND PRODUCTIVITY.

Circle the level that most closely corresponds

Low	Medium	High
Emphasis is on tasks with predetermined outcomes, such as completing commercial worksheets, filling in ditto forms of adult-made pictures, and follow-the-directions activities that yield identical products. Bulletin boards are dominated by look-alike work. Holiday art reflects the same orientation. Heavy emphasis placed on neatness.	Occasional opportunity exists to create a piece of art, write an original story or song, or dance expressively; some opportunities exist for using materials in an open-ended and original manner, but teacher-initiated activities still rely heavily on convergent tasks (look-alike holiday turkeys, for example). The products that go up on bulletin boards are more likely to be adult-initiated than to be children's original work, although both may be displayed.	Children have many opportunities to invent and create across different areas of the curriculum. Children are allowed ready access to scrap materials, as well as basic cutting, writing, construction tools. An appreciation for one's own ideas is reinforced and valued. Flexibility in how children use materials encourages novel solutions and promotes problem-solving abilities. The teacher reinforces deviations from the conventional and displays children's original work. Look-alike, teacher-directed products are not present. *Creativity is viewedas something valued across the curriculum, not confined tothe arts.*

Provide significant evidence supporting the level selected, including verbal interactions, writing and art examples, bulletin boards, and science and social studies examples. Consider the message that the room decorations communicate. (Use a separate sheet, if necessary.)

SUMMARY OF CREATIVITY
Circle the number that reflects an expression of this total characteristic.

1 2 3 4 5 6
Low Medium High

Qualifying comments:

G. SOCIAL-EMOTIONAL ISSUES ARE VIEWED AS AN IMPORTANT PART OF INTELLECTUAL DEVELOPMENT, ARE A PART OF THE CLASSROOM ATMOSPHERE, AND ARE INTEGRATED ASPECTS OF CURRICULUM AND CLASSROOM MANAGEMENT.

ATMOSPHERE

The teacher views the classroom as a small society and works to engender an atmosphere that encourages trust, cooperation, and a sense of community; a minimum of competition; respect for academic, cultural, and social differences; children in charge of their own learning; valuing work and productivity.

Circle the level that most closely corresponds.

Low

Emphasis is placed on doing your own work in isolation. Children are dissuaded from helping one another and giving one another feedback. Stars and other rewards are given to motivate achievement. The teacher sets the standards for right and wrong and for correct ways of achieving and behaving. Differences in style and orientation are not encouraged. Following directions is narrowly reinforced. Little attention is given to group process and working together collaboratively.

Medium

Some attention is given to a sense of group identity, and competition is not encouraged. Some appreciation of cultural and academic differences is apparent. The teacher is not explicit, however, in the way he or she communicates the importance of sharing, helping one another, and letting children know that they have power and autonomy over their own learning.

High

The teacher makes it boldly apparent that there is respect for individual differences, as well as a sense of community. The comments the teacher makes, the actions he or she reinforces, and the activities he or she plans all encourage children to make their own decisions, seeking others' help, solving problems together, and respecting a range of styles and abilities in working. Working hard and taking charge of one's own behavior are key values.

Provide significant evidence of:

- building trust, cooperation, and a sense of community

- respect for academic, cultural, and social differences

- empowering children to be in charge of their own learning

- reinforcing the importance of work and productivity

- Other (use a separate sheet, if necessary):

SUMMARY OF EMPOWERING CHILDREN (ATMOSPHERE)
Circle the number that reflects an expression of this total characteristic.

1	2	3	4	5	6
Low		**Medium**			**High**

Qualifying comments:

SOCIAL-EMOTIONAL ISSUES IN CLASSROOM MANAGEMENT

Circle the level that most closely corresponds.

Low	Medium	High
The teacher states rules frequently, moralizes, and demands obedience. Children have no room to participate in decision making about rules, conflict, or appropriate individual and group behavior Decision making rests with the adult; children have little power. Punishment and shaming are used freely.	The teacher allows some participation by children in establishing rules, regulations, and classroom procedures; spontaneous contributions are accepted but not actively encouraged. The rationale behind teacher expectations for behavior are not made clear.	The teacher uses management and behavioral issues as an opportunity for children to reason, problem-solve, and analyze events; critical thinking and social cognition (understanding social interactions) are clear objectives. The teacher models negotiation strategies. Rules and regulations are used selectively. Helping children achieve autonomy is valued highly.

Provide significant evidence supporting the level selected, including teacher-child interactions and child-child interactions; group time discussions or anecdotes; rules posted on walls, and so on. (Use a separate sheet, if necessary.)

SOCIAL-EMOTIONAL ISSUES IN CURRICULUM DEVELOPMENT

Circle the level that most closely corresponds.

Low	Medium	High
Teacher does not plan lessons and activities which build an understanding of social/emotional issues. Children's spontaneous expressions about what they love, hate, fear, wish for, and so on are not encouraged or developed into learning experiences.	Some opportunity exists for children to express feelings and opinions in group time, open-ended art experiences, stories, and writing, but the teacher does not use subject matter that children initiate as the basis for designing in-depth activities.	Curriculum routinely includes activities that encourage expression of social-emotional issues, and the teacher actively builds understanding of human behavior. Subject matter includes such things as why people fight and become angry; how we show love; understanding people who are different from you; jealousy; friendships, and so on. Motives for certain behaviors are explored. Social cognition is an integral part of curriculum development.

Provide significant evidence supporting the level selected, including examples of children's work in books, drawings, and on bulletin boards; the content of units; the nature of interpersonal discussions at group time; and so on. Look for the way teachers expand understanding of how people behave.

SUMMARY OF SOCIAL-EMOTIONAL ISSUES
(INCLUDING BOTH MANAGEMENT AND CURRICULUM)
Circle the number that reflects an expression of this total characteristic.

1	2	3	4	5	6
Low		Medium			High

Qualifying comments:

H. SINCE YOUNG CHILDREN ARE EGOCENTRIC EMOTIONALLY AND INTELLECTUALLY, SUBJECT MATTER THAT IS OF PERSONAL INTEREST IS AN IMPORTANT WAY TO DESIGN LEARNING EXPERIENCES. CONSIDERATION IS GIVEN TO FAMILY, CULTURAL, AND COMMUNITY CONCERNS.

Circle the level that most closely corresponds.

Low

Subject matter and areas of study are predominantly determined by curriculum guides and conventional worksheets. Stereotyped ideas from commercial sources are presented—fall leaves, spring flowers, farm animals, city workers—with little opportunity for building on children's own backgrounds or expressed interests.

Medium

Children have some opportunity to explore subjects that interest them occasionally, such as in open-ended art activities, dramatic play, and telling and writing stories; the spontaneous is accepted, but ideas identified by children are not integrated into other activities planned by the teacher. Culturally relevant photographs and commercial products may be present.

High

The teacher capitalizes on children's interests, so that certain themes that hold power are explored—fantasy figures, dinosaurs, birthday parties. Family and neighborhood events are strategically integrated into key activities, including language arts and social studies. Interdisciplinary units are designed around areas that are compelling to many children. Differences in culture and language are addressed directly, communicating an appreciation for diversity and individuality.

Provide significant evidence supporting the level selected, including brief anecdotes, examples of lessons, environmental descriptions, material on bulletin boards, children's original art and stories, and so on. (Use a separate sheet, if necessary.)

SUMMARY OF CONSIDERING CHILDREN'S EGOCENTRICITY
Circle the number that reflects an expression of this total characteristic.

1 2 3 4 5 6
Low Medium High

Qualifying comments:

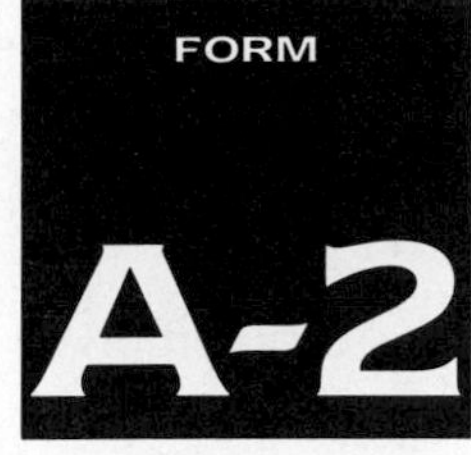

CHARACTERISTICS OF A DEVELOPMENTALLY BASED EARLY CHILDHOOD PROGRAM*

Name of teacher: ______________________ School/town: ______________

Grade level: ________ Observer: ______________ Length of observation: __________

A. THE PHYSICAL ENVIRONMENT IS DESIGNED TO OPTIMIZE CONCRETE LEARNING AND TO ENABLE CHILDREN TO EXPLORE A WIDE VARIETY OF OBJECTS AND MATERIALS.

Low	Medium	High
Tables and chairs dominate. Few objects, toys, or materials readily accessible. Worksheets and structured pencil/paper tasks dominate. Paper/pencil tasks are central materials.	Basic early childhood media present for free play (books; blocks; manipulatives; puzzles; paints; etc.), but not integrated into teacher's instruction. Scope is limited. Materials remain relatively constant from week to week; little variation.	Activity and learning centers are observed. Wide variety of materials for children to explore and use spontaneously. The unique and unusual are present.

Provide significant evidence of physical environment, including listing of objects and materials, nature of tasks, brief anecdotes, environmental descriptions, and so on.

* Abbreviated version.

Check those features in the physical environment that seem to apply:

Positives

_______ Organization communicates a sense of harmony and predictability; clarity and logic in storage (cubbies, bins, shelves are used to organize objects).

_______ Sufficient flexibility and open-endedness in which to explore; acceptance of appropriate messiness.

_______ Children help to maintain the environment; know where things are stored, how to get and return materials; help in cleaning up.

_______ Aesthetics have been considered; plants, beautiful objects, pictures are present; rocking chair, pillows, or other inviting furnishings are present.

Negatives

_______ Messiness and disorganization are present.

_______ Too much attention is given to order and control in the environment; rigidity is communicated.

_______ Children do not make significant contribution to maintaining room; adults do most of the cleanup.

_______ Little attention is given to making the environment beautiful and inviting.

SUMMARY: TOTAL PHYSICAL ENVIRONMENT
Circle the number that reflects an expression of this total characteristic.

1 2 3 4 5 6
Low Medium High

Qualifying comments:

B. THERE IS THE OPPORTUNITY FOR CHILDREN TO WORK ALONE, WITH ONE OR TWO OTHER CHILDREN, IN SMALL GROUPS, AND IN LARGE GROUP SITUATIONS. CHILDREN HAVE SOME OPTIONS IN CHOOSING LEARNING EXPERIENCES.

Low	Medium	High
Except for free play, large group instruction dominates. All children engage in same tasks at same time. Little attention to developmental capabilities.	Some opportunity for children to choose activities. Some small group instruction, but large group instruction dominates. Math and literacy taught primarily in large groups. Some individualization.	Range of options are used (individual, small, and large groups). Interests and developmental levels influence organization of children. Many small group activities. Basic skills addressed frequently in small groups.

Provide significant evidence, including specific nature of groupings, environmental descriptions, attention to developmental levels, and so on.

SUMMARY: ORGANIZATION OF CHILDREN
Circle the number that reflects an expression of this total characteristic.

1 2 3 4 5 6
Low Medium High

Qualifying comments:

C. THE TEACHER OBSERVES, RECORDS, AND ASSESSES CHILD AND GROUP PROGRESS AND BASES INSTRUCTION ON THIS INFORMATION. CHILDREN'S SPECIAL TALENTS, AS WELL AS AREAS OF DIFFICULTY, ARE ADDRESSED.

Low	Medium	High
Standardized testing dominates. No systematic observing and recording of behavior. Activities not differentiated across ability levels.	Teacher aware of individual interests and abilities; some recording occurs. Some individualization of activity, but group needs dominate. Remedial work takes place, but special talents, interests not addressed. Group testing dominates.	Systematic observation and recording takes place. Portfolios, files, and other systems for reviewing children's progress are used and shared with parents and other professionals. Evaluation is a multifaceted process. Children's special needs or unique abilities are addressed.

Provide significant evidence, including folders and portfolios, examples of planned activities for individuals, teacher interviewing, and so on.

SUMMARY: OBSERVATION AND DOCUMENTATION
Circle the number that reflects an expression of this total characteristic.

1	2	3	4	5	6
Low		Medium			High

Qualifying comments:

D. THE TEACHER IS VIBRANT INTELLECTUALLY. UNDERSTANDS THE IMPORTANCE OF MOTIVATIONAL STRATEGIES IN STIMULATING CHILDREN'S INTELLECTUAL AND EXPRESSIVE ACTIVITY AND IS ALERT TO THE TEACHER'S ROLE IN SHAPING THE NATURE OF ACTIVITY. THE NOTION OF COGNITIVE CONFLICT* IS RESPECTED. THE ADULT SHARES INFORMATION, RAISES QUESTIONS, AND PROVOKES EXPERIMENTS IN A WIDE VARIETY OF WAYS.

Low	Medium	High
Teacher relies exclusively on commercial texts and curriculum guides. Heavy emphasis on copying and repetitive tasks. Tasks are aimed at average level; little challenge for some; too difficult for others. Static intellectually; little excitement and variety. Room, including wall displays and bulletin boards, is mundane.	Some interesting lessons, but most are predictable and do not challenge thinking. Objectives for activities are not always clear or purposeful. Open-ended materials may engage children, but adult does not extend thinking significantly. Teacher speech lacks richness and vitality.	Teacher uses variety of teaching strategies to stimulate, is dynamic and interesting. Lessons have clear learning objectives. Teacher asks substantive questions, poses problems, encourages critical thinking. Teacher seizes spontaneous situations for concept development. Teacher language extends intellectual growth. Bulletin boards and room decorations engage thinking. Challenging experiments with media.

Provide significant evidence, including brief anecdotes, exact quotes, motivational techniques, specific lessons, environmental cues, and so on.

* Kohlberg & Mayer (1972)

Comment on the teacher's use of language (vocabulary, use of analogies and metaphors, enunciations, vitality of expression, etc.)

SUMMARY: COGNITIVE CONFLICT
Circle the number that reflects an expression of this total characteristic.

1 2 3 4 5 6
Low Medium High

Qualifying comments:

E. THE ACADEMIC AREAS OF LANGUAGE ARTS AND MATHEMATICS ARE CRUCIAL ASPECTS OF THE CURRICULUM, BUT THEY ARE TAUGHT IN AN INTERDISCIPLINARY MANNER THAT MAKES THEM RELEVANT TO THE CHILD AND BUILDS RESPECT FOR THEIR IMPORTANCE.

Low	**Medium**	**High**
Skills taught in isolation; emphasis on commercial products and workbooks. Phonics exclusive method of reading instruction. Concrete materials not central in math. Little individualization.	Some use of manipulative materials in teaching math skills, but paper/pencil tasks still dominate. Phonics are used in conjunction with other approaches to reading. Some integration of drawing, writing, bookmaking. Some individualization of curriculum.	Academics taught in wide variety of ways; incorporated into activities. Skills are taught in context. Individualization of tasks valued highly. Interdisciplinary curriculum utilized. Reading and math centers readily apparent.

An eclectic approach to teaching literacy is present, including the following:

- the "whole language" approach; the use of "big books"
- phonics as an important resource
- a drawing/writing center for children to make books and journals; the process approach to reading and writing; revisions, "publishing"
- acceptance of children's own phonetic writing (i.e., invented spelling [Chomsky])
- an inviting reading/book area, set up with pillow and a rocking chair to encourage reading and looking at books
- teacher reading to children and telling stories with frequency

An eclectic approach to teaching mathematics is present, including such things as

- Cuisenaire rods, Montessori mathematical equipment, miscellaneous measuring and sorting equipment (rulers, scales, beads, etc.)
- commercial lesson plans rely upon concrete experiences (e.g., *Math Their Way*)
- teacher language addresses mathematical concepts

Provide significant evidence, including the nature of learning centers, reading and mathematics materials, bulletin boards, journals and books written by children, and so on.

SUMMARY: LANGUAGE ARTS AND MATHEMATICS
Circle the number that reflects an expression of this total characteristic.

1	2	3	4	5	6
Low		Medium		High	

Qualifying comments:

F. CREATIVITY IS VALUED HIGHLY; HENCE, EVERY EFFORT IS MADE TO CAPITALIZE ON CHILDREN'S IMAGINATIVE, EXPRESSIVE THINKING & PRODUCTIVITY.

Low	Medium	High
Emphasis on tasks with predetermined outcomes (dittos, patterns, copying). Heavy emphasis on conformity—"rightness" and "neatness." Uniformity of product for all children. Holiday art and academic tasks reflect the trite and the stereotyped.	Some opportunity to create an original story or piece of art and to be expressive. Some open-ended activities, but teacher-initiated tasks emphasize convergent thinking. Some children's original work is displayed but walls are dominated by adult made products and don't reflect originality.	Ready access to media for writing, drawing, constructing. Reinforcement for originality and imaginative, expressive work. Flexibility in how children use materials encourages novel solutions and promotes problem-solving abilities. Teacher reinforces deviations from the conventional and displays children's original work. Look-alike teacher-directed products are not present. *Creativity is viewed as something valued across the curriculum, not confined to the arts.*

Provide significant evidence, including verbal interactions, writing and art examples, bulletin boards, science and social studies examples, and so on. Consider the message that the room decorations communicate.

SUMMARY: CREATIVITY

Circle the number that reflects an expression of this total characteristic.

1 2 3 4 5 6

Low Medium High

Qualifying comments:

G. SOCIAL-EMOTIONAL ISSUES ARE VIEWED AS AN IMPORTANT PART OF INTELLECTUAL DEVELOPMENT AND ARE INTEGRATED INTO BOTH CLASSROOM MANAGEMENT AND THE CURRICULUM.

Classroom Management

Low	Medium	High
Teacher states rules frequently; moralizes and demands obedience. Little room for children's participation in decision making about rules, conflict. Punishment and shaming used freely. Authoritarian atmosphere; children have no power.	Children have some input about rules and conflict. Spontaneous contributions about problems are accepted but not encouraged. Understanding why certain behaviors are unacceptable is not emphasized. Teacher may be warm and accepting, but does not model problem-solving around behavior.	Teacher is authoritative, firm, in charge; supportive, fair. Management and behavioral issues used as an opportunity for reasoning, problem solving, analyzing events. Critical thinking and social cognition (understanding behavior) are objectives. Stating rules and giving didactic commands used *selectively*. Helping children to achieve autonomy and to engage in perspective-taking is valued. Teacher models negotiation strategies. Understanding of individual needs is reflected in teacher's choice of disciplinary methods.

Provide significant evidence, including teacher-child interactions and child-child interaction, group time discussions or anecdotes, rules posted on walls, and so on.

Curriculum Development

Low	Medium	High
Social-emotional issues (fear, anger, love, jealousy, etc.) not meaningful part of curriculum. May be dealt with in a trite manner. Children's spontaneous comments in group time and show-and-tell pertaining to social-emotional issues are not examined.	Open-ended opportunities for sharing feelings, but social-emotional issues are not developed into in-depth experiences. Art expression may allow for spontaneous expression.	Curriculum includes substantive activities around social-emotional issues. Study about such issues as why people fight and get angry; how we show love; understanding similarities and differences among people; friendships; jealousy, and so on. Motives for behavior are explored and concepts are developed. Art, writing, social studies curriculum, and so on, reflect these concerns.

Provide significant evidence, including examples of children's drawings and writing, curriculum units, discussions at group time, and so on. Seek examples of how teachers expand understanding of human behavior.

SUMMARY: SOCIAL-EMOTIONAL ISSUES
(INCLUDING BOTH MANAGEMENT AND CURRICULUM)
Circle the number that reflects an expression of this total characteristic.

1 2 3 4 5 6
Low Medium High

Qualifying comments:

H. SINCE YOUNG CHILDREN ARE EGOCENTRIC EMOTIONALLY AND INTELLECTUALLY, SUBJECT MATTER THAT IS OF PERSONAL INTEREST IS AN IMPORTANT WAY TO DESIGN LEARNING EXPERIENCES. CONSIDERATION IS GIVEN TO FAMILY, CULTURAL, AND COMMUNITY CONCERNS.

Low	Medium	High
Subject matter determined exclusively by curriculum guides, publishers. No development of children's expressed interests and neighborhood events. White middle-class values and lifestyle permeate the curriculum.	Spontaneous expression of interests occurs in drawing, writing, sharing news, but these ideas are not integrated into teacher planned activities. Cultural diversity is represented by photos, objects, and so on, but not examined in depth.	Themes that interest children integrated into key activities (siblings, dinosaurs, neighborhoods, family life, etc.) Language arts and readiness activities build on current interests. Differences in culture and language are addressed thematically.

Provide significant evidence, including brief anecdotes, examples of lessons, environmental description, material on bulletin boards, children's original art and stories, and so on.

SUMMARY: CONSIDERING CHILDREN'S EGOCENTRICITY
Circle the number that reflects an expression of this total characteristic.

1 2 3 4 5 6
Low Medium High

Qualifying comments:

FORM

B CRITICAL QUALITIES OF THE TEACHER*†

1. *The teacher is alert intellectually, vibrant, and responsive to ideas. The teacher models these qualities.*

This is a particularly difficult dimension to observe. Nonetheless, the astute observer will find subtle cues by reviewing the curriculum, children's work, and things on display within the room, as well as teacher-child interactions. The teacher

- remains aware of current events and identifies those issues that are appropriate for children to address.
- is informed about cultural diversity and pays particular attention to learning about the cultures of the children within his or her classroom.
- identifies parents and other key adults as sources for classroom enrichment.
- gathers information about areas of interest initiated by children and their families and builds this information into the program.

Cite examples:

†This form relates to the operational characteristics described in Chapter 4.

2. *The teacher recognizes that the dynamic interaction between adult and child is central to learning. The teacher is not reluctant to take a leadership role in shaping thinking.*

The teacher

- applies understanding of developmental stages in cognition.
- provides many opportunities for skills and concepts to be reinforced through direct contact with materials.
- recognizes that children's errors reveal important data about how they think and does not deal with them negatively.
- identifies children's interests and uses them in designing lessons.
- recognizes that physical knowledge is a crucial part of the curriculum.
- identifies critical dynamic qualities that engage children emotionally and intellectually and addresses these in designing activities.
- understands that when materials are new, it is not usually necessary to provide extensive additional stimulation.
- stretches children's thinking to provide cognitive conflict; ambiguity and problem-solving are highly valued.
- encourages the use of the scientific method.
- recognizes that progression in learning must be applied to expressive, creative areas as well as academic areas of the curriculum.
- is not reluctant to model procedures and skills.
- uses themes as an important part of interdisciplinary teaching and for strengthening skills.
- adjusts expectations when planned activities are met with passivity or resistance.

Cite examples:

3. *The teacher recognizes the power of speech for challenging children intellectually.*

The teacher

- listens to children attentively.
- creates situations in which children can engage in dialogue with the teacher and one another.
- builds on children's spontaneous activity by asking pertinent questions, providing information, and establishing links with prior events.
- guides children verbally to encourage continued thought and involvement.
- is not reluctant to lecture and share information when the situation warrants.
- models rich and vibrant language:

  speaks clearly and articulates well
  stretches thinking through words
  uses language that is descriptive and compelling
  avoids slovenly, hackneyed language
  is free of verbal tics
  doesn't speak too fast or too slowly
  avoids talking "at" children

- questions effectively

  asks probing questions; avoids random, repetitive, rhetorical ones
  avoids questions when children do not have information to answer
  selects questions that allow more than one answer

- recognizes that it is important to wait after asking questions to allow children to conceptualize responses; recognizes individual differences.
- uses metaphors and analogies for expanding concepts.
- praises and reinforces in substantive rather than superficial ways.

Cite examples:

4. *The teacher reinforces the importance of work and productivity and empowers children to expect the best from themselves and be in charge of their own growth and learning.*

The teacher

- helps children to understand the nature of how people learn; that they have control over their own learning.
- helps them to understand that people perform and learn differently from one another, and builds respect for individual differences.
- helps them to understand that achievement and mastery are the result of work and effort, and reinforces attitudes that increase learning potential.
- makes discussion and evaluation of work and the work process part of the program.

Cite examples:

Rank the teacher across the four critical qualities:

1. alert intellectually
2. assumes a leadership role
3. recognizes the power of speech
4. empowers children

Circle the number that is appropriate:

0	**1**	**2**	**3**	**4**	**5**	**6**
Low			**Medium**			**High**

CURRICULUM IN THE DYNAMIC CLASSROOM*†

1. *The teacher observes, records, and assesses progress.*

The teacher

- employs informal and formal techniques for gathering information, uses direct observation for evaluating progress.
- documents progress in ways that may be shared with others.
- recognizes that intellectual capabilities are revealed in a wide assortment of ways; addresses "multiple intelligences" (Gardner, 1983).
- is aware of areas in which children have special knowledge and competence.
- considers how culture impacts on children's participation and performance.

Cite examples:

†This form relates to the operational characteristics described in Chapter 5.

2. *The physical environment optimizes concrete learning. The teacher maximizes its impact.*

ORGANIZATION AND AESTHETICS

- Classroom is organized into activity areas with logic and clarity. Individual areas are clearly defined. Physical organization of the classroom provides space for individual, small group, and large group activities.
- A wide variety of materials are available for children to observe, touch, and manipulate.
- Compelling objects are arranged strategically on tables, shelves to invite close observation and investigation.
- Boxes, bins, cubbies are used to categorize things and make it obvious where they belong.
- Predictability and consistency are apparent in the basic organization of the classroom at the same time that there is novelty and change.
- Aesthetics are apparent. Beautiful photographs, artwork, objects, and plants are present. Things are displayed with care and concern for beauty. There is concern for making the environment warm and inviting (rocking chair, lamps, cozy corner).

Cite examples:

Housekeeping

- The classroom is orderly and well maintained and does not appear disorderly and messy. On the other hand, it has a relaxed, casual quality that invites activity.
- There is sufficient flexibilty in housekeeping to allow for temporary disorder for messy projects and activities.
- Children are expected to help maintain the environment and be respectful of it.

Cite examples:

Teaching Elements

- Bulletin boards, room decorations, and display surfaces are part of the teaching process; they are used to stimulate thinking.
- Children's work is an important part of the environment and is vividly displayed.
- Adaptations are made in the environment for children with special needs.
- Concern for cultural diversity is apparent in the physical environment.

Cite examples:

3. *The academic areas of literacy and mathematics are critical parts of the curriculum, but they are taught in an interdisciplinary manner that makes them relevant and builds respect for their importance.*

- Individual, small group, and large group instruction are all used.
- Distinctions in ability levels are respected and minimized. Flexible grouping occurs.
- Academic subjects are not taught in isolation. Interdisciplinary teaching is apparent; themes are utilized to integrate subject areas.
- Academics are not taught exclusively with trite worksheets and didactic pencil-and-paper tasks. Worksheets, when used, are interesting and engage interest.
- Contemporary approaches to teaching literacy are utilized, such as a writing/drawing center; use of "invented spelling"; integration of whole language and phonics; process writing and book making; a print rich environment; etc.
- Contemporary approaches to teaching mathematics are used, such as concrete manipulatives (rods, blocks, unifix cubes); materials that invite mathematical and quantitative analysis (sorting, classifying; scales, tape measures, rulers); commercial texts emphasizing problem solving.

Cite examples:

4. *The teacher makes curriculum decisions based on the best interests of the child. The teacher negotiates parental and institutional demands that are contrary to what is developmentally appropriate in constructive ways.*

The teacher

- Communicates to parents so they understand his or her objectives and the developmental perspective.
- Is proactive with nondevelopmental colleagues; seeks mutuality and reciprocity; avoids an adversarial position.
- Joins the best of a cultural transmission (traditional) position with the developmental approach.

Cite examples:

Rank the teacher across the four curriculum dimensions:

1. The teacher observes, records, and assesses.
2. The physical environment optimizes concrete learning.
3. Academic skills are of fundamental importance.
4. Curriculum decisions are based on the child's best interests.

Circle the number that is appropriate:

0	1	2	3	4	5	6
Low		**Medium**			**High**	

FORM

D STIMULATING CREATIVE THINKING*†

1. *The teacher reinforces creativity in a variety of ways.*

The teacher

- acknowledges a child's responsibility for a given idea; makes it apparent that originality and expressivity are valued.
- helps children to understand that mistakes may be advantageous.
- communicates that work that is different should not be demeaned; validates an altered perspective.
- follows up on ideas that children contribute; gathers materials, if necessary.
- supports the idea that people can build on one another's ideas.
- is sensitive to the child's ownership of an idea; doesn't impose the teacher's solution on the child.
- recognizes that destroying something is often part of the creative production.
- understands that the process is important; accepts messiness and crude workmanship when they appear to be the natural consequences of creative involvement.
- is flexible in terms of time and schedule to accommodate meaningful activity.

Cite examples:

†This form relates to the operational characteristics described in Chapter 7.

2. *The teacher organizes and maintains the physical environment to promote creative activity.*

- Many examples of children's original work are in the room—representing a range of activities, not just the arts.
- Adult work of a stereotyped commercial nature does not dominate bulletin boards and room decorations. Children's work is an important part of decorative displays.
- Basic art and construction materials are readily available for spontaneous use (markers, glue, scissors, staplers, salvage).
- Novel items are introduced periodically along with basic materials. They may be used spontaneously as well as in conjunction with teacher initiated lessons.
- The teacher makes important materials available for projects children have initiated.
- The teacher allows children to use materials and equipment in ways that differ from how they were intended (within reasonable limits).
- The teacher allows children to move some materials from one area of the room to another (within reasonable limits).
- The teacher places materials in different places, or presents them in an altered or novel way to stimulate children when presenting activities and lessons.
- The physical environment is orderly and well organized. Materials are stored in logical ways, and children are expected to put things away, respect materials, and maintain the environment.
- The teacher understands the importance of the unexpected in the physical environment and charges the room with interesting pictures, objects, and arrangements that promote new ideas.

Cite examples:

3. *The teacher designs curriculum and motivates children to extend creative thinking.*

The teacher

- uses judgment in determining when to intervene in children's play and material use.
- is aware of developmental factors that influence cognition and designs lessons congruent with children's capabilities.
- recognizes that certain issues are central to young children developmentally and addresses these when planning curriculum.
- remains alert to what interests and concerns children; is sensitive to cultural differences and designs curriculum around things that matter to children, rather than to what interests the teacher.
- designs lessons that have creativity and self-expression as central objectives. These lessons are embedded within the entire curriculum, not just the arts.

Cite examples:

- The teacher demonstrates enthusiasm and vitality in stimulating children; models an appreciation of the unique and unexpected; employs fantasy and humor.
- uses a range of motivational techniques to stimulate imaginative thinking—slides, film, video; music and sound; stories; movement; and so on. Speech is not the only way the teacher motivates. The teacher uses heightened affect to stimulate expression.
- models the scientific approach to problem-solving by asking such questions as: "What would happen if . . . ?" The teacher helps children to raise questions and experiment by framing comments in strategic ways.
- uses metaphors and analogies to strengthen children's imaginative capacities; is aware of the power of analyzing similarities and differences and making comparisons.

- models skills and techniques; understands the differences between learning a technique and imitating adult-made products; understands that looking at others' work can challenge thinking and build concepts as long as children are not imitating that work in a mechanistic manner.
- shifts focus when children seem unresponsive or are drawn to an alternative direction.
- encourages an idea that is emerging in cases where a child may have difficulty in following through.
- observes carefully for the right moment to pose a question or dilemma; watches for cues that provide information about the child's intentions; honors the child's motives when extending thinking.
- provides a balance between lessons in which the teacher is central and those in which children can work independently; uses materials and environmental setups as forms of stimulation.
- within a given domain, such as art, considers such variables as change of size; spontaneity versus control; simplicity versus complexity; and so on, as ways of challenging and motivating.
- uses constraints and the elimination of certain expectations as a way of stimulating and challenging.

Cite examples:

Rank the classroom situation across all three criteria:

1. The teacher reinforces creativity in a variety of ways.
2. The teacher organizes and maintains the physical environment to promote creative activity.
3. The teacher designs curriculum and motivates children to extend creative thinking.

Circle the number that is appropriate:

0	1	2	3	4	5	6
Low			**Medium**			**High**

SOCIAL-EMOTIONAL ISSUES*†

Although cognition places limitations on children's capacities to comprehend social-emotional behavior with ease, the teacher recognizes the importance of developing understandings about this complex area in an ongoing way. Knowledge about one's own as well as others' behavior is a fundamental part of intellectual development. Teachers must engage in both spontaneous and planned experiences in this realm.

Part I
The teacher establishes a positive classroom atmosphere and builds an understanding of human behavior.

1. *The teacher models and encourages mutually respectful behavior; the teacher elicits caring and respectful behavior from children.*

The teacher

- interacts with children in a respectful manner, making it clear in everything the teacher says and does that each individual is valued; uses positive speech that does not diminish children's self-respect and encourages the same behaviors from children.
- identifies children's strengths and makes them apparent to others; builds positive understanding of individual special qualities or limitations.
- encourages children to be supportive and considerate of one another; listening and being attentive to others are reinforced.
- helps children to defend their own and others' ideas and convictions in a positive manner.

Cite examples:

†This form relates to the operational characteristics described in Chapter 9.

2. *The teacher helps children to understand how prosocial behavior contributes to work and productivity.*

The teacher

- builds understanding that a variety of points of view must be considered in accomplishing certain tasks (writing a play, building with blocks, taking turns, sharing tools).
- promotes understanding that people need support from one another in order to grow intellectually and work productively; builds positive attitudes toward the ways in which individuals learn and work.
- fosters the importance of individual contributions at the same time that consideration is given to the needs and well-being of the total classroom community; mutuality, group process, and identity are emphasized.

Cite examples:

3. *The teacher incorporates an understanding of social-emotional issues into the curriculum. The teacher introduces some basic understanding of psychology and how people behave.*

The teacher

- helps children to understand that emotions influence behavior, and that adults, as well as children, have strong feelings and emotional needs; encourages the expression of both positive and negative feelings in prosocial ways and provides opportunities for labeling and expressing emotions.
- designs planned curriculum experiences that deal directly with emotions and human behavior—subjects such as anger, jealousy, friendship, love, disappointment, possessiveness, and so on; deals with these in a substantive, not superficial, manner; identifies and teaches key concepts.
- designs curriculum experiences that strengthen understanding of the impact of culture on behavior, such as why people might like or reject certain foods, celebrate certain ideas and holidays, and so on; similarities and differences among people are explored.

Cite examples:

4. *The teacher encourages the development of friendship-making skills, recognizing their critical importance to the child's emotional and intellectual growth.*

The teacher explicitly addresses such issues as how to

- avoid and negotiate conflict.
- initiate contact and share ideas.
- express empathy and concern.
- build on the ideas of others.
- understand what causes others to reject.
- listen to and give feedback to others effectively.

Cite examples:

Part II

The teacher's management of the classroom reflects a cognitive perspective.

1. *The teacher emphasizes knowing and understanding as the basis for shaping children's behavior.*

The teacher

- explains the reasons for certain expectations.
- involves children in discussion about behavior and conflict.
- encourages children's problem-solving about problems, as contrasted to dictating what should occur.
- builds understanding about how some children have special needs in terms of handling behavior.
- helps children to understand that conflict is a natural part of human interaction.

Cite examples:

2. *The teacher involves children in the formation and use of rules.*

The teacher

- discusses why they are important and provides a structure for understanding them; reinforces their importance.
- encourages children's input in creating them.
- reinforces and sets firm expectations for following rules.

Cite examples:

3. *Children are encouraged to participate in thinking about appropriate and inappropriate behavior in a variety of ways, such as*

- labeling, describing, and analyzing behavior.
- problem-solving about the causes and repercussions of certain behaviors; considering multiple views about a conflict.
- taking responsibility for one's own behavior.

Cite examples:

4. *Although the teacher encourages autonomous behavior and children's participation in the process of maintaining a positive classroom climate, the teacher is not reluctant to assert authority in situations that warrant direct teacher intervention. The teacher provides a balance between facilitating understanding and setting necessary limits.*

- When reasons for certain behavioral expectations have been made clear repeatedly, the teacher stops negative behavior when it persists or is threatening to others. The teacher does not allow continuous analysis and discussion to obstruct making the environment safe and predictable.
- Although the teacher strives for fairness and consistency, he or she handles situations with respect for individual need and developmental level.

Cite examples:

5. *The teacher makes alterations in the environment and the program that provide clear boundaries for children, particularly those who have difficulty with impulsivity and interacting with others.*

- Such things as timers, turn-taking cards, and other concrete tools are present.
- Traffic patterns, room arrangement, signs, and scheduling devices reveal concern for reducing disruption.

Cite examples:

Rank the classroom situation across the two criteria:

1. The teacher establishes a positive classroom climate and builds an understanding of human behavior.
2. The teacher's management of the classroom reflects a cognitive perspective.

Circle the number that is appropriate:

0	1	2	3	4	5	6
Low			**Medium**			**High**

Summary

Teacher growth and change are positive factors and are essential components of developmentally based education. This chapter provides six observational forms that can be used to promote ongoing evaluation and development of programs for young children. The forms can be used to assess specific characteristics of developmentally appropriate programs. They are designed to assist in deepening understanding of developmental education and to serve as a guide for the implementation, modification, and amplification of the characteristics that indicate high-quality educational experience for young children (ages three to eight years).

Emphasized is the need to scrutinize the smallest of details, for herein lies the power of classroom observation. Also highlighted is the importance of observing in a systematic fashion. Forms A-1 and A-2 encourage a thoughtfully planned approach to understanding and observing the pervasive characteristics of the developmental model. Forms B through E are designed to aid in the systematic collection and analysis of data relating to challenging children intellectually, stimulating creativity, and incorporating social-emotional issues into curriculum and classroom management. Since the forms are so closely connected to the previous sections of the text, users of the forms are encouraged to refer to the sections in the text in which the respective characteristics are described in detail.

The forms are used in evaluating classrooms that purport to be developmentally appropriate—to determine strengths and weaknesses and to aid in the improvement of quality. The forms facilitate the identification of particular areas in which further development seems warranted, and together with the text provide guidelines for modifications. The forms can also serve as a way of stimulating parent involvement in their children's education and their understanding of educational practices; they can serve as an administrative tool for encouraging program development; and, most important, they can be used by teachers interested in studying teaching and learning in their own and in other classrooms. For educators at all levels of expertise, the process of systematically observing classrooms in action provides an intellectually stimulating professional experience.

Part Five: Questions for Discussion

1. Under what conditions would you use each of the following observational techniques?
   running record
   anecdotal record
   verbal vignettes
   time sampling
   event sampling
2. How can systematic observation be helpful to you as you work with children?
3. Explain the guidelines and provide examples for framing observational questions.
4. Describe what you would expect to see in a classroom that takes into account the fact that young children are egocentric emotionally and intellectually.

BOOKS FOR CHILDREN

Informational Books

AYLESWORTH, THOMAS G. (1982). *Science looks at mysterious monsters*. New York: Julian Messner.

HENWOOD, CHRIS. (1988). *Keeping minibeasts: Spiders*. New York: Franklin Watts.

KNOWLTON, MARYLEE, AND DAVID K. WRIGHT. (1988). *Children of the world: India*. Milwaukee: Gareth Stevens Publishing.

MACAULEY, DAVID. (1988). *The way things work*. Boston: Houghton Mifflin.

MCMILLAN, BRUCE. (1988). *Super super superwords*. New York: William Morrow.

PALLOTTA, JERRY. (1986). *The icky bug alphabet book*. Needham, MA: Charlesbridge Publishing.

PALLOTTA, JERRY. (1986). *The ocean*. Watertown, MA: Charlesbridge Publishing.

PALLOTTA, JERRY. (1989). *The bird*. Watertown, MA: Charlesbridge Publishing.

PRINGLE, LAURENCE. (1973). *Twist, wiggle and squirm: A book about earthworms*. New York: Thomas W. Crowell.

VAN LAAN, NANCY. (1987). *The big fat worm*. New York: Knopf.

WILKES, ANGELA. (1990). My *first nature book*. New York: Knopf.

Books to Stimulate Creative Thinking

AHLBERG, JANET, AND AHLBERG, ALLAN. (1987). *The clothes horse and other stories*. New York: Viking Penguin, Inc.

BAUER, CAROLINE FULLER. (1983). *This way to books: For librarians, teachers and parents: Hundreds of ideas and programs designed to get children and books together*. Bronx, New York: H. W. Wilson.

DE LARMINAT, MAX-HENRI. (1988). *Vassily Kandinsky: Sky blue*. New York: Harry Abrams, Inc.

FLEISCHMAN, PAUL. (1993). *Copier creations: Using copy machines to make decals, silhouettes, flip books, films, & much more*. New York: Harper-Collins.

GWYNNE, FRED. (1976). *A chocolate moose for dinner*. New York: Prentice-Hall.

Haddad, Helen R. (1981). *Potato printing*. New York: Thomas Crowell.
Hoban, Tana. (1992). *Look up, look down*. New York: Greenwillow Books.
Hoban, Tana. (1974). *Circles, triangles and squares*. New York: Macmillan.

Joan, Ann. (1987). *Reflections*. New York: Greenwillow Books.

Kruise, Carol Sue. (1987). *Those bloomin' books: A handbook for extending thinking skills*. Littleton, Colorado: Libraries Unlimited.

Lepscky, Ibi. (1984). *Pablo Picasso*. New York: Barron's Educational Series.

O'Neill, Mary. (1961). *Hailstones and halibut bones*. New York: Doubleday.

Reiss, John J. (1974). *Shapes*. New York: Bradbury Press, Inc.

Scheer, Julian. (1964). *Rain makes applesauce*. New York: Holiday House.
Supraner, Robyn. (1981). *Valentine's Day: Things to make and do*. Mahwah, NJ: Troll Associates.

Van Allsburg, Chris. (1981). *Jumanji*. Boston: Houghton Mifflin.
Van Allsburg, Chris. (1984). *The mysteries of Harris Burdick*. Boston: Houghton Mifflin.

APPENDIX B BIBLIOGRAPHY OF CHILDREN'S BOOKS: A COGNITIVE APPROACH TO SOCIAL-EMOTIONAL ISSUES

The following book list with accompanying annotations represents excerpts from a teacher's literature file. The books are consistent with whole language philosophy and deal with social-emotional issues. The authors express appreciation to Holly Carroll, a literacy center teacher in Cambridge, Massachusetts, for permission to reprint these excerpts.

ADA, ALMA FLOR. (1991). *Gold coin*. New York: MacMillan.
Central American folktale told using the voices of the culture to depict the struggle to develop a sense of self in the face of obstacles. Compare to Frances Hodgson Burnett's *The Secret Garden*. This book worked wonderfully as a literature extension. Watch the development of the character Juan through the vivid illustrations and story development.

ATKINSON, MARY. (1990). *Maria Teresa*. Durham, NC: Lollipop Power Books, Carolina Wren Press.
Lollipop Power publishes nonsexist, nonracist books to counteract stereotypes children may encounter from other sources. The book covers a Mexican-American child's first day in a new school (there are no other Mexican-American children in her school or neighborhood); how to communicate and problem-solve discovering differences and similarities among us.

CARLE, ERIC. (1973). *Have you seen my cat?* Saxonville, MA: Picture Book Studio.
This gorgeous picture book with repetitive text has multicultural illustrations supportive of text, which are accurate and respectful of cultures represented. The book is particularly effective with ESL (English as a second language) learners because two lines of text are repeated in the story. Thus, children are able to read independently. The text lends itself easily to innovation (for example: Have you seen my pencil? book? hat?) and to inclusion of vocabulary from other cultures. As a follow-up (in geography), have children use maps and find countries from which the cats come.

JAMPOLSKY, GERALD G. (ed.). (1982). *Children as teachers of peace*. Written by children. Berkeley, CA: Celestia Arts.
Children from all over the world demand peace using their voices and drawings to help adults understand their vision of a world without war. It is very effective when working with children to use the very real works of other children as a starting place—especially good when working with children from El Salvador, Nicaragua, and Guatemala. Children's voices must be heard.

LIONNI, LEO. (1986). *It's mine!* New York: Alfred A. Knopf.
"Three selfish frogs quarrel over who owns their pond and island, until a storm makes them value the benefit of sharing." Milton, Rupert, and Lydia quarrel over who owns the air. Toad

can't stand the endless bickering. "You can't go on like this." Children experienced huddling together on the "toad," pretending it was a rock. They shared their fears and hopes. Next morning they played together. "Isn't it peaceful! Isn't it beautiful! You know what. It's ours. A fable."

LYON, GEORGE ELLA. (1989). *Together.* New York: Orchard Books.
This beautifully illustrated story is about friendship between two little girls from two different cultures. The use of rhyme supports the story development. Related to a friendship theme, the book lends itself wonderfully to text innovation and self-study of similarities and differences between cultures and the strength of love and friendship as bonds between cultures.

MOST, BERNARD. (1990). *The cow that went oink.* San Diego: Harcourt Brace Jovanovich.
Children delight as the cow "acquires language," learning how to "moo" and retain the ability to "oink" and communicate with a friend, the pig. This wonderful story can serve as a model to help develop sensitivity to second language learners. A perfect story to use as a literature extension; develop your own ending to this story. In Holly's version, all the animals become "multilingual" and are able to understand one another.

PAULUS, TRINA. (1972). *Hope for the flowers.* New York: Paulist Press.
Kindergarten children and graduate students anxiously await the reading of the next chapter to see how two caterpillars, Stripe and Yellow, make decisions regarding their lives and their world.

REDHEAD, JANET SLATER. (1990). *The turkey gobbling frog show.* Austin, TX: Steck-Vaughn.
This book uses repetitive text combined with illustrations supportive of text. The book helps children learn that everybody does something well, and nobody really wins using competition.

WOOD, AUDREY. (1982). *Quick as a cricket.* New York: Child's Play (International) Ltd.
Children's sense of self is developed as gorgeous illustrations are combined with one line of text a page using rhyme and reason, and leading to a surprise ending. This book is effective to use with second language learners to help vocabulary development. First language learners may rewrite the story to explore use of metaphors and adjectives in their native language.

APPENDIX C BOOKS FOR BIBLIOTHERAPY

Bibliotherapy is one approach to helping children address social-emotional issues. In the process of bibliotherapy, teachers help children identify books related to problems they are facing. The children are encouraged to identify with the characters in the book and to develop empathy for the characters' situations. Through this process the children experience emotional release. As they discuss the story, the children acquire insight into possible solutions to their problem. Often this process requires reading several books about a particular problem. For further information about bibliotherapy consult *Bibliotherapy: The Right Book at the Right Time* by Claudia and Charles Cornett (1980), Phi Delta Kappan Fastback, Bloomington, IN. The following books are useful for bibliotherapy.

ALEXANDER, MARTHA. (1981). *Move over, Twerp*. New York: The Dial Press.
Jeffrey goes to school on the school bus, but he is very unhappy about this. The big boys always force him to change his seat. Jeffrey receives all kinds of suggestions for coping with his problem, but he is unable to carry out any of them. Finally Jeffrey gets an idea himself. He paints a picture of a super creature on his tee shirt and then feels better able to stand up to the big boys.

AMOSS, BERTHE. (1972). *The very worst thing*. New York: Parents' Magazine Press.
A story about good things, scary things, and the worst thing of all—facing the first day of school. The story, with its humorous flair, captures the feeling of fear people experience when faced with new encounters.

BROWN, MARC. (1976). *Arthur's nose*. Boston: Little, Brown.
Arthur is a combination person–animal figure who doesn't like his nose. His nose is the same nose as that of other members of his family, but his nose makes him feel different from his friends and not at all happy. After trying several other noses, Arthur decides to keep his original nose. The book ends with a picture of the first grade, each person including the teacher with a different nose. On the opposite page are photos of each member of Arthur's family, each with the same nose as Arthur's: "There's a lot more to Arthur than his nose." Marc Brown is a teacher and illustrator. He lives in the Boston area.

CLEMENTS, ANDREW. (1988). *Big Al*. Saxonville, MA: Picture Book Studio.
Big Al is a big, ugly fish who has trouble making friends. In the story he tries unsuccessfully to hide his appearance. A humorous moment occurs when he covers himself with sand, but his sneeze gives his identity away. One day all the little fish get caught in a net. Big Al uses his strength to bite into the net and free the fish. Then Al gets caught in the net. His new friends are sad. He frees himself: "And now there is one huge, puffy, scary fish in the sea

who has more friends than any one else." A beautifully illustrated book, with batik illustrations full of emotion, its drawings reflect loneliness and the qualities that make friendship real. The book was illustrated by Yoshi.

ETS, MARIE HALL. (1968). *Talking without words (I can. Can you?)* New York: The Viking Press.
An interesting approach to helping children pay attention to body language. The book focuses on the ideas, messages, and moods that people and animals are able to convey without using words. Ets is both the author and the illustrator.

HEIDE, FLORENCE PARY, AND JUDITH HEIDE GILLILAND. (1990). *The day of Ahmed's secret*. New York: Lothrop, Lee & Shepard Books.
This beautiful story takes place in Egypt. A story of universal appeal, it focuses on work, growth, and change. Ahmed has a secret that he keeps to himself all day as he carries out the tasks expected of him. Ahmed is proud of his strength and his ability to work and help his family. Ahmed reflects on how he has grown strong enough to carry the heavy canisters and has learned well from his father how to carry out the responsibility that is now his. He reflects on how he has learned to write his name—the secret he shares with his family at the end of the day.

KEATS, EZRA JACK. (1969). *Goggles*. New York: Macmillan.
A realistic story of the life of a small child in a big city. It is a scary story about Peter, his friend Archie, and dog Willie. Peter finds a pair of lensless motorcycle goggles. He and his friend are on their way to sit on Archie's steps to enjoy their treasure. They encounter some big boys who demand the goggles. The story shows how Peter and Archie use their resources to trick the big boys and manage to retain the goggles. Keats is the author and illustrator.

SENDAK, MAURICE. (1963). *Where the wild things are*. New York: Harper & Row.
Max got into mischief. His mother called him a wild thing. He was punished by being sent to his room. Max uses his imagination to become king of the wild things in his imaginary forest and then longs to be home where someone loves him best of all.

SIMON, NORMA. (1974). *I was so mad!* Chicago, IL: Albert Whitman.
From the author's notes about the book: "Some feelings like love and loyalty are readily acknowledged, but emotions like anger, jealousy and frustration may be repressed or ignored." The book pictures anger and describes children's outer and inner struggles as they try to control their feelings. The illustrator is Dora Leder.

WABER, BERNARD. (1972). *Ira sleeps over*. Boston: Houghton Mifflin.
Ira is invited to a friend's house. His sister asked if he was going to take his teddy bear along. He said that would be too babyish. During the day the two boys played all kind of big boy games—wrestling, magic tricks, dominoes, ghost stories—but at night Ira couldn't sleep without his teddy bear. When he realizes that his friend also sleeps with his favorite teddy, Ira goes home and returns with Rah-Rah.

APPENDIX D

PROGRAMS DESIGNED TO STIMULATE SOCIAL PROBLEM SOLVING

The programs listed here are presented as illustrations of the wide range of curriculum guides that focus on helping children understand feelings, emotions, and interpersonal interactions. These programs differ widely in their approach to this topic—some do, and some do not, have a constructivist orientation. A cognitive-developmental teacher may find these programs useful and could adapt them so that they are consistent with the constructivist philosophy.

"Anti-Bias Curriculum: Tools for Empowering Young Children"

Louise Derman-Sparks and the A.B.C. Task Force, Washington, DC: National Association for the Education of Young Children. (1989).

Includes interesting information about children's development and curriculum suggestions for helping children learn about racial and cultural similarities and differences, disabilities, and gender identity.

"As I Am"

Ingrid Chalufour, Catherine Bell, Jane Weil, Amanda Dyer, and Barbara Peppey, Action Opportunities, Inc., P.O. Box 563, Ellsworth, Maine 04605.

Developed under a grant from the Administration for Children, Youth and Families, U.S. Department of Health and Human Services, Head Start Bureau, DDHS Publication No (OHDS) 88-31542, 1988.

A mental health curriculum focusing on feelings, relating, and thinking. Designed to increase the mental health skills of Head Start teachers. Contains specific ideas appropriate for use with young children.

"DUSO–1(R): Developing Understanding of Self and Others"

Don Dinkmeyer and Don Dinkmeyer, Jr., American Guidance Service, Circle Pines, Minnesota 55024 (1982).

Consists of stories, songs, puppet discussions, and dramatic play activities designed to enhance children's understanding of themselves and help them be resourceful in handling problems.

"Kids and Company: Together for Safety"

Adam Walsh Child Resource Center, Inc., National Center for Missing and Exploited Children, Washington, DC 20006 (1992).

A program for children grades K–6 that "provides children with skills, information, self-confidence and support which will enhance their self-esteem and help prevent abduction and abuse.

"I Can Problem Solve, An Interpersonal Cognitive Problem-Solving Program"

Three versions: Preschool; Kindergarten and Primary Grades; Intermediate Grades. Myrna B. Shure, Research Press, 2612 North Mattis Avenue, Champaign, Illinois 61821 (1992). Contains specific lessons, each with a teacher's script intended to provide a flexible guideline. Focuses on vocabulary and concept building, games, dialogues, and application of concepts in real-life situations.

"Project Charlie"

5701 Normandale Road, Edina, Minnesota 55424 (nd).

Designed to help families build children's self-esteem. Includes suggestions, activities, and discussion topics for parents and children.

"Puppet P.A.L.S.™: Play and Learn Storytime"

Janet Tubbs, Children's Resource Center, P.O. Box 8697, Scottsdale, AZ 85252-8697 (1991).

Consists of a family of puppets, a puppet stage, and scripts on topics such as lying, anger, jealousy, self-esteem, sibling rivalry, and fear of the dark.

"Reach Out to Schools: A Social Competency Program"

The Stone Center, Wellesley College, 106 Central Street, Wellesley, MA 02181-8268 (1987). Pamela Seigle, Project Director

Focuses on building strong relationships in classrooms, creating a cooperative classroom environment, and developing interpersonal problem-solving strategies. Includes a theoretical basis, a commitment to year-long instruction within the classroom setting, and an experiential training model for teachers.

"Second Step: A Violence Prevention Curriculum"

Committee for Children, 172 20th Avenue, Seattle, Washington 98122 (1989).

Includes activities for encouraging interpersonal cognitive problem solving, social skills training, management of anger, and assertiveness training.

"Smiling at Yourself: Educating Young Children About Stress and Self-esteem"

Allen N. Mendler, Network Publications, a division of ETR Associates, Santa Cruz, CA (1990).

Suggestions for teachers, parents, and other care providers of children to age ten. The book includes suggestions for parents and teachers and activities for children. Included is a chapter on solving problems and getting along with others.

"What If I Couldn't . . . ?"

Children's Museum of Boston, 300 Museum Wharf, Boston, MA (1979).

Includes tapes, film strips, booklets, photographs for picture study, and a puppet and script. Focuses on helping children understand disabilities. Included is a section on children who have difficulty managing their feelings.

Accommodation: A Piagetian term that refers to adapting cognitive structures to take into account new information. One of the two complementary organizational processes in cognition—the other being assimilation.

Acquisition-learning hypothesis: A theory that describes an informal, natural process of language learning, as contrasted with the notion that language proficiency develops through the structured learning of grammar rules. According to the acquisition-learning hypothesis, children acquire rather than learn first and second languages.

Affective filter hypothesis: A theory that posits that attitudes of the learner—motivation, self-concept, and anxiety—act to inhibit or enhance experiences necessary for language acquisition.

Anecdotal recording: An observational technique in which a significant event is recorded in abbreviated, summative form.

Apprenticeship: The experience of working alongside someone who has knowledge and competence beyond one's own.

Approximation: A term used in a cognitive-developmental theory to describe the process of learning through modeling. It recognizes children's efforts to match the model even when these efforts fail to come up to the standard of the ultimately desired behavior.

Arbitrary social learning: Information established by the culture and transmitted directly, as contrasted with knowledge or understanding constructed by the individual. For example, names of objects, identification of holidays, customs, skills, and practices of etiquette are forms of social learning.

Assimilation: A Piagetian term that refers to the taking in of new information by means of existing cognitive structures. One of the two complementary, organizational processes in cognition—the other being accommodation.

Attribution theory: Describes the source of influence that one believes controls his or her actions and the actions of others.

Authentic assessment: A process of gathering data regarding children's progress by documenting performance in real-life, meaningful situations, rather than using test-like situations. Includes the processes by which learning takes place, and thus is useful in guiding progress. It could include naturalistic observation.

Autonomy versus shame and doubt: The second developmental stage in Erikson's psychosocial theory that has its roots in the toddler and early preschool period, a time when children are developing their sense of self and need to assert their own will.

Baric tablets: A sensorial material used in Montessori programs to encourage development of children's ability to distinguish among same size tablets of differing weights.

Big books: Both commercially published and child/teacher authored books that are large enough so that a group of children can see the print and participate in shared reading.

Clinical interview: A research method that involves asking open-ended questions in a controlled situation.

Cognitive conflict: A stimulus that challenges the individual's thinking and presents a contradiction or a contest of ideas. In order for cognitive conflict to exist, the learner must be engaged in the situation, disturbed by an aspect of it that is not understood, and/or be interested in figuring it out. Thus, a situation might present cognitive conflict for one individual and not for another. A term used by Kohlberg and Mayer (1972).

Cognitive-developmental: A term used to describe developmental education, particularly as it is related to theories of cognitive psychology. One of the three categories of ideology as defined by Kohlberg and Mayer (1972)—the other two being cultural transmission and romanticism.

Cognitive-developmental theory: A theory that explains how the individual's thinking shifts and changes as part of the developmental process.

Concrete operational stage: A Piagetian term that describes a period of cognitive development characterized by an ability to conserve—that is, to act on more than one variable at a time; to engage in reversible thinking, as long as the thinking is linked to tangible objects.

Constructivism: A particular approach to developmental education that emphasizes the processes of cognitive or intellectual growth as articulated by Piaget and other cognitive psychologists. It describes a way of learning in which the child actively engages with the environment and builds his or her own knowledge and understanding. The teacher's interactions with the children, as well as the setup of the physical environment, play a strategic role.

Creativity: A way of thinking that involves reorganizing, reinventing, and transforming ideas.

Cuisenaire rods: A manipulative math material consisting of many wooden color-coded pieces of different sizes representing units one to ten. They are useful in helping children make mathematical concepts concrete.

Cultural transmission: An educational approach characterized by information being taught and transmitted didactically from the teacher to the learner. One of the three categories of educational ideology as defined by Kohlberg and Mayer (1972)—the other two being the cognitive-developmental approach and romanticism.

Decenter: To view a situation from differing perspectives, especially perspectives other than one's own.

Developmental education: A generic term that refers to a wide range of child-centered programs emphasizing play, concrete learning, and active participation on the part of the child and experiences related to children's interests. The curriculum is matched to each individual child's level of understanding.

Dialectic: Debate and discourse around competing ideas. In Vygotskian theory the term refers to discussion that takes place between a learner and an adult or more knowledgeable peer that provides a vehicle for learning to take place.

Direct teaching model: An orientation toward instruction characterized by transmitting knowledge in a didactic manner and teaching academic skills in an isolated rather than an integrated way. In early childhood, this orientation is associated with Bereiter and Englemann and the Distar curriculum.

Disequilibrium: A Piagetian term indicating an uncomfortable cognitive state that occurs when an individual perceives a problem or an inconsistency and is challenged to address it.

Early childhood education: In this text refers to programs serving children ages three to eight, preschool through third grade. In some cases it also includes programs for children from birth to age three.

Egocentricity: A Piagetian term describing tendencies at the preoperational level (and at the beginning levels of formal operational thinking), in which an individual is able to see things only from his or her own point of view. The term should not be confused with selfishness.

Equilibrium: A Piagetian concept referring to a state of balance that occurs after a conflict about a set of ideas has been worked on and resolved. A term often used synonymously with *homeostasis*.

Event sampling: An observational technique used for gathering information about situations involving a particular behavior, such as shyness, aggression, or cooperation.

Formal operational stage: A Piagetian term referring to the period of cognitive development in which an individual is capable of hypothetical reasoning and abstract thought.

Genetic epistemologist: One who studies the developmental processes associated with the acquisition of knowledge and understanding. A term associated with Jean Piaget.

Geoboards: A manipulative math material consisting of a square board with evenly spaced pegs or nails. Used with elastic bands, allowing children to create forms and explore geometric concepts.

Goodness-of-fit: A term used by Thomas and Chess to indicate the compatibility of temperaments between child and adult.

Head Start: A federally funded preschool program that originated in the 1960s. Provides comprehensive services to young children and their families.

Heteronomy: Being governed by an authority, thereby subordinating one's own thinking to that of others. The opposite of *autonomy.*

Homeostasis: A feeling of being at ease after having achieved a physiological state of balance. Often used synonymously with *equilibrium* to describe the resolution of a cognitive conflict.

Inclusionary philosophy: An educational perspective embodying the idea that children with special needs can contribute and benefit from education in a regular education classroom. Develops realistic self-concepts and focuses on competence and mastery rather than on disabilities. Represents acceptance of the idea that every person is a composite of both strengths and weaknesses.

Industry versus inferiority: The fourth stage of Erikson's psychosocial development theory characteristic of the school-age period, in which mastery of skills is of particular importance.

Initiative versus guilt: The third stage of Erikson's psychosocial development theory characteristic of the preschool period, when exploring, investigating and asserting oneself are of key importance.

Inner speech: Language children use to direct their own behavior. Piaget viewed this as evidence of cognitive immaturity. Vygotsky saw it as the third stage in children's speech development, following the social and egocentric stages, and viewed it as the basis for higher-level thinking.

Input hypothesis: A term used to explain language development, particularly second language learning, which stresses the role of verbal interactions in stimulating language growth.

Interdisciplinary teaching: An approach to curriculum that draws from various disciplines. It often embeds the teaching of skills within the subject being explored.

Intuitive stage: The second substage of preoperational thinking, ages four to seven years, characterized by prelogical thought and the beginnings of concrete operational thinking. The first substage is the preconceptual period, ages two to four years.

Key characteristics: The attributes that reflect the essential components of a developmental program.

Language acquisition device (LAD): A part of the brain that enables human beings to learn language. An innate universal ability to understand and use grammar. A concept postulated by Noam Chomsky.

Language acquisition support system (LASS): The social scaffolding necessary to support language development of the individual within the social context. A term credited to Jerome Bruner.

Learned helplessness: An attitude an individual acquires through repeated experiences of being unable to influence his or her environment; a sense of incompetence and feeling ineffectual.

Locus of control: The individual's belief about whether or not he or she has control over critical circumstances that influence the consequences of one's own actions and well-being. Related to attribution theory.

Logico-mathematical knowledge: A Piagetian term that involves the understanding of relationships in the physical world—the ability to understand rules and to classify, compare, and recognize one-to-one correspondence.

Moral reasoning: The ability to think about right and wrong. According to Piagetian theory, moral reasoning is connected to the level of cognitive competence.

Natural order hypothesis: Second language acquisition follows the same pattern or natural order as first language.

Objective recording: An observational technique in which one documents precisely and explicitly the behavior being observed, free of bias and judgment.

Operational characteristics: Clusters of teaching strategies that enable the teacher to realize key values and objectives inherent in developmentally based programs. Specific elements explain how the various characteristics become realized in the classroom.

Perception-bound: A characteristic of preoperational thought in which the child's thinking ability is bound by what he or she processes through the senses.

Perspective-taking: The ability to view a situation from another's point of view, as well as understanding how others are feeling or thinking.

Phonetic analysis: A process for decoding words that involves focusing on the visual appearance of the letters and the sound the letter represents.

Physical knowledge: A Piagetian term referring to information about the nature of the physical world—for instance, that a wheel rolls, a magnet attracts metal objects, some objects sink in water and others float.

Preoperational stage: A Piagetian term referring to the period of cognitive development characterized by the ability to focus on only one idea at a time and an inability to see another's point of view (egocentricism).

Prepared environment: A Montessori term describing the precise way in which the directress sets up the classroom and the materials in order to provoke children's active exploration.

Preschool: Programs for care and education of children from birth to six years; includes nursery school, day care, child care, and Head Start programs.

Primary creativity: A term used by Abraham Maslow to refer to creative acts that are novel for the individual but not necessarily novel for the culture. Contrasted with secondary creativity.

Process writing: An educational approach that views writing as part of a comprehensive process of learning to read and write in an integrated way. Emphasizes the notion of conveying ideas freely, first in draft form; then, based on conferencing with adults and with peers, revising and editing subsequent drafts.

Project approach: An integrated approach to teaching and learning in which children participate in planning, implementing, and evaluating their experiences. Involves the study of one topic over an extended period of time. A term used by Katz and Chard (1989).

Project method: An approach to teaching based on interdisciplinary units and incorporating active participation on the part of the child. The aim is to help children understand their environment. The term was used by W. Kilpatrick in 1918.

Prosocial behavior: Acting in a way that furthers the well-being and smooth functioning of interpersonal relationships—for example, cooperating, suggesting ideas, and using appropriate conflict resolution strategies.

Psychodynamic theory: A theoretical framework that has its origin in Freud's psychoanalytic perspective.

Psychosocial theory: An orientation within the psychodynamic framework that views social-emotional development as a progressive process, epitomized by Erik Erikson and his followers. It explains growth from the perspective of intrapersonal and interpersonal development.

Reading Recovery: A program that provides an intervention between kindergarten and first grade for children at risk of failure in literacy development.

Reggio Emilia: A city in northern Italy that has established a model for high-quality early childhood programs for children from infancy through six years. The approach includes a commitment to the observational process, a high level of parent and community involvement, teaming among staff members, and careful attention to the documentation process.

Romanticism: One of the three categories of educational ideology as defined by Kohlberg and Mayer (1972)—the others being the cultural transmission and cognitive-developmental approaches. Values a warm, nurturant environment, a minimum of adult intervention, and motivation for learning emanating from the child.

Running record: An observational technique for gathering data. A clear, written description of what occurred, described in a chronological manner.

Scaffolding: The framework or the support that adults provide for children's learning. Used often in connection with language learning and with the concept of apprenticeships.

Secondary creativity: A term used by Abraham Maslow to refer to acts that are boldly inventive; acts that are novel and unique and represent true innovation, as contrasted with primary creativity manifested in acts that are novel for the individual but not necessarily for the culture.

Self-concept: The individual's sense of self-worth, confidence, and perception of his or her own value.

Sensorimotor stage: A Piagetian term referring to the first stage of cognitive development, in which the child processes information through the senses and through his or her own actions on the environment. At the end of this period the child achieves object permanence and has a beginning sense of means-end relationships.

Situated learning: Learning that occurs in a meaningful (real-life) context.

Social cognition: The process of thinking about and understanding social-emotional issues.

Social knowledge: Knowledge about societal conventions transmitted from one generation to the next.

Sociocultural theory: Often referred to as sociohistoric theory. A theory of development postulated by Vygotsky, which explains development in terms of the interaction of the individual within the social or cultural milieu.

Subjective recording: Recording of data in which the observer interjects his or her own biases or judgments. Contrasted with objective recording.

Temperament: The emotional disposition characteristic of an individual. For example, the Thomas and Chess categories, which include easy, difficult, and slow-to-warm up.

Time sampling: An observational technique useful for gathering information regarding the frequency of occurrence of a particular behavior.

Trust versus mistrust: The first stage in Erikson's psychosocial theory. Characterizes the psychosocial conflict of infancy.

Unifix cubes: A manipulative math material consisting of multicolored, one-inch plastic cubes that can be fastened together. Can be used for measurement and exploration of a variety of math concepts.

Verbal vignettes: A compilation of spoken phrases, questions, statements, or comments gathered around a particular observational focus.

Whole language: A philosophy describing how children gain literacy skills by becoming immersed in authentic literacy situations.

Zone of proximal development: The difference between what a child can do independently and what the child can achieve with assistance. On a Venn diagram the intersection between what the child is able and unable to do. The intersection represents the potential at a particular time for development of new understandings.

REFERENCES

AACTE—AMERICAN ASSOCIATION FOR COLLEGES OF TEACHER EDUCATION. (1992, March–April). *Journal of Teacher Education*, 43(2), Theme: Cultural Diversity.

ALEXANDER, K. L., AND D. R. ENTWISTLE. (1988). Achievement in the first two years of school: Patterns and processes. *Monograph of the society for research in child development*, 53 (2, Serial No. 218).

ANDERSON, R. C. (1984). Some reflections on the acquisition of knowledge. *Educational Researcher*, 13(9), 5–10.

ARIAS, M. B., AND T. GRAY. (1977). *The importance of teacher and student language attitudes on achievement in bilingual/bicultural education*. Paper presented at AERA Convention, New York.

ASHER, STEVEN R., AND JOHN D. COIE. (1990). *Peer rejection in childhood*. New York: Cambridge University Press.

ASHER, STEVEN R., AND P. RENSHAW. (1981). Children without friends: Social knowledge and social skill training. In S. Asher and J. Gottman (Eds.), *The development of children's friendships*. New York: Cambridge University Press.

ASHER, STEVEN R., AND G. A. WILLIAMS. (1987). Helping children without friends in home and school. In *Children's social development: Information for teachers and parents*. Urbana, IL: ERIC, Clearinghouse on Elementary and Early Childhood Education.

ASHTON-WARNER, S. (1963). *Teacher*. New York: Simon & Schuster.

AU, K. H., AND C. JORDAN. (1981). Teaching reading to Hawaiian children: Finding a culturally appropriate solution. In H. Trueba and K. H. Au (Eds.), *Culture and the bilingual classroom: Studies in classroom ethnography*. Rowly, MA: Newbury House.

AYLESWORTH, THOMAS. (1982). *Science looks at mysterious monsters*. New York: Julian Messner.

BALABAN, N. (1987). *Starting school: From separation to independence*. New York: Columbia University, Teachers College Press.

BANKS, JAMES. (December 1991/January 1992). Multicultural education: For freedom's sake, *Educational Leadership*, 49,(4), 32–36.

BANKS, JAMES, AND CHERRY A. MCGEE BANKS. (1989). *Multicultural education: Issues and perspectives*. Needham, MA: Allyn & Bacon.

BARATTA-LORTON, MARY. (1976). *Mathematics their way*. Reading, MA: Addison-Wesley.

BARBOUR, NITA H., AND CAROL A. SEEFELDT. (1993). *Developmental continuity: Across preschool and the primary grades*. Wheaton, MD: Association for Childhood Education International.

BARKER, E.(ED. AND TRANS.). (1962). *The politics of Aristotle*. Oxford: Oxford University Press.

BARRON, FRANK L., AND DAVID M. HARRINGTON (1981). Creativity, intelligence and personality. In Mark R. Rosenzweig and Lyman W. Porter (Eds.), *Annual Review of Psychology*, Vol. 32 (pp. 439–476). Palo Alto, CA: Annual Reviews.

BAUCH, J. P.(ED.). (1988). *Early childhood education in the schools*. Washington, DC: National Education Association.

Bazar, J. W. (1976). *An exploration of the relationship of affect, awareness, empathy, and interaction strategic to nursery school children's competence*. Unpublished doctoral dissertation, University of California, Berkeley.

Beaty, J. (1992). *Preschool: Appropriate practices*. Orlando, FL: Harcourt Brace Jovanovich.

Beaty, Janice J. (1994). *Observing development of the young child*, 3rd ed. New York: Macmillan.

Bell, Donald, and R. M. Low. (1977). *Observing and recording children's behavior*. Richland, WA: Performance Associates.

Belsky, J. (1980). Child maltreatment: An ecological approach. *American Psychologist*, 35, pp. 320–335.

Bereiter, C., and S. Engelmann. (1966). *Teaching disadvantaged children in the preschool*. Englewood Cliffs, NJ: Prentice-Hall.

Bergen, D.(Ed.). (1987). *Play as a medium for learning*. Portsmouth, NH: Heinemann.

Berger, Eugenia Hepworth. (1991). *Parents as partners in education: The school and home working together*, 3rd ed. New York: Merrill.

Berk, Laura E. (1991). *Child development*, 2nd ed. Needham, MA: Allyn & Bacon.

Berkowitz, Marvin W. (Ed.). (1985). Peer conflict and psychological growth. *New Directions for Child Development*, No. 29. San Francisco: Jossey-Bass.

Berrueta-Clement, J., J. R. Schweinhart, W. S. Barnett, A. S. Epstein, and D. P. Weikart. (1984). *Changed lives: The effects of the Perry preschool program on youths through age 19*. Monographs of the High-Scope Educational Research Foundation, No. 8. Ypsilanti, MI: High/Scope Press.

Bianco, Margery Williams. (1985). The velveteen rabbit. New York: Knopf.

Biber, B., E. Shapiro, D. Wickens, and E. Glikeson. (1971). *Promoting cognitive growth: A developmental interaction point of view*. Washington, DC: National Association for the Education of Young Children.

Black, Allen, and Paul Ammon. (1992, November–December). A developmental-constructivist approach to teacher education. *Journal of Teacher Education*, 43(5), 323–335.

Bloom, Benjamin. (1963). *Stability and change in human characteristics*. New York: Wiley.

Blumenfeld, P. C., P. R. Printich, K. Wessles, and J. Meece. (1981, April). *Age and sex differences in the impact of classroom experiences on self-perceptions*. Paper presented at the Society for Research in Child Development meeting, Boston, MA.

Blumm, L. (1980). *Friendship, altruism and mortality*. London: Portledge.

Boehm, A. E., and R. A. Weinberg (1987). *The classroom observer: A guide for developing observation skills*. New York: Columbia University, Teachers College Press.

Bond, James T., and Jose Rosario. (1982). *Project developmental continuity: Final report—Executive summary*. Ypsilanti, MI: High/Scope Educational Research Foundation.

Bornlund, Dean C. (1989). *Communicative styles of Japanese and Americans: Images and realities*. Belmont, CA: Wadsworth.

Bottner, Barbara. (1980). *Mean Maxine*. New York: Pantheon Books.

Brandt, Ronald S. (1988). *Content of the curriculum*. Alexandria, VA: Association for Supervision and Curriculum Development.

Braun, Samuel J., and Esther P. Edwards. (1972). *History and theory of early childhood education*. Belmont, CA: Wadsworth.

Bredderman, T. (1983). Effects of activity-based elementary science on student outcomes: A quantitative synthesis. *Review of Educational Research*, 53, 499–518.

Bredekamp, S. (Ed.). (1987). *Developmentally appropriate practice in early childhood programs serving children from birth through age 8*. Washington, DC: National Association for the Education of Young Children.

Bredekamp, Sue, and Teresa Rosegrant. (Eds.). (1992). *Reaching potentials: Appropriate curriculum and assessment for young children*, Vol. 1. Washington, DC: National Association for the Education of Young Children.

Brenner, Avis. (1984). *Helping children cope with stress*. Lexington, MA: Lexington Books.

BRONFREBRENNER, URIE. (1979). *The ecology of human development*. Cambridge, MA: Harvard University Press.

BROWN, J. S., A. COLLINS, & O. DUIGUID. (1989). Situated cognition and culture of learning. *Educational Researcher*, 18(1), 32–42.

BROWN, MAC H., ROSEMARY ALTHOUSE, AND CAROL ANFIN. (1993, January). Guided dramatization: Fostering social development in children with disabilities. *Young Children*, 48(2), 68–71.

BRUFFEE, KENNETH A. (1987, March/April). The art of collaborative learning: Making the most of knowledgeable peers. *Change*, Robin Hood/University of Tennessee–Knoxville, 42–47.

BRUNER, JEROME. (1960). *The process of education*.Cambridge, MA: Harvard University Press.

BRUNER, JEROME S., ALISON JOLLY, AND KATHY SYLVA. (1976). *Play*. New York: Basic Books, 1976. (Quoting L. S. Vygotsky (1933). *Play and its role in the mental development of the child*, pp. 537–554.)

BUKATKO, DONATA, AND MARVIN DAEHLER. (1992). *Child development: A topical approach*. Boston, MA: Houghton Mifflin.

BULLOCK, JANIS R. (1993, September). Lonely children. *Young Children*, 48(6), 53–55.

BUMPASS, L. L. (1990). What's happening to the American family? Interactions between demographic and institutional change. *Demography*, 27, 483–498. (Quoted in Danuta Bukatko and Marvin W. Dachler, *Child development: A topical approach*. Boston, MA: Houghton Mifflin, 1992.)

BURGESS, B. (1986). *Native American learning styles, extracting learning styles for social/cultural diversity, studies of five American minorities*. In Teacher Corps, U.S. Office of Education, *Head Start social services training manual: Participant materials*, U.S. Department of Health and Human Services, p. 14.

BURK, DONNA, A. SNIDER, AND P. SYMONDS. (1988). *Box it or bag it mathematics*. Salem, OR: Math Learning Center.

BURTS, DIANE C., C. H. HART, R. CHARLESWORTH, S. HERNANDEZ, L. KIRK, AND J. MOSLEY. (1989, March). *A comparison of the frequencies of stress behaviors observed in kindergarten children in classrooms with developmentally appropriate vs. developmentally inappropriate instructional practices*. Paper presented at the annual meeting of the American Educational Research Association.

BUSS, ARNOLD H., AND ROBERT PLOMIN. (1975). *A temperament theory of personality development*. New York: Wiley.

BUSS, A. H., AND R. PLOMIN. (1987). Commentary. In H. H. Goldsmith, et al. (Eds.), Roundtable: What is temperament? Four approaches. *Child Development*, 58, 508–529.

BUZZELLI, C. A. (1992, September). Young children's moral understanding: Learning about right and wrong. *Young Children*, 47(6), 47–53.

CALKINS, L. M. (1986). *The art of teaching writing*. Portsmouth, NH: Heinemann.

CAMPIONE, J. C., A. L. BROWN, R. A. FERRARA, AND N. R. BRYANT. (1984). The zone of proximal development: Implications for individual differences and learning. In B. Rogoff and J. V. Wertsch (Eds.), *Children's learning in the zone of proximal development* (pp. 77–91). San Francisco: Jossey-Bass.

CARLSSON-PAIGE, N., AND D. LEVIN. (1985). *Helping children understand peace, war and the nuclear threat*. Washington, DC: National Association for the Education of Young Children.

CARLSSON-PAIGE, N., AND D. LEVIN. (1990). *Who's calling the shots? How to respond effectively to children's fascination with war play and war toys*. Philadelphia: New Society.

CARR, JACQUELYN B. (1991). *Communicating and relating*. Dubuque, IA: Wm. C. Brown.

CASE, R. (1985). *Intellectual development: A systematic reinterpretation*. New York: Academic Press.

CASSIDY, JUDE, AND STEVEN R. ASHER. (1992). Loneliness and peer relations in young children. *Child Development*, 63, 350–365.

CAUDILL, W., AND L. FROST. (1975). A comparison of maternal care and infant behaviour in Japanese-American, American and Japanese families. Urie Bronfenbrenner and M. A.

Mahoney (Eds.), *Influences on Human Development*, 2nd ed. (pp. 229–342). Hindsdale, IL: Drysden.

Cazden, C. (1988). *Classroom discourse*. Portsmouth, NH: Heinemann.

Chalufour, Ingrid, Catherine Bell, Jane Weil, Amanda Dyer, and Barbara Peppey. (1988). *As I am*. Ellsworth, ME: Action Opportunities; U.S. Department of Health and Human Services; Office of Human Development Services; Administration of Children, Youth and Families; Head Start Bureau.

Charlesworth, Rosalind, and Karen K. Lind. (1990). *Math and science for young children*. Albany, NY: Delmar.

Charlesworth, Rosalind, Jean Mosley, Diane Burts, Craig Hart, Lisa Kirk, and Sue Hernandez. (1988, July). *Checklist for rating developmentally appropriate practice in kindergarten classrooms*. Louisiana State University, Baton Rouge.

Charlesworth, Rosalind, and Deana J. Radeloff. (1991). *Experiences in math for young children*, 2nd ed. Albany, NY: Delmar.

Chess, Stella, and A. Thomas. (1977). Temperamental individuality from childhood to adolescence. *Journal of Child Psychiatry*, 16, 218–226.

Chess, Stella, and A. Thomas. (1984). *Origins and evolution of behavior disorders*. New York: Brunner/Mazel.

Chomsky, C. (1971). *Invented spelling in the open classroom*. Unpublished manuscript. Cambridge, MA: Harvard Graduate School of Education.

Chomsky, C. (1971, March). Write first, read later. *Childhood Education*.

Chukovsky, Kornei. (1968). *From two to five*. Berkeley: University of California Press.

Clarke-Stewart, A. (1984). Day care: A new context for research and development. In M. Perlmutter (Ed.), *Parent-child interaction and parent-child relations in child development: The Minnesota symposia on child psychology*, Vol. 17 (pp. 61–100). Hillsdale, NJ: Erlbaum.

Clay, Marie. (1991). *Becoming literate: The construction of inner control*. Portsmouth, NH: Heinemann Press.

Cleverly, J. (1987). *Visions of childhood: Influential models from Locke to Spock*, revised ed. New York: Columbia University, Teachers College Press.

Cohen, D. H., and V. Stern, with N. Balaban. (1985). *Recording and observing the behavior of young children*, 3rd ed. New York: Columbia University, Teachers College Press.

Cohen, E. G., and E. DeAuila. (1983). *Learning to think in math and science: Improving local education for minority children*. Final report of the Walter S. Johnson Foundation. Stanford, CA: School of Education, Stanford University.

Cole, Michael. (1985). The zone of proximal development: Where culture and cognition create each other. In James V. Wertsch (Ed.), *Culture, communication, and cognition: Vygotskian perspectives*. New York: Cambridge University Press.

Collins, Allan, John Seely Brown, and Susan E. Newman. (1989). Cognitive apprenticeships: Teaching the craft of reading, writing, and mathematics. In Lauren B. Resnick (Ed.), *Knowing, learning, and instruction: Essays in honor of Robert Glaser*. Hillsdale, NJ: Lawrence Erlbaum Associates.

Condon, John. (1991). So near the United States: Notes on communication between Mexicans and North Americans. In Larry Samovar and Richard E. Porter (Eds.), *Intercultural communication: A reader*. Belmont, CA: Wadsworth.

Confrey, J. (1991, November). Steering a course between Vygotsky and Piaget. *Educational Researcher*, 20(8), 28–32.

Connecticut State Department of Education. (1988). *A guide for program development for kindergarten: Parts I and II*. Hartford, CT: State Department of Education.

Cornett, Claudia E., and Charles F. Cornett. (1980). *Bibliotherapy: The right book at the right time*. Bloomington, IN: Phi Delta Kappan Fastback.

Corsaro, W. A. (1985). *Friendship and peer culture in the early years*. Norwood, NJ: Ablex.

COWLEY, JOY. (1984). *Greedy cat*. Wellington, New Zealand: Department of Education, School Publications Branch.

CRISPEN, MARIE. (n.d.). *Conditions for learning*. Handout distributed at the New England Kindergarten Conference, Lesley College, Cambridge, MA.

CURRIE, J. R. (1988). Effect in the schools: A return to the most basic of basics. *Childhood Education*, 65(27), 83–87.

DACEY, JOHN. (1989). Discriminating characteristics of the families of highly creative adolescents. *The Journal of Creative Behavior*, 24(4), 263–271.

DACEY, JOHN, AND JOHN TRAVERS. (1991). *Human development across the lifespan*. Dubuque, IA: Wm C. Brown.

DAIUTE, COLETTE. (1989, February). Play as thought: Thinking strategies of young writers. *Harvard Educational Review*, 59, (1), 1–23.

DAMON, WILLIAM. (1977). *The social world of the child*. San Francisco: Jossey-Bass.

DAMON, WILLIAM. (1988). *The moral child: Nurturing children's natural moral growth*. New York: Free Press.

DAY, BARBARA. (1989). *Early childhood education: Creative learning activities*, 3rd ed. New York: Macmillan.

DAY, BARBARA, AND KAY DRAKE. (1983). *Early childhood education: Curriculum, organization and classroom management*. Washington, DC: Association for Supervision and Curriculum Development.

DELPIT, LISA D. (1986). Skills and other dilemmas of a progressive black educator. *Harvard Educational Review*, 56(4), 379–385.

DELPIT, LISA D. (1988, August). The silenced dialogue: Power and pedagogy in educating other people's children. *Harvard Educational Review*, Vol. 58, No. 3, pp. 280–298.

DENNISON, G. (1969). *The lives of children*. New York: Random House.

DERMAN-SPARKS, LOUISE, AND THE A.B.C. TASK FORCE. (1989). *Anti-bias curriculum: Tools for empowering young children*. Washington, DC: National Association for the Education of Young Children.

DEVRIES, RHETA, AND LAWRENCE KOHLBERG. (1990). *Constructivist early education: Overview and comparisons with other programs*. Washington, DC: National Association for the Education of Young Children. (Originally published as *Programs of early education: The constructivist view* (1987), New York: Longman.)

DEWEY, JOHN. (1897). My pedagogic creed. *The School Journal*. (Quoted in Braun and Edwards (1972), *History and theory of early childhood education*, Belmont, CA: Wadsworth, p. 107.)

DEWEY, JOHN. (1938). *Experience and education*. New York: Macmillan.

DIMIDJIAN, VICTORIA J. (1989). *Early childhood at risk: Actions and advocates for young children*. Washington, DC: National Education Association.

DIMIDJIAN, VICTORIA J. (1992). *Play's place in public education for young children*. Washington, DC: National Education Association.

DISESSA, A. (1982). Unlearning Aristotelian physics: A study of knowledge-based learning. *Cognitive Science*, 6, 37–75.

DOLE, J. A., AND D. S. NIEDERHAUSER. (1991, April). *The use of reading in conceptual change*. Paper presented at the meeting of the American Educational Research Association, Chicago, IL.

DOWNEY, G., AND E. WALKER. (1989). Social cognition and adjustment in children at risk for psychopathology. *Developmental Psychology*, 25, pp. 835–848.

DUCKWORTH, E. (1987). *The having of wonderful ideas and other essays on teaching and learning*. New York: Teachers College Press, Columbia University.

DULAY, H., AND M. BURT (1977). Remarks on creativity in language acquisition. In M. Burt, H. Dulay, and M. Finnochiaro (Eds.), *Viewpoints on English as a second language*, (pp. 95–126). New York: Regents.

Dunn, Judy. (1988). *The beginnings of social understanding*. Cambridge, MA: Harvard University Press.

Edmunds, L. (1962). *Rudolph Steiner education: The Waldorf impulse*. London: Rudolph Steiner Press.

Education Development Center. (1971). *Elementary Science Study (ESS)*. New York: McGraw-Hill.

Edwards, Carolyn P., and Lella Gandini. (1989, May). Teachers' expectations about the timing of developmental skills: A cross-cultural study. *Young Children*, 15–19.

Edwards, Carolyn P., Lella Gandini, and George Forman (Eds.). (1993). *The hundred languages of children: The Reggio Emilia approach to early childhood education*. Norwood, NJ: Ablex.

Edwards, Carolyn Pope, with Patricia Ramsey. (1986). *Promoting social and moral development in young children: Creative approaches for the classroom*. New York: Columbia University, Teachers College Press.

Edwards, Tryon. (1955). *The new dictionary of thoughts*. New York: Standard.

Elkind, D. (1967). Piaget and Montessori. *Harvard Educational Review*, 37 (4), pp. 535–545.

Elkind, D. (1976). *Child development and education*. New York: Oxford University Press.

Elkind, D. (1981). *The hurried child: Growing up too fast*. Menlo Park, CA: Addison-Wesley.

Elkind, D. (1987). *Miseducation: Preschoolers at risk*. New York: Alfred A. Knopf.

Elkind, D. (Ed.). (1991). *Perspectives on early childhood education*. Washington, DC: National Education Association Early Childhood Series.

Elkind, David. (1986, May). Formal education and early childhood education: An essential difference. *Phi Delta Kappan*.

Engel, Brenda. (1991). *Evaluation study: Longfellow school literacy project*. Cambridge, MA: Lesley College Graduate School.

Engelmann, S., and E. Bruner. (1969). *Distar reading: An instructional system*. Chicago: Research Associates.

ERIC/EECE Bulletin on Children's Education and Peer Development. *Children's peer relationships*, Vol. 18, No. 3. Urbana, IL: ERIC Clearinghouse on Elementary and Early Childhood Education.

Erikson, Erik. (1963). *Childhood and society*, 2nd ed. New York: Norton.

Erikson, Erik. (1977). *Toys and reasons*. New York: Norton.

Essa, Eva. (1992). *Introduction to early childhood education*. Albany, NY: Delmar.

Evans, Ellis D. (1975). *Contemporary influences in early childhood education*. New York: Holt, Rinehart & Winston.

Farnham-Diggory, Sylvia. (1990). *Schooling*. Cambridge, MA: Harvard University Press.

Featherstone, Helen. (1985). Preschool: It does make a difference. *The Harvard Education Letter*, Cambridge, MA.

Fein, Sylvia. (1984). *Heidi's horse*. Pleasant Hill, CA: Exelrod Press.

Fein, Sylvia. (1993). *First drawings: Genesis of visual thinking*. Pleasant Hill, CA: Exelrod Press.

Feinburg, S. (1977). Conceptual content and spatial characteristics in boys' and girls' drawings of fighting and helping. *Studies in Art Education*, Vol. 18, No. 2.

Feldman, David Henry. (1986). *Nature's gambit: Child prodigies and the development of human potential*. New York: Basic Books.

Fincham, F. D., and K. M. Cain. (1985). *The role of attributions in learned helplessness*. Paper presented to the biennial meeting of the Society for Research in Child Development, Toronto, Canada.

Fischer, John. (1967, April). Rapport, the basic ingredient for teaching. *NEA Journal*, 56 (4), 33.

Fischer, K. W. (1980). A theory of cognitive development: The control and construction of a hierarchy of skills, *Psychological Review*, 87, 477–531.

Fisher, Bobbi. (1991). *Joyful learning: A whole language kindergarten*, Portsmouth, NH: Heinemann.

FISKE, EDWARD B. (1986, April 13). Early schooling is now the rage. *New York Times*.

FLAVELL, J. (1985a). *Child development: Individual, family and society*. St. Paul, MN: West Publishing.

FLAVELL, J. (1985b). *Cognitive development*, 2nd ed. Englewood Cliffs, NJ: Prentice-Hall.

FOGEL, ALAN, AND GAIL F. MELSON. (1988). *Child development: Individual, family and society*. St. Paul, MN: West.

FORMAN, GEORGE. (1989). *Viewer's guide to the exhibit The hundred languages of children*, School of Education, University of Massachusetts, Amherst.

FORMAN, GEORGE. (1990). Lessons from Reggio Emilia. *The Constructivist*, Vol. 5, No. 2.

FORMAN, GEORGE, AND FLEET HILL. (1980). *Constructivist play: Applying Piaget in the preschool*. Pacific Grove, CA: Brooks/Cole.

FORMAN, GEORGE, AND DAVID S. KUSCHNER. (1983). *The child's construction of knowledge: Piaget for teaching children*. Washington, DC: National Association for the Education of Young Children.

FORMAN, GEORGE, AND PETER B. PUFALL. (1983). *Constructivism in a computer age*. Hillsdale, NJ: Erlbaum.

FOSNOT, CATHERINE TWOMEY. (1989). *Enquiring teachers, enquiring learners*. New York: Columbia University, Teachers College Press.

FOX, MEM. (1987). *Teaching drama to young children*. Portsmouth, NH: Heinemann.

FRAIBERG, SELMA H. (1959). *The magic years*. New York: Scribner.

FREEDMAN, D. G., AND H. FREEDMAN. (1969). Behavioural differences between Chinese-American and European-American newborns. *Nature*, 224–229.

FREUD, S. (1964/1938). *An outline of psychoanalysis*, Standard Edition of the Works of Sigmund Freud, Vol. XIII. London: Hogarth Press.

FREUD, S. (1965/1933). *New introductory lectures on psychoanalysis*. New York: Norton.

FROEBEL, F. (1887). *The education of man*. New York: Appleton.

FROSCHL, M., AND B. SPRUNG. (1983). Providing an anti-handicappist early childhood environment. *Interracial Books for Children Bulletin*, 14(7–8).

FURTH, HANS. (1970). *Piaget for teachers*. Englewood Cliffs, NJ: Prentice-Hall.

GALLAS, KAREN. (1991). Arts as epistemology: Enabling children to know what they know. *Harvard Educational Review*, 61 (1), 40–50.

GANDINI, LELLA. (1991, March/April). Not just anywhere: Making child care centers into particular places. *Child Care Information Exchange*, 78, 5–9.

GANDINI, LELLA, AND CAROLYN POPE EDWARDS. (1988). *Early childhood integration of the visual arts*, World Council for the Gifted and Talented. Vol. V, No. 2. Monroe, NY: Trillium Press.

GANNON, S., AND S. J. KORN. (1983). Temperament, cultural variation and behavior disorder in preschool children. *Child Psychiatry and Human Development*, 30, 159–170.

GARDNER, HOWARD. (1983). *Frames of mind: The theory of multiple intelligences*. New York: Basic Books.

GARDNER, HOWARD. (1988, January 27). Getting smart about I. Q. *Education Week*, 7(18).

GARDNER, HOWARD. (1991). *The unschooled mind: How children think and how schools should teach*. New York: Basic Books.

GENISHI, CELIA (ED.). (1992). *Ways of assessing children and curriculum: Stories of early childhood practice*. New York: Columbia University.

GESELL, ARNOLD. (1926). *The mental growth of the preschool child*. New York: Macmillan.

GESELL, ARNOLD, FRANCES ILG, AND LOUISE ARMES. (1977). *The child from five to ten*. New York: Harper & Row.

GESTWICKI, CAROL. (1992). *Home, school, and community*. Charlotte, NC: Delmar.

GILLIGAN, C. (1982). *In a different voice: Psychological theory and women's development*. Cambridge, MA: Harvard University Press.

GILLIGAN, S. G. AND G. H. BOWER. (1984). Cognitive consequences of emotional arousal. In C. E. Izard, J. Kagan, and R. B. Zajarc (Eds.), *Emotions, cognition and behaviors*. Cambridge, MA: Cambridge University Press.

GINSBURG, HERBERT, AND SYLVIA OPPER. (1979). *Piaget's theory of intellectual development*, 2nd ed. Englewood Cliffs, NJ: Prentice-Hall.

GLAZER, JOAN I. (1991). *Literature for young children*, 3rd ed. New York: Merrill.

GLICKMAN, CARL. (1979, February). Problem: Declining achievement scores—Solution: Let them play! *Phi Delta Kappan*, pp. 454–455.

GRACE, CATHY, AND ELIZABETH F. SHORES. (1991). *The portfolio and its use: Developmentally appropriate assessment of young children*. Little Rock, AR: Southern Association for Children Under Six.

GUILFORD, J. P. (1967). *Intelligence, creativity,and their educational implications*. New York: Wiley.

HALE-BENSON, JANICE. (1982). *Black children: Their roots, culture, and learning styles*, rev. ed. Baltimore: Johns Hopkins University Press.

HARTSHORNE, H., AND M. MAY. (1928). *Studies in deceit*. New York: Macmillan.

HARTUP, W. W. (1983). The peer system. In E. M. Hetherington (Ed.), *Handbook of Child Psychology: Vol. 4. Socialization, personality, and social development*, 4th ed. New York: Wiley.

HARVARD EDUCATIONAL REVIEW. (1978). *Stage theories of cognitive and moral development: Criticisms and applications* (Reprint No. 13.) Montpelier, VT: Capital City Press.

HASKINS, R. (1989). Beyond metaphor: The efficacy of early childhood education. *American Psychologist*, 44, 274–282.

HASS, M. (1986). Cognition-in-context: the social nature of the transformation of mathematical knowledge in a third grade classroom. Technical Report, Social Relations Graduate Program, University of California, Irvine.

HAYES, CHERYL D., JOHN L. PALMER, AND MARTHA J. ZASLOW (EDS.). (1990). *Who cares for America's children? Child care policy for the 1990s*. Washington, DC: National Academy Press.

HEAD START BUREAU, OFFICE OF HUMAN DEVELOPMENT, U.S. DEPARTMENT OF HEALTH AND HUMAN SERVICES. (1987). *Easing the transition from preschool to kindergarten*. Washington, DC.

HEATH, SHIRLEY BRICE. (1983). *Way with words*. New York: Cambridge University Press.

HEATH, SHIRLEY BRICE, AND LESLIE MANGIOLA. (1991). *Children of promise: Literate activity in linguistically and culturally diverse classrooms*. Washington, DC: National Education Association.

HEATHCOTE, DOROTHY. (1972). *Three looms waiting* [Videorecording]. New York: Time-Life Multimedia.

HEATHCOTE, DOROTHY. (1991). *Collected writings on education and drama*. Evanston, IL: Northwestern University Press.

HEIDE, FLORENCE PARY, AND JUDITH HEIDE GILLILAND. (1990). *The day of Ahmed's secret*. New York: Lothrop, Lee & Shepard Books.

HENDRICK, JOANNE. (1988). *Whole child: The developmental education for the early years*, 4th ed. Columbus, OH: Merrill.

HENDRICK, JOANNE. (1993). *Total learning: Developmental curriculum for the young child*, 4th ed. New York: Macmillan.

HENDRY, JOY. (1986). *Becoming Japanese: The world of the preschool child*. Honolulu: University of Hawaii Press.

HERBERHOLZ, BARBARA, AND LEE HANSON. (1990). *Early childhood art*, 4th ed. Dubuque, IA: Wm. C. Brown.

HERRON, R. E., AND B. SUTTON-SMITH. (1971). *Child's play*. New York: Wiley.

HETHERINGTON, E. MAVIS, AND ROSS D. PARKE. (1993). *Child psychology: A contemporary viewpoint*, 4th ed. New York: McGraw-Hill.

HEWSON, P. W., AND M. G. HEWSON. (1988). An appropriate conception of teaching science: A view from studies of science learning. *Journal of Research in Science Teaching*, 72, 597–614.

Hidalgo, Nitza, Caesar L. McDowell, and Emilie V. Siddle (1990). *Facing racism in education* (Reprint Series No. 21). Cambridge, MA: Harvard Educational Review.

Higgins, E. Tory, Diane N. Ruble, and Willard W. Hartup. (1983). *Social cognition and social development: A sociocultural perspective*. New York: Cambridge University Press.

Hirsh, E. D., Jr. (1989). *A first dictionary of cultural literacy: What our children need to know*. Boston: Houghton Mifflin.

Hitz, Randy. (n.d.). Certification of teachers of young children: A survey conducted by the Oregon Department of Education.

Hohmann, Mary, Bernard Banet, and David P. Weikart. (1979). *Young children in action: A manual for preschool educators*. Ypsilanti, MI: High/Scope Press.

Hoot, James L., and Ella Bonkareva. (1992, Winter). Understanding the special needs of former Soviet children. *Childhood Education*, 69(2), 82–85.

Howes, C., and M. Olenick. (1986). Family and child care influences on toddlers' compliance. *Child Development*, 57, 202–216.

Howes, Carollee. (1988). *Peer interaction of young children*. Monographs of the Society for Research in Child Development, 53(1), Serial No. 217.

Hunt, J. M. (1961). *Intelligence and experience*. New York: Ronald Press.

Hymes, James L., Jr. (1978). *Living history interviews, Book 1: Beginnings*. Carmel, CA: Hacienda Press.

Hymes, James L., Jr. (1991). *Twenty years in review: A look at 1971–1991*. Washington, DC: National Association for the Education of Young Children.

Hyson, Marion C., K. Hirsh-Pasek, and L. Rescorla. (1989). *The classroom practices inventory: An observation instrument based on NAEYC guidelines for developmentally appropriate practices for 4- and 5-year-old children*. Newark: University of Delaware.

Hyson, Marion C., K. Hirsh-Pasek, and L. Rescorla. (1989, September). *Academic environments in early childhood: Challenge or pressure? Summary report*. Newark: University of Delaware.

Irwin, D. M., and Margaret Bushnell. (1980). *Observational strategies for child study*. New York: Holt, Rinehart & Winston.

Isaacs, S. (1933/1992). *Social development in young children*. London: Routledge & Kegan Paul.

Jackson, P. W., and C. Costa. (1974). The inequality of educational opportunity in the Southwest: An observational study of ethnically mixed classrooms. *American Educational Research Journal*, 11, 219–229.

Jacobs, Francine, and Robert Hollister. (1992). *Embracing our future: A child care action agenda*. Carol R. Goldberg Seminar on Child Care. Boston, MA: The Boston Foundation.

Johnson, David, and Frank P. Johnson. (1987). *Joining together: Group theory and group skills*. Englewood Cliffs, NJ: Prentice-Hall.

Jones, Warren, Jonathan M. Cheek, and Stephen R. Briggs. (1986). *Shyness: Perspectives on research and treatment*. New York: Plenum.

Kabagarama, Daisy. (1993). *Breaking the ice: A guide to understanding people from other cultures*. Boston, MA: Allyn & Bacon.

Kagan, J. (1987, April). *Temperamental bases for reactions to uncertainty*. Paper presented at the meeting of the Society for Research in Child Development, Baltimore.

Kagan, J. (1989). *Unstable ideas: Temperament, cognition and self*. Cambridge, MA: Harvard University Press.

Kagan, Jerome (Ed.). (1967). *Creativity and learning*. Boston, MA: Beacon Press.

Kagan, Jerome. (1984). *The nature of the child*. New York: Basic Books.

Kagan, Sharon L. (1990, December). Readiness revisited. *Phi Delta Kappan*, pp. 272–279.

Kagan, Sharon L., Ann Marie Rivera, Faith Lamb Parker. (1991, January). *Collaborations in action: Reshaping services to young children and their families—Executive summary*. The

Bush Center in Child Development and Social Policy. New Haven, CT: Yale University.

KAGAN, SPENCER. (1992). *Cooperative learning*. San Juan Capistrano, CA: Resources for Teachers.

KAMII, C. (1982a). *Number in preschool and kindergarten*. Washington, DC: National Association for the Education of Young Children.

KAMII, CONSTANCE. (1982b). *Autonomy: The aim of education*. Speech presented at the New England Kindergarten Conference, Lesley College, Cambridge, MA.

KAMII, CONSTANCE. (1987). *Double column addition: A teacher uses Piaget's theory* [Videotape]. Birmingham, AL: Promethean Films South.

KAMII, CONSTANCE (ED.). (1990). *Achievement testing in the early grades: The games grownups play*. Washington, DC: National Association for the Education of Young Children.

KAMII, CONSTANCE, AND GEORGIA DECLARK. (1985). *Young children reinvent arithmetic: Implications of Piaget's theory*. New York: Teachers College Press, Columbia University.

KAMII, CONSTANCE, AND RHETA DEVRIES. (1978). *Physical knowledge in preschool education: Implications of Piaget's theory*. Englewood Cliffs, NJ: Prentice-Hall.

KAMII, CONSTANCE, AND RHETA DEVRIES. (1980). *Group games in early education: Implications of Piaget's theory*. Washington, DC: National Association for the Education of Young Children.

KAMII, CONSTANCE, MARYANN MANNING, AND GARY MANNING (EDS.). (1991). *Early literacy: A constructivist foundation for whole language*. Washington, DC: National Education Association, Early Childhood Series.

KAPLAN, SANDRA N. (1974, June). *Providing programs for the gifted and talented: A handbook*. Ventura, CA: Office of the Ventura County Superintendent of Schools.

KAPLAN, SANDRA N., JO ANN B. KAPLAN, SHEILA K. MADSEN, AND BETTE T. GOULD. (1980). *Change for children: Ideas and activities for individualizing learning*. Santa Monica, CA.

KATZ, LILIAN. (1969). Stage and sequence: The cognitive-developmental approach to socialization. In D. A. Goslin (Ed.), *Handbook of socialization theory and research* (pp. 347–480). Chicago: Rand McNally.

KATZ, LILIAN, AND SYLVIA CHARD. (1989). *Engaging children's minds: The project approach*. Norwood, NJ: Ablex.

KATZ, LILIAN G. (1990, September). Impressions of Reggio Emilia preschools. *Young Children*, 45(6), 11–12.

KATZ, LILIAN G., DEMETRA EVANGELOU, AND JEANETTE A. HARTMAN. (1990). *The case for mixed-age grouping in early education*. Washington, DC: National Association for the Education of Young Children.

KATZ, P. (1982). Development of children's racial awareness and intergroup attitudes. In L. Katz (Ed.), *Current topics in early childhood education*, Vol. 4 (pp. 17–54). Norwood, NJ: Ablex.

KATZ, PHILLIS A. (1976). The acquisition of racial attitudes in children. In P. A. Katz (Ed.), *Toward the elimination of racism*. New York: Pergamon.

KATZ, PHILLIS A. (1983). Developmental foundations of gender and racial attitudes. In R. L. Leahy (Ed.), *The child's construction of social inequality*. New York: Academic Press.

KEANE, SUSAN. (1987, Spring). Teaching children to be learners. MASC *Journal (Massachusetts Association of School Committees)*, pp. 12–14.

KEATINGE, M. W. (1907). *The great didactic of John Amos Comenius*. London: Adam and Charles Black.

KELLOGG, RHODA. (1969). *Analyzing children's art*. Palo Alto, CA: National Press Books.

KILPATRICK, W. (1918). The project method. *Teachers College Record*, pp. 319–335.

KNOWLTON, MARYLEE, AND DAVID K. WRIGHT. (1988). *Children of the world: India*. Milwaukee: Gareth Stevens Publishing.

KOCHMAN, THOMAS. (1981). *Black and white: Styles in conflict*. Chicago, IL: University of Chicago Press.

KOHEN-RAZ, REUVEN. (1977). *Psychobiological aspects of cognitive growth*. New York: Academic Press.

KOHLBERG, L. (1966). A cognitive-developmental analysis of children's sex-role concepts and attitudes. In E. E. Maccoby (Ed.), (1974). *The development of sex differences*. Stanford: Stanford University Press.

KOHLBERG, L. (1969). Stage and sequence: The cognitive-developmental approach to socialization. In D. A. Goslin (Ed.), *Handbook of socialization theory and research* (pp. 347–480). Chicago: Rand McNally.

KOHLBERG, L. (1976). Moral steps in morality: The cognitive/developmental approach. *Moral development and behavior*. New York: Holt, Rinehart & Winston.

KOHLBERG, L., AND MAYER R. (1972). Development as the aim of education, *Harvard Educational Review*, 42.

KOSTELNIK, M. (1992, May). Myths associated with developmentally appropriate programs. *Young Children*.

KOSTELNIK, M., A. K. SODERMAN, AND A. P. WHIREN. (1993). *Developmentally appropriate programs in early childhood education*. New York: Merrill/Macmillan.

KOSTELNIK, M., L. C. STEIN, A. P. WHIREN, AND A. K. SODERMAN. (1993). *Guiding children's social development*, 2nd ed. Albany, NY: Delmar.

KOZOL, JONATHAN. (1991). *Savage inequalities: Children in America's schools*. New York: Crown.

KRASHEN, STEPHEN D. (1987). *Principles and practices in second language acquisition*. Englewood Cliffs, NJ: Prentice-Hall.

KRATHWOHL, DAVID R., BENJAMIN S. BLOOM, AND BERTRAM MASIA. (1967). *Taxonomy of educational objectives: The classification of educational goals—Handbook II: Affective domain*. New York: McKay.

KRECHEVSKY, MARA. (1991, February). Project spectrum: An innovative assessment alternative. *Educational Leadership*, 48(5), 43–48. Reprinted in Joyce H. Munroe and Karen M. Pacioreck (Eds.), *Early Childhood Education*, annual editions, 92–93. Guilford, CT: Dushkin.

KREIDLER, WILLIAM J. (1984). *Creative conflict resolution*. Glenview, IL: Good Year Books.

KUPERSMIDT, J. B. (1983, April). *Predicting delinquency and academic problems from childhood peer status*. Paper presented at biennial meeting of the Society for Research in Child Development, Detroit, MI.

LADD, G. W., AND J. M. PRICE. (1987). Predicting children's social and school adjustment following the transition from preschool to kindergarten. *Child Development*, 58, 1168–1189.

LARSEN, J. M., AND C. C. ROBINSON. (1989). Later effects of preschool on low-risk children. *Early Childhood Research Quarterly*, 4, 133–144.

LAVATELLI, CELIA. (1970–1973). *Piaget's theory applied to an early child curriculum*. Boston, MA: American Science and Engineering.

LAVE, JEAN. (n.d.). *The culture of acquisition and the practice of understanding*. Report No. IRL88-0007. Palo Alto, CA: Institute for Research on Learning.

LAZAR, I., V. R. H. HUBBELL, M. ROSCHE, AND J. ROYCE. (1977). *Summary report: The persistence of preschool effects—A long-term follow-up of fourteen infant and preschool experiments*. Washington, DC: ACYF, HEW, OHDS, 78-30129.

LAZAR, IRVING, RICHARD B. DARLINGTON, ET AL. (1979, September). *Lasting effects after preschool: A report of the consortium for longitudinal studies—Administration for children, youth and families*. Office of Human Development Services DHEW No. (OHDS) 79-30179.

LEE, V. E., BROOKS-GUNN, J., AND SCHNUR, E. (1988). Does Head Start work? A 1-year follow-up comparison of disadvantaged children attending Head Start, no preschool, and other preschool programs. *Developmental Psychology*, 24, 210–222.

LEVINE, ROBERT (1991, Fall). Social and cultural influences on child development. *Harvard Graduate School of Education Alumni Bulletin*, Vol. 36, No. 1.

LEWIS, CATHERINE. (1984, February). Cooperation and control in Japanese nursery schools. *Comparative Educational Review*, 28(1).

LIND, KAREN. (1991). *Exploring science in early childhood.* Albany, NY: Delmar Publishers.

LOUGHLIN, CATHERINE E., AND MAVIS D. MARTIN. (1987). *Supporting literacy: Developing effective learning environments.* New York: Teachers College Press, Columbia University.

LOVE, JOHN, AND MARY ELLIN LOGUE. (1992). *Transitions to kindergarten in American schools: Executive summary.* Final report to the Office of Policy and Planning, U.S. Department of Education. Portsmouth, NH: Research Corporation.

LOWENFELD, VIKTOR, AND W. LAMBERT BRITTAIN. (1982). *Creative and mental growth,* 7th ed. (8th ed. 1987). New York: Macmillan.

LYMAN, LAWRENCE, AND HARVEY C. FOYLE. (n.d.). *Cooperative learning strategies and children.* ERIC Digest, EDO-ps-85-5, ERIC Clearinghouse on Elementary and Early Childhood Education.

MACDONALD EDUCATIONAL CORPORATION. (1973). *Ourselves: A unit for teachers.* London: Nuffield Math Project.

MACHLEM, GAYLE L. (1987, May). No one wants to play with me. *Academic Therapy,* 22(5).

MACLACHLAN, PATRICIA. (1985). *Sarah plain and tall.* New York: Harper & Row.

MAHLER, M. S., F. PINE, AND A. BERGMAN. (1975). *The psychological birth of the human infant.* New York: Basic Books.

MARX, FERN, AND MICHELLE SELIGSON. (1988). *The public school early childhood study: The state survey.* New York: Bank Street College of Education.

MASLOW, A. H. (1963). *The creative attitude.* Modified version of a lecture presented in October 1962 to the Eighth National Assembly of the Canadian Society for Education Through Art held at the University of Saskatchewan in Saskatoon. Greenville, DE: Psychosynthesis Research Foundation.

MASSACHUSETTS DEPARTMENT OF EDUCATION, BUREAU OF EARLY CHILDHOOD PROGRAMS, AND MASSACHUSETTS DEPARTMENT OF PUBLIC HEALTH. (1991a). *A guide to planning transition: For young children and their families.* Malden, MA: Massachusetts Department of Education.

MASSACHUSETTS DEPARTMENT OF EDUCATION, EARLY LEARNING SERVICES. (1991b, March). *Hand in hand: Integrating young children in need of substantial special education supports.* Pub. 16606, Technical assistance paper No. 3. Malden, MA: Massachusetts Department of Education.

MASSACHUSETTS DEPARTMENT OF EDUCATION, THE DIVISION OF SCHOOL PROGRAMS AND THE EARLY CHILDHOOD ADVISORY COUNCIL TO THE MASSACHUSETTS BOARD OF EDUCATION. (1992, April). *Young lives: Many languages, many cultures.* Pub. 17, 138-79-4000-5-92-1, 93-C.R. Malden, MA: Massachusetts Department of Education.

MASSACHUSETTS EARLY CHILDHOOD ADVISORY COUNCIL. (1992, March). Working together: An ethnographic view of interagency collaboration. In *The report on future trends in early childhood education,* Vol. 4. Malden, MA: Massachusetts Department of Education.

MAYHEW, KATHERINE CAMP, AND ANNA CAMP EDWARDS. (1936). *The Dewey school.* New York: Appleton-Century.

MCCABE, ALLYSSA. (1991). *Language games to play with your child,* rev. ed. New York: Ballantine Books.

MCKEE, JUDY SPITLER. (1986). *Play and working, partners of growth.* Association of Childhood Education-International.

MCKEE, JUDY SPITLER (ED.). (1991). *The developing kindergarten: Program, children and teachers.* East Lansing, MI: Michigan Association for the Education of Young Children.

MCLAUGHLIN, BARRY. (1984). *Second-language acquisition in childhood: Volume 1—Preschool children,* 2nd ed. Hillsdale, NJ: Erlbaum.

MCLAUGHLIN, BARRY. (1985). *Second-language acquisition in childhood: Volume 2—School-age children,* 2nd ed. Hillsdale, NJ: Erlbaum.

MCLAUGHLIN, BARRY. (1987). *Theories of second-language learning.* Baltimore: Arnold.

MCMAHON, ELEANOR, ROBERT L. EGBERT, AND JAN MCCARTHY. (1991, September). *Early childhood education: State policy and practice.* Washington, DC: AACTE, American Association of Colleges for Teacher Education.

MEISELS, SAMUEL J. (1992). *The work sampling system™*. Ann Arbor: University of Michigan.

MENDLER, ALLEN N. (1990). *Smiling at yourself: Educating young children about stress and self-esteem*. Santa Cruz, CA: Network Publications.

MILLER, LOUISE, AND J. L. DYER. (1975). *Four preschool programs: Their dimensions and effects*. Monograph of the Society for Research in Child Development, 40(5–6), Serial No. 162, and Eric Ed. 069411.

MITCHELL, ANNE. (1988a). *The public school early childhood study: The case studies*. New York: Bank Street College of Education.

MITCHELL, ANNE. (1988b). *The public school early childhood study: The district survey*. New York: Bank Street College of Education.

MITCHELL, ANNE, AND JUDY DAVID. (1992). *Explorations with young children, A curriculum guide from the Bank Street College of Education*. Mt. Rainier, MD: Gryphon House.

MIZE, JACQUELYN, AND GARY W. LADD. (1990). Toward the development of successful social skills training for preschool children. In S. Asher and J. Coie (Eds.), *Peer rejection in childhood*. New York: Cambridge University Press.

MIZE, J., G. W. LADD, AND J. M. PRICE. (1985). Promoting positive peer relations with young children: Rationale and strategies. *Child Care Quarterly*, 14, 221–237.

MONIGHAN-NOUROT, BARBARA SCALES, AND JUDITH VAN HOORN, WITH MILLIE ALMY. (1987). *Looking at children's play: A bridge between theory and practice*. New York: Teachers College Press, Columbia University.

MONTESSORI, MARIA. (1964). *The Montessori method*. New York: Schocken Books.

MORRISON, GEORGE S. (1991). *Early childhood education today*, 5th ed. Columbus, OH: Merrill.

MOYER, JOAN, HARRIET EGERTSON, AND JOAN ISENBERG. (1987, April). The child centered kindergarten. Position Paper for the Association for Childhood Education International. Wheaton, MD, *Childhood Education*, pp. 235–242.

MUNRO, JOYCE H., AND KAREN M. PACIOREK (EDS.). (1993). *Annual Editions Early Childhood Education: 92–93*. Guilford, CT: Dushkin.

MUNSCH, ROBERT. (1986). *Love you forever*. Willowdale, Ontario: Firefly Books.

NAISBITT, JOHN. (1982). *Megatrends: Ten new directions for transforming our lives*. New York: Warner.

NATIONAL ASSOCIATION FOR THE EDUCATION OF YOUNG CHILDREN AND THE NATIONAL ASSOCIATION OF EARLY CHILDHOOD SPECIALISTS IN STATE DEPARTMENTS OF EDUCATION. (1991). Position statement: Guidelines for appropriate curriculum content and assessment in programs serving children ages 3 through 8. *Young Children*, 46(3), 21–38.

NATIONAL ASSOCIATION OF ELEMENTARY SCHOOL PRINCIPALS. (1990). *Early childhood programs and the elementary school principal: Standards for quality programs for young children*. Alexandria, VA: National Association of Elementary School Principals.

NATIONAL ASSOCIATION OF STATE BOARDS OF EDUCATION. (1988). *Right from the start: The report of the NASBE Task Force on Early Childhood Education*. Alexandria, VA: National Association of State Boards of Education.

NATIONAL ASSOCIATION OF STATE BOARDS OF EDUCATION (NASBE). (1991, December). *Caring communities: Supporting young children and families—The report of the national task force on school readiness*. Alexandria, VA: National Association of State Boards of Education.

NATIONAL COLLEGE OF EDUCATION. (1932). *Curriculum records of the children's school*. Evanston, IL: Bureau of Publications.

NATIONAL COUNCIL OF TEACHERS OF MATHEMATICS. (1991a). *Curriculum and evaluation standards for school mathematics*. Reston, VA: National Council of Teachers of Mathematics.

NATIONAL COUNCIL OF TEACHERS OF MATHEMATICS. (1991b). *Professional standards for teaching mathematics*. Reston, VA: National Council of Teachers of Mathematics.

NATIONAL HEAD START BULLETIN (1987, April/May). *Transition for children and parents: A Head Start priority*. Washington, DC: National Resource Exchange.

National Head Start–Public School Transition Demonstration Project. (1991). (5-6), Serial No. 162, and ERIC ED 069 411.

New, Rebecca. (1990, September). Excellent early childhood education: A city in Italy has it. *Young Children*, 45(6), 4–10.

New, Rebecca. (1991, Winter). Projects and provocations: Preschool curriculum ideas from Reggio Emilia. *Montessori Life*, pp. 26–28.

New Jersey Department of Education. (1981). *Easing the child's transition between home child care center and school*. Trenton, NJ: New Jersey Department of Education.

Nuffield Mathematics Project. (1970). *I do and I understand: Mathematics begins*. New York: Wiley.

Nuffield Mathematics Project. (1967). *Pictorial representation*. New York: Wiley.

O'Neil, John. (1992, March). Wanted: Deep understanding—"Constructivism" posits new conception of learning. *ASCD Update*, 34(3).

Oakes, Jeannie. (1985). *Keeping track: How schools structure inequality*. New Haven, CT: Yale University Press.

Oakes, Jeannie, with Tor Ormseth, Robert Bell, and Patricia Camp. (1990, March). *Multiplying inequalities: The effects of race, social class, and tracking on opportunities to learn mathematics and science*. Santa Monica, CA: Rand Corporation.

Office for Children, Youth and Families. (1987, November). *Executive summary: The transition of Head Start into public school*. Washington, DC: Department of Health and Human Services.

Osborn, Keith. (1991). *Early childhood education in historical perspective*. Athens, GA: Education Associates.

Paley, Vivian Gussin. (1981). *Wally's stories*. Cambridge, MA: Harvard University Press.

Paley, Vivian Gussin. (1984). *Boys and girls in the doll corner*. Chicago: University of Chicago Press.

Paley, Vivian Gussin. (1988). *Bad guys don't have birthdays*. Chicago: University of Chicago Press.

Paley, Vivian Gussin. (1992). *You can't say you can't play*. Cambridge, MA: Harvard University Press.

Palinscar, A. S., and A. L. Brown. (1984). Reciprocal teaching of comprehension-fostering and comprehension-monitoring activities. *Cognition and Instruction*, 1, 117–175.

Pallotta, Jerry. (1986). *The icky bug alphabet book*. Needham, MA: Charlesbridge Publishing.

Paulson, F. Leon, Pearl R. Paulson, and Carol A. Meyer. (1991, February). What makes a portfolio a portfolio? *Educational Leadership*, pp. 60–63.

Perkins, Daniel N. (1984, September). Creativity by design. *Educational Leadership*, 18–25.

Perkins, David. (1992). *Smart schools: From training memories to educating minds*. New York: Free Press.

Perrone, Vito (Ed.). (1991). *Expanding student assessment*. Washington, DC: Association for Supervision and Curriculum Development.

Pestalozzi, J. (1894). *How Gertrude teaches her children*, Trans. Lucy Holland. Syracuse, NY: C.W. Barden.

Pestalozzi, J. (1951). *The education of man*, trans. Heinz and Ruth Norden. New York: Philosophical Library.

Peterson, Rosemary, and Victoria Felton-Collins. (1986). *The Piaget handbook for teachers and parents: Children in the age of discovery, preschool–third grade*, New York: Teachers College, Columbia University.

Pettit, G. S., K. A. Dodge, and M. M. Brown. (1988). Early family experience: Social problem solving patterns and children's social competence. *Child Development*, 59, 107–120.

Piaget, Jean. (1950). *The psychology of intelligence*. New York: Harcourt Brace Jovanovich.

Piaget, Jean. (1951). *Play, dreams and imitation in childhood*. New York: Norton.

PIAGET, JEAN. (1952). *The origins of intelligence in children.* New York: International Universities Press.

PIAGET, JEAN. (1960). *The child's conception of the world.* Totowa, NJ: Helix Books.

PIAGET, JEAN. (1962). *Play, dreams and imagination in childhood.* New York: Norton.

PIAGET, JEAN. (1965). *The moral judgment of the child.* New York: Free Press. (Original work published in 1932.)

PIERSON, D. E., D. K. WALKER, AND T. TIVNAN. (1984). A school-based program from infancy to kindergarten for children and their parents. *Personnel and Guidance Journal*, 62(7), 448–455.

PITCHER, EVELYN, SYLVIA G. FEINBURG, AND DAVID ALEXANDER. (1989). *Helping young children learn*, 5th ed. Columbus, OH: Merrill.

PITCHER, EVELYN, AND LYNN SCHULTZ. (1983). *Boys and girls at play: The development of sex roles*. New York: Praeger.

PLATO. (1954). *Republic*, Trans. Paul Shaney. In Robert Ulich, *Three thousand years of educational wisdom*. Cambridge, MA: Harvard University Press.

PLATT, SUZY (ED.). (1989). *Respectfully quoted.* Washington, DC: Library of Congress.

POWELL, DOUGLAS. (1989). *Families and early childhood programs*. Research Monograph, Vol. 3. Washington DC: National Association for the Education of Young Children.

PRAWAT, RICHARD S. (1989, Spring). Promoting access to knowledge, strategy, and disposition in students: A research synthesis. *Review of Educational Research*, 59(1), 1–41.

RAINES, SHIRLEY C., AND ROBERT J. CANADY. (1989). *Story S-t-r-e-t-c-h-e-r-s: Activities to expand children's favorite books*. Mt. Rainier, MD: Gryphon House.

RAMSEY, PATRICIA G. (1986). Racial and cultural categories. In Carolyn Pope Edwards, *Promoting social and moral development*. New York: Teachers College Press, Columbia University.

RAMSEY, PATRICIA G. (1987).*Teaching and learning in a diverse world*. New York: Teachers College, Columbia University.

RAMSEY, PATRICIA G. (1991). *Making friends in school: Promoting peer relationships in early childhood*. New York: Teachers College Press, Columbia University.

RANKIN, BAJI. (1990). Interaction: The importance of interaction among children and of work in small groups. Unpublished conversation with Loris Malguzzi, Reggio Emilia, Italy.

RAVER, C. C., AND E. F. ZIGLER. (1991). Three steps forward, two steps back: Head Start and the measurement of social competence. *Young Children*, 46, 3–9.

RAVITCH, DIANE. (December 1991/January 1992). A culture in common. *Educational Leadership*, pp. 8–11.

READ, KATHERINE. (1980). *The nursery school and kindergarten: Human relationships and learning*. New York: Holt, Rinehart & Winston.

READ, KATHERINE, PAT GARDNER, AND BARBARA C. MAHLER. (1993). *Early childhood programs: Human relationships and learning*, 9th ed. New York: Harcourt Brace Jovanovich.

REGIONAL EDUCATIONAL LABORATORIES EARLY CHILDHOOD COLLABORATION NETWORK. (1993, Fall). *Continuity in early childhood: Elements and indicators of home, school and community linkages*. Administration for Children, Youth and Families and by the Office of Educational and Research Improvement, U.S. Department of Education.

REGIONAL LABORATORY FOR EDUCATIONAL IMPROVEMENT OF THE NORTHEAST AND THE ISLANDS, ANDOVER, MA. (1992). Early Education–Early Elementary School Linkage Project, supported by the U.S. Department of Education and the U.S. Department of Health and Human Services.

RENZULLI, MARY JO, BARBARA GAY FORD, LINDA SMITH, AND JOSEPH S. RENZULLI. (1976). *New direction in creativity*. New York: Harper & Row.

RICHARZ, ANN SHERRILL. (1980). *Understanding children through observation*. St Paul, MN: West.

ROGERS, CARL R. (1961). *On becoming a person*. Boston: Houghton Mifflin.

ROGERS, CARL R. (1974). In retrospect: Forty-six years. *American Psychologist*, 29, 115–123.

ROGOFF, B. (1990). *Apprenticeship in thinking: Cognitive development in social context*. New York: Oxford University Press.

ROGOFF, BARBARA, AND JAMES WERTSCH. (1984). *Children's learning in the "zone of proximal development,"* New Directions for Child Development. San Francisco: Jossey-Bass.

ROOPNARINE, JAIPAUL L., AND JAMES E. JOHNSON. (1993). *Approaches to early education*, 2nd ed. New York: Macmillan.

ROUSSEAU, JEAN-JACQUES (1762/1911). *Emile, or education*. New York: Dutton.

ROUSSEAU, JEAN-JACQUES (1793/1954). *Emilius or a treatise on education*. In Robert Ulich, *Three thousand years of educational wisdom*. Cambridge, MA: Harvard University Press.

SANTROCK, JOHN W., AND STEVEN R. YUSSEN. (1992). *Child development: An introduction*, 5th ed. Dubuque, IA: Wm. C. Brown.

SAROYAN, WILLIAM. (1972). The first day of school. In Elliott D. Landau et al. (Eds.), *Child development through literature*. Englewood Cliffs, NJ: Prentice-Hall.

SCHWEINHART, L. J. (1991, April). *The High/Scope Perry preschool study, similar studies, and their implications for public policy in the United States*. Paper presented at the Society for Research in Child Development meeting, Seattle, WA.

SCHWEINHART, L. J., H. V. BARNES, AND D. P. WEIKART. (1993). *Significant benefits: The High/Scope Perry preschool study through age 27*. (Monographs of the High/Scope Educational Research Foundation, No. 10), Ypsilanti, MI: High/Scope Press.

SCHWEINHART, LAWRENCE J., AND DAVID P. WEIKART. (1980). *Young children grow up: The effects of the Perry preschool program on youths through age 15*. Ypsilanti, MI: High/Scope Press.

SCHWEINHART, LAWRENCE J., AND DAVID P. WEIKART. (1985). Evidence that good early childhood programs work. *Phi Delta Kappan*, 66, 545–551.

SCHWEINHART, LAWRENCE J., AND DAVID P. WEIKART. (1986, January). What do we know so far? A review of the Head Start synthesis project. *Young Children*, 41(2), 49–54.

SCHWEINHART, LAWRENCE J., AND DAVID P. WEIKART. (1993). *Success by empowerment: The High/Scope preschool study through age 27*. Ypsilanti, MI: High/Scope Press.

SCHWEINHART, LAWRENCE J., DAVID P. WEIKART, AND MARY B. LARNER. (1986). Consequences of three preschool curriculum models through age 15. *Early Childhood Research Quarterly*, 1, 15–45.

SEIGLE, PAMELA. (1990–1991). *Reach out to schools: Social competency program*. Wellesley, MA: Stone Center, Wellesley College.

SELIGMAN, M. E. P., AND S. MAIER. (1967). Failure to escape traumatic shock. *Journal of Experimental Psychology*, 74, 1–9.

SELMAN, R. L. (1980). *The growth of interpersonal understanding*. New York: Academic Press.

SERAFICA, FELICISIMA C. (1982). *Social-cognitive development in context*. New York: Guilford Press.

SEVEREIDE, REBECCA, AND EDWARD L. PIZZINI. (1984, May). What research says: The role of play in science. *Science and Children*, pp. 58–61.

SHANNON, PATRICK. (1990). *The struggle to continue: Progressive reading instruction in the United States*. Portsmouth, NH: Heinemann.

SHAPIRO, EDNA, AND BARBARA BIBER. (1972). The education of young children: A developmental interaction approach. *Teachers College Record*, 74, 55–79.

SHIPMAN, VIRGINIA. (1973). *Disadvantaged children and their first school experience. Educational Testing Service Head Start longitudinal study in compensatory education for children ages 1–8*. Baltimore, MD: Johns Hopkins Press.

SHURE, MYRNA B. (1981). Social competence as a problem-solving skill. In J. D. Wine and M. D. Smye (Eds.), *Social competence* (pp. 158–185). New York: Guilford Press.

SHURE, MYRNA B. (1982). *Interpersonal problem solving: A cog in the wheel of social cognition*. In Felicisma C. Serafica (Ed.), *Social-cognitive development in context*. NY: Guilford Press.

SHURE, MYRNA B. (1992). *I can problem solve: An interpersonal cognitive problem-solving program* (2 vols.: Preschool; and Kindergarten and the primary grades). Champaign, IL: Research Press.

SHURE, MYRNA B, AND GEORGE SPIVACK. (1978a). *Problem-solving techniques in childrearing*. San Francisco: Jossey-Bass.

SHURE, MYRNA B., AND GEORGE SPIVACK. (1978b). *A mental health program for kindergarten children. A cognitive approach to solving interpersonal problems* [Training script] Philadelphia: Hanemann Medical College and Hospital.

SINGER, DOROTHY, AND TRACEY A. REVENSON. (1978). *A Piaget primer: How a child thinks*. New York: Harper Library, Times/Magazine.

SINGER, DOROTHY, AND JEROME L. SINGER. (1992). *The house of make-believe: Children's play and the developing imagination*. Cambridge, MA: Harvard University Press.

SLAVIN, ROBERT E. (1987). *A review of research of elementary ability grouping*. Baltimore, MD: Johns Hopkins University Press.

SLAVIN, ROBERT E. (1990). *Cooperative learning: Theory, research, and practice*.Englewood Cliffs, NJ: Prentice-Hall.

SLAVIN, ROBERT E. (1991, February). Synthesis of research on cooperative learning. *Educational Leadership*, 48(5), 71–82.

SLAVIN, R. E., AND E. OICKLE. (1981). Effects of cooperative teams on student achievement and relations. *Sociology of Education*, 5.5, 174–180.

SLUCKIN, ANDY (1981). *Growing up in the playground; The social development of children*. Boston, MA: Routledge & Kegan Paul.

SMILANSKY, SARA, AND LEAH SHEFATYA. (1990). *Facilitating play: A medium for promoting cognitive, socio-emotional and academic development of young children*. Gaithersburg, MD: Psychological Education Publishers.

SNIDMAN, N., AND J. KAGAN (1989, April). *Infant predictors of behaviorally inhibited and uninhibited children*. Paper presented at the meeting of the Society for Research in Child Development, Kansas City, MO.

SPIVACK, GEORGE, AND M. LEVINE. (1963). *Self-regulation in acting out and normal adolescents*. Report M-45310. Washington, DC: National Institute of Mental Health.

SPIVACK, G., AND M. B. SHURE. (1974). *Social adjustment of young children: A cognitive approach to solving real life problems*. San Francisco: Jossey-Bass.

SPODEK, BERNARD (ED.). (1991). *Educationally appropriate kindergarten practices*. Washington, DC: National Education Association.

SPRUNG, BARBARA, MERLE FROSCHL, AND PATRICIA B. CAMPBELL. (1985). *What will happen if . . . Young children and the scientific method*. New York: Educational Equity Concepts.

STERNBERG, ROBERT J. (1985). *Beyond I.Q.: A triadic theory of intelligence*. Cambridge, MA: Harvard University Press.

SULZBY, ELIZABETH. (1990). *Emergent literacy: Kindergartners write and read*. Bloomington, IN: Agency for Instructional Television.

SUOMI, S. (1987, April). *Individual differences in rhesus monkey behavioral and adrenocortical responses to social challenge: Correlations with measures of heart rate variability*. Paper presented at the meeting of the Society for Research in Child Development, Baltimore, MD.

SUTTON-SMITH, BRIAN. (1971). *Child's play*. New York: Wiley.

SWADENER, BETH BLUE, AND SHIRLEY A. KESSLER. (1992). *Reconceptualizing the early childhood curriculum: Beginning the dialog*. New York: Teachers College Press, Columbia University.

TABA, H., AND F. ELEZY. (1964). Teaching strategies and thought processes. *Teachers College Record*, 65, 524–534.

THOMAS, A., AND S. CHESS. (1977). *Temperament and development*. New York: Brunner-Mazel.

THOMAS, R. MURRAY (ED.) (1988). *Oriental theories of human development: Scriptural and popular beliefs from Hinduism, Buddhism, Confucianism, Shinto, and Islam*. New York: Peter Lang.

THOMAS, R. MURRAY. (1992). *Comparing theories of child development*, 3rd ed. Belmont, CA: Wadsworth.

TIETZE, W. (1987). A structural model for the evaluation of preschool effects. *Early Childhood Research Quarterly*, 2, 133–153.

TOBIN, JOSEPH, DAVID Y. H. WU, AND DANA H. DAVIDSON. (1989). *Preschool in three cultures*. New Haven, CT: Yale University Press.

TRIPP, R. T. (1970). *International thesaurus of quotations*. New York: Crowell.

TURIEL, E. (1966). An experimental test of the sequentiality of developmental stages of a child's moral judgment. *Journal of Personality and Social Psychology*, 3, 611–618.

U.S. BUREAU OF THE CENSUS. (1990). *Statistical abstract of the United States*, 110th ed. Washington, DC: U.S. Government Printing Office.

U.S. DEPARTMENT OF HEALTH AND HUMAN SERVICES, OFFICE OF HUMAN DEVELOPMENT SERVICES, ADMINISTRATION FOR CHILDREN, YOUTH AND FAMILIES, HEAD START BUREAU. (1980, September). *Head Start in the 1980s: Review and recommendations*. Washington, DC: U.S. Department of Health and Human Services.

U.S. NATIONAL COMMISSION ON EXCELLENCE IN EDUCATION. (1983).*A nation at risk: The imperative for educational reform: A report to the nation and the secretary of education*. Washington, DC: U.S. Government Printing Office.

VANDELL, D. L., AND M. A CORASANITI. (1990). Variations in early child care: Do they predict subsequent social, emotional, and cognitive differences? *Early Childhood Research Quarterly*, 5, 555–572.

VERRUSO, SHARIE. (1990). *Children's awareness of racial differences*. Unpublished paper. Cambridge, MA: Lesley College.

VYGOTSKY, LEV S. (1962). *Thought and language*. Cambridge, MA: Harvard University Press.

VYGOTSKY, LEV S. (1978). *Mind in society: the development of higher psychological processes*. H. Cole, V. John-Steiner, S. Scribner, and E. Souberman (Eds.). Cambridge, MA: Harvard University Press. (Originally published 1930)

WALDROP, M. F., & HALVERSON, C. F. (1975). Intensive and extensive peer behavior: Longitudinal and cross-sectional analyses. *Child Development*, 46, 19–26.

WALTER, G., AND L. VINCENT. (1982). The handicapped child in the regular kindergarten classroom. *Journal of the Division of Early Childhood*, 6, 84–95.

WANN, KENNETH D., MIRIAM S. DORN, AND ELIZABETH ANN LIDDLE. (1962). *Fostering Intellectual Development in Young Children*. New York: Columbia University, Teachers College Press.

WASSERMAN, SELMA. (1990). *Serious players in the primary classroom: Empowering children through active learning experiences*. New York: Columbia University, Teachers College Press.

WEAVER, C. WITH DIANE STEPHENS AND JANET VANCE. (1990). *Understanding whole language: From principles to practice*. Portsmouth, NH: Heinemann.

WEBSTER, EVELYN. (1984). *Ideas influencing early childhood education, A theoretical analysis*. New York: Columbia University, Teachers College Press.

WEBSTER'S NINTH COLLEGIATE DICTIONARY. (1984). Springfield, MA: Merriam-Webster.

WEIKART, DAVID, L. ROGERS, D. ADCOCK, AND D. MCCLELLAND. (1971). *The cognitively oriented curriculum*. Washington, DC: National Association for the Education of Young Children.

WEIKART, DAVID, ET AL. (1978). *The Ypsilanti preschool curriculum demonstration project: Preschool years and longitudinal results*. Monograph of the High/Scope Educational Research Foundation, 4. Ypsilanti, MI: High/Scope Press.

WERTSCH, JAMES V. (ED.). (1985). *Culture, communication and cognition: Vygotskian perspectives*. New York: Cambridge University Press.

WERTSCH, JAMES. (1986). *Mind in context: A Vygotskian approach*. Paper presented at the annual meeting of the American Educational Research Association, San Francisco.

WHITE, MERRY. (1987). *The Japanese educational challenge*. New York: Free Press.

WHITEBOOK, M., C. HOWES, AND D. PHILLIPS. (1989). *Who cares? Child care teachers and the quality of care in America*. Executive Summary, National Child Care Staffing Study. Oakland, CA: Child Care Employee Project.

Whiting, B., and C. Edwards. (1988). *Children of different worlds: The formation of social behavior*. Cambridge, MA: Harvard University Press.

Williams, J. E., and J. K. Morland. (1976). *Race, color and the young child*. Chapel Hill: University of North Carolina Press.

Williams, Leslie R., and Doris Pronin Fromberg. (1992). *Encyclopedia of early childhood education*. New York: Garland.

Winitzky, Nancy, Trish Stoddart, and Patti O'Keefe (1992, January–February). Great expectations: Emergent professional development schools. *Journal of Teacher Education*, 43(1), 3–18.

WNET and the Childhood Project, Inc. (1991). *Childhood. Part 2: Louder than Words* [Videorecording]. Jerome Kagan. New York: Ambrose Video.

Wolery, Mark, Phillip Strain, and Donald B. Bailey, Jr. (1992). *Reaching potentials of children with special needs*. In Sue Bredekemp and Teresa Rosegrant (Eds.), *Reaching potentials: Appropriate curriculum and assessment for young children*. Washington, DC: NAEYC.

Wolfgang, Charles, and Mary Wolfgang. (1992). *School for young children: Developmentally appropriate practices*. Boston, MA: Allyn & Bacon.

Wong, Fillmore L. (1976). *The second time around: Cognitive and social strategies in second language acquisition*. Doctoral dissertation, Stanford, CA: Stanford University.

Zigler, E., & Berman, W. (1983). Discerning the future of early childhood intervention. *American Psychologist*, 38, 894–906.

NAME INDEX

SUBJECT INDEX

Page references to figures, tables, photographs, and illustrations are printed in italic type